COMMUNISM AND SOCIAL DEMOCRACY

1914-1931

BY

G. D. H. COLE

George

LONDON

MACMILLAN & CO LTD

NEW YORK · ST MARTIN'S PRESS

1958

MACMILLAN AND COMPANY LIMITED
London Bombay Calcutta Madras Melbourne

THE MACMILLAN COMPANY OF CANADA LIMITED
Toronto

ST MARTIN'S PRESS INC
New York

PRINTED IN GREAT BRITAIN

PREFACE

I HAVE again to acknowledge the ungrudging help given me by many friends in the making of this volume. Three persons for whose judgment I have a high respect — Mr. H. N. Brailsford, Professor Sir Isaiah Berlin, and Mr. Julius Braunthal — read through the entire manuscript and gave me advice that led me to make many corrections and modifications in the opinions expressed. I am again most grateful to them all. I have also many other persons to thank for help with particular chapters, especially in filling in missing dates of births and deaths — for I attach considerable importance to knowing how old my characters were when they did anything worthy of note. Among those who helped me in this respect are M. J. Maitron of the Institut Français D'Histoire Sociale and M. Maurice Dommanget, for France ; Dr. Gerhard Gleissberg and Frau Ruth Gleissberg, for Germany ; Mr. Lloyd Ross, for Australia ; Dr. J. P. L. Wiessing, for Holland ; M. René Renard, for Belgium ; Mr. Branko Pribićević, for Yugoslavia ; Mr. S. K. Evangelides, for Greece ; Professor Iwao Ayusawa, for Japan ; Señor Luis Henriquez, for Chile ; Mr. Mark Starr, for the United States ; Señor Carlos Echagüe, for the Argentine ; Mr. Artero Vartia, for Finland ; Mr. J. W. Ames, for Sweden ; Mr. H. K. Lehmkuhl, for Norway ; Señor Dr. don Felipe de Bustamante, for Peru ; Señor G. Luders de Negri, for Mexico ; M. Charles Barbier, for Switzerland ; Dr. Carlo Doglio, for Italy ; Mr. John Gollan, for Communists from a number of countries ; Mr. V. Richards, of the Freedom Press, for a number of Anarchists ; and Mr. Arthur Lehning, for Socialists from Spain and several other countries. I have also to thank Mr. Z. Najder for reading through my chapter on Poland and for making suggestions which caused me to modify it in a number of respects.

v

There will be, if I survive to write it, one more volume of this history, carrying the record at least to 1945, and possibly further. Looking back, I can see a good deal in my first volume that I should put rather differently if I were writing it now ; but there is no major point on which I see the need for substantial correction. I mean by this, not that I have got everything, or even most things, right, but that I do not think that I could substantially improve what I have written. Great as is the help so many friends have given me, the views expressed are, of course, throughout my own and must not be attributed to those who have lent me their most useful aid.

G. D. H. COLE

ALL SOULS COLLEGE,
OXFORD
December 1957

CONTENTS

PART I

PAGE

PREFACE   v

THE PRINCIPAL CHARACTERS   ix

CHAP.

I. INTRODUCTION   1

II. THREE CONFERENCES: ZIMMERWALD, KIENTHAL, STOCKHOLM   27

III. THE TWO RUSSIAN REVOLUTIONS OF 1917   63

IV. GERMANY IN WAR-TIME, 1914–1918   102

V. REVOLUTION AND COUNTER-REVOLUTION IN GERMANY, 1918–1921   133

VI. RUSSIA IN REVOLUTION AND CIVIL WAR, 1917–1921   172

VII. THE REVOLUTION IN AUSTRIA-HUNGARY: AUSTRIA, HUNGARY, CZECHOSLOVAKIA   213

VIII. THE BALKANS: BULGARIA, RUMANIA, YUGOSLAVIA, GREECE   258

IX. THE RIVAL INTERNATIONALS, 1919–1921   287

X. SOCIALISM AND INTERNATIONALISM IN THE 1920S: COLONIALISM, PEACE, AND DISARMAMENT   343

XI. ITALY TO THE FASCIST VICTORY   367

XII. GREAT BRITAIN FROM 1914 TO THE GENERAL STRIKE   404

THE PRINCIPAL CHARACTERS

	CHAP. REF.		CHAP. REF.
VAILLANT, 1840–1915 [1], [2]	13	S. WEBB, 1859–1947 [2]	12
GREULICH, 1842–1925 [1], [2]	14	JAURÈS, 1859–1914 [2]	13
HYNDMAN, 1842–1921 [1], [2]	12	BRANTING, 1860–1925	15
KROPOTKIN, 1842–1921 [1]	17	TROELSTRA, 1860–1930 [2]	15
GUESDE, 1845–1922 [1], [2]	13	BRACKE, 1861–1955	13
MEHRING, 1846–1919 [2]	5	LEGIEN, 1861–1920 [2]	5
NIEUWENHUIS, 1846–1919 [2]	15	BRIAND, 1862–1932 [2]	13
W. G. SPENCE, 1846–1926 [2]	28	A. FISHER, 1862–1928 [2]	28
SOREL, 1847–1922 [2]	13	SEMBAT, 1862–1922	13
AXELROD, 1850–1925 [2]	3	VLIEGEN, 1862–1947 [2]	15
BERNSTEIN, 1850–1932 [2]	4	DAVID, 1863–1930 [2]	4
GOMPERS, 1850–1924 [2]	23	HAASE, 1863–1919	4
IGLESIAS, 1850–1925 [2]	16	HENDERSON, 1863–1935 [2]	12
LEDEBOUR, 1850–1947	4	CHKHEIDZE, 1864–1926	3
NATANSON, 1850–1919	6	HUGHES, 1864–1952 [2]	28
VOLLMAR, 1850–1922 [2]	4	JOWETT, 1864–1944	12
BLATCHFORD, 1851–1943 [2]	12	SNOWDEN, 1864–1937 [2]	12
ZASULICH, 1851–1919 [2]	3	SCHEIDEMANN, 1865–1939	4
V. ADLER, 1852–1918 [2]	7	N. BANG, 1866–1928	29
MALATESTA, 1853–1932 [1], [2]	11	MACDONALD, 1866–1937 [2]	12
KAUTSKY, 1854–1938 [2]	4	SUN YAT SEN, 1866–1925 [2]	25
DEBS, 1855–1926 [2]	23	VANDERVELDE, 1866–1938 [2]	14
ANSEELE, 1856–1938 [2]	14	WELLS, 1866–1946 [2]	12
BERTRAND, 1856–1943 [2]	14	PILSUDSKI, 1867–1935 [2]	19
HARDIE, 1856–1915 [2]	12	JOGICHES, 1867–1919 [2]	4
MANN, 1856–1941 [2]	12	GORKI, 1868–1936	3
SHAW, 1856–1950 [1], [2]	12	CACHIN, 1869–1958	13
LAZZARI, 1857–1927	11	GANDHI, 1869–1948	27
PLEKHANOV, 1857–1918 [2]	3	EMMA GOLDMAN, 1869–1940	23
SMILLIE, 1857–1940 [2]	12	HILLQUIT, 1869–1933 [2]	23
TURATI, 1857–1932 [2]	11	KRUPSKAIA, 1869–1939	6
ZETKIN, 1857–1933	29	CONNOLLY, 1870–1916 [2]	12
BURNS, 1858–1941 [1], [2]	12	DE BROUCKÈRE, 1870–1951 [2]	14
J. A. HOBSON, 1858–1940 [2]	12	EBERT, 1870–1925	5
KATAYAMA, 1858–1933 [2]	26	KRASIN, 1870–1926 [2]	3
LANSBURY, 1858–1940 [2]	12	LARGO CABALLERO,	
B. WEBB, 1858–1943 [2]	12	1870–1946	16

[1] Discussed also in Volume II.
[2] Discussed also in Volume III.

	CHAP. REF.		CHAP. REF.
LENIN, 1870–1924 [2]	2 etc.	FIMMEN, 1881–1943	15
LUXEMBURG, 1870–1919 [2]	4	FOSTER, 1881–	23
RYAZONOV, 1870–?1935	3	GRIMM, 1881–	14
DAN, 1871–1947	3	KERENSKY, 1881–	3
HOLMAN, 1871–1934 [2]	28	RYKOV, 1881–1938	6
HUYSMANS, 1871–	2	V. TANNER, 1881–	15
K. LIEBKNECHT, 1871–1919 [2]	4	VOROSHILOV, 1881–	6
MERRHEIM, 1871–1925	13	WIGFORSS, 1881–	15
RENAUDEL, 1871–1934	13	DIMITROV, 1882–1949	8
SOUKUP, 1871–1940	7	ATTLEE, 1883–	12
BLUM, 1872–1950	13	KAMENEV, 1883–1936 [2]	3
CHICHERIN, 1872–1936	6	VYSHINSKY, 1883–1955	17
SAVAGE, 1872–1940 [2]	28	ZINOVIEV, 1883–1936 [2]	9
SERRATI, 1872–1926	11	POPOVIC, 1884–1919	8
BOGDANOV, 1873–1928 [2]	3	SANDLER, 1884–	15
BRAILSFORD, 1873– [2]	12	N. THOMAS, 1884–	23
CHERNOV, 1873–1952 [2]	6	CHIFFLEY, 1885–1951	28
MARTOV, 1873–1923 [2]	6	HANSSON, 1885–1946 [2]	15
ORAGE, 1873–1934 [2]	12	RADEK, 1885–	6
RAKOVSKY, 1873– [2]	6	SPIRIDONOVA, 1885–	6
STAUNING, 1873–1942	15	BÉLA KUN, 1886–1936	7
J. H. THOMAS, 1873–1949 [2]	12	BEN-GURION, 1886–	—
GRIFFUELHES, 1874–1923 [2]	13	THAELMANN, 1886–1944	20
NAINE, 1874–?1927	2	DALTON, 1887–	12
KALININ, 1875–1946	6	KÁROLYI, 1887–1955	7
LUNACHARSKY, 1875–1933 [2]	3	MORRISON, 1888–	12
LARKIN, 1876–1947 [2]	12	SOKOLNIKOV, 1888–	6
LITVINOV, 1876–1951	6	BUKHARIN, 1889–1938	9
J. LONGUET, 1876–1938	13	NEHRU, 1889–	27
DZHERZHINSKY, 1877–1926 [2]	6	CRIPPS, 1890–1952	12
U. SINCLAIR, 1878– [2]	23	MOLOTOV, 1890–	3
A. THOMAS, 1878–1932	13	POLLITT, 1890–	21
F. ADLER, 1879–	7	TITO, 1890–	8
JOUHAUX, 1879–1953 [2]	13	NENNI, 1891–	11
STALIN, 1879–1953	17	LASKI, 1893–1950	12
TRANMAEL, 1879–	15	LOMBARDO TOLEDANO, 1893–	24
TROTSKY, 1879–1940 [2]	3 etc.	TOGLIATTI, ?1893–	11
TAWNEY, 1880–	12	BULGANIN, 1895–	17
TOMSKY, 1880–1936	6	HAYA DE LA TORRE, 1895–	24
O. BAUER, 1881–1935 [2]	7	MIKOYAN, 1895–	17
BEVIN, 1881–1951	12	ZHUKOV, 1895–	—

[1] Discussed also in Volume II.
[2] Discussed also in Volume III.

CHAPTER I

INTRODUCTION

THIS fourth volume of *A History of Socialist Thought* covers a shorter period than any of its predecessors — a mere eighteen years as against the sixty of Volume I, the forty of Volume II, and the twenty-five of Volume III. My first intention was to carry the record on in a single volume from 1914 to 1939 ; but on second thoughts I decided that I had better stop short of the essentially new epoch that began with the world economic depression of 1931 and took political shape in the Nazi conquest of power in Germany two years later. I made this decision because, whereas in the decade immediately after the first world war the centre of interest from the standpoint of Socialist thought was the struggle between Social Democracy and Communism for the allegiances of the workers throughout the world, during the ensuing decade, though this struggle continued and even spread over a wider area, it was overshadowed by the Fascist challenge to Socialism and to democracy in all their forms and was also greatly affected by the widespread prevalence of unemployment, the collapse of agricultural prices, and the changes in capitalist economic policy and theory that found expression in Roosevelt's 'New Deal' in the United States and in the restatement of economic theory by John Maynard Keynes. I came to the conclusion that these two periods could not be studied satisfactorily in a single volume, not only because there was too much to compress into such a space, but even more because the central points of interest and attention were too different to allow the unity I had been seeking to achieve.

In effect, the world-wide disturbances and dislocations that arose out of the war, with the Russian Revolution as their essential point of focus, and the beating back of the attempts to turn the Russian upheaval into a World Revolution, provide fully enough material for a distinct study of the years between

1914 and the economic *débâcle* of 1931. It has not, of course, been possible to confine the narrative entirely to the developments of these years. In a few cases I have carried the record on rather further, where 1931 seemed not to be a convenient stopping point in the affairs of a particular country. In at any rate one case — that of the Soviet Union — I have stopped short, in order to avoid breaking off the record of Five-Year planning and agricultural collectivisation at a most inconvenient stage. Nevertheless, broadly speaking, I have gone up to the first onset of the great depression, and have then stopped short of the developments of the 1930s, when every Socialist was confronted with the need to re-think his attitude afresh — even if some of them ended the process by holding almost the same opinions as before.

In such a study, inevitably, the central fact is the Russian Revolution of 1917 — not simply its occurrence, but its success in maintaining itself and its development through the periods of foreign intervention and civil war and of the New Economic Policy which Lenin inaugurated in 1921. Whatever view one may take, either of the successive phases of the Russian Revolution itself or of what came out of it in the realms of thought and action, there can be no question that it has proved itself, for good or ill, or for both, the most important world event since the French Revolution of 1789, and indeed further-reaching even than that vast upheaval because its influence has spread over the whole world and has set all mankind at sixes and sevens. Even among Socialists it has given rise to judgments so divergent that, whereas some have regarded it as providing the pattern for a new world order in which all the contradictions of the older forms of society are destined to be overcome, others have denounced it in unreserved terms as the most terrible of all tyrannies of men over men and have been prepared, Socialists though they may be, to ally themselves with capitalism against it and to incite the peoples subject to Soviet rule to rise in the cause of liberty for its overthrow. It is true that, in the period dealt with in the present volume, this sharp division of judgment was on the whole less in evidence than it has been during the past ten years ; but even at the outset, or at any rate from 1919 onwards, the conflicts between Communism and Social Democracy found expression in sharply divergent social philosophies and programmes of action which made it unrealistic to speak or think of the working-class movement as in any practical sense a single, even loosely unified, force animated by a common object. This does not mean that the entire Socialist movement — much less the entire working-class movement — became divided into two absolutely distinct contending factions, neither of which felt itself to have anything in common with the other. Far from it. Working-class sympathy with the Russian Revolution remained a very lively sentiment among wide masses of persons who rejected the Communist doctrine and the call to imitate the Russian example : even the Social Democratic and Labour leaders who were most vehement in their denunciations of Communist dictatorship and in their appreciation of the principle of parliamentary democracy were, for the most part, careful to disclaim hostility to the new Russia and to urge the Governments of their own countries to take no action against it. Nor was this mere hypocrisy on their part. They could not but rejoice in the overthrow of the Czarist autocracy and feel a keen sympathy for the struggle of the Russians to build up a new society, even if they strongly disapproved of many of the methods which the Bolsheviks not only deemed necessary in their own case but were also determined, if they could, to induce the workers of every other country to pursue.

There were, moreover, especially in the Western countries, a great many Socialists and working-class supporters who found themselves in agreement neither with the Bolsheviks as advocates of World Revolution on the Russian model nor with the out-and-out parliamentarian reformists who utterly condemned the proletarian dictatorship and the one-party system. Many of these middle-of-the-road Socialists were prepared to believe that the Bolshevik method, though inappropriate to the conditions of the more advanced Western societies, might be the only method that was really open in Russia — the only way in which the great Russian Revolution could be defended against its many enemies and used as the foundation for the building up of a Socialist society in a backward country. At the least, many of them were ready to give the Bolsheviks the benefit of whatever doubts were in their minds and to watch the development of the great Soviet experiment in the ardent hope that it would lead, if only in the long run, to the emergence of a really free, democratic society in which the common people would be able to shape their own lives within the framework of public ownership and planned direction of the productive powers at their command. Such observers were always eager to make the best of what they believed to be going on inside the Soviet Union. They watched with intense anxiety the early struggles for sheer survival, and, when at length survival seemed fairly well assured, they exulted in the remarkable achievements of the Russians in the field of industrial development, which they compared with the much slower growth of production in most of the capitalist countries. They were also greatly encouraged by the progress made in the fields of popular education and of the social services ; and many of them came back from visits to the Soviet Union deeply impressed by what they had been allowed to see of the vast works of social and economic construction that were being so energetically pursued. Some of them were even much impressed by the effects of the intense devotion of the Communist *élite*, and came back to contrast the achievements of a disciplined party, highly aware of its objectives and of the need to pursue them with the utmost vigour, with the loose organisation and widespread apathy within the Socialist Parties of the West. Sidney and Beatrice Webb's immense book on *Soviet Communism : a New Civilisation ?* — from whose title the ' ? ' disappeared in a later edition — was the outstanding example of this reaction, the more remarkable as coming from the foremost theorists of Fabianism, the philosophy of Social Democracy in one of its most gradualist and evolutionary guises.

There was, indeed, among Socialists in the advanced capitalist countries, a certain sense of guilt because the Russians, who were deemed so backward, *had* overthrown both Czarism and capitalism and had put a kind of Socialism in their place, whereas in the West the Socialist movements, though numerically much stronger than before the war, seemed in most countries to be still a long way off the achievement of political power. It seemed to be near treason to the Socialist cause to throw stones at men who, in face of prodigious obstacles, were felt to be at any rate attempting to establish a

Socialist way of life. At this stage — I mean in the 1920s — there were relatively few who questioned that this was what the Bolsheviks were setting out to do. It was quite widely believed that the dictatorship and the one-party government that existed in the Soviet Union were temporary expedients, which would wither away as the new society came to be more firmly established, and that an increasing liberalisation of Soviet institutions could be confidently anticipated as the dangers of counter-revolution grew less. The introduction of the New Economic Policy, with its recognition of controlled private enterprise and its abandonment of the policy of agricultural requisitions, strongly encouraged these hopes ; and Trotsky's warnings about the increasing bureaucratisation of the Communist Party under Stalin's influence were not taken very seriously by most outside observers — the more so because Trotsky was himself associated with a policy of sharp dealing with the peasants, of intensified industrialisation, and even of using the Red Army as a conscript labour force. Not until the Russian leaders turned their attention to the rapid collectivisation of agriculture and to the elimination of the so-called *kulaks* as a class were serious fears aroused that the trend might be away from, rather than towards, liberalisation ; and even in face of these developments opinions in the West were sharply divided, for many Western Socialists put high hopes on collectivisation and the improvement in agricultural equipment as means of promoting both higher output and a modernisation of agricultural methods, and the cruelties which accompanied the liquidation of the *kulaks* were not widely understood until a later time.

It must be borne in mind that throughout the period covered by the present volume the outstanding feature of the Soviet economy appeared to be its startling success in restoring and developing industrial production and in overcoming many of the desperate shortages of the civil war period, and that the monolithic character of the Soviet political system was much less in evidence than it came to be later, when the development of the Five-Year Plans and the collectivisation of agriculture had reversed the trends of the N.E.P. period, and, above all, when the great series of trials of alleged 'traitors' and 'saboteurs' had got under way. Even when the situation had changed in these respects, many observers were still misled into mistaking the new Soviet Constitution of 1936 for an advance in the direction of liberal democracy on account of its provisions for universal suffrage and apparently free elections. Moreover, the internal conditions were to some extent hidden from view by the real change in Soviet external policy that came about after the victory of Nazism. In the middle 'thirties the Soviet Union was quite genuinely feeling its way towards an international anti-Fascist front ; and the Communist Parties of the West were attempting to create various forms of 'United Front' that involved a reversal of previous tactics in respect of their relations with other working-class elements. These moves, though rejected by the Social Democratic and Labour Parties in most of the Western countries—except France and, for a time, Spain — did induce many Western Socialists to turn a half-blind eye to the features of the Soviet political and economic system of which they most strongly disapproved.

During the 1920s, however, though the rival Internationals fought the battle of 'dictatorship versus democracy' over and over again, many who were strongly opposed to the splitting tactics of the Comintern, and keenly resented its continuous attacks on the Centre as well as on the Right, drew a sharp distinction in their minds between it and the Soviet Government, despite the control which the latter was clearly in a position to exercise, and did actually exercise whenever it thought fit, over the Comintern's policy and proceedings. Zinoviev and his fellow-protagonists in the Comintern were widely regarded as firebrands to be distinguished from the relatively prudent controllers of official Soviet policy, which seemed to be concentrated more and more on the task of building up 'Socialism in a single country' as the prospect of early World Revolution faded away. The divergence was indeed real ; but it involved, in the 1920s, much less a conflict between Stalin and the Comintern than an agreed demarcation of spheres of action. After the defeat of the Hungarian Revolution of 1919, and the *débâcle* of the Communists in Germany — and still more after the break of the Kuomintang with the Chinese Communists had made havoc of the Comintern's projects of revolution in Asia, the Comintern ceased, for the time being, to be an immediate promoter of World Revolution and became an agency for fostering the growth of Communist movements with the principal purpose of safeguarding the interests of the Soviet Union, while awaiting the advent of the hoped-for world economic crisis that was expected to make international Revolution once more an immediately practicable objective. This change of line was in effect forced on the Comintern by sheer pressure of events ; and one of its effects was to render that body and the Parties associated with it even more subject to Russian control and more definitely instruments of the Russians' desire to build up additional defences for the Soviet Union. Even this, however, was less apparent at the time than it came to be at a later stage.

I admit that I myself had, in the 1920s, no clear appreciation of the strength of totalitarian tendencies in the Soviet Union, and shared the belief that the trend there would be towards increasing liberalisation as the Soviet economy settled down and became able to achieve real advances in the living standards and educational and cultural development of the Russian peoples. Unlike some of my friends and colleagues in the Guild Socialist movement, I was never under any temptation to become a Communist, because my attitude was basically pluralistic and libertarian and I was repelled by the Bolsheviks' conception of a social philosophy based on rigidly determinist principles and involving the unquestionable class-correctness of a single, unified body of doctrine, regardless of considerations of time and place. I believed — and continue to believe — that the essential foundation of liberty is freedom to *choose*, and that any 'good' society must be of such a nature as to allow and encourage this freedom and to include within it a wide diversity of autonomous institutions, each at liberty to shape its own policy within the general framework of a flexible structure of institutions between which real disagreements can find expression and be resolved by open discussion. This attitude, akin rather to that of William Morris, or of P. J. Proudhon, or even of Kropotkin, than to either Communism or orthodox Social Democracy, necessarily held me apart from the Communists, and would have done so even if they had behaved much more sensibly than in fact most of them did. Yet, even if I had been more fully aware than I actually was of the extent of their commitment to the monolithic heresy, I do not think that my view of the proper attitude for non-Communist Socialists to adopt towards the Soviet Union would have been greatly, if at all, affected. It would still have seemed to me a duty incumbent on all Socialists to rally to the help of the Soviet Union, not only against those enemies who continued to hope for its overthrow by counter-revolutionaries within or without, but also against those who attempted, by any means, to build a *cordon sanitaire* for keeping its influence at bay. I believed — and believe to-day — that the Russian Revolution of 1917 — including its Bolshevik phase — was not only an outstanding event in world history but also, on the whole, a beneficent event because it pointed the way towards emancipation from feudal rule and imperialist oppression to a vast section of the world's peoples, and especially to those who were most sorely oppressed and most deeply poor and un-instructed. Communism might have no valid message for the more advanced countries, in which the peoples had already won both substantial democratic liberties and considerable economic, social, and educational gains. It had none the less, in my view, a clear message for a large part of the world — a message which the Social Democrats of the West appeared to have no effective will to transmit, or even to appreciate.

I was, indeed, even at this stage, repelled by the ruthlessness with which the Bolsheviks pursued all who disagreed with them, or refused to accept their will as law. From the very outset it seemed to be taken for granted by the Bolshevik leaders both that 'class-enemies' had no human rights at all and could be killed or maltreated without any sort of com-punction, and that the notion of who were 'class-enemies' could properly be extended to anyone — including any Socialist — who opposed the absolute rule of the Communist Party. I do not mean that I was clearly conscious of this attitude in the early stages of Bolshevik rule, in 1917 or 1918, though I realised later that it had been present all along and formed a definite part of the Communist philosophy of conduct. I became aware of it, I think, only during the civil war of 1919–20, and was then disposed to discount it as an almost inevitable accompaniment of the fighting and to expect that it would come to a speedy end when the civil war was over. I became much more deeply disturbed at the time of the Kronstadt

Revolt early in 1921, when the killing of Socialists by Socialists first appeared as an open element in the struggle of the Bolsheviks to consolidate their political power. At that stage, however, the display of ruthlessness against the Kronstadt mutineers coincided in time with the New Economic Policy, which seemed to indicate a very different tendency ; and, like many other Socialists, understanding but dimly the events at Kronstadt, I was at least half-prepared to give the Bolsheviks the benefit of the doubt, and to explain the growing persecution of Social Revolutionaries and Mensheviks as the outcome of civil war conditions, rather than as the expression of a deliberate policy of exterminating all possible sources of dissident leadership. I simply did not understand the full implications of Leninism as denying the validity of any moral code applicable to all men irrespective of their class connections or attitudes, and mistakenly supposed that the excesses, which I could not but deeply disapprove, were a legacy from the inhumanities of Czarism, aggravated by the critical conditions of semi-starvation and of civil war, and would be repudiated by the Bolshevik leaders themselves as soon as the Revolution had got past the phase of its most acute peril. I see now that I was wrong about this, and that the ruthlessness and the rejection of so-called 'bourgeois' notions of morality formed an integral part of the Bolshevik attitude. But it was much less easy to see this in the years immediately after 1917 than it is to-day, and much easier to discount what one did half-see of it as a largely unavoidable accompaniment of revolution and civil war in a country as devoid as Russia was of any tradition of civilised or tolerant political and social behaviour.

Thus, though I was no Communist and differed profoundly from the Communist version of the Marxist gospel, I was at the same time highly critical of the Social Democratic gospel as it was preached by the Berne International and by its successor, the Labour and Socialist International set up at Hamburg in 1923. The gospel of parliamentary gradualism preached by these bodies seemed to me to involve a disastrous narrowing of the Socialist creed, as if that creed could be applied only to countries which had already passed through the entire course of capitalist development and had acquired the habit of being governed by Western parliamentary methods.

As against this, I stood—and stand—for a conception of Social-ism wide enough to embrace all the world's peoples, without the requirement that they must first experience for themselves the complete process of capitalist domination or must arrive at the acceptance of parliamentary institutions modelled closely on those of Western Europe or the United States. I did not believe either that there was a single road to Socialism by which all peoples must travel in their turn or that the Socialism towards which they must travel would be uniform from country to country, either on the Soviet model or on that of Western parliamentary democracy. I was, indeed, at bottom, less interested in political than in economic and social institutions, holding the environment in which human beings passed their daily lives and did their daily work to be even more important for their well-being and freedom than the large-scale political structures which exercised over them the sovereign powers of governmental authority. In short, I was — and I remain — a Guild Socialist—neither a Communist nor a Social Democrat in the ordinary sense, but something, not betwixt and between these two, but essentially different from both.

Guild Socialism, I am well aware, was never, even at its point of highest influence, an at all widely held version of the Socialist gospel. It remained primarily a British movement, though it had analogues in a number of other countries — for example, in the French movement for 'la nationalisation industrialisée', in the activities of the Histadruth in Palestine, in the American 'Plumb Plan' for the railways, in the Cata-lonian version of Anarcho-Syndicalism, and in many projects for workers' participation in the control of industry in other parts of the world — including Russia itself. It was not, how-ever, strong enough either to stand up to the Trade Union defeats that accompanied the post-war depression or to intrude effectively as a third party into the great dispute between the rival Internationals. In this dispute it could appear only as the rather uncomfortable ally of that Centralist tendency which was represented for a time by the 'Two-and-a-half' Inter-national, the Vienna Union, which was itself before long crushed out by the greater organised weight of the two extremes.

The creation of the Vienna Union was indeed based on a recognition that no single road of advance towards Socialism could really fit the widely different circumstances of all the world's peoples. It was an attempt to persuade Socialists throughout the world to recognise the need for varying methods of struggle and, instead of quarrelling about their differences, to reconstruct a common International within which they could all continue to live together by virtue of common objectives, despite wide differences in the methods by which these objectives were to be pursued. This project of remaking the old Second International on a new basis corresponding to the conditions of the post-war period never stood any real chance of success. The differences were too wide, not merely in themselves, but even more in the strength of the passions they aroused. It was impossible for Communists, who denounced their Socialist opponents as 'social traitors', and Social Democrats, who insisted that parliamentary democracy was a necessary prerequisite of Socialism and any form of 'dictatorship' an unforgivable crime in any circumstances, to work together in a single organisation, however loose. Nor was it possible for co-operation to exist between those who stood uncompromisingly for a centrally controlled International, within which the national Parties would be no more than subordinate local groups, and those who claimed the right for Socialists in each country to settle their own policy in accordance with local — in most cases, primarily electoral — conditions. The organisational unity for which the Vienna Union stood was a chimera ; but that does not alter the fact that a great many Socialists in many countries did have a keen sense of the vital importance of Socialist and working-class unity, and were in sympathy neither with Communism nor with the all-embracing parliamentarism of the Social Democratic leaders. The Centre failed, as this volume will I hope make clear, much less because there was a shortage of Centrists than because, despite their numbers and their individual qualities, they were unable to establish themselves as an effective third party between the Comintern, which had behind it the power and prestige of the Soviet Union, and the revived Second International, which could reckon on the backing of the majority of Socialism's parliamentary protagonists in the advanced countries of the Western world.

It will become evident to readers of this volume that in the post-war struggles within the world Socialist movement, my sympathies were with the Centre, though I never shared its faith in the practical possibility of re-establishing a single International acceptable to the contending factions. When the vision of unity faded, I did not dispute the correctness of the Vienna Union's decision to merge itself in the new Labour and Socialist International, even though that body was clearly cal- culated to ensure the dominance of the parliamentarian right wing. There was, indeed, no other course open. Union with the Comintern was plainly ruled out by that body's intransigent attitude, embodied in the 'Twenty-one Points'; whereas adherence to the L.S.I. did leave open the possibility of working for a less uncompromisingly reformist policy within its affiliated Parties. The L.S.I. was indeed somewhat less dogmatically right-wing than the Berne International which it replaced, though not markedly so in any vital respect. The Italians being reduced to small groups of exiles by the victory of Fascism, and the French Socialist Party having become a shadow of its former self in face of the rise of the Communist Party, the L.S.I. was necessarily dominated by the Germans and the British, with the lesser countries of the West — Austrians, Swedes, Danes, Dutch, Belgians, and Swiss — playing im- portant but secondary rôles in its affairs. The Norwegians remained aloof from it for some time after their final break with the Comintern, and linked up with the L.S.I. only in 1938. In the United States, the American Socialist Party almost disintegrated; and in the rest of the American con- tinent only small and mainly ineffective Socialist movements existed. The Australian and New Zealand Labour Parties remained aloof; and in Asia and Africa, Socialist Parties, as distinct from small and mostly evanescent groups of intellectuals, had hardly begun to emerge except in South Africa, where sharp struggles already existed between rival 'all-White' and pro-African factions. The L.S.I. was to all intents and purposes a loose federation of West European Parties, mainly in countries where parliamentary institutions were strongly entrenched and Communism had but little appeal, as in Scandinavia and in Great Britain, or where the parliamentarians were fighting a rearguard action against in- creasingly powerful reactionary forces, as in Germany and

Austria. In shaping the policy of its affiliated Parties the
L.S.I. was not able to play much part : indeed, it hardly
attempted to do so. Its representatives met from time to time
in general Congresses and in meetings of its bureau ; but,
except when they were making protests against reactionary
violence in Eastern and Southern Europe or drawing up
abortive plans for disarmament and for the strengthening of the
ineffective League of Nations, they hardly tried to do more
than exchange experiences and make available a few data
about the fortunes of the movement in the affiliated countries.

As against this, the Comintern displayed a ceaseless activity
in the affairs of every country into which it was able to penetrate
at all — even where its adherents were few and it had to act
largely through a variety of subsidiary 'front' organisations
lacking in real representative influence. This activity was often
misguided, and even mischievous ; and it often provoked re-
pressions which extended far beyond the Communist ranks.
It provided, however, plain indications of a zeal which, in
many areas, the non-Communist movements and Parties were
quite unable to match. One of its weaknesses was that it was
altogether too apt to ask of its supporters more than flesh and
blood could bear ; another was that it recruited all too many
who were merely disgruntled and presently passed over to
work for movements of a directly opposite kind, as when
former Communists in Germany turned to Nazism in large
numbers during the years of Hitler's rise to power ; or as
Chiang Kai-shek in China, having made use of the Communists to serve his ends, rounded upon them and almost
totally destroyed, for the time being, their influence in the
towns, leaving Mao to build up a new Chinese Communist
movement mainly in the country areas.

A further weakness of the Comintern, even in the 1920s,
was that its policy was constantly dominated by the Russians,
who regarded and treated the Communist Parties of other
countries as merely subordinate auxiliaries in their conflict
with the capitalist world. At first, this subordination was, at
any rate ostensibly, not to the Russians as Russians, but to the
cause of the World Revolution in which Russia was playing
the outstanding rôle. But, from the very beginning, the first
duty imposed on Communists throughout the world was that

of defending the Russian Revolution as the base from which the World Revolution was to be promoted : so that the interest of Russia as *the* revolutionary power was held to come first. Subsequently, when it became clear that the hopes of World Revolution had to be deferred, the Communists of other countries found themselves required to act almost exclusively as supporters of Russian national policies, without direct reference to the furtherance of the Revolution in their own countries or in the world as a whole. The interests of Russia as a world power were simply identified with the revolutionary cause ; and Communist Parties were called upon to act in ways that did not suit their own national conditions simply because that was how the Russians wanted them to act. The pursuance of such a policy was possible only under leaders who were prepared to accept the Russian decisions out of absolute loyalty to the Russians as the protagonists of revolution ; and, because of this, Communist leaders who questioned this attitude were continually being driven out or forced to resign and were thereafter denounced as traitors and apostates. The Comintern was continually denouncing its own children and destroying the local influence of its own parties by compelling them to act as agents of Russia rather than as independent revolutionary parties; and the difficulties of these parties were continually aggravated because the Russians again and again altered the approved party line to suit their own ends in a changing world situation.

The 1920s were thus a difficult time for both Communists and Social Democrats. Even where, as in Great Britain, Sweden, Denmark, and Belgium, the parliamentary Socialist Parties from time to time took office, mostly in coalition Governments but lacking the support of independent majorities of their own, their accomplishments were of necessity very limited, and in some cases their records were hardly glorious. The British minority Labour Governments of 1924 and 1929–1931 both ended in somewhat ignominious collapse. The Scandinavians, facing less difficult situations, did better ; but their main achievements belong rather to the 1930s and were chiefly in the field of improved welfare rather than of positive Socialist construction. As matters stood in 1931, when the world economic crisis reached a critical phase, Western Europe seemed in general as far off Socialism as it had done ten years earlier ; and Communism, though it had consolidated its authority in the Soviet Union, seemed a long way further off achieving World Revolution than it had seemed to be on the morrow of the first world war.

The Socialist record in the 1920s was, indeed, least inspiring of all in the realm of Socialist thought, except for those who are ready to exult in the successes of Communism both in the consolidation of the new Soviet Union and in working out the practical implications of the Leninist conceptions of proletarian dictatorship and one-party rule. The general underlying theory which the Bolsheviks set out to apply after their victory had already been worked out by Lenin over a long period of years, and existed in its main outlines well before 1917. It underwent considerable transformations at the hands of Lenin's successors, particularly Stalin ; but I at any rate find it impossible to regard these developments as advances in Socialist thinking. It is true that a great deal was done to work out the techniques of planning and public accounting in an economy that was mainly socialised except in its still predominant agricultural sector, and that the Bolsheviks showed, on the whole, an unexpectedly high competence in handling the tasks of restoring and expanding industrial output, at any rate in the heavy industries and in the development of electrical power. These successes, however, were achieved at the cost of a progressive destruction of such internal democracy as the Communist Party had possessed at the outset, and of an immense growth of bureaucratic power, accompanied by a deliberate repudiation of equalitarian notions as products of the idealistic petit-bourgeois mind, and by an almost unlimited resort to monetary incentives, of which Stakhanovism became the outstanding symbol. The new order in the Soviet Union involved the steady waning of the power of the Soviets and a parallel growth in that of the increasingly monolithic and centralised Communist Party. It also brought with it the complete subordination of the Trade Unions to the Party, the liquidation of the urban Co-operatives, which were handed over to the State, and the systematic elimination of every sort of group that could possibly have become a vehicle for open criticism of the policy of the ruling *élite*. These things, moreover, took place, not so much while Russia was engaged in a desperate struggle for sheer survival during the Civil War, as increasingly when that war was over, even during the period of apparent liberalisation inaugurated by the New Economic Policy of 1921. The new Stalinist policy reached its high point of oppressive centralisation only later on ; but the seeds of it were being sown steadily from the moment when Stalin began to consolidate his power over the party machine and set to work to secure, step by step, the liquidation of such of his former comrades as were not prepared to cede their wills and judgments unquestioningly to his. The elimination of Trotsky was the first plainly evident sign of this unhappy process ; and Trotsky fared better than the subsequent victims in being allowed to depart from the Soviet Union alive.

The question here arises: how far had Lenin, in his writings up to 1917, already worked out the essentials of the policy which the Bolsheviks actually followed after they took power ? Clearly, Lenin had already formulated his conception of the 'dictatorship of the proletariat', based on an elaboration of the by no means precise ideas contained in Marx's writings, and had combined this conception with that of a Party consisting of, or at any rate dominated by, a corps of professional revolutionists bound together by a very strong corporate discipline. These conceptions, combined, contained in them the germ of the doctrine of 'democratic centralism', in the sense of the disciplined pursuance by the entire Party of the policies decided upon by the members, and of the full acceptance by minorities of decisions arrived at by the majority. The moot question is how far they also carried with them the power of the Central Executive Committee to act as the authoritative interpreter of the Party's will, so as to lead to the imposition of policies by the Central Committee rather than to their formulation as a result of free discussion in the branches, with the Committee acting as interpreter of the members' opinions. It was, no doubt, impossible in practice for the effective decisions on policy to be taken, in the conditions of 1917 and the ensuing years of civil war, by processes of full democratic consultation and building up from below. But in 1917 there was at any rate consultation of Moscow and other accessible local centres by the Central Committee in Petrograd up to the point of the revolutionary assumption of power. As soon, however, as the Bolsheviks had become the Government, the leaders in Petrograd had to act, and to devise their policies, mainly on their own ; and it appears that the notion of 'democratic centralism' as involving the authoritative rule of the Central Committee, if not wholly based on this necessity, was in practice largely influenced by it and led to a radical transformation in the concept of party democracy that prepared the way for Stalin's subsequent bureaucratisation of the Communist Party machine, and served to exclude the rank-and-file membership of the greatly enlarged Party from any effective share in settling its policy. This growth of less than 'democratic' centralism largely preceded in practice its formulation as part of the Bolshevik theory : it had gone a long way in practice before it was invoked as a reason for the official prohibition of 'fractions' within the Party and as a case for muzzling and suppressing the 'Workers' Opposition'. In effect, the internal democracy of the Bolshevik Party, even in the early stages of its tenure of power, hardly extended beyond the members of the Central Committee ; but this was still at these stages a matter of practical necessity rather than of recognised party dogma. Stalin only aggravated and consolidated a practice that had already gone a long way in Lenin's lifetime, but had hardly been proclaimed as a matter of principle before even this element of 'central committee democracy' had been greatly eroded in practice.

In this development of Stalinism, which rested on foundations that had been laid by Lenin while the Revoluton was still to make, I can see nothing that can properly be called a development of Socialist thought, unless one is prepared to regard in that light the acceptance and working out of the idea that it was possible to establish Socialism in a single country, Russia, without waiting for the Revolution to be achieved in the advanced capitalist countries, and without looking to the workers of these countries for any substantial positive help. As we shall see, the Bolsheviks of 1917 were united in taking almost for granted the impracticability of maintaining themselves in power unless the World Revolution, or at the very least, the German Revolution, came to their aid. Hence their almost frantic efforts to foment Communist Revolution in Germany as long as they could find enough support there even for a *putsch* on any substantial scale. As against this attitude it was a real change to entertain the idea of establishing, if not a fully Communist, at any rate a viable Socialist society capable of enduring and developing in a single country, however extensive and well-equipped with exploitable natural resources. It has, however, to be borne in mind that this new idea was a product of necessity, rather than of invention. For, in face of the undeniable set-back to the prospect of World Revolution, what else was there for the Russians to do save to make the best of their own recuperative and creative powers? They set out to build Socialism in a single country, not of choice, but because the only alternative open to them was to admit total failure. Such an alternative was unthinkable for men who were certain that the inexorable forces of history were with them and that the collapse of world capitalism, though it might take longer than they had hoped and expected, was still bound to occur at no very distant time. Their mission, as they saw it, was to hold on grimly until the 'final crisis' of capitalism arrived, and in the meantime to make themselves at all costs as strong as they could for resistance to every sort of capitalist attack or encirclement — which meant that they must strain every nerve to add to their productive power, above all in those industries which formed the essential basis of power in war and of self-dependence in the pressing task of capital construction. In these circumstances, intense concentration on the heavy industries seemed a sheer necessity; and, with population rising fast, it seemed no less indispensable to take drastic measures in order to lift Russian agriculture out of its backwardness by assimilating it as much as possible to the model of large-scale industrialism. The collectivisation of agriculture followed as the intended first step towards an industrialised and mechanised order in farming that would at one and the same time increase agricultural output and assimilate the mind of the peasant to that of the urban wage-earner.

There was a grandeur, or at least a grandiosity, about this conception of a largely primitive country lifting itself by its own unaided efforts to the level of the highest productive achievements of capitalism — and then beyond them — which could readily be regarded as justifying any means, however ruthless, that might be necessary for its realisation. If the

Bolshevik leaders had had any high regard for the 'rights of man' in the sense in which that phrase had been continuously understood in the West, they might have shrunk back appalled at the immediate cost in human suffering of what they were setting out to do. But they had no such regard, partly because their basic theory involved a denial of all 'rights' other than those related to the interests of a particular class — the proletariat—and partly because the society in which they had grown up had itself been so regardless of human costs. Their conception of 'rights' was connected not with individuals or with human beings as such, but with entire classes, or even with a single class regarded as including not only its actual members but also those who were to be raised up into it by the development of industrialisation on the largest possible scale ; and they were unmoved, at any rate for the most part, by the thought of sufferings to be inflicted either on 'class-enemies' or even on persons who could not be identified with the proletariat as a class. In this mood, they found it easy to stretch the notion of 'class-enemies' to include any group they wanted to liquidate in the interests of their grand plan of comprehensive socialisation. This did not prevent them from making large efforts to develop social services and to expand educational opportunities ; for both these things could make important contributions to the establishment of the kind of society at which they were aiming. It did, however, mean that the individual counted for them only as a potential contributor to the success of their immensely ambitious plan, and that they claimed a perfect right both to dispose, by any means, of anyone who seemed to stand in the way of this plan, and to treat any individual — including any member of the proletariat — as an instrument for furthering the collective interest of the class they claimed to represent.

This class conception of 'rights', with its emphasis on the 'collective' rather than the individual human being, is strongly repugnant to those who accept the more individualistic approach of Western believers in the 'rights of man'. In the West, the notion of basic 'rights' has come to be connected closely with that of claims attaching to every human being, by sheer virtue of his or her humanity, and with that of universal brotherhood, as binding men together irrespective of class or creed, or of any special characteristics that differ from person to person. I do not, of course, mean that Western societies have in practice lived up to this universal humanist conception ; but it has at least been widely entertained, and has had positive consequences : in the repudiation of slavery, in the acceptance of universal suffrage, in the gradual development of certain basic social services, and in many other respects. Thus, it seems sheerly immoral to many people in the Western countries, including Western Socialists, to link the notion of rights to a particular social class or to think of rights as applying collectively to the class rather than to individuals. This attitude does, however, appear to fit in with the Marxist denial of social 'solidarity' — that is to say, of any bond among the members of a feudal or capitalist society binding them all together despite class differences — especially if this denial is combined with a rejection of the idea of a common morality by which all men are bound under the law of God or 'nature'. If morality is not 'natural' but conventional, and if there is no common convention uniting all the members of a society made up of contending social classes, there appears to be no room for the notion of basic rights belonging to human beings as such, either within a society or on a world-wide scale. Acceptance of such a view, however, runs counter to the moral habits and traditions of modern Western societies and to modern Christian doctrine. To a great extent the conflict of moral codes between the adherents of humanistic or Western Christian conceptions of the rights of man and the Marxist-Communist conception of class-morality underlay the struggle of the rival Internationals for the allegiance of the world's working-classes and prompted their conflicting manifestoes. The Berne International's assertion of 'democracy' as a prerequisite of Socialism was derived from the notion of a basic solidarity of all, irrespective of class or creed, whereas the Comintern's defiant proclamation of purely proletarian rights emerged from the idea of the class-struggle as paramount, and of morality itself as meaningful only within the framework of class. These contending attitudes could not be reconciled ; and accordingly the attempts of the 'Two-and-a-half' Internationalists to transcend them were bound to fail.

This proclamation by the Communists of the supremacy of proletarian morality resting on the conception of class-war as an overriding historical fact was not a new doctrine born of the Russian Revolution. It had been put forward long before 1917 by Marx and Engels in the *Communist Manifesto* of 1848, and was not wholly new even then. It had been in effect an integral part of the early Marxist gospel, but had been played down, and even half forgotten, by the German and other Social Democratic Parties in the course of their rise to parliamentary influence. It had continued to be a living creed much more among Syndicalists and Anarcho-Syndicalists in France, Spain, and Italy than among the Western Social Democrats of the Second International. It had lived on, and taken on additional sharpness, in Russia and in other areas of Eastern Europe where the struggle was exceptionally bitter, and where the idea of basic social solidarity had found almost no foundation in the facts ; but, even in Russia it had not been acceptable to the Menshevik leaders, who were deeply influenced by Western ideas — or to such old stalwarts of revolutionary Social Democracy as Plekhanov. It had, however, appealed strongly to Lenin, whose deep hatred of the Russian autocracy and essentially Russian angle of vision made it appear to him as a thoroughly correct interpretation of the facts. Lenin, influenced by Auguste Blanqui and, perhaps even more, by Peter Tkachov,[1] the most extreme exponent of the idea of an international revolutionary *élite*, restated this aspect of Marxism in a most uncompromising form, and made it the basis of his determination, from 1914 onwards, to wage relentless war on the 'social patriots' and, instead of attempting to reconstruct the old International, to create a new one on the principles which he put forward unsuccessfully at Zimmerwald in 1915, but persuaded the delegates at Kienthal to accept a year later. The foundations for the Third International were thus laid at the Kienthal Conference ; and both the title and the substance of the opening manifesto of the Comintern in 1919 were a deliberate resuscitation of the *Communist Manifesto* of 1848.

There was, then, nothing new in the basic ideas of international Communism as they were stated in the *Communist Manifesto* of 1919. What was new in the Comintern's policy was the decision, in the light of these ideas, to wage relentless struggle not only against the 'social patriots' of the reviving

[1] For Tkachov, see Vol. II, p. 54.

Second International but also, even more vehemently, against the Centrists who were attempting to reunite the contending factions. This involved splitting the Socialist and working-class movement, not in such a way as to bring over the largest possible number of supporters to the new Communist International, but so as to ensure the purity of its doctrine at the cost of driving away large sections of its potential backers. In this spirit the Comintern drew up its 'Twenty-one Points', threw away a large part of its backing in Italy, in Norway, and in a number of other countries, and forced the reluctant Centrists back into association with the predominantly right-wing, anti-revolutionary Labour and Socialist International. It has to be borne in mind that, at the outset, this strategy was adopted in the belief that World Revolution was both imminent and indispensable to the survival of the Soviet Revolution; but it was persisted in after these anticipations had been falsified because it did follow logically from the principles of Marxism as Lenin understood them, and could therefore not be given up merely because the tactical situation changed. Indeed, this basic attitude was fully as much Stalin's as Lenin's, and was in no respect fundamentally altered by the change of leadership. If, in the 1930s, the Communists seemed for a time to modify their line under pressure of the need to rally all possible supporters for an anti-Fascist crusade, the Nazi-Soviet Pact of 1939 was presently to show that there had been no fundamental change in the Communist attitude, which continued to rest on a denial that 'right' could have any political meaning except in relation to class, and on an assertion that the Soviet Union, as the embodiment of proletarian victory, was fully entitled to shape its course without regard for bourgeois conceptions of right and wrong.

I am saying, in effect, that, however shocked Lenin might have been, had he lived on as an observer, by the developments of Stalinism in later years — and I believe he would have found much in them to shock him — the fundamental philosophy of class-morality and 'class-right' was just as much Lenin's as Stalin's. Indeed, it was really much more so; for Lenin clearly believed in it and did his best to act up to it, whereas it is difficult to regard Stalin as being liberal in anything except his personal 'right' to destroy his enemies and rivals by any and every means. Lenin, when he said 'class-rule', meant class-rule, and did really think of the Communist Party as the veritable representative of the working class. He did value discussion within the Party — at all events, within the central leadership — as a means of arriving at party policy ; and he did understand the need to keep the Party in close and constant touch with the main body of the proletariat it was seeking to represent. He was indeed often insistent on getting his own way, and impatient of critics whom he regarded as either timidly hesitant or unpractical ; but he did set out to persuade rather than to browbeat his direct colleagues, and did assign to the Soviets a real rôle in the processes of government — even though, as we saw, he fell foul of Trotsky in 1917 concerning the respective rôles of Party and Soviet in the moment of actual revolution.[1] On the whole, it is, I think, true to say that Lenin believed in 'class', rather than in 'party', dictatorship ; but with this went a firm belief in the Party as the true representative of the class and in a party discipline which, in effect, involved the dictatorship of the Party rather than of the class. Certainly he did not believe that any proletarian, by virtue of his class, had a right to deviate from the correct class doctrine embodied in the decisions of the Party ; and, within the Party itself, he laid the greatest stress both on ideological correctness, as against individual judgment or opinion based on individual experience, and on the need for the party leadership, at every moment of crisis or important decision on policy, to take full authority and responsibility into its own hands. After Lenin's removal, the party leadership more and more replaced the Party as a whole as the designated representatives of the proletariat as a class. In Lenin's day, under the rule of so-called 'democratic centralism', this replacement had already gone a long way in practice. Stalin carried it further, and raised it to the rank of a dogma, and then proceeded to run beyond it by replacing the collegiate leadership by the supreme authority of a single dominating personality. It is, however, a mistake to regard Stalin as the sole destroyer of democracy within the Communist Party. In fact, it had ceased to exist—so far as it ever had existed — long before he reached a position of exclusive power.

If, in the 1920s, there was much more revival of old Socialist

[1] See p. 89.

doctrine derived from the Marxism of 1848 than of new Socialist thinking on the Communist side, what, we may now ask, was the position on the side of Social Democracy? How much significant new thinking did the theorists of Social Democracy and Socialist Labourism produce? The answer, in terms of major new developments, must, I fear, be that they produced very little. I do not know of any major Social Democratic 'classic' of the war or post-war years. Sidney and Beatrice Webb's *Constitution for the Socialist Commonwealth of Great Britain*, with its proposal for two parallel Parliaments, political and social, is generally regarded as among the least good of their writings; nor is Bernard Shaw's *Intelligent Woman's Guide to Socialism and Capitalism* at all a major work. Nor, again, was H. G. Wells's *Work, Wealth and Happiness of Mankind* nearly so significant as his pre-war writings. Karl Kautsky's later writings include his long study of Socialist attitudes to war, *Sozialisten und Krieg*, and his forthright attack on the Communist theory of dictatorship (in *The Dictatorship of the Proletariat*, published in 1919); but neither of these makes any significant constructive contribution to Socialist theory. In France, nothing of primary importance appeared except in the field of historical studies (*e.g.* the first volume of Édouard Dolléans's *Histoire du mouvement ouvrier*). Italy, torn asunder by the Fascist struggle, produced only occasional controversial writing; Spain, almost nothing until the 1930s. The Scandinavians were active in working out plans of social reform, but made hardly any general contribution to Socialist theory. The Americans published nothing substantial; the Latin Americans, nothing much till the rise of Haya de la Torre's Aprista movement in the later 'twenties. In Belgium, Vandervelde and de Brouckère wrote on, but in the main only in the exposition of ideas already advanced before the war, though de Brouckère's *Le Contrôle ouvrier* (1924) has some claim to be considered as a real contribution to post-war thinking. In Holland, Edo Fimmen's *Europe's Alternative : the United States of Europe or Europe Ltd.* (1924) deserves a mention. So, for Austria, does Otto Bauer's *Der Weg zum Sozialismus* (1919). The total 'bag', however, is not very satisfying. Many of the Social Democratic writers were already more preoccupied with denouncing Communism than with elaborating their own attitudes ; and much of the better writing was concerned with particular projects of reform, or in some cases, of nationalisation, more than with the general issues of Socialist theory and policy.

The principal innovators, indeed, mainly in Great Britain, were the Guild Socialists, who can be classed neither with the Communists nor among their Social Democratic opposites. For the Guild Socialists had, as we saw, a quite distinctive standpoint of their own, especially in their pluralistic conception of social relations and in their insistence on the precedence of economic over political power. Sharing with the Syndicalists and Industrial Unionists an ardent belief in 'industrial democracy' and direct 'workers' control' of industry, they nevertheless accepted the State as a necessary institution for the expression of general interests and sought to find a reconciliation between the claims of political and economic self-government. I was myself too closely connected with the Guild Socialist movement to be in a position to estimate objectively the importance of its contribution to Socialist thought; but in my opinion, for what it is worth, the Guild Socialists did make the outstanding contribution to new non-Communist theories of Socialism during and immediately after the first world war. Guild Socialism had indeed begun before 1914 ; [1] but its influence became considerable only during the war years, and, as we shall see, it faded away in the post-war decade when its adherents broke up into contending groups, partly on issues arising out of the Russian Revolution, and partly when a section of them fell in love with the Social Credit theories of the now almost-forgotten Major C. H. Douglas. The slump of the early 1920s also seriously undermined its influence on the Trade Unions and brought about the collapse of the Building Guilds which had been set up under the inspiration of some of its leading exponents. Guild Socialism was extinguished as a movement ; but it survived as a seminal idea, emphasising the need for industrial as well as political self-government and for the decentralisation of social structures in order to counteract bureaucratic tendencies, and to diffuse social responsibility over as many persons as possible, or a foundation of democratic control through face-to-face working groups.

[1] See Vol. III, pp. 212 f., 223 ff., 236, 242 ff.

In relation to the world scale on which this study of Socialism is conceived, Guild Socialism may seem a small — even a parochial — matter. I cannot feel it so, because I regard its insistence on the need to apply democratic methods of self-government to every aspect of social organisation and at every level, with the face-to-face groups as the essential foundation, as vitally important for the reconciliation of Socialist planning with personal freedom, and for making democracy real in face of the need for large-scale organisation and control. In these matters I feel strongly that both Communism and Social Democracy have gone astray through an undue stress on the notion that centralisation of power is a necessary element in Socialist control, and even that the tendencies of capitalism towards trustification and monopoly are, in their organisational aspect, steps on the road to Socialism. This attitude, as we saw in the third volume of this study,[1] was highly characteristic of German Social Democracy in particular, and was vigorously expressed in the writings of Kautsky, which were widely accepted before 1914 as the classic formulation of the Marxian doctrine. There were, of course, always contrary currents of thought, especially among the Anarchists and Syndicalists — in Bakunin and in Proudhon, and later in Kropotkin, William Morris, and Pelloutier. But among the parliamentary Socialists there was a sustained tendency to favour centralisation and concentration of authority ; and Communism, with its immense stress on the question of 'power' and its dismissal of ethical valuations, made even more strongly for centralised discipline and control. Guild Socialism, and the doctrines akin to it that developed in other countries, mattered because they reasserted, in forms appropriate to the twentieth century, the libertarian aspect, at a time when this needed to be emphasised more than ever before in face both of the immense growth of scale in the modern economy and of the formidable concentration of power, first in revolutionary Russia and later wherever any form of totalitarian gospel was able to impose itself on the affairs of men.

With this preamble, the developments recorded in the succeeding chapters can be left to speak for themselves.

[1] See Vol. III, Part II, p. 970.

CHAPTER II

THREE CONFERENCES: ZIMMERWALD, KIENTHAL, STOCKHOLM

IN August 1914, as we saw in the preceding volume of this work, the Second International collapsed, never to be effectively reborn. While it lasted, despite many disputes on policy both within and between the national groups which made it up, there was at any rate a single International to which almost all the world's Socialists felt themselves to belong, and to owe some sort of loyalty. Moreover, the number of national movements attached to it tended to increase, as Socialist organisation took shape in more countries and as growing attention and anxiety became focused on the International as a potential agency, not so much for the establishment of Socialism as for the prevention of war. Within the Second International there were very wide differences of view concerning the methods of action open to the workers for averting the tragedy of war between the great powers ; and the celebrated resolution carried in 1907 at the Stuttgart Congress papered over these differences rather than resolved them, so that it furnished no clear guidance to action when the time for action arrived. There were differences certainly no less wide about the method of advancing towards a Socialist society ; but, paradoxically, these counted for less in the International's affairs than those connected with the prevention of war. The reason for this is plain : broadly speaking, each national group, and even each faction within it, was free to take up its own line about its methods of action in domestic affairs — though, of course, some methods were practically excluded in some countries by government repression or by other internal conditions. As against this, successful action against war clearly needed to be concerted action, at any rate by the Socialist movements in the countries directly concerned. The Socialists of one country could hope to prevent war only if their country were clearly the aggressor, and if they could bring to bear sufficient pressure to deter its rulers from carrying out their aggressive plans. But even if the aggressor were plain, it by no means followed that the Socialists would be able to deter him ; and in the state of European politics before 1914 it was all but certain that, even though the principal immediate aggressor might be identifiable, there would be at the least some blame imputable to the other party. In such a case it was inevitable that action capable of preventing war would have to be international, involving the participation of the workers of the potential belligerent countries on both sides ; and the leaders of the Second International, despite much argument, had never thought out the practical implications of such action. They had discussed, without endorsing, the proposal to declare a simultaneous general strike ; but they had never even considered counselling their followers to disobey orders calling reservists to the colours, though this was evidently the form in which the call to take part, or to refuse to take part, in a war would necessarily be made first of all to large numbers of the members of the national Socialist and Trade Union movements.

I am not saying that the International should have told its followers to resist mobilisation in any country that was actively preparing to resort to war. But I am saying that, if they were not in a position to do this, their chances of stopping war were bound to be small, as soon as any Government had seriously resolved on a resort to arms. For in any conscript country the call to the colours, if responded to, was bound for the time being both to take the edge off the working-class movement by removing many of its most active militants and to cause many who were not themselves called up to feel a keen sense of the need for giving loyal support to those who were and not 'letting them down' in face of the 'enemy'. Mobilisation was bound strongly to reinforce sentiments of national antagonism from which the working classes of the leading countries were by no means immune. The Germans were bound to be told of the need to resist Russian barbarism and the threat from the East; the French, of the call to avenge the defeat of 1871 and to win back Alsace-Lorraine; the Austrians, of the Russian menace in South-Eastern Europe ; and the British, of the German threat to the Empire and to the 'freedom of the seas' guaranteed by the British navy. Only to the Russians was it unlikely that such appeals would be strongly made — and that only because it would be regarded as unnecessary by the rulers of Russia to explain to their peasant conscripts what they were supposed to be fighting for.

Doubtless the situation would have been different if 1914 had found the working classes of the European countries preparing actively for revolution and moved by an immediate zeal for revolutionary Socialism. But in no country except Russia — and even there only to a limited extent — were any such preparations on foot. In the other leading countries, though the Socialist Parties in some cases looked forward to some sort of revolution as destined to occur some day, Parties and Trade Unions were alike engaged in parliamentary and industrial movements directed to the winning of piecemeal reforms and improvements within the existing order and to the gaining of wider support among the peoples. The really revolutionary groups were everywhere, except in Russia and a few backward countries of Eastern Europe, small minorities even of the organised working class and quite incapable of taking the lead in an effective mass struggle of armed resistance to mobilisation and sabotage of the war effort. Moreover, the Governments knew this, and were in no doubt either that the reservists would obey the call to arms or that the main body of the workers would remain at their tasks and so support the national war effort.

In effect, Socialist resistance to war could have been successful only if none of the leading Governments had been determined to go to war rather than give up its point or even compromise. By 1914 a situation had been reached in which this condition was no longer fulfilled. True, no great power was prepared to proclaim itself an aggressor : each had to find at least a specious case for casting the blame on others. The Austrians blamed the Serbs ; the Russians the Austrians ; the Germans the Russians, and presently the French ; the British the Germans ; and the Italians, who stayed out for the time being, everybody else — and in one country after another the majority of the Socialist and Trade Union leaders, and of their followers, endorsed the nationalist view. Even among the Russians Plekhanov, the doyen of Marxism, an exile in Switzerland till 1917, rallied to the cause of the Allies, holding that a

German victory would be disastrous to the Socialist cause. There was a terrible appearance of inevitability as, one after another, the great powers fell into the places that had been determined for them by the imperialist rivalries of the pre-war decade.

Thus, within a very few days of the outbreak of war in August 1914, the Second International was virtually extinct, though formally it continued to exist. The German invasion of Belgium swept away its headquarters on neutral territory ; and though its secretary, Camille Huysmans, found a new home for it in Holland its capacity to act — or even to discuss — had been utterly lost. Its leaders were scattered to the four winds, and neither able nor willing to meet or attempt to frame a policy for the future. Some of them were speedily enrolled in coalition Cabinets of National Defence — for example, Vaillant in France and Vandervelde, in exile, for Belgium and presently Henderson in Great Britain. Others — Victor Adler in Austria, Ebert and Scheidemann in Germany, and Plekhanov in Russia — were not given the chance of office, but supported their respective Governments from outside. To consider the future of the International there were left only the neutrals — the Italians, the Swiss, the Scandinavians, the Dutch, and the Americans — none of whom, except the Italians, had played a leading part in its affairs up to 1914 or were in a position thereafter to do much more than stand by and wring their hands.

From these bystanders at the great struggle necessarily came such initiative as was designed to keep the old International alive. There was, however, for the time being little they could do. The Italians, in conjunction with the Swiss, were I think the first to attempt any action, though at about the same time the American Socialist Party issued an abortive summons to an international Socialist conference to be held in Washington. The Italian-Swiss Conference, held at Lugano in September 1914, denounced the war as 'imperialist' and denied that any of the Governments involved in it could be regarded as guiltless or free from blame. It agreed with the minorities among Socialists in the belligerent countries who refused to consider in isolation the series of events that had followed the Sarajevo murder and insisted on regarding the war as the outcome of a prolonged period of colonialist and imperialist rivalries and manœuvrings, in the course of which each great power had unscrupulously pressed its own interest in disregard of every principle of international justice and morality. This was essentially the view of Kautsky and Haase in Germany, of MacDonald and the leaders of the Union of Democratic Control in Great Britain, and of Jean Longuet and his fellow-*minoritaires* in the French Socialist Party.

The principal demand put forward by the Lugano Conference was that the International Socialist Bureau, as representing the International, should be called together at once. This request was refused by Vandervelde as Chairman of the Bureau. Émile Vandervelde, as leader of the Belgian Socialists, was in no mood to meet on fraternal terms any German Socialist who supported, or failed to denounce, the violation of Belgium's neutrality ; and in this attitude he was supported by the great majority of the French and British leaders of the International. Instead of convening a full meeting of the Bureau, Camille Huysmans (b. 1871), as we saw, took the initiative in establishing new temporary headquarters for it in neutral Holland ; and it was from the Dutch, in conjunction with the Scandinavian, Socialists that the next attempt to retrieve the International came.

In January 1915 the Socialist Parties of Holland, Sweden, Norway, and Denmark held a joint meeting at Copenhagen, at which they attempted not so much to re-establish the International as to consider possible terms of peace on which the Socialists of all countries could agree. Troelstra of Holland and Branting of Sweden were the two outstanding figures in this attempt, out of which arose the Dutch-Scandinavian Committee that was later to associate itself with the projected Stockholm Conference of 1917.

Meanwhile, events in Italy were moving fast. Though the Italian Socialist Party took up a neutralist, anti-war line, denouncing the 'imperialism' of both belligerent groups, a section within it had already begun to agitate for Italian intervention on the side of the Allies. The leader of this group was Benito Mussolini, who was expelled from the Party on this ground in November 1914. Early in May 1915, shortly before the Italian Government entered the war, the Italian Socialist Party, again acting in conjunction with the Swiss, sent out a call for an international Socialist conference addressed to 'all parties, workers' organisations, and groups' which had 'remained true to the old principles of the International', and were 'willing to fight against the politics of civic peace and for the class struggle and for the united action of Socialists in all countries against war'. This was an appeal, not to the Socialist Parties which had sided with their respective Governments in support of the war, but to Parties not so committed and to the anti-war minorities that were already beginning to take organised form in some of the belligerent countries. The Swiss Socialist, Robert Grimm (1881–1958), became the leading figure in this attempt to rally the anti-war Socialist forces.

The outcome of this call for action was the Conference held at Zimmerwald, in Switzerland, in September 1915 — now regarded as the germ out of which was developed the Third International. It was not a large gathering — no more in all than forty-two delegates ; but it included official delegates from the Socialist Parties, not only of Italy and Switzerland, but also of Holland, Sweden, and Norway in the West, of Russia, Poland, Rumania, and Bulgaria in the East, and of the Jewish Bund. Indeed, three out of the four main Russian Parties — Bolsheviks, Mensheviks, and Left Social Revolutionaries, were represented. From France and Germany there were only unofficial delegates — from the former the leading Syndicalist, Alfred Merrheim (1871–1925), secretary of the Metalworkers' Federation, and Albert Bourderon (1858–1930), a *minoritaire* from the Socialist Party, and from Germany Georg Ledebour (1850–1947) of the Reichstag minority, and Adolf Hoffmann (1858–?) of the Prussian Landtag. The main opposition in these countries had not yet achieved any formal organisation, and remained unrepresented. In Great Britain the Independent Labour Party and the British Socialist Party, both of which had from the first taken, by a majority, an anti-war line, appointed delegates ; but, passports being refused, they were unable to attend the Conference.

The Zimmerwald Conference was definitely anti-war and ready to cast the blame for the war on all the belligerent Governments ; but it was made up of widely different elements. On the extreme left of it was a small group, headed by Lenin, which regarded the Second International as dead and damned by reason of its failure, and wished to use the occasion for establishing a new, definitely revolutionary International and to launch a great offensive against the 'patriots' who, in Lenin's view, were betraying the international workers' movement. But the majority of the delegates were not of this mind. They wanted to stop the war rather than to make it an occasion for World Revolution. Their hope was rather to recall the leaders of the Second International to their senses, or to provide it with a new anti-war leadership, than to throw it over and make a totally new start. Consequently, after the French and German delegates had signed a joint declaration opening with the words 'This is not our war', and pledging themselves to 'agitate tirelessly for peace and to force the Governments to put an end to the slaughter', the Zimmerwald Conference as a whole drew up a resolution placing the blame for the war on reactionary capitalist Governments and their supporters, denouncing the apostasy of the pro-war Socialists in the belligerent countries, and ending with the demand for a peace without annexations or indemnities and with a call to the workers of all lands to unite 'across frontiers, battlefields, devastated cities and countries'. Finally, the Conference set up an International Socialist Commission, commonly called thereafter the 'Zimmerwald Commission', to stimulate and co-operate with the International Socialist Bureau with a view to securing an immediate peace. The Commission consisted of two Swiss — Robert Grimm and Charles Naine (1874-1926) — and two Italian representatives — Oddino Morgari and Angelica Balabanova, a Russian long resident in Italy. It included no Frenchmen or Germans, no Dutch or Scandinavians, and no direct representatives of the Russian Socialist Parties. In effect it was little more than a continuation of the joint Italian-Swiss initiative that had brought the Zimmerwald Conference into being.

As we saw, at the time when the Zimmerwald Conference met, the anti-war forces in both France and Germany were still without any substantial organisation of their own. The more moderate anti-war groups still remained inside the main Socialist Parties. Not until December 1915 did the German minority challenge party discipline by refusing to vote for the war credits in the Reichstag — twenty actually voting against them and another twenty-four abstaining. This challenge led to the deposition of Hugo Haase (1863–1919) from the leadership of the German Party and to the formation of a separate Reichstag group under his leadership. In France, Merrheim and Bourderon formed, in January 1916, a Committee for the Renewal of International Relations which carried on anti-war propaganda, but secured no mass following. The more moderate anti-war groups rallied behind Jean Longuet (1876–1938), who began to get a substantial support inside the Unified Socialist Party. In Great Britain the Independent Labour Party approved the Zimmerwald decisions, and pursued its anti-war policy without severing its formal connections with the Labour Party — though in Parliament the small I.L.P. group increasingly took its own line.

At Zimmerwald, Lenin had demanded that Socialists should not only withdraw their representatives from coalition cabinets and vote against war credits in all countries, but also carry on agitation against the war by illegal as well as legal means, organise street demonstrations against their Governments, conduct propaganda among the armed forces, turn economic disputes into political stoppages, and do their utmost to stir up civil war in each country in order to bring about Socialist revolution. Such a policy, however, was far removed from what most of the delegates either wished for or regarded as practicable. The Scandinavians, the Dutch, and the Swiss, as non-belligerents representing movements that were essentially non-revolutionary, might wish to induce the Socialists of the belligerent countries to cease supporting the war policies of their respective countries, and to join in a common crusade for peace ; but they had not the smallest intention of taking revolutionary action in their own countries, or of calling upon the Socialists of the world to join forces in a great revolutionary crusade. The Italians, just on the point of finding their country involved in the war, were more minded to engage in anti-war activities, but not to the extent of attempting any sort of insurrection. The French and Germans, for their part, were very conscious of representing minority tendencies inside their own national movements, and of being much too weak to carry out such a policy as Lenin advanced. The French, led by Merrheim, were indeed revolutionaries and prepared to resort to illegal anti-war agitation ; but they knew that they did not represent either the majority or the predominant minority feeling within the French Socialist Party. The *minoritaires* in France who were prepared to campaign for peace, but not for revolution, were being led, not by the Syndicalist Merrheim, but by Marx's grandson, the parliamentarian, Jean Longuet, who was steadily gaining support within the Party for a negotiated peace, but was by no means an insurrectionary leader. The two Germans, Ledebour and Hoffmann, belonged, like Longuet, to a parliamentary anti-war minority that was gradually taking shape, but had no thought of carrying out a German Revolution by insurrectionary means, at any rate as long as they lacked the support of a majority among the German workers. Revolutionism, as a practical policy, found support only in Eastern Europe, among the Russians, the Bulgarians, the Rumanians, and the Poles : and the delegates who came to Zimmerwald from these countries by no means represented united movements standing for an agreed policy of Socialist revolution. Lenin's programme therefore stood no chance of being accepted by the Zimmerwald Conference, which would go no further than to call for an immediate peace and to protest against the chauvinistic behaviour of the majority leaders of Socialism in the belligerent countries.

Nevertheless, the Zimmerwald Conference was of real significance as the beginning of an attempt to organise world Socialism in both belligerent and neutral countries as a pressure group challenging, not so much the warring Governments, as the Socialists who had rallied behind them in the name of national unity and defence of their respective countries against their 'national enemies'. Its immediate effects were small because the more moderate anti-war minorities were still, for the most part, unorganised and reluctant to break away from the majorities with which they were still formally united in common Parties and Trade Unions. Moreover, these minorities, even where they had become organised, were most unlikely, in any of the Western countries, to be ready to follow Lenin's revolutionary policy. What most of their leaders were seeking was, not to turn war into World Revolution, but, by bringing the fighting to an end, to regain their chance to resume their previous policies of agitation and electoral struggle in the hope of bringing a majority, not simply of the workers, but of the entire electorate, over to the Socialist side. There were of course in all the belligerent countries some out-and-out revolutionaries, who looked forward to the 'day' when the workers would rise and overthrow the capitalist structure by main force. But, except in some parts of Eastern Europe, the revolutionaries were minorities within the anti-war minorities and had no present hope of being in a position to take the lead.

After Zimmerwald, the International Socialist Commission there set up did its best to act on the resolutions of the Conference by trying to spur on the International Socialist Bureau and to win support for the policy of a speedy negotiated peace. But it met with little success, especially as the entry of Italy into the war, though it did not prevent the Italian Socialists from continuing their anti-war agitation, had left its affairs mainly in Swiss hands. When in the early months of 1916 it decided to convene a further Conference at Kienthal in Switzerland, the groups represented were mainly the same as at Zimmerwald, but there had been a decisive shift of attitude among them towards the left. Lenin no longer found himself in a small minority in urging the need for a decisive break with the pro-war Socialists in both camps ; and the earlier insistence at Zimmerwald on peace as the foremost aim had been largely replaced by a new conviction that no tolerable peace could be made without an international social revolution that would make an end of capitalism and imperialism and set the working class in power as the constructors of a new social order. At Kienthal 'bourgeois pacifists' as well as 'Socialist war-mongers' were roundly denounced, and Socialism, rather than a peace made between the belligerent Governments, was proclaimed as the aim to be pursued by all true Socialists. The Zimmerwald resolutions had called for a peace 'without annexations or indemnities', and for the recognition of national rights of self-determination, but had said little about Socialism, save in the most general terms and as an ultimate objective ; whereas at Kienthal it was declared that there could be no real solution of the conflict without 'the conquest of political power and the ownership of capital by the peoples themselves', and that 'the real durable peace will be the fruit of Socialism triumphant'.

Thus, Kienthal, rather than Zimmerwald, was the true fore-runner of the new revolutionary International which the victori-ous Bolsheviks were presently to set up ; but in 1916 there were few who appreciated its significance. In Western Europe the growing 'minority' groups in the belligerent countries were aligning themselves behind a policy which certainly went no further than the Zimmerwald attitude, if as far. They were demanding 'peace by negotiation', 'peace without annexations or indemnities', and recognition of national claims, but certainly not revolution or a break with the pro-war majorities that was to be regarded as irrevocable or absolute. They had no desire to set up a new International based on Leninist principles : on the contrary, while censuring the International Socialist Bureau for its failure to act, they hoped to spur it to action and before long to win over a majority of workers in the various countries to support their demand for a negotiated peace. Even in refusing to accept the discipline of the pro-war majorities in their several parties and in establishing their own separate organisations they remained parliamentarians and not revolu-tionists, and looked forward to the re-establishment of Socialist unity, both national and international, as the will for peace gained ground.

The main bodies of anti-war Socialists in Western Europe were indeed very reluctant to take any action that would formally split their parties on the war issue by setting up separate minority parties. In Germany, though the 'Independ-ents' formed a separate Reichstag group as early as March 1916, a new Independent Social Democratic Party was not formally constituted until April 1917, by which time the position of the minority inside the old Social Democratic Party had been made sheerly intolerable. In Great Britain the Independent Labour Party, though it took a consistent anti-war line and its small group of Members of Parliament acted throughout virtually as a party of their own, maintained its affiliation to the Labour Party throughout the war and made no attempt at formal separation. The British Socialist Party, the successor of the Social Democratic Federation, also took up an anti-war attitude, defeating its old leader, Hyndman, who presently broke away to form a small National Socialist Party, but had no considerable following. The Socialist Labour Party, active mainly in Scotland, had never been attached to the Labour Party : it took a strong anti-war line, but had little influence except on Clydeside, where it formed close links with the left wing of the shop stewards' movement. In France, the main group of *minoritaires*, headed by Jean Longuet, remained within the Unified Socialist Party and directed its energies to winning support in the regional Federations on which the party structure was based. In 1917 they were reinforced by a Centre group, headed by Marcel Cachin (b. 1869) ; and this group set itself to the task of maintaining party unity while moving party policy by stages towards the left. Before that, in 1916, Jules Guesde (1845-1922) and Marcel Sembat (1862-1922), who had been the first Socialists to join the Government in 1914, had resigned office, leaving Albert Thomas (1878-1932) as the principal Socialist in office. Not until July 1918, after a struggle that had gone on for three years, did the French minority become the majority, by winning a majority on the National Council of the Party — a victory confirmed in October 1918 at the Party Conference, by a vote of 1528 against 1212. Even then the victory was not for revolutionism, but for Longuet's parliamentarian leftism, which closely resembled that of the German Independents and of the British I.L.P. There was, however, among those who supported Longuet, a much bigger revolutionary minority than in either Germany or Great Britain ; and the victory of the *minoritaires* helped to prepare the way for the subsequent decision of the French Socialists to throw in their lot with the Third International.

In Austria, the majority of the Social Democratic Party had followed Victor Adler's lead in 1914 and had supported the war. But a minority under his son, Friedrich Adler (born 1879), took an anti-war, internationalist line ; and this group gained steadily in influence as the war proceeded. In 1916 Friedrich Adler assassinated the Chancellor, Count Sturgkh, in protest against his refusal to take part in an inter-party conference called for the purpose of re-establishing constitutional government. Adler used the opportunity offered by his trial to make a celebrated speech, in which he denounced the Government's war policy and affirmed his faith in international Socialism ; and thereafter the strength of the anti-war fraction steadily and rapidly increased, culminating in the general strike of January

1918 and in a series of agitations which included mutinies within the armed forces. By that time the Austro-Hungarian Empire was already in an advanced stage of disintegration, which prepared the way for the Emperor's abdication in November 1918 and for the establishment of the succession States.

Finally I come to the Belgians, whose territory had been overrun by Germany in 1914, so that many of their outstanding political leaders were thereafter in exile. Émile Vandervelde, who was President of the International Socialist Bureau as well as leader of the Belgian Labour Party, had become a Minister in the war-time Coalition Government ; and the main body of the Party, so far as its views could be known, supported him in his pro-war policy. The expatriated Belgians indeed became the most intransigent element in the International, taking a strong stand against meeting the German Socialists as long as the war continued. At the outbreak of war the Executive of the International, which acted for it between meetings of the International Socialist Bureau, was entirely in Belgian hands ; and this was an important factor in paralysing its action, though its office was transferred by its secretary, Camille Huysmans, to neutral ground in Holland and before long Dutch Socialists were installed to act provisionally as an executive committee in place of the Belgians. In Belgium itself there could be under the German occupation little opportunity for the discussion of Socialist policy ; but it is unquestionable that most Belgian Socialists agreed with Vandervelde's war attitude. This was shown when, in December 1918, the Belgian Labour Party's first post-war Congress gave full support to Vandervelde's policy and to his position in the Government.

Thus, in all the Western belligerent countries except Italy, there were, up to 1917, official Socialist and Labour Parties supporting their respective Governments and resolutely opposed to any negotiated peace that would not accord victory to their own side. Arrayed against these majorities there were in all the countries, except Belgium, organised minority groups which remained, at any rate formally, attached to the pro-war parties but were struggling inside them to win over adherents to their point of view. These minorities were made up, in each country, mainly of advocates of peace by negotiation, including both out-and-out pacifists (not very numerous) and critics of the imperialist policies of the rival powers who did not wish to see either side win and believed that a peace based on stalemate offered the best hope for the resumption of constitutional Socialist advance. To the left of these parliamentarian minorities there were more revolutionary groups, still for the most part small, in some cases acting with the peace-seeking minorities and in others independent of them, especially after the Kienthal Conference. In the West, among belligerents, only the Italian Socialist Party had a clear anti-war majority.

In Eastern Europe the situation was entirely different. Of the Russians, both the Bolsheviks and the Mensheviks and also the main group of the Social Revolutionary Party were officially represented at Zimmerwald. Only a small fraction, headed by the Social Democratic veteran, George Plekhanov (1857–1918), and by Boris Savinkov (1879–1925) of the militant and terroristic section of the Social Revolutionary Party, supported the war while Czardom still remained in being. The Hungarian, Rumanian, and Serbian Socialist Parties were anti-war. The Bulgarians and the Poles were divided : in Bulgaria the 'Broad Socialists' were pro-war and the 'Narrow Socialists' anti-war, and in Poland the party of Pilsudski, the P.P.S., worked with the Austrians, but a left wing split away from it. Rosa Luxemburg's rival Polish Social Democratic Party was from the first anti-war, in a revolutionary sense, and was fully prepared to co-operate with the Russian proletariat in overthrowing the Czarist régime.

It remains to consider the attitudes of the Socialist Parties and groups of the countries not involved in the European War. We have already seen that some of these began to press for international action practically as soon as the fighting had begun. After the abortive call of the American Socialist Party, in September 1914, to an international Socialist conference to be held in the United States, similar demands for action came in swift succession from the Italians, not yet at war, and from the Danes, the Norwegians, and the Swedes. The first actual International Conference after 1914 took place at Copenhagen in January 1915, and was confined to Socialists from neutral countries—actually to those of Holland and the three Scandinavian States. This Conference of Neutrals, moving with caution, merely called on the International Socialist Bureau to convene a meeting 'as soon as circumstances allow', and in any case 'not later than the opening of peace negotiations'. This was the first of many proposals that a meeting of Socialist representatives from all countries should be held simultaneously with that of an inter-governmental conference designed to restore peace, and with the purpose of bringing working-class pressure to bear on such a conference. The following month a Conference of the Socialist Parties of the Allied countries — France, Belgium, and Great Britain, together with a section of the Russian Social Revolutionaries, but not the Bolsheviks or the Mensheviks, who alike refused to attend — met in London and declared that the workers of all countries must join forces in the International at the conclusion of the war, but made no proposal for action to bring the war to an end. Two months later the Socialist Parties of the Central Powers — Germany, Austria, and Hungary — met at Vienna and pronounced in favour of a continuance of international Socialist relations and of the activities of the various Parties during the war, but made no move towards a reconciliation of the divergent points of view of the opposing groups, limiting itself in the main to a discussion of the future of international Socialist relations when the war was over. Before this, in February 1915, Clara Zetkin (1857–1933), as Secretary of the Second International's Women's International Council of Socialist and Labour Organisations, had succeeded in getting together at Berne, in Switzerland, an International Women's Socialist Conference, which was attended by delegates from both blocs of belligerent countries as well as from neutral States. Such Women's Conferences had been part of the regular machinery of the pre-war International; but it it was no small feat to bring about a meeting in 1915, especially as the lead came from an outstanding figure in the German minority.

After this round of meetings, neutral, Allied, and Central, there was a lull. In each country, the struggle continued between the opposing factions ; and on the whole the attitude of the pro-war groups hardened as the minorities became organised and more articulate than during the first few months of warfare. Grimm, from Switzerland, and the Italians continued their efforts to mobilise anti-war opinion ; and in

Holland, Huysmans and the new Dutch Executive of the International Socialist Bureau continued, with the support of the Scandinavians, to sound the Parties of the belligerent countries in the hope of inducing them to resume relations. At length, in July 1916, a second Conference of Neutrals was held at The Hague, with Troelstra of Holland, Branting of Sweden, and Algernon Lee of the American Socialist Party among the leading participants. This meeting called for an early convocation of the full International Socialist Bureau and set Huysmans and the Dutch committee to work in the hope of persuading the Parties of the warring countries to agree to attend such a gathering, at which an attempt would be made to reach agreement between them on acceptable terms of peace. The Socialist Parties of the Allied countries, however, were not yet prepared for such a meeting. They preferred, for the time being, to attempt to work out an agreed statement of Allied Socialist War Aims, which they could then press upon their respective Governments and in due course carry to the Peace Conference as embodying the common policy of the Socialist Parties of the Allied countries, or at any rate those of Western Europe.

At the beginning of 1917, with the new Coalition Government under Lloyd George in power in Great Britain with an increased Labour Party participation, international Socialism appeared still quite incapable of any effective action to bring the war to an end, and still more of doing anything to carry out the international revolutionary policy proposed by the Kienthal Conference. But, during the next few months, the situation was thoroughly transformed by the outbreak of revolution in Russia. The breakdown of the Czarist régime under the strain of war did not indeed mean either an immediate assumption of power in Russia by the Socialists, or the immediate defection of Russia from the ranks of the Allies. Nevertheless the fall of Czardom and the institution of a Republic could not but be greeted with enthusiasm by the Socialists of all countries, as well as by many non-Socialists who regarded the new Russia as a potential recruit to the ranks of liberal democracy. Among pro-war Socialists in the other Allied countries, however, there were mixed feelings, arising out of the fear that the Russians might be driven to make a separate peace with Germany, and thus set the German armies free to direct their entire weight against the Allies in the West. There were, accordingly, almost frantic efforts to induce the new Russian Republic to carry on the war, and even to launch, despite the exhaustion of the Russian armies, a mass offensive designed to relieve the heavy pressure on the Western Front. The new Governments which succeeded one another between the two Russian Revolutions of 1917 by no means wished to abandon their allies or to enter into a separate peace on terms which were bound to be very hard in view of Russia's military weakness. They would gladly have carried on the war, had they been in possession of the means. It was, however, all too plain that the great desire of the conscripts was to go home, above all when the occurrence of the Revolution had aroused their hopes of land distribution, in which they might miss their chance to share unless they could get back to their villages in good time. Moreover, most of the military leaders not only felt no loyalty to the new Governments which had taken the place of the Czar and his ministers, but were strongly hostile to them, and in some cases much more willing to wage war on the Revolution than against the Germans.

To an ever-increasing extent Russia, between the Czar's abdication and the seizure of power by the Bolsheviks, had no effective Government, and the vast centralised structure was breaking up. In the capital, in Moscow, and in other cities the new Councils of Workers' and Soldiers' Deputies — the Soviets — came by stages to constitute a parallel structure of authority unco-ordinated with the formal structure of government and administration, and strong enough to veto almost any act of the latter of which they disapproved. Until some sort of Constituent Assembly could be elected and convened, the formal Government was left in the air, with no real foundation for its authority and no power to enforce its decrees. The Soviets, however, though from June onwards they gathered much power into their hands, remained without the equipment and central co-ordination needed for making them the basis of an alternative Government, and were a long way off the possession of a common or clearly conceived policy for the future of the Russian peoples. At the outset the Bolsheviks made up only a small minority of the deputies ; the Social Revolutionaries and the Mensheviks still commanded much larger bodies of popular support. Nor were even the Bolsheviks at all clear or fully united about their future course of action, or even sharply marked off from the Mensheviks until after Lenin's arrival in Russia in April 1917. There was, however, one issue on which the great majority of both Social Democrats and Social Revolutionaries were at one — the urgent need for peace ; and it was on this issue that the Russian Socialists first made their impact on the outside world.

When the Russian Revolution occurred, Camille Huysmans and the Dutch members of the war-time Executive of the I.S.B. were still pursuing their discussions with the Socialist Parties of the warring countries with the object of inducing them to agree to take part either in a fully representative meeting of the Bureau or in a full International Socialist Conference open to all countries ; but they were making scant progress in face of the objections of the Allied Socialist Parties to any meeting with the Socialists of the Central Powers. The success of the Revolution in Russia seemed to Huysmans and to the Dutch to constitute an immensely strong new reason for bringing all the Socialist Parties and groups together both to press for an immediate end to the fighting and to formulate, if possible, agreed terms of peace consistent with Socialist principles. The Dutch, as we saw, had been working in close touch with the Scandinavian Socialists ; and it now seemed desirable to give this collaboration a more formal shape. There was, however, the serious difficulty that the war-time Executive of the I.S.B. formally included the Belgians who had composed it before the war, as well as the Dutch, who had been added to it when the Secretariat moved to Holland. The Dutch, accordingly, felt themselves unable to act in the name of the I.S.B. without the consent and collaboration of their Belgian colleagues. This could not be procured : Vandervelde was at Le Havre and a minister, Louis Bertrand and Edouard Anseele were in Belgium and could not leave the country to attend an international meeting. Besides, of the three, only Anseele was in favour of an international Conference at which the Germans would be represented on equal terms.

The solution chosen by the Dutch Socialists was that their representatives on the I.S.B. Executive should take action, not

as representing the I.S.B., but in the name of the Dutch
Socialist Party, which should take the initiative in setting up,
with the Scandinavian Parties, a special Dutch-Scandinavian
Committee which was to invite the help of the I.S.B. Secretariat in summoning an International Socialist Conference. In
order to achieve this, the Dutch delegates, in April 1917, went
from Holland to Stockholm to meet their new colleagues, and it
was decided to make Stockholm the venue for the Conference,
partly in order to be within easy reach of the Russians, whose
prospective part in it was still quite undetermined. The I.S.B.
Secretariat simultaneously transferred its temporary headquarters to Stockholm, and on April 22nd sent out to all
affiliated Parties and groups a definite invitation from the
Dutch section of the International to send delegates to an
International Socialist Conference to be held at Stockholm on
and after May 15th, 1917.

The Dutch-Scandinavian Committee, which was not fully
constituted at the beginning of May, consisted of Pieter
Troelstra, J. W. Albarda, and H. Van Kol from Holland
(with W. H. Vliegen and F. M. Wibaut as substitutes);
Hjalmar Branting, Gustav Moller, and Ernst Söderberg
from Sweden ; Thorvald Stauning from Denmark (with Nina
Bang as substitute) ; and J. L. Vidnes from Norway. It
appointed Camille Huysmans of Belgium as secretary, with a
Swede, Arthur Engberg, as assistant. The Committee soon
found that there were still many difficulties to be surmounted
before a full International Conference could be expected to
meet ; and it decided not only to postpone the meeting, but
to begin with a series of bilateral meetings at Stockholm with
representatives of each separate country and group, and to ask
each Party or group to submit its own proposals both about
the conditions in which the full Conference should be held
and about the terms of peace it advocated. The Committee
made it clear that it considered these bilateral meetings as
mere preliminaries to the full Conference, which it considered
already decided on in principle ; whereas the Belgians and
some other sections, while agreeing to send delegates to these
preliminary meetings, reserved the right still to refuse to
attend any general Conference with Socialists who were 'supporting the imperialist policies of the Central Powers'.

While these negotiations for bilateral meetings were still in progress, the Russians dramatically intervened by sending out from Petrograd an appeal of their own to the Socialists of all countries to attend an International Socialist Conference to be held in a neutral country on an unspecified date. The Dutch-Scandinavian Committee, which had already been corresponding with the Russians in the hope of associating them with its plans, thus found itself confronted with an independent action which would clearly wreck the Stockholm project unless the Russians could be brought in. This danger was averted when, on May 18th, the Organisation Committee of the Russian Social Democratic Party telegraphed its willingness to participate in the Stockholm project, together with a brief manifesto for transmission to all Socialist Parties urging their attendance and the need to provide for the representation at the Conference of both majority and minority groups. There was, however, still no thorough co-ordination of the two projects, and no participation of the Russians in the Dutch-Scandinavian Committee or in its preliminary meetings with the delegates from the various countries. These delegates arrived at Stockholm at various dates during May and June, and the consultations in fact went on from May to July and were resumed towards the end of August, continuing into November. They were by no means fully representative, though memoranda were received from a number of Parties which did not send representative delegations. The fullest consultation took place between the Committee and the German delegates, who included Ebert, Scheidemann, Molkenbuhr, Sassenbach, Legien, and Richard Fischer, for the majority, and Kautsky, Bernstein, Haase, and Ledebour on behalf of the recently formed German Independent Social Democratic Party. The Austrians too sent a strong delegation, headed by Victor Adler, and including Renner, Ellenbogen, and Hueber, the Trade Union leader. The Russians, headed by Paul Axelrod, also held a long series of sessions with the Committee. Hungary was another country which sent a strong delegation; and both Vandervelde and Louis de Brouckère represented the Belgian majority, while two other delegations came from Belgian minority groups. Among other countries represented were Armenia, Bohemia, Bosnia, Bulgaria (the 'Broad' Socialists), Croatia, Finland, Italy (Irredentist group),

Poland, Serbia (Duchan Popovic), Turkey, and the Austrian Ukraine, and also, outside Europe, Egypt, India, Palestine, Persia, the United States, and a number of Moslem groups and Parties from the Caucasus, Algeria and Tunis, Morocco, Tripoli, and Turkestan. Only one delegate, not well known, came from Great Britain (J. West), and no one at all from France.

This, however, did not mean that the French or the British were unconcerned in what was happening. It meant rather that they preferred other methods of dealing with the matter. The French, who had been very cool in their attitude to the Dutch-Scandinavian Committee, suspecting it of acting under indirect German influence, were very much interested in any initiative coming from Russia. Marcel Cachin and Marius Moutet (1876–?) had been sent at an early stage by the French Party on a mission to Russia, whence they returned enthusiastic advocates of an International Conference. On May 27th, after hearing their report, the National Committee of the French Socialist Party carried unanimously a resolution taking note of what had been done by the Dutch-Scandinavian Committee and welcoming the Russian initiative for an International Conference. The resolution went on to declare for the sending of a delegation to Stockholm to carry the French support for 'common action destined to prepare for a peace in accordance with the principles proclaimed by the Russian Government and the Socialists of Russia'. At the same time the French National Committee set up a special commission to work out the terms of the French reply to the questionnaire sent out by the Dutch-Scandinavian Committee and to formulate the conditions under which the proposed International Conference should be held. This delayed matters ; but the British were still slower. In May the British Labour Party Executive, sharply divided on the Stockholm issue, decided to defer its response to the Dutch-Scandinavian Committee pending the report of a delegation which was to proceed to Russia in order to consult with the Russian Socialists. The delegates were to be G. H. Roberts (1869–1928), who was a pro-war extremist and held minor government office, William Carter (1862–1922) of the Miners' Federation, and Ramsay MacDonald of the I.L.P. group, representing the minority. The British

Government, however, at first refused to issue passports to the delegation, and decided itself to send Arthur Henderson, who represented the Labour Party in the War Cabinet, on an official mission to Russia. Henderson, having reached Petrograd, where the Kerensky semi-Socialist Government had recently assumed office, cabled home urging the Government to grant passports to the delegates. The Government acted on his advice ; but MacDonald and his colleagues were held up at Aberdeen by the refusal of the Sailors' and Firemen's Union to allow MacDonald to sail.

In June, while Henderson was in Russia, the Kerensky Government launched its ill-starred offensive against the Germans, which met with immediate disaster. When the collapse came, Henderson was already on his way home, convinced that the offensive was doomed and that the Russians would be forced to make a separate peace unless the Socialists of the West came to their rescue by showing their readiness for a general peace. He therefore strongly favoured the Stockholm Conference and British participation in it ; but when he put his view before the Labour Party Executive there was still much opposition, and it was decided to defer any decision until Henderson and MacDonald had been to Paris to confer with the French Socialists. There was also much dispute over the question whether, if the Stockholm Conference were held, it should be entitled to reach decisions mandatory on the Parties represented, or should be merely consultative. Henderson took the latter view, with which he persuaded the French to agree ; and he came back from Paris determined to press the case for Stockholm even in face of opposition from his Cabinet colleagues, to whom he had already proffered his resignation when they had taken objection to his attitude and proceedings. Under his influence a special Labour Party Conference held on August 10th, 1917, voted in favour of Stockholm by a majority of more than three to one, but added a rider that the British delegation should consist exclusively of delegates from the Labour Party and the Trades Union Congress, thus denying representation to the I.L.P., as the exponent of the minority view, despite the I.L.P.'s membership of the British Section of the old International. This exclusion ran directly counter to the terms of the Stockholm invitation, which had provided expressly for the representation of minority views. It drew a strong protest from the Russian delegation which had by this time arrived in England. This issue, however, was swept aside a few days later by the news of Henderson's resignation — or exclusion — from the War Cabinet as a result of his stand over the Stockholm Conference. It might be supposed that the treatment of its leader would have led to the Labour Party's withdrawal from the Coalition Government; but it did not. The pro-war engineer, G. N. Barnes, replaced Henderson in the War Cabinet, and on the surface the Coalition continued as before.

The decision of August 10th put the advocates of Stockholm in a difficulty ; for the Labour Party had no power to prevent the I.L.P. or the other Socialist societies from sending delegates to Stockholm if they wished — and if the Government allowed them to go. Accordingly, the Special Conference was adjourned in order to allow the Party Executive time to consider the position and find a way out if it could. By the time it re-assembled on August 21st there had been a tremendous press campaign against its decision to be represented at the Stockholm Conference, which was widely denounced as a German manœuvre ; and the opposition insisted on reopening the entire issue. This time, the proposal to send a delegation to Stockholm was carried by the bare margin of 3000 votes — 1,234,000 to 1,231,000 ; and the rider excluding the I.L.P. and the other Socialist groups was reaffirmed. This, in effect, destroyed the possibility of British representation. When the British Labour Party met the Parties of the other Allied countries on August 28th for the purpose of agreeing on a common attitude at Stockholm, the other Parties insisted on the minorities being represented and also referred a Statement of War Aims, which had been drawn up by the British Labour Party for Allied endorsement, for further consideration at a resumed Allied Socialist Conference to meet at an unspecified future date. This ruled out the sending of any immediate delegation to Stockholm and, in effect, brought the entire Stockholm project to an untimely stand.

I have been forced, in giving this account of the fate of the Stockholm project in the Allied countries, to run ahead of the record of its development elsewhere, particularly in Russia. In the confused state of Russian affairs and in face of the dualism of effective authority as between the official Government and the Soviets, it was not easy for the Dutch-Scandinavian Committee or for the Socialist Parties of the West to know what bodies to treat as the effective representatives of the Russian workers, or of the Revolution. As we saw, the message of May 18th expressing readiness to co-operate with the Dutch-Scandinavian group came from the Organisation Committee of the Russian Social Democratic Party — which meant, in effect, from the Mensheviks, who were still the predominant group. But from the beginning of June the initiative passed to the Petrograd Workers' and Soldiers' Council, which on June 1st issued an appeal to the Socialist Parties and Trade Union Centres in all countries, calling upon them to struggle for 'a peace without annexations or indemnities, based on the right of nations to self-determination'.

The Petrograd Soviet went on to recall its own earlier appeals for international working-class action and the steps it had taken to compel the successive Provisional Governments to endorse its policy. The new coalition Government, it pointed out, had been forced by the pressure of the Soviets to make the quest for a peace on the lines proposed the first point in its declaration of policy. The Petrograd Soviet then expressed the view that the required peace could not be brought about 'save by the combined international efforts of the working-class Parties and the Trade Unions of both belligerent and neutral countries, united in an energetic and passionate (*acharnée*) struggle against the universal massacre'. It accordingly called for a conference to organise this international movement, and laid down as the first task of the conference the achievement of 'an agreement among the representatives of the Socialist proletariat to liquidate completely the policy of national unity with the Governments and the imperialist classes'. Such liquidation, it said, was the indispensable prologue to the organisation of the struggle on a grand scale and on an international foundation ; and it claimed that such a course would be no more than the fulfilment of the policy laid down by all previous Socialist Congresses — *i.e.* by the Second International. The resolution went on to express the 'firm conviction' that all the organisations which responded to its appeal would 'enter into an undertaking to carry out inflexibly all the decisions reached at the proposed International Conference'. In conclusion, without any mention of the Dutch-Scandinavian Committee, it summoned the Conference to meet in Stockholm on July 8th in response to the invitation contained in its appeal.

Thus, the Petrograd Soviet took action on its own responsibility; and there was still no effective co-ordination between the Russian initiative and that of the Dutch-Scandinavian Committee. On the same day as the Petrograd Soviet sent out its summons, the Dutch-Scandinavian Committee telegraphed, not to the Soviet, but to Axelrod and to the Socialist Ministers in the Russian Government, claiming somewhat prematurely that all the Parties and Trade Union bodies affiliated to the International had now adhered to its plans for the Conference, which 'elementary prudence' made it necessary to convene in a neutral country, and adding that a Russian delegation, if it were sent to Stockholm, could speedily settle the remaining problems and 'set the common work on foot'. After some delay, a Russian delegation did arrive in Stockholm early in July, and on July 11th agreement was reached to transform the Dutch-Scandinavian Committee into a Russian-Dutch-Scandinavian Committee and to combine the conflicting initiatives under the auspices of the new body.

From this point, the Committee included, in addition to its previous members (except Stauning of Denmark, who was replaced by Borgbjerg when he joined the Danish Ministry), five Russians: H. Ehrlich, G. Goldenberg, W. Rosanov, N. Roussanov, and E. Smirnov. Later, when the Russian delegation returned home, the Russians were represented at the Stockholm Conference by Goldenberg and Axelrod. In the meantime the Russians left Stockholm on a series of missions to the Allied countries, designed to prepare the way for the meeting of the general Conference. The centre of activity then shifted to London and Paris, where the British and French Socialists, as we saw, were engaged in a fierce contest over their attitudes to the Stockholm project. On July 29th Henderson telegraphed, after meeting the Russians, a recommendation, endorsed by them, to postpone the Conference until August 22nd, in order to allow time for the Allied Socialists to meet and agree on their policy and for their conclusions to be endorsed by a further Conference of the British

Labour Party. This telegram was followed by another, on August 1st, following on the meeting of the British and Russians with the French, endorsing in their joint names the Stockholm project, recommending that minorities as well as majorities should participate and that the Trade Union Centres of the various countries should be asked to send delegates, and proposing that the Stockholm meeting should be postponed until September 9th. But a few days later it was announced that the Governments of the Allied Countries had decided to refuse to issue passports to the respective delegations. This refusal preceded Henderson's resignation from the British Cabinet on August 13th. In the debate on his resignation and in many newspapers in the Allied countries, it was categorically denied that the Russian Government any longer favoured the Stockholm project — which brought from Kerensky a few days later a counter-denial, affirming the Russian Government's continued support. It was, however, clearly useless to hold the Conference unless the Socialists from the Allied countries could be in a position to attend ; and there were, apart from this, difficulties arising out of the British refusal, reaffirmed on August 21st, to allow the British minority to be represented.

The Russian delegation returned to Stockholm from its travels on September 10th, and a fortnight later, on September 25th, the Russian-Dutch-Scandinavian Committee issued a new manifesto, in which it announced that the Conference would not be given up, though no date could now be fixed for its meeting. 'Stockholm', it was stated in the Manifesto, was not merely a Conference but a 'permanent organisation' ; and the Committee would proceed with its discussions with the various Parties and would draw up, on the basis of their several declarations of policy and war aims, a 'preliminary project' of its own, to be submitted to the Parties for approval and to be laid before the full Conference when it was able to meet. This announcement provoked some criticisms that the Committee was usurping the functions of the full Conference ; but the Committee went on with its work and issued its 'preliminary project' on October 10th. The 'project' was in two parts — a résumé of the views expressed to it, orally or in writing, by the representatives of the various Parties and groups, and an outline for a general peace settlement on lines intended to be acceptable to world Socialist opinion. This plan, after declaring that the impossibility of settling international conflicts by war had been fully demonstrated, went on to describe arbitration as the sole remaining resource. It demanded general disarmament and a cessation of violence, and the establishment of a League of Nations. It also called on the world's workers to launch an immediate campaign against imperialism and annexationism in all countries.

That was where matters stood when the entire Stockholm project, which had come to depend greatly on Russian backing, was in effect swept aside by the outbreak of the second Russian Revolution. The Bolshevik seizure of power removed all semblance of authority from the delegates who had been taken hitherto as speaking in the name of the Russian Revolution, and thus left the Dutch-Scandinavian Committee high and dry. The Committee, deprived of the power to do anything more about the Conference, set to work to compile a full record of its proceedings, prefaced by an account by Camille Huysmans of what it had attempted to do. This document, issued in January 1918, embodied an account of the discussions at Stockholm with the various national delegations it had interviewed, as well as statements by the various Parties and groups and the analysis and 'preliminary project' which the Committee had prepared. For a while the Committee still attempted to regard the Stockholm Conference as only postponed ; but in practice the entire project was dead.

I have told the story of Stockholm at some length — though with the omission of many particulars — because, though the Conference never met, the proposal to convene it held the centre of the Socialist stage in the West during the critical months that followed the first Russian Revolution. Throughout these months there were many in the Allied countries who regarded Stockholm as essentially a German manœuvre, despite Branting's well-known favour of the Allied cause and even despite the fact that the Russian delegates could by no stretch of imagination be regarded as siding with Germany. It was the case that the German and Austrian Socialists favoured the Stockholm project — for peace feeling was gaining ground rapidly among the workers of the Central Powers ; and this was enough to stir up strong feeling against the Conference among those who were set on a fight to a finish and the destruction of Germany's military power. There was, moreover, after the widespread enthusiasm which had greeted the overthrow of Czardom, a recoil of feeling in the Allied countries as the fear grew of the Russians making a separate peace. This fear might well have made — and did make in some quarters — for an increased support for Stockholm as the possible means of bringing about a general peace ; but there were more among the leaders of the majorities in the Allied countries who were still supporters of a fight to a finish and rejected any idea of conferring with the Germans unless, and until, they were prepared fully to admit Germany's 'war guilt', and to present themselves as suppliants rather than as equals. Even those who understood the sheer inability of Russia to carry on the war effectively were disposed, none the less, to regard a separate peace as treason to the Allied cause, and to press the Russians to declare categorically that no such peace would be made. The Russian Socialists who participated in, or supported, the Kerensky Government mostly agreed with this view ; and the Dutch-Scandinavian Committee, in its quest for a general peace, was also hostile to a separate peace between Russia and Germany, and even pressed the Russians for an assurance that no such peace would be made. Thus, the Stockholm Conference became, most of all, an issue between the advocates of a fight to a finish and the advocates of peace by negotiation ; and, despite Henderson's efforts in Great Britain and the growing strength of the minority in France, it proved impossible to rally Socialist opinion in these countries at all solidly behind the Stockholm project. The pressure of the minority was strong enough in both countries to prevent Stockholm from being rejected outright, but not to line up the French and British movements solidly behind it.

Thus, although Arthur Henderson was out of the Government and set free to devote his energies to rebuilding the Labour Party's organisation with a view to its position after the war, the Labour Party continued to be represented in the Lloyd George Coalition right up to the end of the war ; and in France and Belgium, Albert Thomas, Émile Vandervelde, and other Socialists were in a similar position. The French *minoritaires* did not become the majority until July 1918. The Italian Socialist Party, being anti-war, was differently placed and remained unaffected by ministerial responsibility ; but it followed from its attitude that little account was taken of it by the majority Socialists in the other Allied countries.

With the victory of the Bolsheviks in Russia the situation of international Socialism was deeply changed. The contest over Stockholm had been, in the main, a struggle between opponents who were on the same side on the general issue of reform versus revolution, and were divided only, or at any rate chiefly, on the issue of a fight to a finish versus peace by negotiation. This does not quite hold good for the Russians, who had been almost by necessity revolutionaries up to the first Revolution of 1917. But the Russians who appeared at Stockholm were not Bolsheviks, but Mensheviks or Social Revolutionaries for whom their revolution had already taken place. They were not contemplating a further revolution : their chief desire was to end the war in order to be free to concentrate on the consolidation of what had been won and on the defeat of the counter-revolutionary forces inside Russia. They by no means shared Lenin's view that the duty of Socialists everywhere was to use the situation brought about by the war to consummate world revolution on a basis of proletarian dictatorship. They did indeed find it difficult to understand why the Socialists of the West showed so little inclination to overthrow their own Governments or to take part in a general anti-imperialist crusade. Nevertheless, their main task, as they saw it, was to put an end to the fighting in order to secure a chance to straighten out the terrible tangle of difficulties that faced them at home. They were accordingly very ready to fall in with the objectives of the essentially unrevolutionary Dutch-Scandinavian Committee and to work for a peace without annexations or indemnities in co-operation with those whom the Kienthal Conference had denounced as 'bourgeois pacifists' and 'social patriots', even if they could not quite see eye to eye with them or feel at home in the parliamentarian atmosphere of the West. Conscious of the collapse of Russian military power and of the need for peace to rescue the Russian Revolution from its enemies at home and abroad, they yet shrank from a separate peace with the Germans because they foresaw how hard upon Russia its terms were likely to be. That made them all the more anxious for a general peace, on almost any terms that would leave the first Russian Revolution an accomplished fact. The Bolshevik view was entirely different; for the Bolsheviks were practically all agreed that revolution could not be successful in Russia unless it were complemented by revolutions in the more advanced capitalist countries of the West — above all, in Germany. For the Bolsheviks, at this stage, the Russian Revolution was only the opening phase of a world revolutionary upheaval. Unless there were a German Revolution, they saw no means of preventing the Germans from overrunning their territory, annexing the Baltic provinces and probably the Ukraine, or at the least setting up there and elsewhere puppet régimes which would make the position of the new Russian Republic untenable and give rise to counter-revolutions they would be unable to resist. Moreover, apart from the immediate threat from Germany, they were convinced that the capitalist Powers would enter into a league against them and would either dismember the Russian territories or restore the Czarist régime. They felt, on these grounds, an imperative need to do everything in their power to foment revolution in the West and most of all in Germany, as the only means of saving the Revolution in Russia.

The Bolsheviks, however, also had their qualms about a separate peace, which, by setting free the German armies on the Eastern Front, threatened to strengthen the established German régime instead of helping on the German Revolution. It was Lenin, rather than the Bolshevik Party, who was prepared to face even the most unfavourable terms of peace that Germany could impose because he saw the utter impossibility of continuing the war without ensuring the victory of counter-revolution inside Russia. Well aware of the dire disadvantages of making peace with Germany on whatever terms German imperialism might impose, he nevertheless saw the only hope in agreeing to such a peace and then appealing to the German masses to denounce it and rise up in revolt against their rulers. It was Lenin who insisted, against Trotsky, on the signing of the Brest-Litovsk Treaty, as allowing at any rate a temporary maintenance of the Revolution within a restricted territory, though he did not believe it could maintain itself, even there, unless revolution in Western, or at least in Central, Europe were to come speedily to its aid.

Thus Lenin, and presently the Bolshevik Party under his masterful influence, did their best to act on the principles that had been laid down at Kienthal and to make the Bolshevik Revolution the prelude to world revolution without the countenance of more than small revolutionary groups in the Western countries. For the rapidly growing anti-war minorities both in Germany and in the Allied countries were still mainly under the leadership of men who had no sympathy with Lenin's brand of revolutionary doctrine, who regarded the victory of Bolshevism with deep misgivings, and who were thinking and planning in their own countries in terms of a conquest of power by constitutional parliamentary means, or at most of a 'revolution' of which the outcome would be the establishment of responsible parliamentary government and not of any sort of dictatorship by class or Party.

No doubt there were within these minorities groups, mostly small, of a much more revolutionary outlook, and among the rank and file of the minorities many who did not know at all clearly where they stood. But these revolutionary groups nowhere dominated even the minority Parties or fractions which were demanding a negotiated peace. Time was needed before the minority Socialists in the various countries — or indeed the majority Socialists — could arrive at any clear estimate of what had taken place in Russia or at any evaluation of the morals of the second Russian Revolution in their bearing on Socialist policies in the West.

Accordingly, from the moment of the Bolshevik victory in Russia the attempt to revive the pre-war International either as an instrument for the achievement of peace or as the engineer of the peace settlement passed out of the field of practical politics, though the cry for peace by negotiation continued to become louder and more widespread. The attempt to hold an International Socialist Conference at the same time as the official Peace Conference made no headway. The Socialist Parties of the Allied countries continued, without the Russians, to hold conferences of their own for the formulation of 'War Aims'; and within the Central Powers the challenge to the established Governments grew more intense. But the attempt at restoration of the International was deferred until after the end of the fighting, and then took shape in the struggle between those who wished to rebuild the Second International on much the old foundations, those who supported the new Third International under Russian leadership, and those, at first numerous, who found themselves caught between two fires and sought to achieve some sort of unity between the main contestants.

The attempt of the Socialists in the Allied countries to formulate an agreed definition of their war aims was based on a mixture of considerations and motives. In part, it was a direct outcome of war weariness, or of the consciousness among the leaders of the growth of critical feeling about the policies that were actually being followed by the Governments on both sides, and threatened to involve an indefinite continuance of the war until the one or the other achieved complete victory, and was thus put in a position to impose its own terms on the vanquished. Even those Socialists who supported the war were for the most part unwilling to trust their own Governments to behave with justice under such circumstances, and were ready to press their Governments to declare their war aims in order to reassure the critics that victory would not be abused. To this was added, from the moment of the first Russian Revolution, the pressure of the Russians for an immediate peace as a means of saving the Revolution and of defeating the Jingo extremists in both the hostile camps. The Stockholm project, moreover, brought with it a definite call from the Dutch-Scandinavian Committee to the Socialists of all the belligerent countries to declare unequivocally the conditions in which they were prepared to take steps to end the fighting ; and each national Party, in framing its reply to the Stockholm invitation, found itself under the necessity of defining its own attitude on this issue much more precisely than it had done so far. Under these impulsions the British Labour Party took the initiative in drawing up a statement of war aims, drafted by Henderson, MacDonald, and Sidney Webb in consultation with Camille Huysmans of the International Socialist Bureau ; and this statement was submitted to, and approved by, a special Conference, representing the Trade Unions as well as the Labour Party, in December 1917 — that is to say, soon after the Bolshevik Revolution in Russia. An earlier draft of this statement, as we saw, had been submitted by the British Labour Party in August 1917 to an Allied Socialist meeting, which had been called to consider the reply to be made to the request sent out by the Stockholm Committee. The Allied delegates had then fallen out sharply, the supporters of a fight to a finish objecting to any statement of war aims that implied a preparedness for peace by negotiation with the Central Powers. By December, however, the situation had been radically changed, not only by the Bolshevik victory in Russia, but also by the publication in *Izvestia* of the secret treaties by which the Allied Governments had committed themselves to plainly unjustifiable measures of annexation. In these circumstances, the British Labour Conference endorsed the statement of war aims drafted by Henderson, MacDonald, and Webb; and it was decided that this statement should be submitted to the Allied Socialist Parties as the basis for an agreed statement declaring their common objectives. With only minor modifications it was subsequently endorsed by the French and Belgian Socialists, and thus became a common declaration of Allied Socialist policy, to be urged upon the Allied Governments both immediately and at the peace negotiations whenever they were begun.

The British War Aims Statement, published as a pamphlet before its submission to the Allied Socialist Parties, received very wide publicity, in the United States as well as in Europe. Its publication immediately preceded the proclamation by President Wilson of his 'Fourteen Points', with which it had much in common, though it was more detailed and explicit and covered a still wider field. It was, indeed, a very remarkable document, embodying a conception of the terms of peace that went a long way towards satisfying both the critics who had been most outraged by the revelations of the Secret Treaties and the advocates of a world settlement designed to make an end of imperialism and war; and to set up a supra-national authority armed with real power to bring about the reign of justice in world affairs; and to promote the general well-being on foundations of self-determination; and of international action for the economic development of all peoples. It also satisfied most of the pro-war Socialists because it included provisions for the full restoration of Belgian independence, for the settlement of the problem of Alsace-Lorraine in accordance with the wishes of the inhabitants, and for the self-determination of the peoples of the Austro-Hungarian and Turkish empires. It thus rejected the notion of a peace 'without annexations or indemnities', such as the pacifists had been demanding, and clearly contemplated that the war must be carried on until these objectives could be secured. As against this, however, it sought to limit 'annexations' to what could be justified on grounds of national self-determination, and, while allowing for the exaction of limited reparations for war damage, ruled out all forms of punitive 'indemnity'. Moreover, in relation to imperialism, it went to the length of preparing a plan for the unified administration and development of the whole area of tropical Africa under the auspices of the League of Nations, of which it strongly urged the establishment on a basis that would enable it both to prevent future wars and to play an active rôle in world development, economic as well as political. The League, it urged, should set its face against economic warfare waged by means of protective tariffs and capitalist monopolies. It called for international co-operative action to secure the sharing out of world supplies of foodstuffs and raw materials on the principle that 'none should have cake till all have bread'; and it advocated that all claims for reparations on account of war damage should be assessed by an international commission before which Governments should bring the cases of their respective nationals.

The War Aims Statement thus accomplished to a great extent the difficult aim of satisfying the majority of both the pro-war and the middle Socialist groups in the Western Allied countries, though not, of course, the extremists on either side. Taken in conjunction with President Wilson's 'Fourteen Points' it exercised a great influence on opinion in Germany and Austria-Hungary as well as in the Allied countries and the United States, by strengthening the movements aiming at a just peace and compelling the advocates of war to the bitter end to moderate their more outrageous demands. At the same time it struck a special blow at those who called for peace at any price, and sharply dissociated its sponsors from the Bolsheviks, who insisted that peace could come only as a by-product of universal revolution and called for 'revolutionary defeatism' as the correct Socialist answer to the 'social patriots' who were supporting the causes of their respective Governments. If a case could be made for the 'social patriots' among the Allied Socialists, the statement on war aims made that case clearly and well, with fully enough Socialist idealism to carry wide conviction except to out-and-out revolutionaries. But that, of course, made it all the less acceptable to the Bolsheviks and to their revolutionary supporters in the rest of the world.

Immediately, the statement on war aims could have no effect on the course of events. Within two months of its adoption, Russia was out of the war under the Brest-Litovsk Treaty ; and there was no possibility of the German Government accepting the terms proposed until it had been forced to abandon all hope of military victory. Nor was there any prospect of the Allied Governments accepting them, despite the 'Fourteen Points', unless they on their side had to abandon their hopes of driving Germany down to utter defeat. Accordingly, what occurred was that the Germans, reinforced by the armies set free by the ending of the war in the East, launched their great Western offensive in the hope of breaking the Allied resistance before the Americans could come effectively to the aid of the Western powers ; and only when this final onslaught had been beaten back and the intensified submarine campaign held in check did any real prospect of an ending of the struggle arise. When that stage was reached, in the summer of 1918, the breakdown in Austria-Hungary was undoubtedly much assisted by the combined impact of the 'Fourteen Points' and of the war aims statement ; and the ensuing German collapse was also hastened by the popular hope that these declarations would help in securing tolerable terms of peace — a hope that was speedily frustrated by the intransigent attitude of the Allied Governments towards the newly founded German Republic.

The Allied war aims statement had been drawn up without the participation of the American Federation of Labor, which, under the leadership of Samuel Gompers, took up a strong line against any sort of negotiated peace and refused to take part in the discussions of the Allied Socialist and Trade Union movements. It had been the intention of the Allied Socialists that their representatives should take a recognised part in the peace negotiations and should present the statement for acceptance by the Peace Conference through an international Socialist Conference that was intended to meet simultaneously with the official Conference of Governments. But when the time came, the Allied Governments were by no means prepared to accept the claim of the Labour movements to have a share in making the peace ; and the Labour Conference which met at Berne in February 1919 could do no more than lay its case before the representatives of the Governments, who rejected it outright in all its more significant features, and allowed Labour participation only in the special discussions which led to the establishment of the International Labour Organisation. As we shall see, the terms of peace and the constitution of the League of Nations set up at Versailles bore no resemblance to what had been demanded by the Allied Socialists. The statement on war aims played its part in rallying the Allied Socialists to continued, though critical, support of the Allied war effort during the final year of the struggle, but had little or no effect on the terms enforced on Germany after its military collapse.

CHAPTER III

THE TWO RUSSIAN REVOLUTIONS OF 1917

Russia entered the war in August 1914 as the ally of France and the United Kingdom against the Central Powers, but as an ally of which many in the West could feel only ashamed, though Russian liberals were for the most part well pleased at the alliance and hoped to use it as an instrument for liberalising and westernising the behaviour of the Russian State. The Constitutional Democrats (or Cadets), Milyukov's party, were particularly keen supporters of the war and supported highly chauvinistic war aims, including the annexation of Constantinople by the Russian State ; and not only the more moderate Social Revolutionary leaders but also a considerable section of the Mensheviks supported the war effort, while opposing chauvinistic projects of annexation and demanding that the Government should cease from persecutions and be given a character more representative of the main currents of political opinion. Only the Bolsheviks, under Lenin's influence, took up an unequivocal anti-war attitude of 'revolutionary defeatism' and urged that the war situation should be used to intensify revolutionary activity, so as to be made the basis for an actual revolution which, they hoped, would come about in all the belligerent countries and make the proletariat masters of European society. Even among the Bolsheviks in 1914 it was the general opinion that Russia was not far enough advanced economically for Socialist, proletarian revolution to be practicable ; but whatever the nature of the coming Russian Revolution, they had no doubt that the proletariat would be called upon to play a leading part in it, or that the war ought to be treated primarily as an opportunity for bringing it about.

The Mensheviks, more numerous than the Bolsheviks, were also united in disbelieving in the possibility of proceeding straight to a Socialist revolution, and in holding that in Russia the expected Revolution would need to take for the time being a bourgeois form. They agreed in regarding capitalism as a stage through which each country needed to pass on its road to Socialism, though they differed considerably about the rôle to be played by the proletariat, both in bringing the bourgeois Revolution to birth and in collaborating with the bourgeoisie to maintain it until Russia had developed far enough economically to make the transition to Socialism practicable. They also differed sharply about the attitude Socialists ought to take towards the war. One group, headed by G. V. Plekhanov (1857–1918), the doyen of Social Democracy in Russia, threw itself ardently on the side of the Allies and urged the need to overthrow the militarist imperialism of the Central Powers, to liberate the subject peoples of Austria-Hungary, and to unite the Russian peoples in the cause of democracy and of Western 'progress' : a second, led by Yuly Martov (1873–1923), took up an 'internationalist' position, saw all the warring States as sharers in a common imperialist guilt, and held that the primary duty of Socialists in all countries was to work for a speedy peace based as far as possible on social justice, and on recognition of the rights of self-determination for all the peoples. Many Mensheviks hesitated between these two views, or found themselves impelled towards the second, as disaster after disaster overtook the Russian armies and as the social structure began visibly to disintegrate under the intense pressure of war.

Plekhanov's adhesion to the Allied cause came as a severe shock to many Russian Socialists ; for he was the 'grand old man' of Russian Marxism and was held in high respect as an outstanding theorist of Socialism. He was, moreover, the Russian Social Democrat who had had both the greatest respect in the Second International and the closest connections with German Social Democracy, and had held the German S.D.P. in highest esteem. As Lenin's early teacher and most prominent collaborator in the early years of *Iskra*, he had great prestige in Bolshevik as well as in Menshevik circles, especially among those who still hoped that the breach in the Social Democratic Party could be healed.

The Social Revolutionaries were a much more heterogeneous group than the Social Democrats and had in all a much larger following than Bolsheviks and Mensheviks combined. They were essentially an agrarian party, depending mainly on peasant support, though they had also a considerable following in the towns. Identified till quite recently with a policy of individual terrorism,[1] they had nevertheless a substantial following of moderates, in terms of social and economic aspirations, and had links with the non-Socialist progressives who were active in the *zemstvos* and in promoting Co-operative activities ; but at the other extreme they included many near-Anarchists. Very decentralised in structure, the Social Revolutionary Party had a much more widely dispersed following than either faction of the Social Democrats, and spread into every region of the vast Russian empire. Its followers, for the most part, were much more conscious of local than of national or international problems : they made up an ever-fermenting mass rather than a coherent body capable of formulating a common policy. They were affected by the war chiefly because of the vast numbers of peasants who were continually being called up and taken away for war service, and because of the increased pressure on the countryside to provide food for towns and armies. Their leaders, indeed, were for the most part educated men, who had views on national and international issues ; but there was little or no pressure from the followers upon the leaders to take up any particular attitude on such questions, and in practice the widest divergences were consistent with remaining within the Party. In the Fourth Duma they were not represented as a Party, though the small group of Trudovics (Labour Party), headed by Kerensky, was fairly closely associated with them, as were a few other deputies described as of no, or of unknown, party allegiance. For the most part they worked underground, endeavouring to focus peasant discontents as the means to a social revolution, which they hoped to base on the peasant masses, with the industrial proletariat playing an important, but only a secondary part.

From 1914 onwards, some of the S.R.s and of the groups loosely associated with them espoused the Allied cause with much greater enthusiasm and single-mindedness than most Mensheviks. This applies particularly to the Populist groups

---

[1] From 1906 the S.R.s had officially restricted terrorism to particular cases approved by the Central party authority, and had rejected indiscriminate terrorism or acts of terrorism instigated by local groups.

round the veterans N. V. Chaikowsky (1850–1926) and Felix Volkhovsky (1846–1914) and to many of the other exiles who had found refuge in Paris or London. But at the opposite extreme there were S.R.s who opposed the war quite as bitterly as any Bolshevik and were no less ready to treat it as an opportunity for revolutionary action involving national defeat. The S.R. Party, as we saw,[1] had already split into Maximalist and Minimalist factions on the occasion of the earlier Russian Revolution of 1905 ; and their left wing had continued to advocate terrorism when the majority of the Party suspended terrorist action. No further formal split occurred in 1914 ; but the S.R.s of the left shared, though on different grounds, the anti-war revolutionary attitude of the Bolsheviks, with whom they were to be associated for a time after the November Revolution. Between the two extremes there were many intermediate groups, ranging from Victor Chernov's (1873–1952) primarily agrarian followers to Kerensky's Trudovics, and in war attitude from support of the Allies to a position akin to Martov's 'internationalism'.

During the period that followed the assassination of Stolypin in September 1911, the Czarist Government had followed a persistently reactionary course. Stolypin's successor, Count V. N. Kokovtsev, was a thoroughly conservative official who curried favour with the court and made no attempt to cooperate even with the conservative majority in the Duma, which he completely antagonised. Under him the Czarina was able to press her reactionary views and to procure the appointment of intransigent anti-democrats to key positions ; and the sinister influence of the abominable Rasputin was enabled to grow apace. In the long run, Stolypin's agrarian reforms might have brought into being the minority of relatively well-to-do, technically progressive, and anti-revolutionary peasants on whom his hopes were set, and therewith, on a part of the land, the improved, more capitalistic methods of cultivation at which he aimed. But for the time being the position of most of the peasants got worse and worse as pressure on the limited lands held by them increased with rising population. Stolypin was largely successful in destroying the old collective systems of ownership and cultivation, and in transferring a large part of

[1] See Vol. III, Part I, p. 471.

the land to individual ownership. But for the time this made matters worse, as most of the peasants had neither the knowledge nor the resources required for the application of better methods, and the tiny and often scattered holdings were very unproductive. Consequently, after a lull which followed the ruthless suppression of the 1905 Revolution, peasant unrest soon began to grow again — and to be met with a resumption of the old ferocity. Unrest also developed rapidly in the towns, among the industrial workers ; and in this case too the increasingly numerous strikes and disturbances were met with violently repressive measures against the Trade Unions and the Socialist agitators, at whose door the blame was laid. From 1912 to 1914 there was a succession of big strikes in St. Petersburg, Moscow, and other industrial centres ; and things were already blowing up for a new revolution before the outbreak of war.

There were also, during these years, serious scandals arising out of corruption in high official quarters, especially in relation to the military administration. Abroad, Russia was attempting to follow an imperialist policy, which brought the Czar's Government into sharp conflict with Austria-Hungary and Germany, especially over Balkan affairs. The Russians helped to foment the first Balkan war, from which they hoped to profit by increasing their influence throughout the Near East ; but in the great power negotiations that followed the second Balkan War they suffered a serious diplomatic set-back when they failed to save their Bulgarian protégés from defeat. The Czarist Government did not then feel strong enough to go to war without the assurance of support from its Western Allies. It was left smarting under a sense of defeat and in no mood to take further Austrian or German aggression lying down. Accordingly, in 1914 Russia, by rallying to the support of the Serbs after the Austro-Hungarian ultimatum, took the plunge and therewith brought Germany into the conflict, thus dragging in France and presently Great Britain as its allies. In this mood Russia entered into a world war for which it was utterly unequipped, both because the armed forces were in a thoroughly bad state and, even more, because its productive resources and its means of transport were entirely unequal to meeting the strain. The Russians lacked not only staying power but also the means of rapid manœuvre. All they could do was to throw immense masses of undertrained, grossly under-equipped and ill-clothed, ill-fed conscripts into the field, with no means of keeping them adequately supplied. These masses, with the aid of Allied supplies, could be used to win immediate military successes by the sheer impact of numbers ; but despite the individual bravery of the soldiers in battle and the presence of not a few able military leaders, they could not last out when they had to meet sustained opposition from forces much better organised and supplied.

The Russian Government, instead of attempting in this situation to share its responsibility with the parties and groups that were prepared to co-operate in the war effort, used the war as an occasion for intensified repression. After the severe defeats which occurred in the spring of 1915, both the military and the internal situation got rapidly worse. There was indeed an attempt to rally the wealthier classes behind the national effort and to improvise voluntary services to aid the nation in its emergency ; and the *zemstvos*, under the leadership of Prince Lvov and with the support of the bourgeois Cadets, including many from the ranks of the professional class, did something to organise hospital services and necessary supplies. But these efforts were largely stultified by the insensate behaviour of the Government and the court, where Rasputin was in greater favour than ever. The Czar presently left for the front to assume personal command — and still more to escape from the stifling atmosphere of the capital ; but this in no way checked the Government's behaviour or mended the administrative breakdown. During 1916 there were constant desertions from the front, and starving soldiers began to roam the countryside in search of food. A strike at the Putilov works was put down with the utmost violence. The Duma, which had been suspended since the outbreak of war, was called together in 1916 to deal with the mounting financial crisis ; but its calls for a more responsible Government were unheeded. Both the armies and the half-starving town populations were getting near the end of their tether. Revolution was getting nearer ; but there seemed to be no one to lead it. Most of the outstanding Socialist leaders, of all parties, were in prison or in exile, either in Siberia or abroad ; and the bourgeois parties of the opposition — except Milyukov and his followers among the Cadets —

were not, for the most part, prepared to lead a revolution that they felt themselves impotent to control — the more so because revolution in war-time seemed to most of them to involve a betrayal of the national cause, which they supported, and also, if it were to get out of hand, the danger of a breach with the Allies, on whom Russia depended for war supplies. Accordingly, month after month, nothing happened except fresh military disasters and a more and more rapid deterioration of conditions at home.

In the end, the Revolution was not planned, or led. It simply happened. It was brought on by the bread riots, which the army was called on to suppress, and was made, in effect, by the soldiers, not at the front, but first of all in Petrograd — the new name given to St. Petersburg after the outbreak of war. There had been mutinies before March 1917 ; but they had been sporadic and had been put down, and the Cossacks, the most reliable part of the Czarist army, had remained loyal to their officers. Then, quite suddenly — and for no particular reason — for suffering and frustration and the sense of being made fools and victims by an incompetent and oppressive Government were hardly *particular* reasons — regiment after regiment of the Petrograd garrison refused to obey orders and began marching about the city, hardly knowing what it would be at. The workers from the factories poured out on the streets and began to hold huge demonstrations. Leaders arose out of their ranks and delivered fervent orations, each according to his bent. The soldiers, called upon to disperse the civilian demonstrations, refused and mutinied, many handing over their arms to the unarmed workers. Rebellious soldiers occupied and held key buildings ; but there was still no plan, no central leadership, no knowledge what was to be done next. The Duma, taken entirely aback by the outbreak, had no notion how to react. The majority of its members were monarchists and reactionaries: the Octobrists — the Party which came nearest to representing constitutionalist landlordism and high finance, and the Cadets — the Party of the more progressive landowners, industrialists, and merchants, and also of the bourgeois intellectuals and the professional classes — had between them fewer seats than the parties of the right. The surviving Socialists and Trudovics were only a handful. But something had to be done ; and, even in such a Duma, exasperation with the Czar's Government was intense. Octobrists and Cadets got together and, as news of the sheer collapse of authority came in from all sides, decided that there was no alternative to the Czar's abdication, to demand which they sent emissaries to army headquarters. They hoped, however, to save the monarchy, while jettisoning the monarch. The Czar, on the emissaries' insistence, agreed to abdicate and nominated his son as his successor, then changed his mind and named the Grand Duke Michael instead. The Duma Parties formed a Provisional Government, with the moderate aristocrat Prince Lvov, the head of the *zemstvo* organisation, as Prime Minister, the Octobrist leader, A. I. Guchkov as War Minister, the Cadet Paul Milyukov as Minister of Foreign Affairs, and Alexander Kerensky (b. 1881), to represent the left, as Minister of Justice. This Ministry — at first, without Kerensky — was actually formed in great haste the day before the abdication — in haste, because on the same day there had come into being a rival body which, it was feared, might challenge the Duma's authority and try to carry the Revolution further instead of arresting it at the stage already reached. This new body was the Petrograd Soviet of Workers' and Soldiers' Deputies, consisting of members chosen directly by the soldiers and workers in their regimental and factory groups, and removable and replaceable at any time by the groups that had elected them.

The Soviet which thus sprang suddenly into being during the critical March days was, of course, a harking back to the great days of 1905, when a similar body of workmen's deputies — without the same basis of regimental support — had played, under Trotsky's chairmanship, a vital part in the earlier Revolution.[1] It was natural that this precedent should be called to mind and made use of by the workers' leaders who were striving to give order and direction to the sheer incoherence of the outbreak. It was also natural that the appearance on the scene of such a body should cause deep forebodings in the minds of the party leaders in the Duma, whether they wished to crush the Revolution or only to prevent it from getting out of hand, and to use it as a means to the establishment

[1] See Vol. III, Part I, p. 464.

of constitutional government under a modified Czarist system. In the eyes of the Duma Parties of the centre — Octobrists, Cadets, and bourgeois Progressives — the immediate need was to establish some sort of constitutional authority able to hold the allegiance of the vast civil service machine and of the military leaders, to administer the country, and to carry on the war. The new Government would have preferred to do this under a new Czar, prepared to serve as a constitutional monarch and to give the Revolution the sanction of legality. But the Grand Duke Michael, understanding the mood of the people better than the politicians, declined the succession, and left Prince Lvov's Government to face the future without his aid.

The new Government thus found itself republican against its will, and dependent for its authority on the forces let loose by the Revolution. For the moment it was successful in holding the allegiance of the Civil Service and in securing the adhesion of the military commanders ; and it was also, after a week's uncertainty, recognised by the Allied Governments, which were anxiously watching the course of events and were in a panic that the new masters of Russia might refuse to go on fighting the Germans and enter into a separate peace. In that event, the German armies that were held on the Eastern front would be set free for transference to the West, where the military pressure was already severe enough ; and, unless the Americans came in, the Central Powers would be bound to win the war. Indeed, even if the Americans did intervene, it was doubtful whether they could arrive in time to avert disaster. The Western Allied Governments therefore felt it necessary to subordinate every other consideration to keeping Russia in the war and to accept whatever Russian Government would take over Czardom's commitment to the Triple Entente. They had been watching with dismay the growing disintegration of Russia under the impact of prolonged fighting and extreme maladministration, and they had assuredly no love for the corrupt, incompetent, and brutally reactionary Czarist system. Nevertheless, the Revolution dismayed them, and their one thought was to halt it at a point which would leave the Russians still committed to carrying on the struggle against the Central Powers.

In both France and Great Britain the Russian alliance had

long been regarded with many misgivings, not only by the working classes but also by most liberal and progressive groups ; and the behaviour of the Czarist Government during the war had added greatly to its unpopularity, not only among progressive but also among the more conservative elements in Western politics. In every country the victory of the Revolution in Russia was hailed with enthusiasm by the working classes ; and it was also welcomed by many bourgeois progressives who hoped that it would mean the recruitment of a new great country to the cause of parliamentary democracy. Only the more extreme reactionaries were prepared to speak out against it ; but there were others, including most of the leaders of the Governments in the Allied countries, whose attitude was ambivalent because they feared its effects on the Allied cause. These latter, however, were compelled, whatever their feelings, to extend a welcome in public to the new Russian Government, in the hope of inducing it to remain at war and even to launch a new offensive designed to relieve the severe pressure on the Western Front.

Singularly ill-informed by their own embassies in Petrograd, whose members hobnobbed chiefly with reactionaries and had little knowledge of the state of feeling among the peoples of Russia, the Western Governments had very little notion of what was really happening inside that country, or of the extent to which the dislocation had proceeded even before the dramatic disappearance of Czardom. They believed that the new Government, having secured the allegiance of the military authorities and the Civil Service, would be in a position to take over control of the country and to carry on at least no worse than its incompetent predecessor. At first they attached little importance to the presence in Russia of a rival authority — the Petrograd Soviet — which was as yet making no claim to be the Government or to seize power against Prince Lvov and his colleagues. They did not realise that, in Petrograd, the regiments would not obey orders unless these were endorsed by the deputies whom the soldiers had elected to represent them, or that Soviets resembling that of Petrograd were springing up everywhere, not only among worker and peasant groups, but also in the armies on the various fronts. To be sure, these many Soviets, no more than that of Petrograd, claimed governmental authority, or knew at all clearly what they meant to do. They did, however, collectively constitute the real power set loose by the Revolution, whereas the Provisional Government, even while the Soviets issued no formal challenge to its right to rule, held only the shadow of authority and could do nothing positive without their support.

The Soviet was, indeed, in the situation of Russia in 1917, a magnificent revolutionary instrument. It emanated directly, in each area, from the working groups that had been held in sharp repression by the autocracy and were now learning eagerly how to act for themselves. It was, moreover, an entirely flexible instrument, changing from day to day in response to every change in attitude or opinion among the working masses and commanding confidence because no member of it had any security of tenure if he failed to reflect his constituents' feelings and desires. It was altogether unlike a Parliament or any body constitutionally elected for a formal term, and therefore able for the time being to act as it might think fit, even against the opinion of its constituents. This no doubt meant that it was inherently unstable, as long as it kept its original character. But, in the situation that had to be faced, this very instability was at the root of its power.

At the outset, the new Soviets, in Petrograd as well as elsewhere, consisted largely of unknown men who were thrown up by the Revolution itself. Naturally, however, there appeared among the members most of the active Socialists, of any brand, who were on the spot ; and these militants were continually reinforced by returning exiles from Siberia or from abroad and, especially in the rural areas, by conscripts who found their way, usually as deserters, back to their villages. At first there was no central co-ordination. Each local Soviet acted for itself, mainly in sheer ignorance of what was going on elsewhere. But soon communications began to be established, and presently a pattern of central organisation emerged. There were regional Congresses covering larger or smaller areas, and then national Congresses both of Workers' and Soldiers' and of Peasant Soviets from all parts of the Russian empire.

Through all the earlier phases of the March Revolution the Soviets, including the Petrograd Soviet, were dominated by the more moderate Socialist Parties — in the big towns especially by the Mensheviks. N. S. Chkheidze (1864–1926), a leading Menshevik from Georgia, was President of the Petrograd Soviet : the Bolsheviks were everywhere no more than a small minority. This was the situation which Lenin found in existence when he returned to Russia from Switzerland early in April ; and it had hardly changed when Trotsky arrived from America a month later. There were, moreover, among the Social Democrats a number of groups which had refused to identify themselves with either the Bolshevik or the Menshevik faction. Among these were the group round Maxim Gorki (1868–1936) and his journal *Novaya Zhizn* (*New Life*), which was strongly anti-Bolshevik, and — of more importance — the Mezhrayonka, or Inter-borough Organisation, founded in 1913 with Trotsky's support from abroad. The Mezhrayonka included a galaxy of leaders already well known before the Revolution — A. V. Lunacharsky (1875–1933), D. B. Ryazonov (1870– ?1940), M. N. Pokrovsky (1868–1932), A. Yoffe (d. 1923), D. Manuilsky (b. 1883), M. Uritsky (1873–1918), and V. Volodarsky (1881–1915) — and others who were later to become prominent servants of the new Soviet State, such as L. Karakhan (1889–1937). It was indeed mainly a group of orators and leaders, with no large or clearly defined popular following, but with an appreciable influence. This was the group to which Trotsky, still not a Bolshevik, gravitated on his return to Russia ; and through its merger with the Bolsheviks he presently became a Bolshevik and appeared, with Lenin's backing, as a leading figure in the Bolshevik Party and in the making of the November Revolution. For some time after his arrival, however, the Mezhrayonka continued as an independent group, in broad agreement with the new policy to which Lenin had won over the hesitant Bolshevik Party, but differing from it in being less prepared to dismiss the Menshevik majority as traitors to the Socialist cause.

The great question for the Bolsheviks, at the moment of Lenin's arrival in Russia, had been that of the kind of revolution it was their business to promote. By tradition, Lenin and the Bolsheviks, equally with the Mensheviks, had stood for the view that Russia was too undeveloped economically for a Socialist revolution to be practicable, and that the Revolution would need to be halted temporarily at the bourgeois stage, with the Socialists not attempting to form the Government but exerting independent pressure on it in the workers' interests. It had, however, been apparent from the very formation of Prince Lvov's first Government, based on the Octobrists and the Cadets, that these Parties were lacking in the popular support needed for the exercise of real power ; and from an early stage the Petrograd Soviet had been of necessity much more than a mere pressure group influencing it from the outside. The Soviet was before long virtually compelled to act in many respects as an independent power — for example, in endorsing Government orders which neither the regiments nor the workers in the factories would have obeyed without its sanction, and in forcing the Government to publish pronouncements which ran sharply counter to its actual views. The dualism of authority between the Provisional Government and the Soviet had become important, at any rate by June, not because the Soviet deliberately planned it, but because the realities of power made it indispensable to the Government's continued existence. Leading members of the first Provisional Government were not at all prepared to accept any sharing of power with the Soviets as lasting. The Octobrists in particular revolted against acceptance of the Soviet as having any independent authority and wanted to bring back the old Duma to give some sort of legality to their position in the Government. Their leader, Guchkov, as Minister of War, was set on restoring discipline in the army and on getting rid of the regimental Soviets, without whose endorsement the soldiers refused to take orders from their officers. When he failed to achieve this, he resigned, and in doing so largely contributed to making the Government's position untenable.

The final blow to the first Provisional Government, however, was dealt by the Cadet leader, Milyukov, as Minister of Foreign Affairs, when he declared, in response to pressure from the Allied Governments, that the new Russia would take over the war aims of the old and would stand by the treaties in which these aims had been embodied. This declaration, which would have committed Russia to a fight to a finish in support of the imperialist policies of Czardom, provoked so great an outcry that Milyukov in his turn had to resign and the entire Government broke up. The question then was, what was to take its place ? The bourgeois parties clearly could not carry on without Socialist support ; should the Socialists then agree to a coalition with them, or with what was left of them after Guchkov's and Milyukov's removal ? The only alternative appeared to be the formation of an entirely Socialist Government, or no Government at all — which would have meant that the Soviets would have had to take the whole power into their own hands. But the Soviets were not organised in such a way that they could take such power. The first National Soviet Congress had still to meet ; and the Socialist Parties were not at all disposed to form a Government which the army leaders and the Civil Service would probably refuse to recognise or to obey. The Bolsheviks were indeed by this time raising the cry 'All power to the Soviets!' and they rejected the idea of any coalition with the bourgeoisie. But their influence was still small : it was the Mensheviks and Social Revolutionaries who had to make up their minds how the situation was to be faced.

Most of them came down on the side of coalition, not because they liked it, but because they did not see what else to do. They decided, in fact, to support a new Provisional Government still led by a non-Socialist — Prince Lvov — and in which the Socialist Ministers were in a minority. Indeed, many Socialists found it easier to swallow such a coalition than they would have found it to accept one in which the Socialists were to hold the leading place. There were several reasons for this. One — very important in their eyes — was that a mainly Socialist Government could hardly have failed to follow a broadly Socialist policy, whereas the Mensheviks at any rate were mostly sure that Russia was not ripe for such a policy and needed a Government that would foster rapid capitalist development. A second reason was that the Government needed to secure the continued obedience, if not the allegiance, of the armed forces, which a Socialist Government would have found very difficult, if not impossible. A third reason, I think, was that many of the Socialists were actually afraid of power in the very difficult conditions that had to be faced, and many also wanted a government which the Soviets could criticise and, if need arose, coerce, rather than one they would need to recognise as representing themselves.

At all events, the second Lvov Government was formed, with eight non-Socialist and six Socialist Ministers ; and among the latter were Kerensky as Minister of War, Victor Chernov (1873–1952) as Minister of Agriculture, M. I. Skobelev (1885–1930) as Minister of Labour, and I. G. Tseretelli (1882–?) as Minister of Posts and Telegraphs. Of these, Kerensky and Chernov were Social Revolutionaries, Tseretelli a leading Menshevik, and Skobelev a former collaborator of Trotsky who had been active as a Menshevik in the fourth Duma.

The first National Congress of Soviets, heavily dominated by Mensheviks and S.R.s, had still to be convened when the new Provisional Government assumed office ; and it was the Petrograd Soviet that was called upon to pronounce on the question of Socialist participation. It did so, in favour of participation, by a very big majority, after a debate in the course of which Trotsky, the day after his arrival in Russia, expressed his sense of the danger of the coalition and his conviction that the next step must be the taking of full power into the hands of the Soviets as the representatives of the toiling masses. Coalition, he said, would not end the dualism of control : it would only transfer the dualism into the Government itself. Trotsky thus made his first public appearance as the ally of the Bolsheviks, though he did not yet fully realise this ; for he had not yet discovered how drastically Lenin had already succeeded in changing the Bolshevik policy towards what had previously been his own. In the past it had been Lenin who had insisted that the Russian Revolution could be only, in the first instance, a bourgeois revolution ; whereas Trotsky, as we saw,[1] had argued that the sheer pressure of events would force the workers to take the lead and make the Revolution their own. Lenin had now come over to this view, and had persuaded his Party, in face of Kamenev's opposition, to espouse the slogan 'All power to the Soviets !', which involved a declaration of war on the Provisional Government. This did not mean that Lenin had been simply converted to Trotsky's views : on the question of the correct form of party organisation and of attitude to the other Socialist Parties they were still a considerable distance apart. But Lenin had changed his view about the nature of the Revolution that was working itself out in

[1] See Vol. III, Part II, p. 955.

Russia, mainly because he saw the situation as completely changed by the war. Russia's unripeness for Socialism was no longer a valid reason for holding back, because the Revolution in Russia could no longer be regarded as standing by itself. It had to be envisaged as a part of the World Revolution for which the war had provided the opportunity. Lenin held that, even if Russia, standing alone, was not ripe for Socialism, capitalist Europe as a whole was ; and in his opinion the Russians were called upon by the circumstances in which they found themselves to act as the pioneers of the World Revolution and to summon the proletariats of the more advanced countries to follow their example by overthrowing their rulers and seizing power for themselves. This was the Kienthal policy of 1916 applied to the Russia of 1917 ; and in the prevailing circumstances it would be betrayal of the World Revolution for the Russian proletariat, despite its backwardness, to stop short of making the Russian Revolution its own. The necessity of passing through the successive phases of capitalistic development could not in any event be escaped ; but now this would have to be done, not under the control of the bourgeoisie, but under proletarian rule. There would need to be a period of State Capitalism, with the proletariat taking the place of the capitalists as the controlling and directing power.

For the time being, both Lenin and Trotsky were voices crying in the wilderness. When the first National Soviet Congress met at the beginning of June 1917, five-sixths of the deputies were either Mensheviks or S.R.s of the right and centre ; and the Bolsheviks, Left S.R.s, and other left-wing groups made up only a small fraction of the whole. In vain both Lenin and Trotsky told the Congress that the time had come for the Socialists to form their own Government as the direct expression of the workers' power manifested in the Soviets. The Cadets and the rest of the bourgeois groups, Trotsky told the Congress, no longer had any following that mattered ; and it was high time to sweep them away. This, of course, would have meant, had the Congress accepted their bidding, that power would have passed into the hands, not of the Bolsheviks and their allies, but of the very same moderate Socialist groups as were already represented in the Government. But it would have meant also that the Ministers would have become clearly answerable to the Soviets, whose composition was subject to continual change ; and under such conditions they would have been irresistibly impelled to the left by the growing urgency of the demand for peace and by the refusal of the soldiers and peasants to leave the settlement of the land question over till a Constituent Assembly, as yet unelected, could meet to deal with it. Any Minister who refused to endorse either of these demands would have found himself speedily displaced in favour of someone who was better able to assess the mood of the workers and peasants, and to comply with their wishes.

Not only the Socialist Ministers, but also the Parties that supported them, were well aware of this ; and accordingly the advocates of 'All power to the Soviets !' were voted down, and the Provisional Government received the endorsement of the Congress. The left wingers were indeed in a difficult position. Lenin, at the Congress, called on the Socialist Ministers to break with the Cadets and form an entirely Socialist Government responsible to the Soviets. This would have meant a Government of Mensheviks and S.R.s, responsible to bodies in which these two parties were in an overwhelming majority. It would have left the Bolsheviks and their supporters still in opposition to such a Government, but under a difficulty in opposing it as long as it had a firm basis of support in the Soviets. There was, however, nothing else for the Bolsheviks to propose at that stage ; for Lenin and his fellow-leaders were entirely opposed to any attempt to seize power until they had a majority behind them in the Soviets, at least in the main centres. There were others, including some of the Left S.R.s and the Anarchists, who wanted an immediate move to overthrow the Government by force, even if it had the support of the Soviets. These elements argued that, even though the Soviets voted in favour of the Government, most of their members were in reality hostile to its policies — above all to the continuance of the war in conjunction with the Allies — and would rally behind anyone who would promise them peace and land. Lenin, on the other hand, knew that, though working-class opinion in Petrograd was moving very rapidly leftwards and it might be quite possible to overturn the Government by a *coup*, this was much less the case in the provinces, and a successful *coup* in Petrograd might only isolate the capital and let loose counter-revolution elsewhere. He therefore strongly urged holding back ; and when a projected mass-demonstration of the left to demand an all-Socialist Government was banned by the Congress of Soviets he persuaded his Party to accept the ban. The Soviet majority then proceeded to arrange for a mass-demonstration of its own, to march past the assembled Congress. This took place on June 18th, when, to the dismay of its organisers, the demonstrators, or a large part of them, turned out under banners calling for the resignation of the non-Socialist Ministers and for the taking of all power into the Soviets' hands. The demonstration, however, was orderly ; and no attempt was made to turn it into a revolutionary *coup*. It served only to show how far opinion in Petrograd had run ahead of the attitude of the delegates who had been chosen some time before to attend the Congress of Soviets, and to indicate the precariousness of the Coalition Government's tenure.

Through the rest of June the Lvov Government, with its Socialist minority, lasted on into July. Kerensky, as War Minister, launched the ill-considered offensive that was soon to show how little fight was left in the armies inherited from Czardom ; and behind the lines disintegration grew greater, and the Socialist Ministers continued to reveal their impotence. Then came, early in the new month, the 'July Days', about which there was at the time and has been since so much dispute. Without any appearance of acting under any concerted orders, soldiers and workers again poured into the streets, demanding — it was not clear what : bread, peace, resignation of the Government, all power to the Soviets.

At the time, many, including not a few of the moderate Socialists, said — and probably believed — that the 'July Days' were the outcome of a plot by the Bolsheviks and their allies to seize power. But all the evidence I know of is against this view. On the contrary, it seems fairly clear that the Bolshevik leaders, unable and probably unwilling to prevent the demonstrations, did all they could to keep them short of leading to a revolutionary *coup*, for which Lenin, as well as the more cautious members of the Central Executive Committee, felt the situation to be still unripe. The underlying causes of the huge, mainly spontaneous movement among both soldiers and workers appear to have been the growingly acute shortage of food and other supplies, the sharp and continuous rise in prices, and the widespread distress among the population of Petrograd, aggravated by the additional demands of the armed forces in connection with the ill-fated military offensive. With the distress went a more and more urgent demand for peace and a swelling protest against the continuance of the war in support of the war aims of British and French, as well as of Russian imperialism, and therewith a developing sense of the futility of Socialist participation in a Government in which the Cadets were still the predominant Party. Political and economic factors went together ; but the latter seem to have been the more important in the precipitation of the mass-movement. The aimless and unco-ordinated behaviour of the various groups of demonstrators seems to show the absence of any central direction ; and, because there was none, the movement gradually petered out as the soldiers went back to their barracks and the workers to their factories, not knowing what to do. But the 'July Days', though they ended without a climax, did in many respects fundamentally transform the situation — the more so because almost simultaneously with their ending came the news that the military offensive had collapsed. There followed an intense campaign against the Bolsheviks, who were accused not only of having staged a rising that had failed, but also of being German agents and responsible for the military disaster. Not only Lenin, but also Trotsky and many others, were openly accused of being German spies. The episode of Lenin's transit through Germany in a sealed train and allegations that he was receiving funds from Germany to be used in disrupting the war effort were widely publicised in proof of this charge — which was in fact partly true ; for Lenin did receive German money, as well as help in reaching Russia, and was doing anything he could to obstruct the prosecution of the war and to stir up rebellion in the armed forces, though he of course acted in these ways, not in Germany's interest, but in pursuance of his own revolutionary purposes. The charges, however, did much for the time to discredit the Bolshevik Party and to narrow the basis of its support. Leading Bolsheviks were arrested and gaoled wholesale ; and before long the arrests spread to others who were supposed to be in sympathy with them, including Trotsky and Lunacharsky. Even Chernov, the S.R. Minister of Agriculture, was forced to resign from the Government because he had taken part in the Zimmerwald Conference of 1915, though he had been in fact giving strong support to the war effort. A general hue and cry set in against the left ; but, as against this, the collapse of the offensive made the position of the Lvov Government finally untenable. The Cadets were not forced out, but Kerensky became Prime Minister in a new Coalition Government in which moderate Socialists held for the first time the leading offices. Lenin and Zinoviev, after some hesitations and under pressure from their party colleagues, went into hiding. It was left to the Mensheviks and right-wing Social Revolutionaries to try their hand at riding the storm ; but any chance they might have had was fatally prejudiced by their continued governmental alliance with the Cadets and by their persistence in carrying on the war.

The Cadets, for their part, were seriously disturbed at their reduced rôle in the Government ; and, many of them, during the anti-left frenzy that followed the 'July Days', began to coquet with ideas of counter-revolution. Strongly hostile to Socialism, committed to a continuance of the war in partnership with the Allies, and intense believers in Western parliamentarism as the only proper basis for the government of Russia, they saw the country drifting towards Socialist solutions of its economic problems, towards a separate and disastrous peace on Germany's terms, and towards Soviet rule. They had committed themselves, equally with the Socialist Parties, to the convening in due course of a Constituent Assembly that would settle the future constitution of Russia ; but they were reluctant to proceed to elections for the Assembly because they realised their own electoral weakness and feared that its composition would turn out overwhelmingly Socialist. Many of them began to think that the only way back to sanity — that is, to liberal parliamentary government — might lie through a counter-revolution which they hoped to be able to prevent from going too far, and seeking to undo the whole Revolution.

Counter-revolution, however, could come only from the

generals and officers of the army ; and the open question was whether the soldiers would follow them if they led the way. Even if they would, it was not easy for generals in the field to order their troops away from the military front and turn them against their own people. What the Government would have preferred would have been, not open counter-revolution, but the backing of reliable army units against the disaffected regiments which formed the major part of the Petrograd garrison, and, if possible, the removal of these elements from the capital. The regiments of the garrison, however, refused to move ; and Kerensky's attempts to bring in more 'reliable' units from the front only prepared the way for General Kornilov's rebellion and, after its failure, for the Bolshevik seizure of power.

Of course, not all the Cadets turned their thoughts towards counter-revolution. Not a few of them were sympathetic to social reform, and had no desire to see a reversion to the old, bad order of Czarism. Some even became Socialists, joining the Mensheviks or the Social Revolutionaries, while ardently opposing the Bolsheviks and the threat of Soviet rule. But most of those who moved leftwards as they came to realise the bankruptcy of the bourgeois parties continued to support Russian participation in the war and to attach high importance to the war alliance as linking Russia to the Western parliamentary democracies, in whose image they desired to refashion the Czarist State. Such persons supported in turn each Provisional Government and wagged their heads at the growing disintegration of the armed forces under the influence of the Bolsheviks' subversive propaganda for immediate peace.

Meanwhile, the soldiers who formed the Petrograd garrison and had made the February Revolution by their refusal to act against the demonstrators were the target of incessant propaganda from the Bolsheviks and their allies. Having by their action dethroned the Czar and having set up Soviets which their officers did not dare to disobey, they were in a position to decide for themselves what orders to accept or to refuse and, in particular, whether to allow themselves to be drafted away from Petrograd to take part in the renewed offensive or to insist that their task was to remain in the capital in order to defend it, as need arose, either against the Germans, should they march upon it, or against counter-revolution, or even against the Provisional Government, should it attempt to suppress the workers by armed force. The Bolsheviks, in their attempts to bring the soldiers of the garrison over to their side, had the great advantage that few among them felt any urge to participate actively in the war, and that most of them much preferred to stay in Petrograd under the relaxed conditions of discipline and popular prestige which their action in the Revolution had won for them. They were prepared to fight, if it became necessary to defend Petrograd against a German attack, but not to be sent away to face the hardships of the front in a cause in which they did not believe, or to be used either by counter-revolutionary plotters or by a suspect Government to suppress the workers. This attitude made them more and more ready to listen sympathetically, not so much to the Bolsheviks as such as to the emissaries of the Petrograd Soviet irrespective of their party connections. As the Soviet gradually went Bolshevik, the regiments of the garrison changed in harmony with it, until in the final stages of preparation for the November Revolution, most of them were prepared to accept the call of the Soviet's Military Revolutionary Committee and to play their part against Kerensky in the *coup* that carried the Bolshevik Party and its allies into power. But at the time of the Kornilov rebellion this stage had not yet been reached. Indeed, both Kerensky's attempts before the rebellion to bring more 'reliable' military units from the front to the capital, and thereafter the rebellion itself, played important parts in converting the regiments of the garrison into aiders and abetters of the Second Revolution.

As far as I know, the circumstances that led up to the attempted Kornilov *putsch* have never been clearly demonstrated. Kerensky was accused at the time by the Bolsheviks of having connived at it ; but it is an undoubted fact that, when Kornilov had actually raised the standard of revolt against him, he invoked all the help he could call upon to put the counter-revolution down. Kerensky had been active since the 'July Days' in persecuting the Bolsheviks and in disarming the Red Guards who were the protagonists of the factory workers ; but no sooner had Kornilov announced his intention of marching on Petrograd and liquidating the Revolution than the Ministers were reduced to appealing to the Soviets to stop him and to the garrison and the sailors at Kronstadt, who were on the extreme left, to rally to the Government's defence. The Bolsheviks and their allies were then in some difficulty in making up their minds what to do. They had no desire at all to defend Kerensky or his Government ; but they had even less to connive at the overthrow of the Revolution by military force. When a deputation from the Kronstadt sailors visited Trotsky in prison and demanded his advice, Trotsky told them unhesitatingly that their duty was to defend the Revolution against its enemies, even if that meant, in the immediate emergency, coming to Kerensky's aid. The sailors responded ; and so did the regimental committees and the Bolshevik leaders. The defeat of Kornilov was accomplished, not in open fighting, but by propaganda carried out mainly by the Bolsheviks and their allies. Instead of attacking the capital, Kornilov's soldiers, after advancing almost to its boundaries, melted away, leaving Kerensky nominally victorious, but in fact nearly helpless against the rapidly swelling forces of the left. The remaining Cadet Ministers resigned from the Government in protest against Kerensky's invocation of the left-wing 'traitors' against the Kornilov *putsch* ; and the Socialist Ministers also resigned because they disapproved of Kerensky's alleged intrigues with Kornilov prior to the *putsch*. Kerensky, unable to get together a popular Ministry, governed as best he could for the next month with the aid of a very unrepresentative small Directorate, which commanded hardly any popular support.

What were the real nature and significance of the Kornilov *putsch* ? Its purpose was undoubtedly to make an end of the anti-war elements that were dominant in Petrograd and to bring Russia back into the war under authoritarian leadership, but not necessarily to restore the Czarist régime. Kornilov seems to have been not so much a Czarist as a believer in authoritarian rule ; and it is significant that he had the support of Savinkov, the former leader of the terrorist section of the Social Revolutionaries, who was certainly no Czarist, whereas Kerensky in the event opposed him. The truth seems to be that Kornilov's rebellion, by its failure, greatly strengthened the Bolsheviks and discredited all the right-wing groups, whether they had really been implicated in it, or even favourable to it, or not. Kerensky realised, if only at the eleventh hour, that if Kornilov were to capture Petrograd the only possible outcome would be civil war, in which both his Government and the middle course he was trying to uphold would be swept away. He therefore appealed to the left for help against the *putsch* ; but the effect was that the left, having defeated Kornilov, gained immensely in popular esteem, whereas Kerensky lost almost at a blow the great prestige he had apparently built up with the army as the inspirer of the military offensive. Up to the *putsch*, Kerensky had been riding on a wave of patriotic feeling : the almost simultaneous collapse of the offensive and of Kornilov's *putsch* lost him his support from the right without gaining him any continuing support on the left when the *putsch* was over. In a very real sense, these were the direct causes of the big swing of support to the left from August onwards : the failure of Kornilov and of the war effort cleared the road for the Bolshevik victory.

The defeat of Kornilov was followed by a sharp change of attitude in the Petrograd Soviet, hitherto under Menshevik control. Trotsky, who had been released on bail on September 4th, moved five days later in the Soviet a resolution of no confidence in the Soviet's Menshevik Presidium and, to the astonishment of many, his resolution was carried. At last, the Petrograd Soviet had gone over to the Bolsheviks : a new Presidium, which they dominated, replaced the old one, and on September 23rd the Soviet elected Trotsky as its President, thus raising him to the office he had so notably occupied twelve years before. Soon afterwards, Moscow and other big towns followed Petrograd's lead. The day was at hand when 'All power to the Soviets !' would mean 'All power to the Bolsheviks and their immediate allies !' and no longer 'All power to the Mensheviks and S.R.s !'

Trotsky, however, unlike Lenin, was not yet disposed to claim all power for the Bolsheviks, whom he had only just joined as a Party member through the amalgamation with them of the Mezhrayonka, becoming at the same time a member of the Bolshevik Central Executive Committee. He insisted against Lenin that on the new Soviet Presidium each party should be given representation according to its numerical strength. He was not prepared, as Lenin was, to write off as counter-revolutionary traitors all those Socialists who opposed the Bolsheviks and stood either for a moderate all-Socialist Government or even for a further attempt at coalition. He agreed with Lenin, who, from his place of concealment, was already bombarding the Bolshevik Executive with demands for an insurrectionary seizure of power, that the time for such action had arrived ; but he still wanted to organise the new Revolution under Soviet rather than under Bolshevik party auspices and to carry with him the largest possible following in the Soviets and base the new order directly on the Soviet power. With this in view he set about organising the Soviet in Petrograd as a military as well as a civil power. On October 9th the Petrograd Soviet, under his influence, set up a Military Revolutionary Committee, which actually came to be the principal organiser of the November Revolution, though its main purpose at the outset was to provide for the defence of the capital against a possible German attack.

In the meantime Kerensky and his supporters had been searching for an alternative to the Soviets as a façade behind which to carry on the Government. On September 14th the moderate Socialists brought together a Democratic Conference representing a very miscellaneous collection of bodies, largely non-political, including *zemstvos* and Co-operative Societies, and called upon it to advise what should be done. Out of this gathering, from which the representatives of the left walked out after a challenging speech from Trotsky, arose the so-called 'Pre-Parliament', which was announced as the forerunner of the still unelected Constituent Assembly that was to settle Russia's future. After the secession of the left, the Democratic Conference voted by a small majority in favour of a new Coalition Government, but also rejected further co-operation with the Cadets, many of whom had become involved in the Kornilov affair. Kerensky, ignoring the latter vote, proceeded to constitute a new Ministry, in which Cadets were included ; but its authority was almost negligible. It was at the Soviets' mercy, as soon as they were ready to push it over.

On September 21st, when the new Government took office, neither the Petrograd Soviet nor the Bolsheviks, despite Lenin's insistence, were yet quite ready to overturn it. Trotsky did not become President of the Soviet till two days later ; and the Bolshevik Executive was still rent by sharp internal divisions.

Among its members Zinoviev, in hiding with Lenin, and Kamenev, who was at large, were strongly opposing immediate insurrection. Zinoviev was petitioning the Executive to allow him to come out of his concealment in order to oppose Lenin's policy ; and Kamenev was consistent in his hostility to immediate revolutionary action. There was indeed a case for waiting a little longer. A second National Congress of Soviets was scheduled to meet in the fairly near future ; and the Bolsheviks confidently expected it to produce a majority in favour of their policy. Should they not at least wait till the Congress had met, or was on the point of meeting ? Lenin said no, both because he expected that the moderate Socialists would put the Congress off, rather than allow it to declare against them, and also because he was exceedingly apprehensive of a further counter-revolutionary movement, better planned and much more dangerous than Kornilov's. Trotsky preferred a short, but only a short delay, to allow for proper preparation, because in both matters he was less apprehensive than Lenin. In the event he had his way, not because his arguments were accepted — for he was between two fires — but because the Bolshevik Executive could not make up its mind.

Between Lenin and Trotsky the difference was not felt by either to be fundamental. As against Kamenev and Zinoviev they were united in calling for insurrection ; and it seemed a secondary matter that the one preferred the Soviet and the other the Party as its principal instrument. Trotsky did not share the fundamental belief in the Party that was a cardinal article of faith with Lenin and with the 'Old Bolsheviks' such as Stalin. For Trotsky, filled with memories of 1905, the Soviet was the true revolutionary instrument of the toiling masses, capable of carrying along with it many workers whom a purely Bolshevik Revolution would only alienate. It was, however, a much stronger bond between Lenin and Trotsky that both were determined on insurrection than it was a ground for cleavage that they differed about the mechanics of the uprising. They were allies, not opponents ; and Trotsky's open presence and his position in the Petrograd Soviet gave him an immense advantage over Lenin in getting his own way, despite the suspicions entertained of him by some of the 'Old Bolsheviks' who resented his rapid rise to leadership. Lenin, indeed, unable to appear in person to urge his policy, and unable to persuade the Bolshevik Executive by his written exhortations, was at a severe disadvantage during the critical period that followed the formation of Kerensky's last *simulacrum* of a Government.

Only in retrospect, years later, was this question — whether the Revolution should be conducted under the auspices of the Petrograd Soviet or of the Bolshevik Party — erected into a vital issue of party discipline, and used against Trotsky by those who wished to call his loyalty to Communism into question. That he did not feel it to go without a question that the Party should direct the entire operation should not be at all surprising ; for he had only just joined the Bolsheviks and had differed sharply from them over a number of years. He had, moreover, joined them much more because he believed them to be broadly right in the situation of 1917 than because he thought he himself had been at fault in earlier differences. Indeed, he probably put it to himself that the Bolsheviks were shedding some of their old sectarianism under the pressure of events, rather than that he had changed his attitude. Such a state of mind, and the demeanour that resulted from it, were intolerable to some of the Bolshevik Old Guard, who regarded Trotsky as a gate-crasher and outsider and resented his popularity as much as they needed his help. This was certainly true of Stalin, who, after being the foremost Bolshevik on the spot in Petrograd in the earlier phases of the Revolution, had found himself diminished in stature by the return of the exiles and by the 'dilution' of the Party with what he regarded as 'unreliable' recruits from the Mezhrayonka and elsewhere.

There was of course no doubt in either Lenin's or Trotsky's mind that the Bolshevik Party would need to play a key part in organising the Revolution, as well as in ruling Russia after its success. That was not the issue, which concerned primarily the formal auspices under which the Revolution was to be made. Yet the issue was not *merely* formal. Trotsky wanted the Soviet to be put in the forefront, not only because he believed it would secure the wider popular support, but also because he was anxious to carry along with it as many as possible of the waverers in the active Socialist ranks. He was quite prepared to denounce as apostates those who failed to take sides with the new Revolution at the critical phase ; but he was much less ready than the 'Old Bolsheviks' to exclude those who might yet be induced to come down on the left side of the fence. His past record as a 'Conciliator' expressed an attitude that was as natural to him as suspicious exclusiveness was to some of his instinctively critical collaborators. In this respect he differed deeply from Lenin, as well as from Stalin.

It has further to be borne in mind that the Bolshevik 'Old Guard', far from being united behind Lenin in the demand for immediate revolutionary action, was deeply divided on this very issue. Not only Kamenev and Zinoviev, but also for a time Stalin, were for rejecting Lenin's advice that the Party should decide unequivocally for an armed rising. Not until October 10th did the Bolshevik Executive, at a session attended by Lenin in disguise, declare for revolutionary action by a vote of 10 to 2 — Kamenev and Zinoviev constituting the minority. Nor did even this finally settle the question ; for the two dissentients refused to give way and appealed to the wider organisations of the Party against the Executive's decision, and for the time being the Executive did nothing to give effect to it beyond appointing its first 'Political Bureau', among whose members were Kamenev and Zinoviev as well as Lenin, Trotsky, Stalin, S. N. Sokolnikov (1888–1937) and A. S. Bubnov (b. 1883) — certainly not a group capable of working together to plan a Revolution to which two of them were fundamentally opposed.

In these circumstances the centre of the revolutionary stage continued to be held by the Petrograd Soviet and its Military Revolutionary Committee, of which also Trotsky was chairman. The Military Committee had been set up ostensibly, not to plan a rising against the Government, but to ensure the military defence of the capital against either attempted counter-revolution or a threatened German advance upon it, following the further disasters at the front. There were many rumours that the Government was intending to leave Petrograd and to dispatch the revolutionary regiments of its garrison to the front ; and it was felt to be vital to prevent both the fall of the capital to the Germans and its capture by counter-revolutionary forces tougher than Kornilov's had shown themselves in resisting revolutionary propaganda. During the first half of October

Trotsky, as chief spokesman and organiser of the Petrograd Soviet, was doing his utmost to prepare the way for the coming *coup* without too plainly declaring his intentions. Immediately his principal objectives were, first, to get the Menshevik-controlled Executive, left in charge by the first National Congress of Soviets, to summon at once the further Congress that had been promised, and secondly to make sure that the regiments of the garrison would obey the Petrograd Soviet's orders to remain if Kerensky attempted to order them out of the capital. He felt confident that in a new Soviet Congress the Bolsheviks and their allies would have a clear majority which would either declare for a new Revolution or approve it if it had already occurred ; and he hoped to make sure that the garrison would not only refuse to leave the capital, but would also respond to orders from the Soviet to rise against the Government and occupy the key points when the Soviet was ready to act. On the first of these matters, when he could not get the Executive of the Soviet Congress to act, he decided to act on his own, by sending out from the Petrograd Soviet a wireless message summoning all Soviets to send their delegates to the Congress. On the second, he obtained on October 16th a decision from the garrison regiments that they would refuse to obey any order from the Government to quit the capital and would remain to defend the Revolution against either foreign or domestic enemies. This decision was of crucial importance ; for, though nothing was said about a coming insurrection, it did mean that, in effect, the garrison was prepared to side with the Soviet against the Government when the call came. On the same day Trotsky acted on this assumption by ordering the issue of 5000 rifles from the military stores to the workers' Red Guard.

These developments brought Lenin, again in disguise, to a further meeting of the Bolshevik Executive, attended also by party delegates from Moscow and other centres. At this meeting Lenin insistently demanded that the date for the rising should be fixed ; and it was fixed provisionally for October 20th, the day before the Soviet Congress was expected to meet. Kamenev and Zinoviev were again outvoted, though others also expressed doubts concerning the readiness of the workers and soldiers to respond to the call. But, even then, the two dissentient leaders refused to accept the decision of the majority, and went to the length of communicating their views to Gorki's newspaper *Novaya Zhizn* an article in which had already blown the gaff and thus largely destroyed the effect of Trotsky's clever manœuvring to prepare the way for the *coup* without showing his hand. Naturally, this action by Kamenev and Zinoviev roused Lenin to fury, and he at once demanded that the offenders, whom he accused of a crime equivalent to 'strike-breaking', should be expelled from the Party. The remarkable thing is that he found no support for this proposal, and that, when Kamenev offered his resignation from the Executive, it was accepted only by a vote of 5 to 3. Zinoviev, who was still in hiding, was not even removed from his Executive position. The Bolshevik leaders were terribly afraid of the effects of a split in their own ranks ; and even Trotsky was against expelling the dissentients from the Party, though he voted for accepting Kamenev's resignation from the Executive.

The Party's deliberations at this stage still left it uncertain whether the *coup* was to be carried through in its name or in that of the Petrograd Soviet, as most of the Bolshevik leaders themselves, in opposition to Lenin, thought best. In effect, the issue was settled in favour of the Soviet by the Party's vacillations and hesitancy. The rising did not, however, take place on the day that had been provisionally fixed for it. The date for the opening of the Soviet Congress having been put off for a few days, the day of revolution was put back correspondingly ; and up to the final moment both the Government and the anti-Bolshevik Socialist leaders remained miraculously unaware of its imminence. In the middle of the uncertainty, on October 23rd, Kerensky tried to hit back by closing the editorial offices of *Rabochyi Put* (*Workers' Road*), the name under which the Bolshevik *Pravda* had reappeared after its suppression in July. Trotsky hit back by sending revolutionary troops to break the seals on the doors and to defend the Bolshevik organ. This armed challenge to the Government precipitated the rising. Kerensky announced his intention of arresting the Soviet's Military Committee, including Trotsky, and of sending forces to deal with the revolutionary sailors at Kronstadt. But before he could act, on the night of October 24-25th, Red Guards and soldiers occupied the key positions in the capital, and carried out a bloodless revolution. Before morning Kerensky had fled from Petrograd, leaving his Ministers to wait for him vainly at the Winter Palace, where they were soon besieged.

The following day the Second National Congress of Soviets opened at the Smolny Institute, already the headquarters of the victorious Revolution. More than two-thirds of the delegates were Bolsheviks : with their supporters, the Left S.R.s, the Bolsheviks had about three delegates out of four on their side. The Congress began with violent mutual recriminations. The right-wing Mensheviks and S.R.s, after denouncing the *coup*, walked out. The anti-Bolshevik left and centre stayed to demand a coalition Government of all the Socialist Parties, and, when this was refused, walked out too, leaving the revolutionary majority in possession of the field. During the debate the cruiser *Aurora* could be heard bombarding the Winter Palace with blank ammunition. Lenin had already come out of hiding, to assume the leadership of the new order : Kamenev, at almost the last moment, had renounced his opposition and had taken his part in the final preparations for the rising. The Petrograd Soviet, which had organised the whole affair, at once handed over authority to the new Soviet Congress. But it was the Bolshevik Party alone that formed the new Government — the first Council of People's Commissars. The Left S.R.s, invited by Lenin to enter the Government, preferred for the moment to remain outside it, and to try to bring over the waverers among the main body of S.R.s to the side of the new Revolution.

In the capital itself the victory of the insurgents was complete ; but it had still to be established over the rest of the country. Moreover, Kerensky was in the near neighbourhood, at Gatchina, where he was preparing, with General Krasnov's Cossacks, for an attack on Petrograd. There followed a strange episode. The Cossacks advanced towards the capital, and Trotsky ordered the regiments of the garrison to move out against them. But neither army had any stomach for the fight ; and after an artillery bombardment by the revolutionary forces and a little skirmishing, Krasnov's army melted away. It was, however, touch and go. The Cossacks did not give way, as General Kornilov's troops had done, without any fighting at all ;

and the forces of the Revolution were not easily induced to do even the little fighting that was needed to disperse them. Kerensky came within a very little of retaking Petrograd, though he could hardly have held it, or have reconstructed any sort of Government even if he had won the opening round. When the tide turned, Trotsky hoped to capture him ; but he again escaped. Krasnov, who was captured, was released on parole, and promptly broke it to organise a new rebellion.

While the fighting outside Petrograd was still going on, the officer cadets in the city attempted a counter-revolutionary rising, and captured, among others, V. Antonov-Ovseenko (1884–1938), the new Commissar of War, who had been one of the chief organisers of the Soviet *coup*. The cadets were, however, speedily suppressed and taken prisoners ; and at last there was a brief breathing-space in the capital. Not so elsewhere, where the fate of the Revolution still hung in the balance. In Moscow, for example, it took a week's fighting to establish the Bolsheviks in control. Thereafter, however, success was rapid and widespread, in the countryside as well as in the towns. Well before the second Revolution the peasants in many areas had been following the Bolsheviks' advice by seizing the land for themselves and dividing it up without waiting for the still non-existent Constituent Assembly to provide a legal basis for their action. The soldiers, deserting from the armies and flocking back to the villages, had played an outstanding part in this movement. Many châteaux had been burnt, and the landlords' title-deeds destroyed ; and the peasants who had taken the land had no intention of allowing themselves to be dispossessed. The victors at Petrograd had but to legitimise their action by proclaiming that the land was theirs, to be sure of a wide body of popular support among the landless and the poorer peasants.

Land, however, was not by itself enough to ensure the consolidation of the victory. The demand for peace was even more overwhelming, coming as it did from town and country alike, and from the soldiers equally with the civilians. It was a comparatively simple matter for the new Government to declare that the land was the peasants', though thus to sanction its parcelling out in individual peasant holdings went sorely against the grain of Bolshevik policy. It was a much more difficult matter to make peace, either separately with the Germans or by inducing the Allied Governments, bitterly hostile to the new Revolution, to take part in immediate negotiations for a general peace, or agree to a cease-fire. Yet, in one way or another, peace had to be made ; and the task of making it was the hardest of all the Revolution's pressing problems.

When the Bolsheviks set to work to form their Government, Lenin proposed that Trotsky, as the chief organiser of the insurrection, should lead it ; but everyone else, including Trotsky, regarded Lenin as the only possible leader, and Lenin reluctantly accepted the fact. He then proposed that Trotsky should be Commissar of Home Affairs, with the task of implementing the Revolution at home and of suppressing counter-revolution ; but Trotsky refused, fearing that his Jewish origin would seriously prejudice his chances of success, especially in the rural areas. He became, instead, Commissar for Foreign Affairs, and thus took on the most difficult task of all — that of making the peace.

As one looks back over the period of only a few months between the first and second Russian Revolutions of 1917, what stands out most of all is the immensity of the gulf between them. In the earlier Revolution, the Czar was forced to abdicate, but it was by no means taken for granted that he was to have no successor. Not only the Octobrists, but also many of the Cadets, were monarchists, and would have greatly preferred a constitutional monarchy of the Western type to a Republic. What defeated them for the moment was the lack of an acceptable candidate who was prepared to ascend the throne under the conditions they deemed to be necessary. The accession of the Czarevitch, who was a child, would have involved either a Regent or a Council of Regency ; and the deposed Czar refused the conditions put forward by Prince Lvov's emissaries for his acceptance. The Grand Duke Michael, who was then offered the succession, refused so uneasy a mandate ; and the first Provisional Government found itself forced to carry on without a monarch for the time being. Its leaders did not, however, thereupon become Republicans. They continued to maintain that the future form of Government in Russia must be settled by a Constituent

Assembly — which, nevertheless, they were in no haste to see elected, because they feared that in the disturbed state of the country it would turn out to be much too revolutionary for their taste. Leading Cadets, including Milyukov and Nabokov, continued to express their hopes that a monarchical constitution on Western parliamentary lines, providing for a constitutional monarch working with a democratically elected Parliament and a responsible executive Government, would be adopted in due course ; but for the time being both because there was no monarch and under pressure from the Soviets and the Socialist Parties, they had to adopt what were in effect republican methods, though they did their best to avoid any action that would commit them officially to sanctioning a republican régime.

As against this attitude of the Parties upholding Prince Lvov's Governments, the Socialists of all parties and factions were of course Republicans ; but it did not follow that they all wanted a Republic to be immediately and definitely proclaimed. Many of them were deeply committed to supporting the war effort of the Allies and were afraid that the open proclamation of a Republic might prejudice the position of Russia as an ally and deprive the country of help from the West. Moreover, some of them held, as conscientious 'democrats' in a parliamentary sense, that the entire question ought to be left to a properly elected Constituent Assembly, while fully expecting that such a body would declare in favour of a Republic.

It has to be borne in mind that at the beginning of the Revolution both the Social Democratic Parties — Bolshevik and Menshevik — and also most of the groups not fully attached to either Party — still held as their official doctrine that the Russian Revolution, because of Russia's social and economic immaturity, would have to be a bourgeois and not a Socialist revolution. What precisely this meant might be in dispute ; but it was, at any rate, commonly held to mean that the revolutionary Government would have to be a bourgeois Government, and that it would govern in conjunction with some sort of Parliament or Duma in which, for the time being, the majority would be supporters of bourgeois parties and policies. There were differences over the question whether Socialists ought or ought not to enter into coalitions with bourgeois parties ; but most Mensheviks, much more strongly than most Bolsheviks, were against this, and held that the Socialists should support the bourgeois parties from outside in defence of the bourgeois Revolution, but should stay independent in order to press the claims of the working classes and to make sure that the bourgeoisie did not betray the Revolution for fear of letting it go too far.

It was Trotsky, rather than any other Social Democrat of stature, who was — and had been right back in 1905 — a heretic in relation to this conception of the necessarily bourgeois limits of revolution in Russia. It was Trotsky who, holding that the proletariat would necessarily play the leading part in any real revolution, drew the conclusion that a revolution, once started with the proletariat as its driving force, could not in practice be arrested at the bourgeois stage, but would be bound to lead on directly to a Socialist revolution. This was indeed the foundation stone of the theory of the 'permanent revolution', discussed already in the preceding volume of this work.[1] This theory had not found acceptance in either Bolshevik or Menshevik circles. Among most Social Democrats of both factions, a belief in the necessarily bourgeois nature of the Revolution still held sway during the early months of 1917. The main controversy during this period was not on that issue, but concerned the nature and extent of the pressure which Soviets and Socialist Parties ought to apply to the bourgeois Provisional Government.

The situation in the Social Revolutionary Party was of course quite different ; for the Social Revolutionaries either put no stress on the distinction between a bourgeois and a Socialist revolution or, where they did, drew it in quite another way. Social Democrats — Bolsheviks and Mensheviks together — were at one in wishing to see Russia develop, as rapidly as possible, a more highly capitalistic economy, as a necessary step on the road to Socialism, because they held it to be impossible to by-pass the capitalistic phase of economic evolution. Social Revolutionaries, far from accepting this necessity, denied that Russia need become industrialised or capitalistic before it could become Socialist, and wanted to base Socialism in Russia on the foundations of the communal

[1] See Vol. III, Part I, p. 452, and Part II, p. 956.

elements in village life and land tenure. They were primarily agrarian Socialists and opponents of westernisation, and therewith hostile to the Social Democratic theory that capitalist centralisation was the necessary means of preparing the way for a Socialist conquest of power. There were indeed many shades of opinion among them, from terrorists and near-Anarchists at one end of the scale to moderate agrarian reformers at the other ; but they were all decentralisers and advocates of basing the Revolution, in a high degree, on spontaneous mass action. In theory, most of them were prepared to follow the mass revolution whithersoever its spontaneity might lead, without any inhibitions about passing at once from a bourgeois to a Socialist stage. In practice, they differed widely in their preparedness to co-operate with the bourgeois Parties — or indeed with the Social Democrats — in dealing with the immediate issues that had to be faced, and also in the degree of importance they attached to the use of formally democratic methods — for example, to the election of a Constituent Assembly by universal suffrage as against demanding that all power should be taken over by Soviets representing only workers, soldiers, and the peasant masses. In the Left Social Revolutionary Party, which broke away from the main body largely because of differences of this kind, Anarcho-Syndicalism and near-Anarchism were strongly marked tendencies. For the time being, Bolsheviks and Anarchists appeared to be allies, because they were united in contempt of bourgeois democracy and in support of the claims of the Soviets to control the Government ; but behind this apparent unity lay the deep difference between belief in centralised party discipline and in free, spontaneous action by militant minorities infecting the troubled masses of the common people.

At the outset, then, the Left S.R.s, who felt no qualms about pushing on with the Revolution to the furthest possible limit, constituted the main element on the extreme left, with the Bolsheviks taking a much more cautious, and indeed an uncertain, line. Not until Lenin arrived in Petrograd in April 1917 did the Bolsheviks even begin to face the question of a possible second Revolution, though they had of course from the outset favoured strong Soviet and proletarian pressure on the bourgeois Provisional Government. It was Lenin who, in apparent contradiction of his earlier view that the Revolution would have to halt at its bourgeois stage, began immediately after his return to demand, not indeed a new revolution at once, but a determined attempt — by demanding 'All power for the Soviets !' and by winning the Soviets over to Bolshevism — to establish the conditions that would make it practicable to carry the Revolution on to the stage of proletarian dictatorship — with the Bolshevik Party, as the true representatives of the industrial proletariat, in the key positions of control. For the understanding of what happened between Lenin's arrival and the November Revolution, it is of the utmost importance to understand what it was that had caused Lenin to change his mind.

There is no doubt on this matter. Lenin, when he agreed that only a bourgeois revolution was practicable in Russia, had been thinking in terms of a revolution in Russia alone, or at any rate dependent on purely Russian conditions. But after August 1914 he was no longer thinking or arguing in these terms, as he made plain both at Zimmerwald, where he was outvoted, and at Kienthal, where he got his way. From the moment when war broke out and the Second International collapsed, Lenin's mind was fixed on World, or at least on European, Revolution as the destined outcome of the fighting and as the necessary basis for an acceptable peace. Hence his scorn of the 'bourgeois pacifists', as he called them, who dominated the Zimmerwald proceedings : hence his fury against the 'chauvinists' and 'social traitors' who were supporting the war efforts of their respective Governments : hence his repudiation of every suggestion that the old International should be reconstructed or any accommodation reached with the old leaders of the Socialist Parties that were supporting the war. Lenin did not merely *hope* that the war would end in general revolution : he was firmly convinced that it would, and most convinced of all that Germany would be, if not the first to rise, at any rate the principal means of transmitting to the West a revolution beginning in Russia as the weakest link in the capitalist-imperialist chain.

Trotsky, no less than Lenin, was convinced of this ; and it was also common ground between them that Socialist Revolution, if it began in Russia, could not maintain itself unless it spread to the more advanced countries of the West. In such a situation, with war clearing the road for general revolution, the economic and political backwardness of Russia became irrelevant; for the Revolution in Russia would be only a part of a wider European movement, and the proletariats of the more advanced countries would be able to come to the help of the Russians and to enable them to begin at once on the task of building a Socialist society — not as a separate structure of 'Socialism in one country', but as a constituent of a new, essentially international society. The criterion of 'ripeness' for Socialist revolution, therefore, was not the degree of maturity reached in Russia, or in any one country, but that of the European economy regarded as a single whole. The outbreak of war, in both Lenin's and Trotsky's view, had carried the 'contradictions of capitalism' to a point which ruled out the reconstruction of the capitalist order in Europe, and absolutely required a Socialist remedy. Any doctrine resting purely on considerations of the degree of maturity in Russia alone was therefore obsolete. The war had changed the entire situation; and the time was ripe, in Russia or indeed anywhere in Europe, for the Socialist Revolution.

That these confident anticipations of European revolution proved false in the event does not alter the fact that they were immensely influential on the course of affairs. Unless both Lenin and Trotsky had believed in the imminence of revolution in Europe generally, they would have found it vastly more difficult to persuade even the Bolsheviks to take the lead in a second Revolution in Russia; and it is fully possible that Lenin at any rate would not have wished to do so. It was by driving this expectation of coming revolution all over Europe — and above all in Germany — into the minds of their colleagues that Lenin and Trotsky were able in the end to win the support of the majority both in the Bolshevik Party and in the new Presidium of the Petrograd Soviet after it had gone over to the left. Not even the Bolsheviks were all persuaded: as we have seen, Kamenev and Zinoviev remained among the sceptics to the very end, and what most held them back was not their fear of failure to seize power in Russia, but their lack of faith in the speedy outbreak of revolution in Germany or elsewhere. The belief in the certain coming of *international* revolution was the great myth that made possible the second Russian Revolution of 1917.

It may be argued against this view that, even in the absence of this belief, the Bolsheviks would have been forced, in the course of their struggle against the successive coalition Governments, to take power into their own hands. But even if this would have been the case, they would certainly have taken much longer to screw themselves up to the point ; and it is highly likely that by the time they had done so, they would have been too late. Petrograd might easily have fallen, either to the Germans or to a counter-revolutionary attack ; and Russia might easily have dissolved into sheer chaos without the Bolsheviks — or anyone else — having the means of putting it together again. Lenin realised this : hence his immensely vehement insistence on the folly of delaying even for a moment, after he thought the conditions ripe for a Bolshevik seizure of power. This may be held to show that he was, at bottom, less confident of the sheer inevitability of the Socialist Revolution than he believed himself to be ; but it in reality shows only that he feared Russia might fail to take its chance to lead the Revolution — which he intensely wanted it to do. What Lenin held to be inevitable was an immediate Socialist Revolution, not in Russia, but in the capitalist world as a whole ; and such a view was fully consistent with deep uncertainty about the part that Russia would play in its making.

Lenin and Trotsky, then, played their parts in forcing on the Bolshevik Revolution not as a *Russian* revolution, but as the opening move in an international uprising of the proletariat against capitalist imperialism and all its works. Only when this greater Revolution had plainly failed to occur did they have to think again, and to decide what could be done to save the Revolution in Russia when it found itself encircled by the capitalist world. No considerations of this order presented themselves in 1917 : then it was only a question of the best way of holding on until help came and, in order to do this, of holding the counter-revolution at bay by giving the Russian people what it was most imperatively demanding — land and peace, and, so far as possible, bread for the already half-starving towns.

CHAPTER IV

GERMANY IN WAR-TIME, 1914–1918

WHEN the European War broke out in August 1914, the German Social Democratic Party rallied immediately to the support of the Reich Government. In the Reichstag the Socialists decided to vote for the war credits. In the party meeting a minority of 14 out of 110 favoured abstention, but agreed to accept the verdict of the majority. Consequently the party leader, Hugo Haase (1863–1919), though personally one of the minority, made the official speech in favour of the majority view, and for the time being kept his position as leader and Chairman of the Party. The same attitude existed in the Party outside the Reichstag, including the groups in the various States of the Reich ; and the dissentients were fewest of all among the leaders of the Trade Unions, whose influence on the Party had been rapidly growing since the Russian Revolution of 1905. Even those who disagreed with the party line bore witness to the immense strength of popular feeling in favour of the war, and for the most part accepted the impracticability of making, at that stage, any effective protest. Nor was there much change of attitude, except in the direction of still greater vehemence of support for the war, as long as all went well with the German *Wehrmacht* and as most Germans continued to believe in the assurance of German victory.

It may not be difficult to explain this attitude, in the light of the Party's record before 1914 ; but it does need explaining. The dissentients included not only Haase, who had recently taken August Bebel's place as leader, and the outstanding personalities of the pre-1914 left wing, such as Rosa Luxemburg (1870–1919), Franz Mehring (1846–1919), and Karl Liebknecht (1871–1919), but also both the theoretical protagonists in the internal struggle over Revisionism, which had come near to splitting the Party in the early years of the twentieth century. In the new emergency, Karl Kautsky (1854-1938), the apostle of Marxian orthodoxy, and Eduard Bernstein (1850-1932), the apostle of Revisionism, found themselves, as internationalists, on the same side ; but, just as they had shrunk back from splitting the Party on the earlier occasion, so they shrank back now. The S.P.D. — the German Social Democratic Party — had been, from the days of its persecution under Bismarck, a highly disciplined machine, in which the concept of loyalty ranked very high. The Party had set before itself the purpose of winning a majority of the whole people to its side on the basis of a policy in which both its great objective — Socialism and the destruction of the existing social system — and its short-run programme of political and economic reforms were clearly laid down ; and its leaders had postulated unity in pursuance of these objectives as the indispensable condition of success. As we saw,[1] this had meant in practice that the Party, whatever differences might arise within it, could never afford to expel any group of dissentients strong enough to threaten the setting up of a rival Party : the most it could do was to make it difficult for dissentients to get or hold key positions of influence either in the party organisation or in the party press. It could depose Karl Liebknecht, on account of his anti-militarist activities, from the leadership of its Youth organisation, and could set Friedrich Ebert in his place. It could put obstacles in the way of Rosa Luxemburg as a party journalist, though it could not silence her, and it could go a long way towards staffing the party headquarters and its official agencies with 'safe' men. But it could not suppress the expression of minority opinion within the Party without losing its prospects of continued electoral advance ; and it had also to allow considerable latitude to the party groups in the various States which together made up the German Reich.

The minorities within the Party, for their part, largely shared the belief in the need for unity, and had no thought of breaking away unless their position in it were made utterly unbearable. They too, for the most part, believed that the Party, which had won big electoral victories in 1912, was destined to go on from strength to strength until it came to represent a clear majority of the whole people, and thus became

[1] See Vol. III, Part I, p. 303.

democratically entitled to claim its right to constitute the
Government and to put an end to the irresponsible power of
the monarchy and the ruling classes. Revisionists and their
opponents, save a very small semi-Anarchist minority headed
by the poet, Gustav Landauer (1870–1919), held this belief
in common and looked forward together to the 'day' of democratic triumph. They differed, no doubt, about what would
and should happen thereafter. The official view was that the
winning of an electoral majority, followed by the assumption
of governmental office, would *be* 'the revolution', or at least
would set the revolution immediately on foot ; whereas the
Revisionists preferred not to speak or think of 'the revolution',
but rather to envisage a succession of gradualist reforms which
could be greatly speeded up by the acquisition of political
power, but could be started even well before the Socialists had
become a majority of the people. Neither of the main groups,
broadly speaking, envisaged the coming victories in other than
electoral and parliamentary terms, save to a quite minor extent.
Both assumed that, given a Socialist majority among the
electors, it would be impossible for the irresponsible rule of the
Kaiser and the governing classes to be maintained and that a
responsible democratic régime would be able to replace it,
either without serious resistance or any rate without the
necessity of really embittered civil war. Those who did not
accept this view — for example, Rosa Luxemburg — were
hardly less at odds with Kautsky and Bebel than with Bernstein or Georg Vollmar : they constituted a third group on
the extreme left of the Party, and were very conscious of the
smallness of their influence in its counsels, and indeed of the
diminution of their influence as the right and centre groups
moved closer together after the excitements of 1905.

Indeed, well before 1914 the controversy over Revisionism
had almost ceased to count, and questions of international
policy had taken an increasingly important place in party
affairs. As we saw,[1] the occasion of the Russian Revolution of
1905 had led the Central Trade Union Commission, under
the leadership of Karl Legien (1861–1920), to declare decisively
against the policy of the political general strike, of which Rosa
Luxemburg was the most vehement advocate ; and throughout

[1] See Vol. III, Part I, p. 312.

the subsequent discussions at the International the Germans had strongly opposed such a policy, though they had finally accepted under some pressure the ambiguous resolution passed at Stuttgart and reaffirmed at Copenhagen concerning the attitude to be taken up by Socialists in face of a threatened, or of an actual, European War. These discussions, we saw,[1] had turned partly on the question of participation in 'national defence'; and the German delegation had made plain its endorsement of the view that, if Germany were *attacked*, the Social Democratic Party should accept the obligation to take part in defending it. Jaurès had taken the same line for France, with the support of a part of the French delegation; but nothing had been laid down on this issue in the Stuttgart resolution — or it would never have received general endorsement. The Germans, in defending their attitude, had always chosen as their example a threatened or actual attack on Germany from the East; and there had been frequent references to the defence of German civilisation against barbarian invasion by the 'Asiatic hordes of Czarist Russia'. In Prussia especially, anti-Russian feeling had been very strong, among Socialists as well as among supporters of the existing German régime; and the triumph of reaction in Russia after 1905 had strengthened this feeling and had made it easier to reconcile with Socialist sentiment. It was largely hatred of Russia that impelled many of the leaders of German Socialism during the years before 1914 into an attitude of increasing hostility to France and Britain, as Russia's allies, and thus made them the readier to take the side of Germany, on such issues as that of colonial policy and the 'drive towards the East' through South-Eastern Europe.

No doubt, in spite of this growing tendency to line up behind the German Government in the recurrent international crises of the pre-war years, most of the leaders of German Social Democracy remained honestly wishful to avoid the outbreak of war between the great powers, and to do what they could by constitutional action to curb German aggressiveness. Indeed, when the crisis did arrive in July 1914, they did try to exert a restraining influence on the German Government and to prevent it from pledging its full support to Austria-Hungary as

[1] See Vol. III, Part I, p. 61.

long as they saw a chance of localising the conflict. They would have been well content if Austria-Hungary had been allowed a free hand to deal with the Serbs without interference from any other of the great powers ; and the Party as a whole did make an attempt to induce the Austrian Government to take a less intransigent line — an attempt which the Austrian Socialists deemed themselves unable to press in face of the strength of warlike feeling in Austria itself. As soon, however, as the Russian Government made plain its intention to intervene on the Serbs' behalf, Socialist sentiment inside Germany changed very fast. It was obviously to the German Government's advantage, whatever pledges it had already given to Austria-Hungary, to make it appear that Germany was being driven to enter the conflict by the aggressive policy of the Russian Government, which threatened to undermine the whole position of Germany in Eastern Europe and even to launch a direct attack on Germany itself. This was the light in which the sequence of events that followed the Sarajevo assassination was made to appear to the German people, who were driven to a frenzy of anti-Russian feeling by all the arts at the disposal of the German ruling classes. The German Socialists, by the time they had finally to make up their minds what attitude to take up towards their Government's demand for war credits, were already confronted with an internal situation in which any attempt to oppose the war was likely to lose them a large part of their support among the German people and would probably have disrupted the Party.

I point this out, not in order to exculpate the German Social Democratic Party, but rather in order to explain its apparently sudden *volte-face* immediately before the actual beginning of hostilities in the West. Hugo Haase, when he met the French and Belgian Socialists in Brussels on July 28-29th, 1914, seems quite honestly to have thought it most unlikely that the Party would break with its traditions so far as to vote for the war credits in the Reichstag, and still to have hoped that its members would at the least decide to abstain. That was what Haase himself, as a sincere internationalist and a strong critic of German imperialist policy, wished the Party to do ; and he then still believed that its well-established policy of refusing to support the imperial budget would be maintained, even if many of its members hoped that, in a struggle against 'Russian barbarism', their own country would be victorious. Haase made far too little allowance either for the widespread belief, even among Socialists, in the superiority of German culture, and in Germany's mission to dominate Europe as a major civilising influence, or for the effect of the still more widespread belief that Germany was called on to defend itself against Russian aggression. This latter belief would have been much less easily accepted had not the 'myth' of German cultural pre-eminence and of Russian backwardness already infected so deeply the international outlook of a large section of the Party. Haase, as soon as he got back to Germany, encountered the full blast of patriotic sentiment, and found himself one of a small minority who continued to maintain that the German Government, by its support of Austrian intransigence, had played a key part in rendering European war unavoidable. He, and those who agreed with him, had then to make the very difficult choice between accepting the verdict of the majority of their party colleagues — and of the great mass of public opinion inside Germany — and persisting in the line of conduct which they held to be both objectively right and in harmony with the traditional practice of the Party — and with loyalty to the spirit of the International. This second course would have meant flouting party discipline, and thus going counter to the no less strongly established tradition of party unity, as well as facing not merely great unpopularity among the mass of their countrymen, but also the practical certainty of persecution and suppression by their political enemies. It would not be fair to say in general that, in this crisis, their courage failed them : it was rather that they felt themselves irresistibly impelled to put party loyalty before faithfulness to their personal convictions and were induced to do so above all by the immense strength of the party tradition in favour of unity. In effect, they did what Bernstein had done when his Revisionist doctrine had been decisively rejected by the Party : they accepted the claim of the majority to enforce conformity of action upon them, but refused to renounce their convictions or to abandon their attempt to bring the majority over to their views. Haase himself actually kept for the time being his position as party leader ; and for the time being the victorious

majority refrained from pushing its victory to the boint of
driving out the minority, or even of preventing it from continuing to express its dissentient views. Even Karl Liebknecht,
who stood far to the left of Haase, accepted at this point the
need to be bound by party discipline as a Reichstag deputy.

At this stage, in August 1914, only 14 Socialist members of
the Reichstag, out of 110, voted in the minority at the party
meeting ; and all of these, save perhaps one who was absent
when the vote was taken in the Reichstag, subsequently voted
in favour of the war credits, thus saving the solidarity of the
Party at the expense of its international professions. Nor did
even these 14 advocate voting against the credits : they
urged only abstention, as the utmost there was even the faintest
chance of getting the Party unitedly to accept. There were
no doubt a few more besides the 14 who had misgivings
and gave their votes with reluctance, either because they understood something of the active part which Germany had played
in bringing the war about, or because they were Socialist
enough to dislike breaking the long tradition of Socialist opposition to the Kaiser's Government and to the German ruling
classes. But during the weeks that followed the violation of
Belgium's neutrality, with the German armies advancing
swiftly in the West and a rapid, victorious end to the struggle
apparently well in sight, the minority, far from gaining new
converts, actually lost ground while the majority's enthusiasm
for a German victory grew more extreme and rendered it a
good deal more intolerant of the opposition within the Party.
A struggle began with the purpose of ousting supporters of
the minority from positions of vantage in the party press and
in its local organisations, and of purging the Trade Unions of
trouble-makers. Only when the German advances had been
halted short of Paris, and the possibility of a prolonged war on
two fronts began to be seriously faced, did the minority take
heart a little and win a few, at first hesitant, converts to the cause
of a negotiated peace. When, after the military check, the
question of war credits came up again in December 1914, the
number of dissentients at the party meeting had risen to 17,
and Karl Liebknecht had at length made up his mind to flout
party discipline by casting a lone hostile vote in the Reichstag.
Liebknecht, whose statement of his position was refused a

place in the official record, not only voted against the credits but published his case in a pamphlet which was widely circulated and set going a considerable pamphleteering campaign inside the Party. His case, in broad outline, was that the war was an outcome of capitalist imperialism and would benefit only the imperialist forces that were behind it, that it would be used to crush the Labour movements of the belligerent countries, including Germany, and that it was being fought by Germany, not in self-defence, but with annexationist aims. Liebknecht's pamphlet included a strong protest against the German violation of Belgium's neutrality, and against the state of siege and military dictatorship that was being imposed on the German people. It was a hard-hitting, extremist pronouncement, and it brought down on Liebknecht the violent denunciation of the spokesmen of the majority, who accused him of acting as a traitor both to his country and to his Party. It went far beyond anything the main body of the minority was prepared to assert and was the beginning of a rift in the minority that was to have momentous effects at a later stage.

This was not because Liebknecht was on the side of the Allies. If he felt above all else the call to fight against the war-makers in his own country and was prepared to denounce the war as the product of an Austro-German imperialist conspiracy, he also attacked the imperialisms of Russia and France and Great Britain and called upon the workers in all countries to dissociate themselves from their imperialist Governments and to assert the peoples' rights. He was no 'bourgeois pacifist', seeking a negotiated peace between the warring capitalists, but a proletarian internationalist, whose anti-militarism rested on a foundation of class-war doctrine. From the moment of his stand, a small group of pre-war leftists, among whom Rosa Luxemburg and Franz Mehring were the outstanding figures, rallied round him and began to lay the foundations for what later became the Spartacus movement and, still later, the nucleus of the German Communist Party. Such an attitude was widely different from that of the main opposition group, of which Haase, Kautsky, and Bernstein were the best-known leaders ; for its members — though they agreed in condemning Germany's part in precipitating the war and were also alive to the presence of capitalist-imperialist tendencies on the side of the Allies — were primarily parliamentarians and wished to appeal rather to the whole people than to the workers alone. Their aims, as far as they were clear even to themselves, were not to stir up the proletariat to mass strikes or armed insurrection, but to bring the Socialist Parties of the warring countries back to their senses, and thus to set on foot a powerful movement in favour of a negotiated peace which would render it possible for Socialism to resume its interrupted advance towards the conquest of power by political means. This is perhaps an over-simplification ; for there were, in the minority, some who occupied a position midway between the parliamentarians and the out-and-out revolutionaries, hoped that the war would end in the overthrow of the economic, militarist, and governmental forces that had brought it about, and were prepared to contemplate the use of revolutionary methods, should these prove to be necessary to effect the transformation. Georg Ledebour (1850-1947) was the principal figure in this intermediate group ; but at this relatively early stage the position of the opposition was still largely undefined, and the whole minority was held together by the comprehensive denunciations with which the majority was attempting to overwhelm it.

In this majority the outstanding figures were the saddler Friedrich Ebert (1870-1925), the leading figure in the party bureaucracy, the glib politician Philipp Scheidemann (1865-1939), and the formidable Karl Legien (1861-1920), who had for many years ruled over the 'Free' Trade Unions with an iron discipline. There were, however, lesser figures than these who made more noise on the extreme right wing of Socialism and outdid them in support of even the most unbridled German war aims. Among these an outstanding figure was Eduard David (1863-1930), who had been for a long time prominent in the reformist wing of the Party and had been a vigorous upholder of the duty of 'national defence' at the Congresses of the International. Wolfgang Heine (1861- ?) too had belonged to the pre-war right wing, and Konrad Haenisch (1876-1926) had also taken a leading part in maintaining Germany's right to expansion during the pre-war conflicts on questions of colonial and imperial policy. As against these, Paul Lensch (1873- ?), who soon became the most extreme advocate of German expansionism, had been an active protagonist of the left wing up to 1914, and changed sides abruptly only after the actual outbreak of war. All these — especially Haenisch and Lensch — vigorously campaigned for the view that German expansionism, and not British 'liberalism', stood for the cause of progress, and pointed the way towards European Socialism under German leadership. They contended energetically for the belief that the war was clearing the way for the complete unity of the German people through the absorption of Austria, which would assure the European pre-eminence of German culture and the integration of Europe under German economic and ideological hegemony.

These and other protagonists of the war party in the S.P.D. showed for the most part a high arrogance in maintaining the thesis of German superiority in an otherwise decadent Europe. In 1914 they were concerned chiefly with drawing a contrast between German civilisation and Russian barbarism, and with upholding the thesis that the war was for Germany one of sheer self-defence against unprovoked Russian aggression. This was indeed, in August 1914, the quintessential S.P.D. line ; and it is a notable fact that the German invasion of Belgium did almost nothing to alter it. The Reichstag group, when it first decided to vote for the war credits, did not know that the invasion had actually occurred — though many must have known that it was contemplated. The German march into Belgium was publicly announced in Germany only in the Chancellor's Reichstag speech demanding the credits — that is, after the Party had taken its critical decision ; but the announcement did not cause the Party, after hasty consultations, to change its attitude. Indeed, many German Socialists defended the German army's right to march through Belgium, on the ground that the Belgians had forfeited any claim they might have had to have their neutrality respected by entering into military consultations with the French ; and not a few were prepared, even apart from this, to maintain Germany's right to sweep Belgian claims aside on the plea that doing so would shorten the war by improving the chance of a speedy knock-out blow. To most of the leaders of the German majority, the Belgian issue seemed too trivial a matter to affect their general attitude.

There was, however, at this early stage no such chorus of

'hymns of hate' against either France or Great Britain as came to be heard as soon as the German armies had encountered their first serious check. Indeed, the S.P.D. seized eagerly on the German Government's assertion that it was not fighting a war of annexation, and that its aims were strictly defensive ; and it was on this interpretation of German policy that the Party agreed to vote for the war credits. The French and the British were denounced for not keeping out of the war and for not giving Germany a free hand to deal with Russia. But hopes were expressed that, when the French had learnt their lesson, amicable relations between victorious Germany and defeated France could be established on terms not too humiliating to the French people. There was more anger against Great Britain for intervening ; and the British action was attributed to imperialist motives — above all, to Great Britain's desire to keep its world monopoly of trade and colonialism and to destroy the prospects of its greatest challenger as a world economic power. Not a great deal, however, was made of this during the opening phases of the war : the great anti-British diatribes of such writers as Paul Lensch appeared mainly in or after 1915.

The anxiety of the German Socialists to rebut the charge that they had been unfaithful to international Socialism and to their own pledges at the Congresses of the International was shown by their zeal in sending delegations to neutral countries to explain their conduct. It was argued by these German missionaries that the terms of the Stuttgart resolution were clearly inapplicable where a country was the victim of foreign aggression — said in this case to be Russia's. The delegates were able to point to the fact that German representatives from Bebel downwards had made it clear at repeated International Congresses that the S.P.D. accepted the obligations of national defence against an aggressor and had consistently opposed the suggested international mass strike against war on the ground, among others, that no country could declare such a strike with any firm assurance that others would do the same, or without exposing itself to defeat if they did not, however good its cause might be. These delegations, sent out in the first months of warfare, far from putting the case for German world domination, took their stand on the thesis that Germany had gone to war reluctantly, and solely in self-defence, and that only on this assurance from the German Chancellor had they given him their support. They found it difficult, however, to convince foreign Socialist listeners that the German war aims were as impeccable as they were said to be, or that there had been no going back on what the S.P.D. had agreed to at Stuttgart and at subsequent meetings of the International.

It is, I think, undeniable that, up to the moment when Russia's entry into the war was seen to be imminent, the S.P.D. was sincere in its wish to avert the major conflict. It protested strongly against the terms of the Austrian ultimatum to Serbia and did what it could — which was not much — to stiffen the Austrian Socialists' faint-hearted efforts to moderate the Austrian Government's attitude. Thereafter it tried its hardest to prevent Russia and Germany from being involved, and thus to limit the conflict. Only when its leaders came to believe that the Russian Government was determined to intervene did they begin to waver ; and only when they had come to believe that the Russians were set on attacking Germany did they go over *en masse*, save only a few convinced internationalists, to support of the war. Certainly the S.P.D. leaders did not want the war : up to that point they had done their best to prevent it, within the limits of constitutional action and public demonstrations all over Germany. But no sooner had popular feeling against Russia been raised to boiling point than they saw themselves faced with the loss of their hold on the people, including the main body of the workers, and with the probable suppression and destruction of their Party if they were to maintain their opposition. This danger they simply could not face. Regarding themselves as essentially the interpreters of the mass will of the German working class and its allies, they were entirely incapable of going against the evident trend of popular feeling. The Socialist leaders were, of course, not immune from the influence of the violent russophobia which swept over Germany during the opening days of August. How could they be, when the almost universal sentiment of Socialists in all countries had been for so long detestation of the Czarist régime as the most reactionary of all, and when it had so long appeared a holy mission to keep the Czarist hordes away from Western Europe ? But in Germany this sentiment, in no way peculiar to the Socialists, had taken a special form because it was combined with a strong sense of German superiority, not only to Russia, but also to the countries of Western Europe. The German Socialists had been used to being regarded, and to regarding themselves, as the head and forefront of the Socialist movement, and to having their well organised and rapidly growing Party looked up to as the guide and philosopher of the International, imitated and emulated by other Socialist Parties only from a respectful distance. The threat to their country's military and diplomatic power appeared to them as a threat to their own predominance in the counsels of International Socialism, and they were unable to conceive that it might be incumbent upon them, in the service of Socialism, to allow the Russian 'barbarians' to invade their country and destroy, not merely the German political régime to which they had been opposed, but also the power of German Socialism which they had been building up against it.

In this discussion of the underlying causes of the attitude of the German Socialist Majority in 1914 I have so far said nothing of the influence of Marx and Engels, upon whose doctrines the S.P.D. had been so largely based. Marx's writings had, to say the least, provided strong encouragement to the view of Germany as the cultural leader of Europe and as the champion of European culture against the 'barbarous' Slavs. Marx, though he had taken his stand against Lassalle on the question of co-operation with the Prussian-dominated German Reich, had endorsed the notion of German predominance over the Slavs in Bohemia and Moravia and of the inclusion of the Czechs, as a privilege, in a Greater Germany. He had also, in 1870–71, favoured a German victory over France, while opposing the annexation of Alsace-Lorraine by the German Reich. The main Marxist tradition in German Socialism thus included a large element both of anti-Slavism and of assertion of German claims to cultural superiority ; and this traditional attitude undoubtedly played its part in deciding the policy of the Majority Socialists in 1914. At a later stage, attempts were made to attribute the jingo elements in the German Socialist attitude in 1914 to the continuing influence of Lassalle rather than of Marx ; but the truth appears to be that in this matter there was no great difference between them, except that the

Lassallians were readier than the Marxists to accept the consequences of supporting the war on the relations of the Socialist movement with the dominant forces of the German imperial régime.

The consequence was a sudden and dramatic change in the attitude of the S.P.D. to the whole structure of the German establishment. The Social Democrats, who had been hitherto almost outlaws, excluded from all share in the government of German society, found themselves suddenly invited to take part in the task of organising the German nation to meet the needs of national mobilisation and defence, and told that, if they accepted the call, they would be treated no longer as helots, but as recognised co-operators in the common cause. They were sure that the mass of their followers looked to them to accept, and for the most part they could see no alternative to doing so. They could not, however, accept without a very far-reaching reversal of an attitude to which they had clung with determination in their struggle with the Revisionists and Reformists in their own ranks. It had been an axiom of German Marxists that the Socialist Party must stand aloof from all entanglement with the existing State régime, and that constructive work for Socialism could begin only after they had won political power with a majority of the people behind them. All coalition with the bourgeois Parties — even with those of the bourgeois left — had been ruled out as contrary to the precepts of Marxism ; and culturally as well as politically they had built up their own Socialist institutions in active hostility to those of the established order. If they were to become now co-operators in a common national effort, transcending class and political differences, this policy had to be drastically reversed. The class struggle had to be put into cold storage, and the Socialists had to accept service, side by side with their erstwhile enemies, in improvised national agencies for coping with war-time emergencies on the 'home front'.

So sharp a change of attitude and behaviour could not be accomplished at all easily, and could scarcely have been accomplished at all had the Party, up to 1914, been nearly as monolithic as it professed to be. But in practice the non-participation practised by the majority of the leadership had already been undermined, especially in South Germany, by sections of the

Party which had been merely reproved, and not disciplined, when they had collaborated with bourgeois and peasant Parties in a number of the German States, and still more by the Trade Unions, which, as their numbers grew, had taken more and more to peaceable collective bargaining with the employers. It cost the Trade Union leaders, and the South Germans generally, much less effort to adopt their new rôle than it did the Prussians or the Saxons, who had been engaged in a much bitterer and more uphill fight with reaction. In the Reich Constitution there was at least an element of democracy, in that the Reichstag was elected on a basis of manhood suffrage and the Reich Chancellor could not govern without its support — though its power was seriously limited by the entrenchment of reaction in the Prussia-dominated Second Chamber and by its lack of control over the Government's executive authority. In Prussia, on the other hand, there was not even any semblance of democratic government. The Prussian Diet was elected on a three-class system of voting which made it impossible for the Socialists to win even a single seat except with the aid of the progressive bourgeois Parties ; and the Social Democrats had only recently given up their policy of boycotting the Prussian elections. In 1914 they were engaged in a bitter struggle for the reform of the Prussian Constitution ; and throughout the war they continued to press for this reform, only to be put off with vague promises that something should be done about it when the war was over, coupled with statements that so controversial a matter could not be dealt with while the country was engaged in a national struggle for survival. This made it peculiarly difficult for Prussians — or indeed for Saxons ; for conditions in Saxony were much the same — to rally behind the German Government in support of the war effort ; but, as against this, the threat from Russia was felt most of all in the Prussian borderlands, and Prussia seemed to most Germans the great bastion of Germany against the danger from the East. Accordingly, even in Prussia and Saxony, most of the Socialists endorsed the policy of the S.P.D. leadership.

This change of front, when once it had been made, exerted a powerful influence on the ideas of the Party as well as on its immediate behaviour. Having moved so far, the majority

Socialists soon found it easy to move further and to convince themselves that the true interests of Socialism would be best served by a German victory, involving the destruction of the rival imperialisms of the Entente powers and the establishment of German hegemony in Europe — under which the S.P.D. would be able to lead the entire European proletariat in its march towards democracy and Socialism.

This drift towards a German imperialist Socialism was speedily strengthened in the course of the majority's struggle with the minorities which refused to accept the new gospel. These minorities, as we saw, included a revolutionary minority which aspired, in accordance with the closing paragraph of the Stuttgart resolution, to use the war as an opportunity for ending the rule of the capitalist class, by stirring up the masses to revolt, without regard to the effect on the war effort. This group, however, was small, and served at the outset chiefly as a means to discrediting the whole opposition by accusing the rest of it of being the accomplices of the extreme left. In fact, the main body among the minority was behind, not Liebknecht and Rosa Luxemburg, but Haase and Kautsky, who stood, not for proletarian insurrection, but rather for a speedy peace without victory for either side — that is, for a peace which would show up the futility of war and, made without annexations or indemnities, would lead to a general acceptance of arbitration in international conflicts, to disarmament, and therewith to the triumph of democracy at the expense of discredited militarist and imperialist ruling classes. The establishment of this new order might require revolutions in some countries, where the reactionaries refused to accept defeat ; but its essence was not revolutionism, but rather pacification and the victory of reason over violence. In the ensuing conflict within the S.P.D. this group was impelled leftwards, just as the majority was impelled rightwards by its entanglement with the ruling powers. But, both before and after the Russian Revolutions of 1917, most of its members stopped short of accepting the full insurrectionary gospel ; and after the Bolshevik Revolution, a part of it, headed by Kautsky, reacted violently rightwards through hatred of the policy of dictatorship upheld by Lenin as the antithesis of bourgeois 'democracy'.

I do not wish to suggest that, even at the height of the

struggle, the German Majority Socialists ever quite forgot their Socialism or went over whole-heartedly to support of the annexationists. Some did ; but they remained a minority : the Party never officially endorsed their attitude. While it denounced in extreme terms the imperialist policies of France and Britain, as well as of Russia, and accepted the need for a German victory in the field, it continued to protest against the more extravagant claims of the militarists and to assert its desire for a 'just' peace, paying at least lip-service to the principles of democracy and national self-determination — though its interpretation of these principles usually reflected its major insistence on German interests, for example, in Alsace-Lorraine, and in relation to the Polish and Belgian questions. It has to be recognised that most of the German Socialist leaders were convinced that Germany was fighting an essentially defensive war and did make some attempt to prevent it from being turned into a war of unashamed imperialist aggression. This became more evident in the later stages of the struggle, as the prospect of victory grew less and the possibility of sheer defeat had to be seriously faced. The policy of a negotiated peace without annexations or indemnities then became increasingly attractive not only to the Majority Socialists but also to many in the bourgeois Parties ; and the Reichstag's peace resolution of July 1917 reflected this change of mood. The German Socialists, moreover, opposed the unrestricted submarine campaign of January 1917, which brought the United States into the war, and from this point became growingly critical of imperial war policies. It is of course possible to argue that this change of attitude was no more than a reaction to the deteriorating military position and to the increasingly severe privations of the German people from the intense food shortage and the extreme militarisation of the home front under stress of total war. It would not, however, be quite fair to regard it as due solely to these factors. There were, throughout the war, Majority Socialists whose consciences were troubled by their implication in imperial war policies of which they could not but disapprove, and who honestly believed themselves to be acting as good Socialists in the cause of national defence. I think Philipp Scheidemann must be regarded as ranking in this group.

I do not propose to discuss in this book to what extent the Germans can be convicted of responsibility for the war of 1914, or how great a share of the blame is properly attributable to the pre-war diplomacy of the Entente countries. This issue can be, and has been, argued about so much that I have nothing fresh to contribute. I can only recall my own feelings and opinions at the time. I was under 25 in August 1914, and, though already active and well known as a Socialist writer, had concerned myself mainly with industrial affairs and knew what seems to me now singularly little about foreign politics, about which I had written nothing at all. I was, however, by instinct a pacifist, looking on war as a horror nothing could justify and regarding it as the imperative duty of the working class in all countries to use every possible means of preventing it. I therefore followed with keen sympathy the manifestations of the Socialists against war and the appeals to international working-class solidarity that followed the Sarajevo murder and the Austrian ultimatum to Serbia. I was guileless enough to have great difficulty in believing that war would really come, and critical enough of the Liberal Imperialist policy of Asquith and Grey to believe that, if it did, a substantial share of the blame would rest on the British Government. Even when it had become clear that there would be war, and that not only Russia and Germany but also France would be involved in it, I still wanted Great Britain to keep out. I was deeply shocked when the Germans invaded Belgium, and said so publicly ; but even then I remained opposed to British intervention, though I felt that Germany had put itself clearly in the wrong. My pacifism was too deeply seated to be even shaken by the violation of Belgium's neutrality, crime though I held it to be. From the moment the war began, I wanted it to end without victory for either side, in as speedy as possible a negotiated peace. I was in fact what Lenin scornfully called a 'bourgeois pacifist', and to that attitude I adhered throughout. In spirit I was in due course a Zimmerwaldian, but not a Kienthalian ; and I was of course a strong supporter of the Stockholm Conference project. In 1917 I welcomed both the Russian Revolutions ; but I did not become a Bolshevik or wish for a British Revolution on the Russian model. For Russia I could see no viable Socialist alternative to Bolshevism ; but I continued to hope that, at any rate in Great Britain, Socialism could be won without civil war or dictatorship. I remained, in short, a 'liberal' Socialist of the left, held back not only by personal pacifism but also by a belief in the value of toleration and freedom of choice from joining the revolutionary extreme left, with which I nevertheless sympathised much more than with the strictly constitutionalist right wing of the Socialist movement. I was wittily described at the time as having 'a Bolshevik soul in a Fabian muzzle'; but I do not think this was quite correct. My soul was not 'Bolshevik' but Guild Socialist, and my muzzle not 'Fabianism' but half pacifism and half a belief in the liberal democratic tradition.

I have tried to give a candid account of my own attitude in 1914 and in the years that followed, not because what I felt was of any outstanding importance, but solely because my personal sentiments are bound to affect my interpretation of the events I need to describe and to evaluate in their relation to Socialist thought. I found myself in agreement with the majority Socialists of the Allied countries in censuring very strongly the attitude of the German majority, but differing from them only a little less strongly in their determination to pursue the war against Germany to the bitter end and to refuse discussion with German Socialists about the possible terms of a negotiated peace. In common with many Socialists in all the belligerent countries I found myself becoming more vehemently 'anti-war' as the struggle went on, with no end in sight. If one side had to win, I continued to prefer an Allied to a German victory; but more and more strongly I wished for peace without victory and for the rebuilding of Socialism as an international force — though I was not at all clear, I admit, how this rebuilding was to be achieved in face of the betrayal of Socialist principles by so many of the leading Socialists in many countries — and most of all in Germany.

Having said this, I can leave my personal attitude and come back to the consideration of what happened to German Socialism under the stress of war. As the prospect of a speedy and conclusive German victory began to fade, the opposition inside Germany began to gather strength, not only among Socialists but also, to a smaller extent, among the bourgeoisie, which found itself increasingly opposed to the militarists who dominated the social structure and enforced a sharper and sharper discipline on the civil population. It was, however, neither among the Majority Socialists nor among the bourgeoisie that active opposition began : it was on the extreme left — among those who followed Karl Liebkecht and Rosa Luxemburg. After voting against the war credits in December 1914, Liebknecht issued the following month a pamphlet reprint of a speech in which he roundly attacked the S.P.D. as deserving 'neither confidence nor respect' and thus started a big controversy inside the Party. In March 1915 a second deputy, Otto Rühle (1874–?), joined Liebknecht in voting against the war credits, which then came up as part of the general budget, and no fewer than 31 other deputies abstained from voting. Thus, not far short of a third of the Reichstag deputies refused to follow the official party line, though some of them were opposing not so much the war credits as the reversal of the traditional party policy of voting against the Government's budget.

Through the rest of 1915 there was a ding-dong battle of growing acerbity between the Socialist factions. In August the Majority Socialists issued a statement of war aims which provoked a violent retort from the 'International' group headed by Liebknecht and Rosa Luxemburg. This group's 'Junius' pamphlet, *War and the Proletariat*, vehemently attacked the attempt to suspend the class-struggle during the war and insisted on the need for international proletarian struggle against the imperialist warmongers in all the belligerent States. It contended, against the Majority, that Germany had no right to maintain its hold on Alsace-Lorraine, that the Austro-Hungarian Dual Monarchy ought to be destroyed, and that only international working-class action could bring the war to a tolerable end. This extreme group, however, had still only a small following. A better sign of the growth of opposition to the Majority was the manifesto signed in June 1915 by a thousand office-bearers in the S.P.D. and its subsidiary organisations. This was primarily an attack on the Majority for agreeing to the suspension of the class-struggle and thus acquiescing in the 'militarisation' of the nation and in a denial of the Party's essential purposes. It did not deal with the question of war aims ; but soon afterwards Haase, with Kautsky and

Bernstein, published an appeal in which they denounced the perversion of the alleged war of defence into an aggressive war and declared that this made it impossible for the minority any longer to obey party discipline by voting for the war credits. In December 1915, 31 deputies voted against the credits at the party meeting and 20 carried their opposition to the point of giving hostile votes in the Reichstag itself.

This defiance brought the crisis in the S.P.D. to a head. In March 1916 the Majority decided to exclude the Minority from membership of the party group in the Reichstag, but had no power to turn them out of the Party, which was not in a position to hold a fully representative congress. The Minority, for their part, were unwilling to secede from the S.P.D., in which they felt they were gaining strength. Not till January 1917 did they set up any formal organisation of their own. Then they established a Working Union, still without actual secession. This, however, provoked the Majority to further action, and, during the next few months, there were widespread expulsions. At length, at Easter 1917, the Minority groups took the plunge and founded an entirely new Party — the Independent Social Democratic Party (U.S.P.D.). Almost at the same moment, in April 1917, the extreme left under Liebknecht formed the Spartakusbund, which attached itself loosely to the U.S.P.D., but kept its separate organisation and right of independent action.

By this time revolution had broken out in Russia. The Czar had abdicated, and Prince Lvov's Government was in office, though hardly in power. Naturally, the Russian Revolution had an immense impact on opinion in Germany. The new Russian Government was attempting to continue the war in conjunction with the Western Allies ; but the Russian armies were already threatening to disintegrate, and their military position was very bad. From the Russian people, peasants and workers alike, there was going up a more and more insistent cry for peace. But what sort of peace was it to be ? At this stage the Russian Government was in the hands of the bourgeois parties, which were deeply committed to the Western alliance and had by no means abandoned their aggressive war aims. The newly established Soviets at Petrograd and elsewhere were dominated by the Social Revolutionaries and

Mensheviks, with the Bolsheviks and their allies still forming only small minorities. Neither Lenin nor Trotsky was yet back in Russia. The Social Revolutionary and Menshevik leaders were divided in their war attitudes. Many of them were, up to a point, supporters of the war, and most of them were very reluctant to contemplate a separate peace with Germany, on what seemed likely to be very unfavourable terms. There was, however, no doubt about the ardent desire of their followers — above all, of the soldiers in the ranks — for a speedy peace ; so that the real question that faced them was whether there was a hope of bringing about a general peace by negotiation, including all the belligerents, or whether the Western powers would refuse to negotiate and thus force them to choose between separate peace negotiations and attempting to continue the fighting. The Western Governments, for their part, were desperately afraid of the Russians making a separate peace, but were also determined to fight on in hope of victory. They were accordingly pressing the Russian Government not merely to continue resistance but if possible to launch an offensive in order to retrieve the military position on the Eastern front.

Clearly, in this situation, a great deal depended on the state of affairs inside Germany. It was well known that the privations of the German people were severe, and that a great deal of discontent existed among them. In April 1917 there were big strikes in progress, and the newly established U.S.P.D. was gaining ground rapidly. The Spartacus group and other left-wing elements had been carrying on a vigorous campaign of propaganda in the *Political Letters* of 1916 and in the *Spartacus Letters* which began to appear in September of that year. There were not a few, both in Russia and in the West, who entertained hopes that Germany might be almost on the point of cracking under its internal difficulties, and that the Revolution in Russia might be speedily followed by a German Revolution. If these hopes had any basis, there seemed to be strong reasons for Russia to remain in the war at least for a little longer, with the prospect of being able to make peace on more favourable terms. As against this, the unrestricted submarine campaign had only recently begun — in February 1917 — and only at the beginning of April had the United

States definitely entered the war. It was still on the cards that Britain might be starved into submission before American help could be mobilised on a sufficient scale. The outcome of the war as a whole thus still seemed highly uncertain : it was a question which country would come to the breaking point first.

As the year advanced, it became clear that, despite the intensive submarine campaign, the Germans' promise to starve the British into submission before the harvest would not be made good, and that the chance of a German victory depended on a military break-through in the West before the Americans could arrive in Europe in force. But it also became ever more evident that the Russians' power of resistance was almost at an end. In May the Petrograd Soviet, reinforcing the efforts of the Dutch-Scandinavian Committee, sent out its appeal for a Socialist Peace Conference to prepare the way for a general peace ; and in June the Russian Government was forced to make its appeal for a general peace without annexations or indemnities. In July the Germans, who had been marking time, launched their big offensive on the Eastern front, driving the Russians before them in a disorderly retreat. In August they overran Rumania, and at the beginning of September they captured Riga and came almost within striking distance of Petrograd itself. The Provisional Government in desperation had launched in July its impracticable counter-offensive, which was immediately defeated ; and by the end of August the abortive counter-revolutionary move of General Kornilov had prepared the way for the Bolshevik seizure of power.

During these critical months the peace movement in Germany continued to gain strength. On July 19th the Reichstag passed its celebrated resolution in favour of a negotiated peace, and on August 1st the Pope issued his peace proposals to the belligerent powers. At Stockholm the Majority and Minority of the German Socialists presented their rival statements of war aims to the Russian-Dutch-Scandinavian Committee. Both declared themselves in favour of a peace without annexations or indemnities and of the general right of self-determination for the peoples ; but they put widely differing interpretations on these principles. The general line of the Majority was that there should be a return to the *status quo ante bellum*, except that the right of independent nationhood should be accepted for Finland and for Russian — but not for Prussian or Austrian—Poland, which were to be given only some degree of autonomy within the German and Austrian empires. The Majority further declared that Alsace-Lorraine must become permanently part of the German empire, with internally autonomous institutions ; it accepted the restoration of Belgian sovereignty, but subject to safeguards that would prevent that country from becoming a satellite of any power. Finally it required the restoration of the colonies taken from Germany during the war. Essentially, what it demanded was a peace that would leave Germany's power intact and would ensure it the means of continued advance ; and it rejected altogether the claim that Germany should make good the damage done to Belgium or to any other country invaded by its armies during the war. The Majority, in effect, while opposing the policy of the extreme German militarists, was not prepared to recognise that any greater blame rested on Germany than on the Allied powers.

The Minority took a very different line. It declared un-equivocally in favour of ending the war at once and of applying the principle of national self-determination over the widest possible field, provided that this did not mean continuing the fight for that purpose. It called upon Socialists in all countries to cut themselves free of entanglement with the imperialist Governments, and to make a peoples' peace. In the case of Belgium it advocated complete restoration of political and economic independence and in addition payment towards making good war damage ; and it urged that the future of Alsace-Lorraine should be settled by a plebiscite of the in-habitants, which all countries should pledge themselves to accept as finally deciding the issue. It declared in strong terms against colonialism in all its forms and expressed its support for the colonial peoples in their struggle for self-determination, but was not in favour of making this support — or indeed any-thing at all — a reason for continuing the war. Its general attitude was that peace should be made at once and war out-lawed for the future, and that the terms of peace should be laid down by the workers and enforced on the Governments. On the issue of 'war guilt' it said nothing directly ; but it implied that the German Government had been guilty of wrongs it

would be called on to set right, though it by no means ex-
onerated the Allied Governments from a share in the blame.
Only Ledebour went so far as to call on the workers of all the
warring countries for strike action to bring the war to an end.
The U.S.P.D. delegation at Stockholm, as a whole, called
not for World Revolution but for an immediate negotiated
peace.

For this, however, the conditions did not exist. In both
France and Britain the majority groups in the Socialist and
Labour movement were still behind their respective Governments in seeking victory and in rejecting any settlement that
would leave German power intact. In both countries, and also
in Belgium, there was great reluctance to meet the German
Majority on equal terms, even in a Socialist Conference ; and
the German Majority, though quite ready to meet the Allies,
were not at all prepared to accept any basis of discussion that
would imply either German 'war guilt' or a German military
defeat. The prospects of the Stockholm Conference being
able to meet in full session died away ; and in all countries
except Russia more intensive mobilisation set in with a view
to a decisive struggle in the following year. When, towards the
end of 1917, Germany resorted to the Hindenburg plan of
general industrial mobilisation under military control, the
German Trade Union Commission, dominated by the Majority
Socialists, agreed to co-operate ; and the rift between the
Majority and the Minority became yet wider. Before that, in
October 1917, the Spartacists and their allies had set to work
to establish revolutionary Workers' Councils in the war factories;
and the sending of many militants into the armed forces, while
it may have weakened the industrial front, served mainly to
spread unrest in these forces.

Meanwhile, in Russia, the Bolshevik victory had settled the
issue in favour of a separate peace. Negotiations for an
armistice were begun on December 3rd, and the armistice terms
were signed on December 15th. On the same day the Bolsheviks dispersed the Russian Constituent Assembly. A week
later peace negotiations opened at Brest-Litovsk, and the
Russians were made painfully aware that the German authorities
intended to treat them hard.

In Germany the Bolshevik Revolution deeply affected the

internal situation. Greeted with enthusiasm on the extreme left, it was regarded with deep hostility by the Majority Socialists and also by a section of the Independents, who strongly denounced the dispersal of the elected Constituent Assembly, and rejected the dictatorship of the proletariat — which they said, was really that of the small Bolshevik minority — as a betrayal of Social Democratic principle. Kautsky, old comrade of many of the displaced Menshevik leaders and strongly in sympathy with Martov's Internationalist fraction of the Menshevik Party, soon became the leading theoretical antagonist of Bolshevism ; and under his influence the parliamentary element in the U.S.P.D. began to move sharply rightwards. Others, such as Ledebour, took the opposite line, and moved into closer relations with the industrial left. In January and February 1918 the strike movement in Germany assumed vast dimensions and spread rapidly from town to town under the leadership of the rapidly growing Workers' Councils. Richard Müller, the U.S.P.D. chairman of the Berlin Council, became the most prominent leader. On March 3rd the Russians, who had broken off the peace negotiations for a time, but had given way before Lenin's insistence that peace must be made at any cost, signed the Brest-Litovsk Treaty, on terms which involved an immense loss of territory and resources, including recognition of an independent German-occupied Ukraine as well as the separation of Finland, the Baltic States, and Russian Poland from the new Russian State. In March, the Germans, with the Eastern pressure thus relaxed and the food situation bettered by the prospect of supplies from the Ukraine, launched their great offensive in the West and brought the Allied armies to the very brink of disaster. Not until June was their advance halted : it was even resumed for a few days in July, just before the Allied counter-offensive began. The war was at length entering on its final, decisive phase. The attempted Austro-Hungarian offensive of June had already broken down. There were bread riots in Vienna that month ; and the whole Austro-Hungarian empire was manifestly breaking up under the pressure of nationalist movements in Bohemia and other Slav areas. Already in May, Lloyd George had been able to announce that the Allies were sinking U-boats faster than the Germans could build them, and building new tonnage faster than the Germans could sink it. Before the end of July the German armies in France were already in retreat ; and through August and September they suffered a series of disasters. On September 24th, Army headquarters informed the German Government that it was necessary to ask for an armistice : the Hindenburg line was broken three days later. Reinforced by American contingents the Allies swept on through France and Belgium ; and the invasion of Germany itself became an imminent threat. On October 3rd the German Government fell, and Prince Max of Baden was appointed as Chancellor. The following day both Germany and Austria-Hungary sent notes to President Wilson asking for an armistice on the basis of his 'Fourteen Points' proclaimed on January 8th.

The end had come, not with a negotiated stalemate, but with an Allied victory in spite of Russia's military collapse. The German people, however, still had no idea of what was in store for them. They did not know that their armies had been finally beaten in the field ; and most of them still hoped for a peace, inspired by the 'Fourteen Points', that would leave Germany still a great power, while bringing with it a more democratic constitutional régime that would enable them to resume their pre-war agitation for better conditions. President Wilson, however, was no more minded than the European Allies to come to terms with an intact Germany still under militarist and junker control. His answer to Prince Max made it clear that he insisted on German capitulation. Prince Max, in despair, asked the German High Command about the prospects of continuing the war in hope of better terms, and was told that this was out of the question, and that a sheer collapse might come at any moment. As news of the desperate military situation leaked out, there began to be talk of placating President Wilson by persuading the Kaiser to abdicate ; and the Majority Socialists, who had agreed to be represented in Prince Max's Government, began to press for this solution. The Kaiser, as early as October 3rd, had left Potsdam and taken refuge at army headquarters, where he remained throughout the next few weeks. Prince Max—aware of the mounting state of feeling in Germany, which turned more and more against Wilhelm II as the knowledge of disaster spread abroad—wished for a voluntary abdication but refused to press the reluctant 'All-Highest' to renounce his authority, and still hoped that the monarchy could be saved. The Kaiser, however, refused to abdicate, and the situation continued to get worse while the Government still hesitated to accept the American terms. On October 24th the German navy, which had been cooped up — mainly at Kiel — through most of the war, was ordered by the naval authorities to get ready to put to sea for a last desperate engagement with the enemy. The sailors, already seething with unrest, refused ; and the arrest of their leaders served only to bring rebellion to a head. On November 3rd the sailors at Kiel mutinied and elected Sailors' Councils to take charge of affairs ; and the mutinies spread rapidly to other ports. On the following days revolt broke out all over Germany. In one city after another, revolution was proclaimed, and provisional governments based mainly on the Workers' and Soldiers' Councils assumed temporary authority. On November 7th the revolution spread to Bavaria, where a Socialist Government under the Independent Socialist Kurt Eisner (1867–1919) assumed office. Two days later Berlin itself declared for the revolution, and a manifesto of the Berlin Workers' and Soldiers' Council, signed by, among others, Haase, Ledebour, and Liebknecht, called for a German Republic. On the same day, Prince Max resigned and handed over the Chancellorship to Friedrich Ebert (1871–1925), the most right-wing of all the Majority Socialist leaders. Ebert accepted the office, though his constitutional status was by no means clearly defined. The Kaiser, right up to the last, was still refusing to abdicate, despite the advice of a sequence of emissaries sent to army headquarters from Berlin. Moreover, almost to the last, the Majority Socialists, though they regarded his abdication as necessary, refused to raise any public demand for it for fear of increasing the revolutionary ferment : indeed, they appear to have held out hopes that a constitutional monarchy might still be accepted if the Kaiser and the unpopular Crown Prince could be got out of the way. Only at the very last, in fear of their followers going over *en masse* to the U.S.P.D., did the S.P.D. leaders present Prince Max with an ultimatum that, unless the abdication were received by the day following, they would be forced, in self-defence, to take matters into their own hands. Even this ultimatum, presented on November 8th, did not induce the

Kaiser to yield. The 'fact' of his abdication had to be announced for him, without his consent; and even then Ebert seems to have hoped that it might still be possible to maintain the monarchy in a constitutional form Finally the Republic was proclaimed, not by Ebert but by Scheidemann; and this was done in order to forestall Karl Liebknecht, who was said to be on the point of proclaiming not merely 'the Republic', but the *Soviet* or Workers' Council Republic on the model of what had been done in Russia a year earlier. Scheidemann tells in his *Recollections* that Ebert was furiously angry with him for proclaiming the Republic in any form; but the thing was done, and the seal was set on it by Wilhelm's flight to Holland as soon as the news reached him. Abdications at once became the order of the day: all over Germany, kings, grand dukes, and petty rulers tumbled from their thrones with hardly an attempt at resistance.

At this first stage the German Revolution was almost entirely bloodless. The soldiers away from the fighting lines took very little part in it beyond the passive rôle of refusing to make any attempt to repress it and in some cases openly fraternising with the demonstrators who thronged the streets. In many cases the regiments elected Soldiers' Councils; and away from the front discipline largely broke down. But at the front order and discipline were preserved, both while the armistice discussions were in progress and subsequently, while the German armies evacuated such occupied territory as they still held and executed an orderly retreat beyond the lines fixed on November 11th. Only as they neared home did their discipline at length give way as the weary conscripts made for their homes. Most of them showed much less desire to make a revolution than to get back to civilian life as fast as they could. The war was over; and Germany was left almost without an armed force, either on the side of the revolution or against it. Even the Kiel sailors, whose revolt had started off the revolution, accepted Gustav Noske (1868–1947), the Majority Socialist who had gone to Kiel the day after the outbreak in the hope of restraining them with fair words. They showed, indeed, much more zeal for the redress of their own grievances — bad food, bad conditions, and intolerably harsh discipline — than for the wider revolutionary cause. Power passed from the old Government of the Reich neither to a revolutionary army nor immediately to any new central authority. For the time being it was widely diffused in the hands of local or regional improvised Governments of widely varying complexion, with Workers' and Soldiers' Councils appearing to constitute the main basis of authority over the greater part of industrial Germany, or at any rate in the major cities.

The Allies and President Wilson, in demanding the deposition of the Kaiser and the ending of the militarist régime, had in effect invited Germany to revolt. They were, nevertheless, in great fear of the German Revolution going too far and coming to model itself on the Bolshevik Revolution in Russia. There were some who would have had the Allied armies march on into Germany and dictate terms of peace in Berlin itself, making an end both of Germany's imperialism and of proletarian revolution at a single blow. This, however, was easier to say than to do ; for if they destroyed both the old régime and its antagonist, what sort of new Government were they to set up, and what measure of support would it receive ? To most of them it appeared preferable to let the German armies manage their own demobilisation and for the time being to stand aside, maintaining a blockade that could be used, if need arose, to starve the revolution into submission. They were not yet ready to declare the terms of peace. For the time being lip-service had to be paid to President Wilson's 'Fourteen Points,' on the basis of which the Germans had accepted the armistice. Months of wrangling lay ahead before they could agree among themselves how best to circumvent the American President's inhibitions and confront the German Government, whatever it might be by then, with a treaty it could be forced to accept without further argument. In November 1918 most Germans still had no conception of the peace that was to be thus imposed on them. They were too busy with their own problems, and too thoroughly down-and-out to be thinking much about the terms of peace.

Thus, the German Revolution of November 1918 happened, not because it was planned by any body of men capable of taking power into their own hands in the disastrous conditions that were facing the country, but because Germany's military power had at length given way under the terrific strain of war, and because the Kaiser's obstinacy had stood too long in the way of every attempt to avert revolution by establishing the constitutional régime that would have fully satisfied the Majority Socialists, as well as the bourgeois Parties of the left and centre. It happened despite the Majority Socialists, who were thoroughly scared of it and did their best to stall it off. It happened because the exasperated people, sick to death of the war lords who had brought disaster upon them, could not help making a revolution when the old authorities collapsed in ruins at their fi st appearance in the streets, when the dispirited armies offered no resistance, and when power appeared to be ready for the hands of the first taker who could put himself at the head of the mass. It was soon to be made plain that the main body of the German people — even of the German workers — had made the revolution without meaning to do more than upset the discredited dynasty and its reactionary hangers-on, and with no clear notion of what was to be done thereafter. There were, of course, groups of revolutionaries who knew well enough what they wanted to do ; but they were few, and the disciplined ranks of the S.P.D. were against them no less than the bourgeoisie and the Junker and militarist reactionaries. A revolution made in such conditions could not succeed : the story of its failure must be left to be recorded in the next chapter.

CHAPTER V

REVOLUTION AND COUNTER-REVOLUTION IN GERMANY, 1918-1921

EARLY in November 1918 the great Hohenzollern empire suddenly dissolved in ruin, and the Socialists found themselves forming a Government to hold the pieces together, because there was literally no-one else to take charge. In this extremity the two sharply opposed Socialist Parties joined hands, but not hearts, in a common Government with Friedrich Ebert, ex-saddler and Majority Socialist politician, at its head as Chancellor. The new Government consisted at the outset of three Majority Socialists — Ebert, Scheidemann, and Otto Landsberg — and three Independent Socialists — Hugo Haase, Wilhelm Dittmann (1874-1954), and Paul Barth. These six's first problem was to end the war, by getting the armistice, already arranged for, duly signed. This was done at once. Its next problem, hardly less urgent, was to decide what sort of Government it was. Was Germany still a monarchical State, or had it become a Republic ? As we saw, Scheidemann, to Ebert's annoyance, publicly declared that the Republic had been set up ; and the Kaiser put the seal on this declaration by fleeing to Holland. But the question remained — Was the German Republic a totally new State that would need to create for itself an entirely new set of institutions, resting on quite different foundations from the old ; or did it inherit the administrative machinery of the old Reich ? This question was of the utmost importance : it involved so many vital matters — among them that of the federal structure of the State. As princely rule collapsed in one part of Germany after another, it had to be decided immediately whether the old territorial divisions were to be kept intact, or whether the new Republic should be constituted from the outset as a single centralised State. Secondly, there was the immediate problem of the armed forces, which had to be brought home and demobilised in one way or another. Were they to remain for this purpose under the existing General Staff and subject to the orders of the old officer caste ; or was power to be handed over to the rank and file, acting through elected Soldiers' and Sailors' Councils such as already existed in some, but by no means in all, units ? Thirdly, what was to be done about the Civil Service and the government departments ? Were they to go on as before, with the existing official hierarchies, subject only to being called upon to take their orders from a new Government ; or were the old bureaucrats to be turned out and replaced by an improvised team of Socialist amateurs, who would then have to learn their jobs as best they could ? Fourthly, what about the judges and the courts of law ? Were they, despite their notoriously reactionary composition, to go on administering the existing body of law until there had been time and opportunity to change it ; or were they to be swept away and a new judiciary improvised to administer a new body of law — not yet in being — in their place ?

These were all difficult questions : taken together, they added up to the question whether the Revolution meant a complete change of system or only the dethronement of the monarch, and a reform, rather than a destruction, of the old machinery of State. There was, of course, no doubt in the minds of the Socialists — Majority or Minority — that such gross anomalies as the three-class Prussian franchise would have to be swept away and many other democratic reforms introduced. There was, however, a very real division of opinion between those who wanted drastic structural changes to be made at once, in the name of the Revolution, and those who held that, as far as possible, such questions should be left over to be settled by a Constituent Assembly, to be elected as soon as practicable on the widest possible franchise. The leaders of the Majority Socialists argued for the latter course, as alone consistent with democracy ; and some of the Independents agreed with them. Most of the Independents, however, did not : they wanted to strike while the iron was hot and to establish the foundations of a new order as firmly as possible *before* calling on the people to elect its Assembly to confirm the change and give it constitutional form. Some Independents and groups on the extreme left, including, of course, the

Spartacists and some of the Revolutionary Shop Stewards, went further and wished the victorious proletariat of workers, soldiers, and sailors to declare itself, through its elected Councils, the true representative of German democracy, and to take all power into its hands ; and some wished a revolutionary *élite* to seize power, even if the Councils were not behind it, in the faith that where the few led boldly, the majority would follow. There existed, however, at the moment of the Revolution's success, neither any general Congress of Councils to which power could be handed over nor any organised revolutionary *élite* capable of acting on a national scale. There was as yet nothing corresponding either to the Congress of Soviets which had given its endorsement to the *coup* of November 1917 in Russia or to the disciplined revolutionary Party that had made the *coup* possible.

There were thus three main streams of Socialist opinion ; but none of them coincided exactly with a particular Party. The Majority Socialists, or at all events their leaders, were solidly for using as far as practicable the existing state machine, with a Socialist President in place of the Kaiser, until a Constituent Assembly could be brought together to draft a new constitution and bring the laws into conformity with the needs of the new order. Most of the Independents agreed with them about the need for a Constituent Assembly, but were much more hesitant about carrying on, for the time being, through the machinery of the old State. Most of the Independents wanted to place power, for the time being, in the hands of the Workers' and Soldiers' Councils, to bring the Councils together at once in a National Congress, to which the Government would be responsible, and to introduce fundamental social, economic, and political changes *before* the Constituent Assembly was elected. These were the two major tendencies. The third, represented by groups partly inside the U.S.P.D. and partly outside it, had no use at all for the Constituent Assembly at any stage, rejecting it as an instrument of outworn 'bourgeois democracy', but was divided, though not yet clearly, between advocates of a 'mass dictatorship' of the workers and advocates of the seizure of power by a small revolutionary *élite*. Both these groups naturally claimed to be following the Russian example, and to be calling for a 'Soviet' Revolution ; there lay between them the shadow of earlier differences between Lenin and Rosa Luxemburg concerning proper and improper forms of dictatorship, and of still older differences between the followers of Blanqui and of Marx.

The first issue of all that the new Government had to decide, was what to do about the government departments and the Civil Service. If the people were to be fed and the country held together at all, it seemed imperative to keep the Civil Service and the departmental machines at work. But they could clearly not be trusted not to sabotage the Revolution unless they were firmly controlled ; and the new junta of six was not ready with a team of its own to replace the old departmental chiefs. It was decided to leave the old administrators at the head of the departmental ministries, but to attach to each ministry a Socialist from each wing to keep an eye on them and to ensure their conformity to the Government's orders. This was a fateful decision, however difficult to avoid ; for its effect was to carry over the old bureaucracy, in which a strongly anti-Socialist sentiment was almost universal, into the new order. Similarly, though many, even of the Majority Socialists, would have liked to destroy Prussian hegemony and to establish the Republic as an unitary German State, so big an upheaval seemed for the moment impracticable, and nothing was done to alter the federal structure pending the decision of the coming Constituent Assembly. The judges and the law courts too were left to carry on ; and the work of demobilisation remained in charge of the military administration and of the High Command under General Hindenburg.

Some of these arrangements filled the Independents with deep misgivings ; but they could not make up their minds what to do. From the very first, it was with Ebert and the Majority, and not with the U.S.P.D. Ministers, that the old administrators and military leaders consented to work. The Independents were nominally equal in the Government with the S.P.D. ; but in practice no such equality existed. The Independents could only protest, as they did again and again : they could not make their protests effective without a clear-cut alternative policy of their own. But they were unable to frame such a policy, partly because they disagreed among themselves, but still more because they had no majority behind them in the

Councils for whose claim to power they ostensibly stood. When the National Congress of Councils met on December 16th it was dominated by the Majority Socialists and decided almost at once to hand over power at the earliest practicable moment to the forthcoming Constituent Assembly. This left the Independents without any solid foundation for an alternative course, unless they were prepared to go with the extreme left towards an armed rising designed to set up a minority dictatorship — and most of them were not.

Not even in Berlin did the left wing command a majority in the Workers' and Soldiers' Council. The Councils which sprang up all over Germany and in the armed forces during the Revolution represented many different tendencies. Generally speaking, the Independents and the extreme left were strongest in the big industrial cities and in the home units of the army : the Majority Socialists controlled most of the smaller towns, and were also predominant in the armed forces in and behind the fighting lines. But there were many exceptions. Some of the areas in which the S.P.D. and the free Trade Unions had been traditionally weak, such as the largely Catholic Ruhr, now showed a strong leaning to the left ; and in Bavaria, the only area in which Peasant Councils developed on any considerable scale, the U.S.P.D. held the predominance as long as Kurt Eisner was at the head of the regional Government. Bavaria was indeed a region of extremes, and of great political instability, as was speedily to appear when it became the main centre of civil war a few months later. Bremen was a notable centre of extreme left activity, inspired largely by the Pole, Karl Radek (1885–?) ; and Saxony too was a stronghold of the left. In Berlin itself, Richard Müller, the U.S.P.D. chairman of the Revolutionary Shop Stewards' organisation, was a considerable influence, and was working closely, at the outset, with Karl Liebknecht and his Spartacus group ; but a dangerous rift very soon appeared between the Spartacists and the Shop Stewards over the two vital issues of the left's attitude to the Trade Unions and to political action. These two issues, indeed, played havoc with the unity of the left's forces.

The German free Trade Union movement, strongly centralised and controlled by the masterful veteran, Karl Legien, had thrown its weight heavily into the war effort and

had worked in closely with the Majority Socialists. Its influence, however, though considerable in many branches of
industry, was limited. Right up to the Revolution the railwaymen, as state employees, were not allowed to belong to it ;
and in the Catholic areas it was weak in face of the competition
of the separate Catholic Unions, which had links with the
Centre Party. Even where it was strong, its war attitude prevented it from taking any effective part in the development of
war-time strike movements or in the political agitations of the
left ; and these movements grew up for the most part in
association with the Independents, except where they were
under the influence of the extreme left. Even the Spartacists,
up to the Revolution, were loosely attached for the most part
to the U.S.P.D. Thus, when the Revolution broke out, it was
not unnatural for the left to look on the official Trade Unions,
and particularly on their leaders, as its enemies and to consider
the possibility of building up a rival mass movement of their
own. The Trade Unions, seeing this danger, made haste to
participate in the Revolution when it became, almost overnight,
an accomplished fact. They pressed hard for immediate industrial concessions — for higher wages to meet rising prices,
for the eight hours' day, and for freedom to organise all types
of workers ; and the Provisional Government made haste to
grant their demands without waiting for the Constituent
Assembly. Consequently, Trade Union membership rose by
leaps and bounds — from a pre-war figure of about 2 millions
attached to the Free Trade Union Commission to about 8
millions before the Revolution was a year old. The Unions
officially continued to hold aloof from politics, and restricted
themselves to purely industrial claims. They made no demands
for nationalisation, which was widely regarded as impracticable
for the time being, in view of the chaotic state of industry at the
end of the war. But in practice they threw their weight on the
side of the Majority Socialists and against not only the extreme
left but also the main body of the U.S.P.D.

The workers flocked into the Trade Unions, irrespective of
their political sympathies, because the Unions were the
champions of their immediate industrial demands. This put
the left in a quandary. One policy, clearly the only sensible
one in the circumstances, was to accept this fact, to urge the

workers to join and play an active part in the Unions, and to endeavour to win them over to the side of the U.S.P.D. But there were not a few on the extreme left who, regarding the existing Unions as hopelessly reactionary, wanted to break away from them and to set up a rival movement of mass Industrial Unionism on a class basis, using the war-time shop steward organisation as a nucleus and giving the new Unionism a definitely political and revolutionary Socialist character. The difficulty about this policy was that in practice such a movement was most unlikely to succeed in detaching the main body of members from the older Unions, so that it would lead only to a minority breakaway that would be unable to negotiate effectively for the immediate concessions which chiefly interested most of the workers. The section of the extreme left which looked forward to the speedy seizure of power by a small revolutionary *élite* was not deterred by this prospect ; but most of the U.S.P.D. stalwarts were deterred, save in areas where the old Unions were exceptionally weak. The majority, even of the Revolutionary Shop Stewards, refused to follow the lead of the intransigents and remained within the existing Unions. Even on the Spartacist left, Rosa Luxemburg, who hated sectarianism and put her hopes in the revolutionary potentialities of the masses, vainly opposed the intransigents and was forced to follow them reluctantly in a course of action which she knew was likely to lead to disastrous defeat.

The second issue — that of parliamentary political action — also sharply divided the left. Practically the whole of the left was at one in holding that the Provisional Government ought, without waiting for a Constituent Assembly, to set to work consolidating the Revolution by destroying the foundations of Junkerdom and militarism, breaking up the great estates in the eastern regions, democratising the Civil Service and the judiciary, bringing the police forces under the firm control of the new order, creating armed detachments of revolutionary workers, and subjecting industry and finance to central public regulation with a large element of workers' control. They differed, however, about the form to be taken by the new political institutions of the Reich. Some — for the time being a majority among the activists — stood for some form of 'Council' Government ; that is, for making the Government lastingly subject to Councils representing the workers, to the exclusion of the old ruling classes and of the bourgeoisie. Others, while they regarded the Government as properly subject for the time being to the Councils, wished also for a democratically elected Constituent Assembly which would in due course determine the future structure of the Reich on a foundation of universal citizenship. These latter, for the most part, also wished to defer the election of the Assembly until the Revolution had been carried to a stage which would rule out the restoration of the old order and would ensure the Socialist character of its successor. The Majority Socialists, on the other hand, wanted the Assembly to be elected as soon as possible, and the decision about the new order to be left for it to make. When it had been decided, with the support of the Congress of Councils, to press on with the elections at once, the left had to make up its mind what attitude to adopt. The main body of the U.S.P.D., though it had wished to defer the elections, was in no doubt that it should take part in them ; but the extreme left was sharply divided. The Spartacists and their allies were well aware that they had no chance of securing more than a few representatives in an election based on universal suffrage. They desired, not merely to postpone the calling of the Assembly, but to dispense with it altogether in favour of Council Government ; and they decided to boycott the elections rather than participate in them merely as a fraction of the U.S.P.D. Towards the latter end of December the Spartacists, meeting in national conference, outvoted Liebknecht and Rosa Luxemburg, broke away from the U.S.P.D., formed themselves into a German Communist Party, and decided to boycott the elections for the Constituent Assembly. In taking these decisions, the Spartacists no doubt believed themselves to be following faithfully the Russian example. As the Bolsheviks had seized power in Russia, they hoped to seize power in the name of the proletariat in Germany. But, whereas the Bolsheviks had waited until they had behind them the assurance of a majority both in the Petrograd and Moscow Soviets and in the National Congress of Soviets, the Spartacists had no such majority, even in Berlin. The second Revolution which they set out to make could be at most no more than a Blanquist coup.

Yet they had a case, which to many of them seemed overwhelmingly strong. The Russians, who had achieved their Revolution in a backward country, unripe according to traditional Marxist ideas for any sort of Socialism, had justified their action on the plea that the world, or at any rate Western Europe, was ripe for proletarian rule, even if Russia were not, and that the war was bound to end in a great European Revolution, in which Germany would play the leading part. Manifestly the Revolution that had actually occurred in Germany in November 1918 was not that which the Russians meant : it was at most only a first stage, the equivalent of the February Revolution that had tumbled the Czar from his throne. It had to be followed up by a further Revolution, corresponding to the Bolshevik uprising of October 1917. Not only was Germany *ex hypothesi* ripe, as the most advanced of industrial countries, for such a revolution : for it not to occur would be betrayal of the Russian Revolution, and would lead inevitably to its defeat at the hands of its capitalist-imperialist enemies. The Bolsheviks themselves were of this opinion, and regarded proletarian revolution in Germany as the inevitable next step towards the predestined World Revolution. It would be sheer treason for the German left to hang back, merely because they could not command the support of a majority of the German workers. It was part of the historic mission of the German proletariat to save the Russian Revolution from defeat : if the mass of the German workers failed to see this, they must be made to see it by the determined action of the few who did.

The Spartacists were not alone in being inspired by a sense of obligation to press on with the German Revolution beyond its first inconclusive stage, or in wishing to come to the help of the hard-pressed Russians. Strong disapproval of the terms forced on the Russian Government at Brest-Litovsk had been a substantial factor in winning support for the Independents in Germany ; and the whole U.S.P.D. saw that real revolution could not be achieved without a decisive attack on the established order and an effective transference of authority at all levels into Socialist hands. Most of the U.S.P.D. leaders, however, soon realised that they had too little support to be in a position to make a second Revolution in face of the hostility of the Majority Socialists and the Trade Unions — and indeed of the greater part of the armed forces, whose great wish was to get out of uniform and to return home. The Independent Ministers in the Provisional Government therefore remained uneasily at their posts, unable to prevent their Majority colleagues from taking every step they could to hold the Revolution in check and to keep the old machine of State in being till a new Constitution could be duly drawn up and approved.

A critical matter at this stage was the possession of enough military force to hold the revolutionary left in check. In fact, however, neither the Government nor its opponents had any considerable force on which they could depend. In the early days of the Revolution, small bodies of armed men had been enrolled to defend the Republic; but the allegiance of these groups was, for the most part, uncertain. In Berlin the Majority Socialist Otto Wels (1873–1939) had been made commander of the garrison; but the police were under the command of the Independent Emil Eichhorn, and the Marine Division, which occupied the castle, had drawn in a preponderance of left-wing recruits and was ready to make trouble. A number of regiments back from the fighting fronts were stationed round Berlin; but it was quite uncertain whether they would accept orders to act against the left. The Government, or at any rate its Majority members, wanted to disband the Marine Division, or at least to reduce it to a skeleton force; but the Division was resistant and was clamouring for back pay, which the authorities were refusing to hand over unless their conditions were accepted. As an outcome of this dispute, the Marine Division took action, arrested Wels in his own office, and occupied the chancellory when Ebert refused to receive a deputation.

Ebert thereupon telephoned to General Groener, the head of the War Department, and called upon the army to liberate the chancellory. Groener moved soldiers into the city, and prepared to make war on the recalcitrant Marines. The Independent members of the Government tried to prevent this; and even Ebert recoiled when the military announced their intention of bombarding the castle, the headquarters of the Marine Division. But he allowed himself to be overruled by the War Office, or perhaps even acquiesced in its decision. On the morning of December 24th the bombardment began — the first open blow of the counter-revolution. The soldiers' hearts, however, were not in the fight. When the Marines released Wels and agreed to come to terms with the Government, General Groener's forces began to evaporate, and the engagement was called off with the Marine Division still in possession. At that moment, the left had probably its best chance of seizing power ; but it was not ready. Instead, what happened was that the U.S.P.D. Ministers resigned from the Government in disgust and thus handed power over entirely to the Majority Socialists, who were thereby given freedom to carry on with the support of the reactionaries, under the pretext of maintaining law and order.

The Majority Socialists had, however, been seriously shaken by the behaviour of the armed forces whose aid Ebert had invoked. In their search for a force that could be relied on to act against the left, they were driven to a disastrous expedient — the organisation of 'Free Corps' made up mainly of former officers and non-commissioned officers from the old army, which was being rapidly demobilised. These 'Free Corps' units, the first of which arrived in the neighbourhood of Berlin a week after the fighting at the castle, were to become, almost at once, the storm troops of the counter-revolution against the left. Though they acted on behalf of the Majority Socialist Government, they had no use for it save as an immediate provider of work and pay and as a means to bringing the revolting proletarians to heel. Gustav Noske, who had shown his capacity by subduing the mutinous sailors at Kiel in the early days of the Revolution, became the responsible head of this movement as Minister of Defence in the new, all-Majority, Provisional Government. He justified himself by saying, in his customary rough way, that someone had to take the odium of being the 'bloodhound'. Meanwhile Wels, who had not covered himself with glory, was replaced by Anton Fischer, formally a Franciscan friar, as commandant of Berlin, and the right and left in the capital made their preparations for a renewal of the struggle.

It has been said again and again that the U.S.P.D. made a disastrous mistake in leaving the Provisional Government and thus giving the Majority exclusive control. It is indeed clear that this enormously helped the Majority Socialists in gaining dominance over the regional and city authorities which had come to power during the Revolution. It is not, however, easy to see what else the Independents could have done. If they had remained in the Government they would have become responsible, jointly with the Majority, for the authorities' action against the left; for, however strongly they protested, they were not in a position to stop Ebert and Scheidemann from acting in their names. If it had come to a conflict of orders, the War Department and the Civil Service would have obeyed the Majority Ministers, and not them. They were, in effect, forced into a position in which they had either to resign or to surrender. Mere resignation, however, was not enough: if they were to achieve anything they had to go into resolute, activist opposition. This, however, meant coming to terms with the extreme left and being prepared to fight the Government in arms, and not merely in debate. Some of them — for example, Georg Ledebour, who had opposed coalition with the Majority Socialists from the first — were ready for this; but most of them hung back, chiefly because they were aware of, and largely shared, the desire of many of their followers for peace rather than civil war. For the U.S.P.D., as we have seen, was a mixture of many elements from pacifists and anti-militarists to ardent believers in proletarian revolution, and from parliamentarians to those who regarded parliamentary institutions as a mere cloak for the 'dictatorship of the bourgeoisie'.

The Independents, then, could only protest as the new Provisional Government went on with its preparations for a decisive reckoning with the left. Thereafter events moved swiftly. The Spartacists turned themselves into a Communist Party: the Government, on January 4th, 1919, dismissed Eichhorn from his position as chief of the Berlin police. The following day the capital was thronged with mass demonstrations against the Government. The demonstrators, meeting with little resistance, occupied the police headquarters and the offices of *Vorwaerts*, the chief newspaper of the Majority The U.S.P.D., which had hesitated at first to accept the challenge of Eichhorn's dismissal, threw itself into the fray with a call for a general strike, and on January 6th the strike began, with considerable mass support. The next day Noske joined the Government as Minister of Defence, with the task of suppressing the outbreak. The left, seeing that the time for compromise had passed, declared war on the Government and set up a Military Revolutionary Committee, with Ledebour, Liebknecht, and Paul Scholze as joint chairmen, but without the participation of Richard Müller, the head of the powerful organisation of Revolutionary Shop Stewards. Müller, indeed, like many other U.S.P.D. leaders, disapproved of the whole affair, which he believed to have been deliberately provoked by the Majority Socialists. There was a brief pause, while Noske mobilised his Free Corps forces for an attack on the left-wing strongholds. Then the Free Corps moved in, shelling and destroying the buildings occupied by the inadequately armed insurgents. There was no question of the Government's new armed forces refusing to fight : they were eager to be set at the rebel riff-raff and to do their worst. The occupied buildings were retaken, and the centre of the city cleared ; and then the Corps moved into action against the working-class suburbs, where some attempt was made to hold out. The numbers who fought on either side were fairly small : most of Berlin's population only looked on. By January 13th the fighting was over ; and the defeated U.S.P.D. called off the general strike. The leaders of the left went into hiding or escaped from the city. Two days later a detachment of the Free Corps caught and arrested Karl Liebknecht and Rosa Luxemburg, who had remained in Berlin, and murdered them instead of handing them over for trial. Not long afterwards Leo Jogiches (1867–1919), Rosa Luxemburg's closest associate over many years, was similarly murdered.

These deaths were a disaster for the German extreme left, which lost at a blow its principal leaders. Karl Liebknecht, indeed, had never been much of a theorist of Socialism ; but he had been the left's outstanding orator and had commanded deep respect for his complete and passionate sincerity and his deep hatred of every sort of militarism. Long before 1914, with the prestige of his father's name behind him, he had fought passionately against the patriotic nationalist trend in the German Socialist Party, and had been ousted from his position as leader of its Youth Movement. During the war he had relentlessly pursued his anti-militarist campaign. In 1915 he had been drafted into the army, where he had agitated among the soldiers. Gaoled for his activities, he had remained a prisoner till he was released by the amnesty proclaimed by Max of Baden's Government on the eve of the Revolution. He had immediately resumed his place at the head of the Spartacus League, of which he had been a chief inspirer. Thereafter he had been overruled by still hotter heads within his own organisation, but had felt it his duty to go with them when the crisis came. He was not, perhaps, a wise leader : certainly he was bad at planning and lacked the talent of organisation. But he was supremely devoted and single-minded ; and there was no-one capable of taking his place.

Jogiches was entirely unlike Liebknecht ; he was a planner and plotter who did his work behind the scenes and had no wish to claim the credit for it. As a Pole, he had worked long underground with Rosa Luxemburg in the left-wing Polish Social Democratic Party, and had been her lover as well as her faithful coadjutor. Though he wrote almost nothing, he was a theorist even more than a man of action ; and what she wrote often owed much to his ideas. During the war years he had flung his energies into the German left — especially into the Spartacist movement. His death, too, was a bad blow for revolutionary Socialism.

But, of course, by far the greatest loss was that of Rosa Luxemburg. Her career and her conceptions of Socialism and of Socialist strategy have been discussed in the preceding volume of this study and need not be reconsidered here.[1] Of all revolutionary Socialists Rosa Luxemburg alone can bear comparison with Lenin, with whom she had disputed as well as agreed over many years, on questions both of nationalism and of revolutionary strategy. On the nationalist issue she had stood out against Lenin's insistence on the national right of self-determination, proclaiming against the Polish national Socialists that the Polish and Russian Socialists must make common cause against Czarism and that the proletariat must transcend national frontiers in an essentially international struggle for freedom. She refused to make the concessions Lenin deemed necessary to the claims of subject nationalities to secede and set up Governments of their own ; for she thought in terms of a World Revolution which, far from creating new frontiers, would abolish those which existed already. She had

[1] See Vol. III, Part I, Chapter XI.

also, at any rate during the last year of her life, serious doubts about the policy which Lenin had followed in the Bolshevik Revolution ; for though she was an advocate of proletarian dictatorship, the dictatorship she stood for was that of the proletariat, and not a dictatorship over it by a centralised and authoritarian party deeming itself the vanguard of the working class. Rosa Luxemburg, unlike Lenin, had no faith in a disciplined *élite* of professional revolutionaries. She believed in the revolutionary *élan* of the masses and in their capacity to make and mould the Revolution for themselves. She had fears after November 1917 of the advent in Russia of a new professional bureaucracy which, in the name of the Revolution, would set out to subject the masses to itself. Not until 1921, when Paul Levi (1883-1930) published her writings on the subject, did these fears of hers become widely known ; and even then, for a time, they were little noticed or understood.

Rosa Luxemburg, even if she had her fears about party 'centralism', was faithful always to the Revolution, for which she lived. In Germany she was the one great intellectual force on the revolutionary side, and also the one great international figure of the younger Socialist generation. In addition to her political and economic eminence, she was also a woman of wide and deeply rooted cultural interests. She had been the close friend of Jaurès, despite their political disagreements ; and despite her deformity — she was a hunchback — she had great personal attraction. Her murder was felt and spoken of as an outrage all over Europe.

The deaths of Rosa Luxemburg and Karl Liebknecht took place only four days before the elections for the National Assembly, which were held on January 19th. The result clearly showed up the weakness of the Independents, who won only 5 per cent out of the total seats, as against the 39 per cent of the Majority Socialists. But it showed also that the two Socialist Parties, taken together, were in a minority, and that the reorganised bourgeois and right-wing Parties, though divided among themselves, were a force fully capable of re-asserting itself in the affairs of the new German State. In face of these results, the Socialists could no longer have claimed, even if they had been united, to govern the country in the name of parliamentary democracy ; and, far from being

united, they were fighting among themselves with ever-
increasing bitterness. With nearly 11½ million votes out of
30 million, the Majority Socialists were much the largest
Party in the Assembly ; but the Catholic (Centre) Party got
more than 6 million, the Democrats over 5½ million, and even
the extreme Conservatives more than 3 million, whereas the
U.S.P.D. polled hardly more than 2¼ million. There seemed
to be no way out save a coalition with the less reactionary
bourgeois Parties ; and the Majority Socialists accordingly
agreed to share office with the Democrats and the Catholic
Centre. This gave them a handsome majority in the Assembly,
but not for Socialism, for which they had no longer any mandate. The most that could be expected of such a coalition
was that it would confirm the Republic and provide it with a
parliamentary constitution in accordance with traditional liberal
ideas, and that it would hold the right-wing extremists in some
sort of check.

Even this last, however, was none too easy in view of the
nature of the forces on which the new Government was relying
in its warfare against the left. Neither the Berlin defeat nor
the election results had made an end of the left-wing opposition.
The Congress of Councils, indeed, promptly resigned the
authority it had been supposed to exercise over the Government into the Assembly's hands ; but the more left-wing local
Councils maintained their opposition, and the U.S.P.D., smarting under its defeat and threatened more and more by Noske's
Free Corps, moved sharply leftwards. In March 1919 the
U.S.P.D. Conference declared in favour of Council as against
parliamentary government and thus ranked itself by a majority
on the revolutionary side.

Before this, there had been sharp struggles in many parts
of Germany. In Bremen, a great stronghold of the revolutionaries, the left-wing Socialist Government was overthrown
at the beginning of February. In Bavaria, Kurt Eisner, newly
returned from denouncing the Majority Socialists at the Berne
International Socialist Conference, was assassinated on February
21st by a reactionary fanatic —Count Arco ; and in him the
moderate left lost one of its few outstanding leaders. Bavaria,
by tradition a stronghold of Catholicism and reaction, had
declared early for the November Revolution, largely because

its people hated the Prussians and rejoiced in the fall of the Prussian autocracy. Bavaria, as we saw, was the only part of Germany in which Peasant Councils were set up on any considerable scale ; and for a while it seemed that Eisner, though a Jew as well as an Independent, had established his Socialist Government firmly in power. The Bavarians, however, had not really changed their allegiance : they were only more set than ever on maintaining their regional independence and on dissociating themselves from the Prussian disaster. The death of Eisner removed the one personality capable of holding the Government together. His left-wing supporters invaded the Diet, where he had been shot, killed two bourgeois deputies, and severely wounded the Majority Socialist Minister, E. Auer (1874–1945). The Diet was dispersed ; and the Munich Workers' and Soldiers' Council took over authority in the city. But the greater part of Bavaria would have none of 'Council' Government : a Congress of Bavarian Councils rejected this, and the two Socialist Parties, under pressure, joined forces to establish a new Socialist Cabinet, headed by Adolf Hoffmann. This Government now came forward with an ambitious social programme, including measures of socialisation which antagonised the peasants as well as the bourgeoisie. Under pressure it agreed to re-convene the dispersed Bavarian Diet, in which the Socialists were in a minority. The Munich Council, fearful that the Diet would overturn the Government, declared in favour of 'Council' rule ; and the Government took fright, became reconciled with the bourgeois Parties, and removed itself from Munich first to Nuremberg and then to Bamberg, in Northern Bavaria, where the left wing had but little following. The Munich rebels then set up a 'Council' Government of a very strange kind ; for it consisted of Majority Socialists and Independents, with the Communists refusing to co-operate. This curiosity, however, lasted for only a brief period, before its own Republican Guard attempted to overthrow it and to bring the Hoffmann Government back. This brought the Communists, who had hitherto stood aside, into the field. Headed by the Russian Jew, Eugen Leviné (?–1919), an experienced revolutionary in the Russian movement, the Communists both defeated the Republican Guard and expelled the 'Council' Government, which they replaced with a new Soviet Government under their own control. They formed a miniature 'Red Army', under the command of the young U.S.P.D. intellectual, Ernst Toller (1893–1939), then aged 25, and proceeded to organise the city under proletarian dictatorship. They had, however, but little support, even among the Munich workers, and practically none in the rest of Bavaria. The Hoffmann Government, too weak to attack Munich by itself, appealed for help to the Governments of Württemberg and of the Reich, and both of these sent forces to its aid. These forces soon advanced upon the city, and captured it with but little resistance. At the final stage, yet a third Soviet Government, led by Toller, had expelled Leviné and assumed power, but collapsed as soon as the invaders reached the city.

Many allegations were made subsequently that the Bavarian Soviet Governments — no fine distinctions being made between them — had been guilty of savage butcheries of the bourgeoisie during their brief tenure of power. There is, however, no evidence that they killed even a single person until the very last moments of their resistance, during which seven or eight hostages were undoubtedly shot by members of the disorganised remnants of the Red Army. The killings, apart from this, came later, and from the opposite side. The victorious counter-revolutionaries celebrated the fall of 'Red' Munich by a massacre, which extended to a group of twenty-one Catholic workers assembled at an entirely unpolitical social gathering, as well as to other innocent victims. The executions followed — among them that of Leviné. Gustav Landauer (1870–1919), a well-known intellectual of the anarchistic left, was killed in the fighting. Toller escaped, to become celebrated later as a dramatist of the left.

The uprooting of the Munich revolutionaries, and the establishment of military rule which ensued, destroyed Bavarian Socialism and made the city into a stronghold of counter-revolution in its most extreme forms. Munich became the chief breeding-ground of Nazism and the scene four years later of Hitler's first abortive attempt to seize power as the ally of Ludendorff and the extreme nationalist right. The history of its Soviet Governments would be merely ludicrous, if it were not tragic as well. For in truth Bavarian Socialism never had any roots among the people or the smallest chance of establishing itself by a revolutionary *coup*. The adventures of Landauer and Leviné simply played into the hands of the reaction, and gave Noske's thugs a grand chance of gratifying their lust for blood.

While the Munich tragi-comedy was being played out, terrible events were taking place in other parts of Germany. Most terrible of all was the renewed fighting in Berlin during the second week of March 1919. During the previous month extensive strikes had broken out in many parts of Germany, and especially in the Ruhr coalfield, where the miners had organised a powerful new Union. This Union was demanding the recognition of Workers' Councils, for which it claimed the right to participate in the control of the industry ; and similar claims were being put forward in other industries and areas. Over a large part of central Germany there developed a general strike which for a time practically isolated the National Assembly, then meeting in Weimar to draw up the new Constitution and to decide on the changes needed in the German economic structure. At the beginning of March the strike spread to Berlin under the leadership of the Berlin Workers' Council, of which Richard Müller was chairman. As a consequence of the strike, but not of any orders from its leaders, crowds appeared in the streets and sporadic fighting broke out between the remnants of the Marine Division and other left-wing groups and the Berlin police, now under the command of the Majority Socialist, Eugen Ernst (1864–1954). Noske's Free Corps were brought in to reinforce the police ; and the insurgents, retreating from the centre of the city, tried to entrench themselves in East Berlin. A terrible massacre followed, as Noske's forces advanced into the working-class quarters. There were doubtless atrocities on both sides ; but out of more than a thousand killed not one in ten was a soldier, and much of the killing was of workers who were found to possess arms, even if they had made no attempt to use them. Thirty men of the Marine Division, though they had taken no part in the fighting, were shot in cold blood by orders of an officer, after they had been made prisoners. Many stories were circulated and published about atrocities alleged to have been carried out by the insurgents ; but in the subsequent investigation it was shown that many of these stories were simply untrue. The military authorities had made up their minds to make an end once for all of the trouble-makers of 'Red' Berlin ; and they did their work ruthlessly while most of the population stood helplessly by.

It is by no means clear who was responsible for the incidents that brought on the fighting. Neither the U.S.P.D. nor the Workers' Council which was conducting the strike had any part in the affair ; and the Communist Party also repudiated any connection with the outbreak. On the insurgent side it seems to have been a spontaneous uprising, with no real organisation behind it, brought on in the first place by the behaviour of small disorderly elements and by the methods used by the reorganised police in repressing them. The actual insurgents were few, and were easily and decisively beaten. The main loss of life was the work of Noske's Free Corps.

After the Berlin tragedy the strike movement gradually died away, as concessions were made to the demands for recognition of the Works Councils, though not to the claim that the workers should be granted by law a measure of participation in the control of industry, or to the demands for socialisation put forward especially by the miners in the Ruhr. As we saw, at the time of the November Revolution most of the Socialist leaders, including many in the U.S.P.D., had rejected immediate socialisation of industry as impracticable in view of the state of the German economy and the imperative need to maintain production undisturbed. This view may have been partly correct ; but it need not have prevented the Provisional Government from introducing at once some measure of general control designed to provide for a workable interim structure of industrial relations, and to compel employers to conform to public requirements. In fact, however, almost nothing was done beyond decreeing the introduction of the eight hours' day and the signing of an agreement providing for Trade Union recognition between the Trade Union Commission and a central body of employers. The wider issues were shelved until the National Assembly could find time to deal with them. This delay caused much dissatisfaction, as it involved, in effect, the restoration of capitalist enterprise and the surrender of powers which many Workers' Councils had assumed during the November days. The Trade Union leadership, however, was in the hands of Majority Socialists, and readily acquiesced in the Government's decision. The protests came, in growing volume, from the shop stewards and Workers' Councils, re-inforced by the new Unions which had sprung up during the Revolution, especially in the mines.

The volume of protest was strong enough, even before the strikes of March 1919, to make the Government realise that it would lose its following among the workers unless some con-cessions were made to the demand that recognition should be given to the Workers' Councils. The Majority Socialists were, however, entirely opposed to the demand that the Councils should be allowed any share in political power, which belonged in their view exclusively to the National Assembly and to the elected Diets of the various States. They therefore fell back on the idea of responding to the workers' claims by making limited concessions in respect of economic power, and met the wave of strikes by promising to establish by law a structure of Economic Councils through which the workers would be able to participate at every level both in the determination of work-ing conditions and welfare and in the settlement of economic policy. The agreement concluded at Weimar on March 15th, 1919, provided for the setting up, under the new Constitution, of representative Workers' Councils in the factories and other establishments, and also for the formation of joint councils at higher levels to discuss and regulate matters of production and to draw up plans for socialisation and regulation of industry in the public interest. A declaratory clause based on the agree-ment was actually included in due course in the Constitution of the Weimar Republic ; but it could have no effect unless laws for implementing it were also passed. One part of the scheme — the establishment of statutory Works Councils with limited powers over such matters as working conditions, work-shop discipline and dismissals — was actually passed into law ; and these Councils remained in being throughout the life of the Weimar Republic. The proposed higher Councils were never legislated for, and were never established. In the matter of socialisation, laws were passed laying down the principle of socialisation for the coal-mines and the generation of electrical power ; but the coal-mines were never in fact socialised. All that happened was that the pre-war Rhenish-Westphalian Coal Syndicate, in which the State had a share, was reorganised as a general co-ordinating agency for the German coal industry, which remained in private hands. The general question of socialisation was dealt with by the National Assembly by setting up a Socialisation Commission to report, and by appointing to it most of the leading economists of both the Socialist and the middle bourgeois Parties. This Commission duly produced a report recommending socialisation of a very limited group of so-called 'ripe' industries, the required conditions being that they should be both subject to monopoly control and unlikely to need further technical development or new markets or new sources of materials — a requirement which ruled out practically every important candidate. These proposals were naturally quite without practical effect. Only the law on Works Councils made any practical difference ; and even its value was to the Government in damping down industrial unrest rather than in making any real concession to the demand for workers' participation in the control of industry.

It is worth while to pursue a little further the attitude of the German Socialists in 1919 to the questions of socialisation and workers' control. The left wing, including most of the U.S.P.D., was in the main interested much more in getting political power for the Workers' Councils than in the matters covered by the Works Council law. It cried out for socialisation, but for the most part envisaged this, not as State ownership and administration, but as meaning that the workers would take over the running of industries on some sort of Co-operative basis, so as to avoid bureaucratic or parliamentary control. The Majority Socialists, on the other hand, denounced this as meaning that each body of workers would be set free to exploit the public and that it would lead to both inefficiency and inflation, as prices would be forced up in order to increase wages. They said that Germany, which imperatively needed to build up its industries, would be priced out of the world market. The Majority Socialists were, however, no less opposed to socialisation in the alternative form of State ownership and management. The State, they argued, was not a suitable body for running industries ; and in pursuance of this argument they were led into the most remarkable laudation of the virtues of capitalist enterprise and of *laissez-faire*. They did not, to be sure, reach this position at a single bound : they began mainly by arguing that the economic situation was too bad and critical for socialisation to be immediately practicable. It soon became plain, however, that their objections went far beyond this. As we saw earlier in this study,[1] the orthodox German Social Democrats before 1914 had always regarded socialisation as something that would come on the morrow of the attainment of a Socialist political majority, and had refused to discuss what form it would then take. They had been hostile to socialisation before 'the Revolution', because it would add to the power of the existing State, which was their enemy ; and they had dismissed as 'utopian' all attempts to forecast the structure of the future society. What some of them now said — for example, the Austrian, Adolf Braun, who had become a regular writer on Socialism in the German Social Democratic press — was that Marx had never envisaged socialisation except on the assumption that there would be highly productive capitalist industries ready to be taken over, whereas in Germany in 1918 capitalist industry lay in ruins and would present the State with insoluble problems of reconstruction that would only discredit Socialism if it were taken over. Socialism, Kautsky proclaimed in a work published just after the Revolution but written before it, 'cannot remove the poverty that is due to general want in society. It can only remove the load of want amid abundance.' This was his reason for opposing any attempt at early socialisation.

If the Socialists would have neither workers' control nor state operation, there was nothing for it but a continuance of capitalism. Rudolf Wissell (b. 1869), the Majority Socialist who became Minister of Economy early in 1919, did indeed attempt to work out a comprehensive scheme for a controlled capitalist economy based on government planning. But he did not remain long in office, and under his Majority Socialist successor, Robert Schmidt (1864– ?), his plans were rapidly dropped.

While the Weimar Assembly was setting up its Socialisation Commission and listening to Wissell expounding his projects, the civil war between the Government and the left was proceeding apace. Saxony and the Ruhr were the chief remaining

[1] See Vol. III, Part I, p. 267.

strongholds of the left; and of these the Ruhr had been temporarily placated by the March agreement about Workers' Councils. In Saxony, the U.S.P.D. was the leading party. On the pretext that the Saxon Government had been engaging in a dictatorial policy and that there had been serious disturbances in Dresden and Leipzig, Noske's forces marched into Saxony in May 1919 and occupied both cities. Saxony, in the early days of the Revolution, had been ruled by a Government based entirely on the U.S.P.D. In January there had been serious disturbances, and this Government had given place to one dominated by the Majority Socialists. Thereupon the left had organised mass protests throughout Saxony, and sporadic fighting had occurred. In April a 'Council' Government had been proclaimed in Leipzig; and this provided the pretext for action which Noske required. He sent in General Märker with instructions to suppress the left; and the Reichswehr took over control. There were further troubles in Chemnitz and other areas during the following months. In the Reich, in October, the S.P.D. entered into a coalition Government with the Democrats, and this lasted till April 1920, when, as a sequel to the Kapp *putsch*, the two Socialist Parties came to terms and formed a joint administration. Noske's forces, after the summer of 1919, had passed on to other 'disaffected' areas.

When the Reichswehr marched into Saxony in May 1919, the German Government had just received the draft Peace Treaty drawn up in Paris by the Allied Ministers. It was received with howls of execration, in which the Majority Socialists loudly joined. The proposed terms were denounced as a flagrant violation of President Wilson's Fourteen Points, on the basis of which the German Government had sued for peace. So, indeed, in many respects they were; but the protests went far beyond what could be justified on this ground. The Majority joined to the full in the demand for the retention of Alsace-Lorraine, for the return of the German Colonies, and for the establishment of frontiers which would recognise the complete unity of the German people. There were clamant demands that the Government should refuse to sign the Treaty, or indeed any Treaty that branded Germany with any sort of 'war guilt' or treated her as a defeated enemy. There were loud assertions that the German armies had never been defeated in the field, but had been the victims of a 'Dolch-stoss' — a 'stab in the back' — from the collapse of the home front. The left was accused of having brought this collapse about not only by the militarists, but also by some of the Majority Socialists. Scheidemann himself announced that nothing would induce him to sign so dishonouring a surrender as the Versailles Treaty. The Government rejected the proposed peace terms, and sent counter-proposals to the Allies. These were for the most part promptly rejected, though some modifications were made ; and the German Government actually considered the possibility of renewing the war, only to be told by Hindenburg and the other generals that no chance existed of offering successful military resistance. There were some who still preferred even a hopeless war to a 'shameful' peace ; but to most of the leaders it had become plain that there was no real alternative to accepting the Allied terms. Scheidemann, however, persisted in his refusal and, on June 20th, resigned his office as Chancellor and was replaced by Gustav Bauer (1870-?), the Trade Union leader, who liked the Treaty no better, but took a more realistic line. Scheidemann soon afterwards retired from politics and returned to his native Cassel, where he became burgomaster and continued to serve till he fled abroad from the Nazis in 1933. The Treaty was signed on June 28th, and finally ratified on July 9th ; and the Allied blockade of Germany, which had been maintained throughout the preceding months, was lifted on July 12th.

This continued blockade of Germany, long after the fighting had come to an end, had hung as a constant threat over the Germans throughout the successive phases of the Revolution. Already at the time of the military collapse, shortages of food and raw materials had been exceedingly severe and the German people had been enduring very serious hardships. The evacuation of the occupied territories made the situation worse, and there were also great difficulties over transport and distribution due to the loss of railway equipment and vehicles and to the heavy demands of demobilisation. Germany, at the end of the fighting, was in urgent need of imports both of foodstuffs and of the raw materials required for putting industry into operation on a peace-time basis. The victorious Allies, however, were in no mood to come to the relief of the Germans by allowing supplies to enter the country until the terms of peace had been laid down and accepted. Moreover, the refusal of supplies served a political purpose not only as a means of compelling the Germans to accept whatever terms the victors might decide to impose, but also in damping down the German Revolution by forcing the German Government to consider what attitude the Allies would be likely to take up if, after dethroning the Kaiser, the Germans proceeded to measures designed to lay the foundations of a Socialist system. If, for example, any attack were to be launched on capitalist property, or even on the class of great landlords, might not the Allies seize the excuse to march into Germany, in order to put down Bolshevism and restore the authority of the old ruling classes, or at least to establish an anti-Socialist bourgeois régime? These, it has to be remembered, were the days of attempted Allied intervention in Russia against the Bolsheviks; and it was feared that, if the German Revolution seemed to be taking a Socialist shape, no nice distinctions would be drawn by the Allied Governments between Bolshevism and democratic Socialism.

The German Majority Socialists had therefore, from the moment when the Revolution carried them into office, an extremely difficult situation to face. In view of the condition of the country they had to do their utmost to get the blockade ended; and the best chance of this appeared to lie in doing as little as possible to offend the Allied Governments, either by attacking private industry or by entering into relations with Bolshevik Russia. This argument, as well as the others referred to in this chapter, was widely used as a reason for doing nothing, at least for the time being, to socialise industry or to encourage the workers' claims to take it into their own hands. It is true that, by acting in this very circumspect fashion, the Majority Socialists did not succeed in getting the blockade removed until the Peace Treaty had been accepted; but who can say with any assurance what measures the Allied Governments might have resorted to had the Revolution in Germany been given its head? I am not suggesting that, in fact, the German people would have gone Bolshevik, or even Socialist, in 1918 had the Majority Socialists taken a different line; but I am arguing that one very powerful reason why there was so little zeal for Socialism in Germany was that a great many Germans were afraid that any attempt to establish it by forcible action might lead to drastic Allied intervention, including invasion of the country, and might add greatly to hardships that were already almost too much to be borne.

In the Allied countries, especially in Great Britain, there were some who protested strongly against the continuance of the blockade after the fighting was over and pleaded on humanitarian grounds for action both to relieve the immediate distress and to help the Germans to get production restarted as speedily as possible. But this was not the general mood, which was one of sharp vindictiveness against Germany as the country mainly responsible for the war and of insistence on making the Germans pay the penalty both financially and in suffering for their past misdeeds. The same process of intimidation by blockade was used against Austria and Hungary as against Germany, and created great difficulties for Károlyi in Hungary and for the newly founded Austrian Republic. It is, perhaps, no cause for surprise that this should have been the prevailing attitude among the statesmen who favoured the Versailles Treaty and were at the same time in daily terror of the spread of revolution from Russia to other parts of Europe. But the continued blockade involved making ruthless war on the populations of the defeated countries in defiance of all the principles of human decency of conduct ; and it is to the credit of the Western Socialist Parties that they soon began to protest against it, though they were in no position to make their protests effective.

I have stressed the very great difficulties that confronted the German Majority Socialists in 1918–19, not in order to justify their general conduct, but only because, in common fairness, account has to be taken of these difficulties in assessing the blame. The Majority Socialists had excuses, and reasons, for not pursuing a Socialist policy ; but I think it is also plain that, had these particular reasons not existed, they would have found — as they did in fact find — others. The German Revolution, though they had been contemplating it so long, took them by surprise when it came, and found them altogether unready with any workable plans for establishing a new social order. Though they had long purported to be a revolutionary Party, Ebert was but voicing a widespread sentiment when he said that he 'hated revolution' — by which he meant any change not carried through in strict constitutional form. Moreover, during the war the Majority Socialists had deeply committed themselves to the support of aggressive, annexationist, even pan-German policies which rendered them incapable of facing the realities of a situation involving utter German defeat. Their attitude does not excuse the Allies, or justify the continued blockade ; but it does show that something more than fear of what the Allies might do held the Socialists back from an attempt to use the Revolution for laying the foundations of a really new German social order.

At all events, under irresistible Allied pressure, the German Government finally accepted the Versailles Treaty ; but its terms were bitterly resented, and during the next few years a succession of German Governments did their best to avoid carrying it out. It was known in Germany as the 'diktat' of Versailles ; and the act of the Socialists in signing it was held up against them first by the militarists and conservatives, and later by the Nazis. They had, however, no real choice.

Thus, Philipp Scheidemann, who had been, even more than Ebert, the active leader of the Majority Socialists during and after the Revolution, passed out of the political world. Among the most vehement supporters of the war and, during the Revolution, among the strongest opponents of the left, he was nevertheless a great hater of the Kaiser and of the militarist clique that surrounded him and, according to his lights, a convinced adherent of democracy. He actively disliked Ebert, with whom he had to collaborate closely, and, even in his most right-wing moments, remained well to the left of him. He had qualms about Noske and his Free Corps ; but when it came to the point he was prepared to use *any* methods to defeat the left. In common with most of the Majority leaders he had a horror of Bolshevism and a firm belief that it was his business as a statesman, not so much to lead as to do whatever was decided on by a majority vote. Democracy to him meant parliamentarism, based on universal suffrage, and nothing else. As an ardent admirer of Germany and German culture, he was quite unable to conceive that Germany deserved anything but victory in the war, or that after the defeat there could be any justification for the imposing of punitive terms. A fluent speaker and a lively personality, he had no clear ideas of his own beyond this democratic Germanism ; and he was entirely incapable of making any contribution to Socialist thought. As Chancellor, he was impelled, by the internal struggle after the war, further and further to the right and at any rate experienced some discomfort at the behaviour of some of his even more right-wing colleagues. But he had no will to resist them ; for his first belief was that Germany must be saved by crushing Bolshevism wherever it raised its head. When he resigned rather than sign the 'shameful' Treaty, he gave place to men who fully shared this attitude and were prepared to carry on no less relentlessly the war against the German left.

While the wrangle over the Peace Treaty was proceeding, the Weimar Assembly, under the guidance of the Democrat, Professor Hugo Preuss, was busy drafting the new Constitution, which was finally promulgated on August 11th. The Weimar Constitution established the new Germany as a federal Republic, retaining the old state boundaries with some amalgamations of the smaller prewar States into bigger units. It was in a formal way highly democratic in a parliamentary sense, in that it provided for universal suffrage and for proportional representation under a multi-party system, and for responsible government. What it involved in practice was that the Socialists definitely resigned their claim to govern alone unless they could win a clear majority of the electors to their side — by no means a probable contingency in view both of their own divisions and of their failure to attract any substantial part of the peasantry into their ranks. Proportional representation, which the Majority Socialists regarded as a matter of democratic principle, meant that the Republic would have to be governed by party coalitions either with or without Socialist participation. It meant weak and fluctuating governments, where strong government was badly needed. It meant that the German Revolution had definitely failed to establish a Socialist order.

Was there at any point a chance that it would ? Hardly ; and none at all unless the Socialists had been ready, at all risks, to seize their opportunity promptly in November 1918. Their one chance lay in using the immediate crisis, not merely to dethrone the Kaiser and proclaim the Republic, but to depose the army command — to tell the peasants and labourers of

Eastern Germany to seize the land, and the workers of all Germany to occupy and work the factories and mines as public property — and to dismiss the higher ranks of the public officials and put new ones, however inexperienced, in their places — and, at the same time, to create swiftly a new armed force under Socialist leadership for the defence of the Revolution against its enemies at home — and in addition to face the possibility that the Allies, despite the Armistice, would march on into Germany in order to destroy the Revolution together with its domestic opponents. To recite this list of necessary actions is enough to show how entirely out of the question it was that the German Majority Socialists should act in any such way. They were Germans much before they were Socialists : they felt the defeat of the German armies not as an opportunity but as a disaster. They were, moreover, strict constitutionalists and had a passionate belief that even revolution ought to be made in an orderly fashion and required a mandate that could be given only at the ballot box, by a majority vote. Even if they had had a plan for making a Socialist society — which they had not — it would certainly not have been the sort of plan that could possibly have been carried out in 1918 or 1919. They had deeply disapproved of the Bolsheviks for seizing power even when they had a majority in the Soviets ready to endorse their *coup* : were they to attempt to monopolise authority when they had no such assured majority for doing so, even in the Councils ? Their answer was bound to be an emphatic no — the more emphatic because it was not for civilised Germans to imitate the methods of barbarian Russia. Therefore, paradoxically, while backward Russia, where even the Bolsheviks had supposed till nearly the last moment that only a bourgeois revolution was possible, went on to make the proletarian revolution a fact, Germany, the home of advanced capitalism and of the reputedly strongest Socialist movement in the world, halted at the bourgeois revolution, and before long slipped back even from that. The sheer weakness of capitalism made the position of bourgeois revolution untenable in Russia : the very strength of the constitutional Socialist movement made Socialist revolution impossible in the German Reich.

It is indeed pertinent, at this point, to consider whether the experience of the German Social Democratic Party and its very marked success in building up an organisation for the conduct of an essentially parliamentary struggle did not unfit it for the task of conducting a successful revolution. Of all Socialist Parties — and indeed of all Parties that existed up to 1914 — the S.P.D. was the most highly organised, both for its electoral tasks and for imposing itself as a powerful influence on the lives and attitudes of its members. In these respects only the Austrian Party could be compared with it; and the Austrian Party was but the leading element in a loose federation of Parties representing the distinct nationalities of the Austrian empire. The Germans in the German Reich had built up a solid organisation, resting on a basis of mass membership and directed to the purpose of winning a Socialist majority in the Reichstag and of holding the supporters of Socialism together in a closely knit fraternity in opposition to the German imperialist régime. In pursuance of these objectives the S.P.D. had become involved in a wide range of business transactions, arising out of its ownership of an extensive party press, office buildings and meeting halls, and so on. It had, accordingly, a considerable stake in the maintenance of orderly conditions and a marked tendency so to carry on its affairs as not to frighten away its more moderate supporters. In some degree these conditions necessarily apply to any large-scale Party that has become accustomed to carrying on its agitation under legal and constitutional conditions. It had been argued much earlier by certain outstanding revolutionaries, such as Bakunin, that for this reason all highly organised political Parties would necessarily fail to take a really revolutionary line and, even if they became involved in a revolution, would draw back in the moment of crisis for fear of sacrificing their established position and pulling down the structures they had been at such pains to build. Clearly, even if this generalisation is not fully accepted, there is some substance in it; and the inhibitions against forthright revolutionary action were particularly strong in the S.P.D. despite its reiterated assertions of its essentially revolutionary character. I discussed this matter at some length in an earlier volume of this History, and need not pursue it further here.[1] It was sufficiently apparent from the very beginning of the German Revolution in 1918 that the main body of

[1] See Vol. III, Part II, Chapter XXVIII.

the S.P.D. leaders, far from wishing to encourage the forces that desired to carry it through to completion as a Socialist revolution, were set on holding it to the greatest practicable extent within the bounds of legality and strictly constitutional reform, and that in taking up this attitude they had the full endorsement of the Trade Union leaders, who were much more concerned with strengthening their position in respect of constitutional collective bargaining with the employers than with any measures designed to bring the capitalist system to an end.

Such was the attitude of the chosen leaders of the S.P.D. and the Trade Unions in their hour of trial ; and there were large elements in the U.S.P.D. leadership which differed from them only in holding that the German militarists had been mainly responsible for the disaster. These elements could not share in the real indignation with which the Majority Socialists received the Allies' peace terms ; but they were in agreement that any attempt to advance towards a Socialist society must be made in due order and in strict accordance with the principles of parliamentary democracy. This view was probably not shared by most of the U.S.P.D. rank and file, who would have been quite ready to go ahead on a basis of 'Council' Government without a Constituent Assembly. But the U.S.P.D. was clearly not in a position to act effectively alone ; and the only possible basis for action by it was knocked away when the Majority Socialists easily captured a majority in the Congress of Workers' Councils. There remained only the possibility of some sort of Blanquist *coup*, by a small revolutionary *élite* ; and that was not a policy which the U.S.P.D. leadership, or any substantial part of it, was prepared even to consider. It became the policy of the new Communist Party, formed out of the Spartacus League, only against the advice of its outstanding leaders, who realised the hopelessness of the adventure, and thereafter of a succession of disappointed and angry left-wing Socialists, who saw the defeat of the Revolution and could not bear to accept defeat without striking a blow, however wild.

The Communists, for a time after the strikes and the fighting of the early months of 1919, appeared to have learnt their lesson. Paul Levi (1883–1930), who had become their leader after the murder of Liebknecht, was determined on a change of policy. He wanted the Communist Party to give up its refusal to take part in parliamentary elections and to attempt to build itself up as a mass Party ; and he also urged it to abandon its attitude of hostility to the Trade Unions, as strongholds of reaction, and to set out to capture them instead. At the second Party Congress, held in October 1919, he sprang on the delegates a series of theses embodying the new policy, and got a substantial majority — upon which the dissidents, accusing the majority of treasonable opportunism, seceded and attempted to set up a rival Communist Labour Party, which speedily faded away. Meanwhile the U.S.P.D. had been moving leftwards, shedding in the process some of its right-wing members, such as Eduard Bernstein, but gaining recruits rapidly, as discontent with the Majority Socialists increased. Before the end of the year the U.S.P.D. had not only reaffirmed its support for 'Council' Government as against parliamentarism, but had also refused to participate in reviving the Second International and had opened negotiations with Moscow with a view to joining the newly founded Third International. Before this, the U.S.P.D., too, had lost its leader, Haase, who was mortally wounded by an assassin early in October 1919, and died a month later.

Hugo Haase was an honest and intelligent but in no sense a great man. He had been in the Reichstag for more than twenty years, and in 1912 had become joint leader during Bebel's illness, and also joint chairman of the S.P.D. During the war he had shared the party chairmanship with Ebert and had been leader of the Reichstag group, despite his anti-war views, till he was driven out of the Party in 1916. Primarily a parliamentarian, he belonged by instinct to the more moderate group in the U.S.P.D. ; but circumstances drove him further to the left, and he became a supporter of 'Council' Government, though he never went over to the U.S.P.D. left wing. As a theorist he was of no considerable account ; but he was widely respected, and his death left the U.S.P.D. without a leader capable of holding it together. Ledebour, the most distinguished of those left to it, was old — 68 when the Revolution broke out — and too far to the left to be acceptable. Clara Zetkin (1857-1933), also in her sixties, had already thrown in her lot with the Communists. Eisner was dead. Rudolf Hilferding (1877-1942), the Austrian-born financial expert, and

Kautsky were much too far to the right. There remained Ernst Däumig (1868–1922) and Wilhelm Dittmann (1874–1954), neither an outstanding figure, and Arthur Crispien (1875–1946), on whom the choice fell to lead the Party through the crisis which arose out of its attempt to come to terms with the Third International.

The Peace Treaty came into force in January 1920, and later in the month the Dutch Government refused to hand the ex-Kaiser over to the Allies for trial. In Germany there was a pause before the next storm, which broke from the right, entirely unexpected by Noske and indeed by the whole Government. On March 13th came the Kapp *putsch* — a revolt of Noske's new army against the Government that had organised it to crush the left. The Ministers fled precipitately from Berlin to Stuttgart, while in the capital General Lüttwitz proclaimed the Government's deposition and set the notorious Dr. Wolfgang Kapp, a founder of the extremist Fatherland Party, in its place. Old Karl Legien, the right-wing Majority leader of the German Trade Unions, remained in Berlin and thence issued the call for a general strike. The response was immense, and within a few days the *putsch* simply collapsed in face of it. Legien, disgusted at the Government's pusillanimous conduct, called on the two Socialist Parties to sink their differences and form a coalition Government, and even asked the Communists to give their support. In the Ruhr the workers rose *en masse* and defeated and disarmed the military units. In Chemnitz, Majority Socialists and Communists joined forces in a 'Council' Government led by the Communist, Heinrich Brandler (b. 1881), who thus rose to prominence in his Party. In Leipzig, the Independent Socialists avenged the military occupation of the previous year. In Hamburg and in many other areas, the Socialists triumphed without firing a shot. It seemed as if, miraculously, the German Revolution had been given a second chance.

Among the leaders of the rival Socialist Parties, however, feeling was too bitter for sustained common action to be possible. The U.S.P.D. rejected Legien's proposal ; and, instead of an all-Socialist Government, the Majority Socialists formed a coalition with the Catholic Centre, Hermann Müller (1876–1931) replacing Gustav Bauer as Chancellor. Instead of attempting to punish the leaders of the *putsch*, the new Government let them go scot-free, and actually left most of the military ringleaders in possession of their commands. Only a week after Müller had assumed office, the Reichswehr advanced into the Ruhr to stamp out the rebellious workers who had dared to defy it during the *putsch*. The Ruhr district was controlled at this time mainly by left-wing elements of the U.S.P.D., which had formed a 'Red Army' during the *putsch* ; but some areas, including Essen and Duisburg, were in the hands of the extreme left. The Müller Government first appealed to the workers to disband their forces and to give up their arms ; and after negotiations the Independents agreed, as they saw no prospect of successful resistance and were promised that there would be no reprisals. The extreme left in the Western Ruhr refused : and the Reichwehr marched in and took their revenge for their earlier discomfiture. What resistance there was was soon beaten down, and the 'Red' Ruhr was shattered. Noske himself had been displaced by the change of Government : he was too unpopular to be used again. But the Kapp *putsch*, despite its failure, ended in pushing the Majority Socialists further along the road of reaction, and in rending the German Labour Movement still further asunder on the morrow of its great demonstration of solidarity. The U.S.P.D., at its conference in June 1920, confirmed its refusal to enter into coalition with the S.P.D., and decided to send a delegation — Crispien, Dittmann, Ernst Däumig, and Helene Stöcker (1869–1943) — to Moscow to negotiate on the terms of admittance to the Communist International.

When the U.S.P.D. delegates got to Moscow, in time to attend as observers the second Congress of the Third International, they found themselves confronted with a formidable list of conditions for membership. The Eighteen Points put forward in February 1920 became Twenty-one and now included the exclusion by name of the leading party members who were regarded as belonging to the anti-Communist right wing or centre, and were therefore branded as 'social traitors'. There will be more to say in a later chapter about this fateful Congress, which irrevocably split the international Socialist movement. Here, we are concerned only with its effects on the German movement. After the return of the delegates the

U.S.P.D. held a Congress at Halle to consider their report, and Zinoviev attended it on behalf of the Communist International. After fierce debates, the U.S.P.D. voted by a majority to accept the Twenty-one Points hook, line, and sinker. This, of course, meant a split : the dissentients withdrew and re-formed the U.S.P.D. as an independent Party. Out of about 800,000 members of the old U.S.P.D. roughly 300,000 became members of the new amalgamated Communist Party, while about 200,000 joined the new U.S.P.D. The rest either dropped out or went back to the Majority Socialists. The German Communist Party thus acquired for the first time something of the character of a mass Party and began again to dream of a mass-uprising that would bring with it a real German Social Revolution on the Russian model.

While the Comintern was conferring in Moscow, the Russian armies had been advancing on Warsaw, and it had seemed to be well on the cards that a military victory would put them in a position to bring powerful aid to a Communist rising in Germany. But in August the Russians had been flung back by the Poles, aided by the French, and this hope had vanished. Simultaneously with the Halle Congress the Poles and Russians were concluding an armistice, which was signed on October 12th. The Comintern moved on to its next task, that of inducing the Italian Socialist Party to accept the Twenty-one Points ; and the German Communists settled down to the job of absorbing and indoctrinating their U.S.P.D. recruits. Meanwhile the Russians were finishing off General Wrangel's forces in the Crimea, and were thus bringing the civil war to a close. The German Government was already engaged in an acrimonious dispute with the Allies about reparations. Inside Germany there was for a few months a deceptive calm.

This pause came to an abrupt end early in the following year. In February 1921 the Italian Socialists met in order to decide whether to accept the Twenty-one Points ; and at their Leghorn Congress the Comintern was represented by Matthias Rakosi of Hungary and Christo Kabakchev, the leading theorist of Bulgarian Communism, who took a high line in demanding the expulsion of Turati and other leaders, but failed to carry the day. The Italian Party was thus lost to the Comintern.

Rakosi, on his way back, came to Germany and demanded that the German Communists should endorse his action at Leghorn. Paul Levi, who had been at Leghorn and had tried to mediate between the disputants, opposed Rakosi and was joined by Clara Zetkin and by most of the U.S.P.D. leaders who had come over to the Communist Party. Rakosi obtained a narrow majority on the central committee, and the dissentients resigned from it.

At this point the French, correctly alleging that Germany was not carrying out the disarmament provisions of the Versailles Treaty, marched into the Ruhr and occupied Düsseldorf ; and the Comintern sent Béla Kun to represent it with the German Communists. Early in March, serious troubles broke out in the copper-mines at Mansfeld in Prussian Saxony, a Communist stronghold ; and Hörsing (1874– ?), the Majority Socialist Governor of the province, sent in police to occupy the area. The miners rose in rebellion and seized the mines ; and immediately afterwards the chemical workers at the great Leuna works, near Halle, joined the revolt. The new Communist leadership, egged on by Béla Kun, thought it saw its chance to bring about a general rising. It called for a general strike and urged the proletariat to seize power throughout Germany. There were a few local risings — for example, at Hamburg — and a good many sporadic acts of violence and sabotage — buildings blown up, railway traffic interrupted, and so on. But there was no mass strike, and the Government was able easily to suppress the movement. Mansfeld and the Leuna Works were taken by the military, and the whole affair collapsed — and with it the mass membership of the German Communist Party, which within a few months lost more than half of its 350,000 adherents. The Comintern at first gave its full backing to Béla Kun ; but Clara Zetkin went to Moscow, where she managed to see Lenin and persuade him that the rising had been a disastrous mistake. Nevertheless Levi, who had meanwhile been actually expelled from the K.P.D., was not restored to favour ; for he had published a pamphlet, *Our Road*, in which he vigorously attacked the entire strategy of the Party as calculated to divide, instead of unifying, the proletarian forces. A principal count in his attack was that the K.P.D. had set itself to stirring up the unemployed against the employed workers, by using the unemployed to beset work-places where the call to strike was not obeyed — a method which had led to internecine fighting among the workers and had disastrously alienated mass proletarian support.

Paul Levi, the most intelligent of the German Communist leaders, thus passed out of the movement, in which he had never been personally popular. A wealthy intellectual and a connoisseur of the arts, he had alienated many by his upper-class way of living and his airs of superiority. He was, however, a sincere left-wing Socialist, with a clear appreciation of the real state of social forces inside Germany and a sharp disapproval of the 'infantile disease' of leftism from which German Communism was suffering. His place in the leadership was taken by Heinrich Brandler (b. 1881), the leader in the Chemnitz revolt of the previous year, with August Thalheimer (1883–1948) and Paul Frölich (1884–1953), the ardent admirer of Rosa Luxemburg, as his principal lieutenants.

The troubles of the Communists did not end with the suppression of the attempted rising. *Vorwaerts*, the Majority Socialist organ, got possession of a large mass of documents containing the Communists' plans for acts of violence, and began to publish them in instalments in order to bring discredit on the Party. In face of these revelations, Ernst Reuter-Friesland (1889–1953), the secretary of the K.P.D., and other leading members resigned from the Party ; and those who remained at its head temporarily changed their policy and adopted a cautious attitude which endured for the next two years, until it was drastically reversed during the Ruhr crisis of 1923. Russia, in the meantime, had also changed its line with the inauguration of the New Economic Policy in April 1921 and the accompanying retreat from the attempt to force the pace of revolution in Western Europe.

Only for a few months, in later 1920 and early 1921, had the German Communists come near to becoming a mass Party by taking over the left wing of the U.S.P.D. This opportunity they had foolishly and recklessly thrown away, largely under the influence of the Comintern, then in its most intransigent mood. Zinoviev, Rakosi, and Béla Kun between them had played a major part in bringing disaster on the suddenly enlarged Party. Attempting to split the world Socialist movement into rival revolutionary and anti-revolutionary masses, they had succeeded in both Germany and Italy only in splitting the left, so as to reduce it to impotence, without making any impression at all on the masses. Right up to this point, Comintern policy — and, indeed, Russian policy too — had been dominated by the mistaken notion that, despite all appearances to the contrary, the proletariats of the Western countries *must* be ready for the Socialist Revolution, if only they were given a forthright lead. In this, no doubt, the wish fathered the thought ; for the Russians had been hard pressed both by the civil war and by their prodigious internal economic difficulties, and revolution in the West had seemed to offer the only prospect of release and help. In this hope Lenin had striven his hardest for a victory over the Poles that would have enabled the Russians to bring help to the German revolutionaries, and Zinoviev, as head of the Comintern, had sought to get the full Bolshevik gospel accepted by the left-wing Socialists of the West. But after the troubles in Petrograd in the early months of 1921, after the Kronstadt Rising, and after the ignominious collapse of Communism in Germany, it had to be recognised that the Russians' first task was to deal with their internal difficulties and that all hope of immediate Socialist Revolution in Western Europe had to be given up. The Russians were still convinced that the World Revolution was on its way ; but they could no longer look to it to help them towards an immediate solution of their own pressing problems.

CHAPTER VI

RUSSIA IN REVOLUTION AND
CIVIL WAR, 1917–1921

BOTH the Russian Revolutions of 1917 were, on the surface, urban. The most spectacular events of both were staged in Petrograd. There, when the soldiers had refused to turn their weapons on the demonstrators, the first Provisional Government was formed and the Republic proclaimed ; and there, less than nine months later, the Bolsheviks and the Military Revolutionary Committee carried out their almost bloodless seizure of power. But of course in neither case was what took place in Petrograd the decisive factor. The capital city gave the signal ; but what happened elsewhere, in the towns, in the countryside, and in the armed forces, settled the outcome. In and after February 1917, over the whole of Russia's vast territory, the old order rapidly crumbled away ; and, though it took very much longer after October for the new order to establish itself over all that was left of this territory, a substantial part of it came immediately under Soviet rule and, even where Lenin's writ did not run, power passed almost immediately in most areas into the hands of bodies which had no intention of letting the newly won land slip back into the possession of its former owners.

Over most of Russia the Revolution was, above all else, an agrarian Revolution. It had to be ; for despite the rapid growth of industry during the twenty or so years up to 1914, Russia remained overwhelmingly an agricultural country, with peasants — landed or landless — as by far the largest class. There could have been no Revolution without the peasants, not only because they were the main producers, but also because the army was made up mainly of peasants — and there could have been no Revolution had the army been prepared to suppress it. No doubt, it is equally true that the peasants could not have made either Revolution, in anything like the same form, without the townsmen. If the first Revolution had been exclusively a peasant affair it might have destroyed Czarism ; but it would have destroyed Russia, too, by breaking it up into fragments over which no common Government could have been re-established by any means. And, of course, if the matter had been left to the peasants, the second Revolution would not have occurred at all. There would have been a *jacquerie*, and a redistribution of the land in forms differing from place to place. There would have been in a sense a separate peace, even if there had been no peace treaty ; for the armies would have melted away in disorder and made for home. But there would have been neither the tragi-comic months of dual powers divided between the Provisional Governments and the Soviets nor the establishment, when this dualism finally broke down, of a new central authority capable of restoring unity and of creating a new Russia strong enough to terrify the capitalist world.

Nevertheless, the peasants did ensure the victory of the Revolution by one thing above all others — by seizing the land, instead of waiting in hope of a Constituent Assembly that would give it to them in due form. No doubt the Constituent Assembly, had it been allowed to continue its sessions, would have agreed to the handing over of the land to the peasants, if only because they had already taken it before the Assembly met. Dominated by the Social Revolutionaries, the Assembly could hardly have wished to take any other course. But would it have been summoned, or elected, when it was, had not the peasants, after months of vain waiting, taken matters into their own hands ? Certainly the Provisional Government was in no haste to call it together, at any rate until the peasants had confronted them with a largely accomplished fact. No less certainly, what subsequently ruined the chances of the counter-revolution was the fixed determination of the peasants not to be deprived of the land they had won. This it was that made every district occupied by a reactionary general utterly unsafe at every point not actually controlled by his armed forces, and so cut his supply lines and faced him with an impossible task in maintaining order. The peasants were no Communists, except where the reactionary invaders made them so against their will and instinct ; but they were revolutionaries against the old régime and against every attempt to resurrect it. Without their aid the Red Army could not have won the civil war.

True, the peasants contributed hardly any leaders of note to the new order. Even their own Party, the Social Revolutionary Party, was led not by peasants but mainly by intellectuals, such as Chernov, Avksentiev, and, on the extreme left, Marie Spiridonova and Steinberg. Peasant leadership, where it existed, was local, and did not look far beyond the village or group of villages. Even in the mainly peasant army, the spokesmen of the regiments came largely from workmen or members of the lower bourgeoisie. The peasants and peasant soldiers knew what they wanted — land and peace and, while they remained in the army, bread to eat. They hated the autocracy, the landowners as a class, and the officials who levied taxes on them, took them away as soldiers from their villages, and contemned them as inferiors. Beyond these desires and hates their politics did not go far. These, however, were enough to make the old order unrestorable when once it had broken down.

Any Government that hoped to establish itself in place of the vanished Czarist autocracy had to do everything it could to get the peasants on its side, at least to the extent of acquiescence in its authority. But none of the Provisional Governments dared in fact do much to meet the peasants' wishes. They were all committed to carrying on the war, either to the bitter end or at least until they could induce the Allied powers to join them in making peace ; and as the Allies would not agree to a negotiated peace, this meant in practice that all the Provisional Governments were committed to carrying on the war indefinitely, or as long as there were any soldiers left to fight. The Provisional Governments could neither give nor even promise peace. Nor could they even promise the peasants the land, on terms the peasants would accept, without destroying the foundation of their own precarious existence ; for the bourgeois elements in the successive coalitions under Lvov and Kerensky could assuredly not have been induced to agree to simply letting the peasants divide up the land among themselves. The most the Provisional Governments could even promise was that the land question should in due course be remitted for settlement to the Constituent Assembly — when it met ; and even that was too much for some of them when they considered of what elements the Assembly was likely to be made up. As for bread, somehow the armies and the cities were supplied with just enough food to keep them alive ; but even that the Provisional Governments could achieve only with the co-operation of the Soviets and the Trade Unions, which controlled the actual movement of supplies. In effect, the Provisional Governments — at any rate from June onwards — could not govern : they could only maintain a façade of authority by inducing the Soviets to countersign their orders.

When leading Social Revolutionaries and Mensheviks became members of these Governments, nothing was really changed. The men who were chosen for office were among those who were committed to carrying on the war and to maintaining a common front for this purpose with the liberal bourgeoisie. They could neither make peace nor acquiesce in the peasants' seizure of the land without breaking with their allies and setting up an entirely Socialist Government. This, however, they were wholly unwilling to do, both because most of them would not contemplate a separate peace on what were bound to be very unfavourable terms and, still more, because they were positively against turning the Revolution into a Socialist Revolution. Their reasons for being against this, to be sure, differed from man to man. The Menshevik members of the Government were hostile on principle, because they believed Russia to be unripe for Socialism and held that there must be a period of intensive industrial development under capitalism before it could become ripe. This did not prevent the Mensheviks from being in favour of socialising the land ; but they were altogether opposed, on Socialist grounds, to allowing the peasants to take it for themselves and divide it up. They were not, like Lenin, prepared to give up socialisation for peasant proprietorship in order to win peasant support. The S.R.s in the Government did not suffer from the same inhibition as the Mensheviks on the score of Russia's unripeness for Socialism ; but either they were wedded to making the great change in due democratic order through the Constituent Assembly, or they shrank back from a rupture with the bourgeoisie while the war was still in being. No less did they shrink back from the necessary condition of a purely Socialist Government — alliance with those Socialists who were against the war and prepared to make an end of it on almost any terms. During the months between February and October there was time for personal and factional antagonisms between Socialists to deepen and grow intensely bitter — above all, after the 'July Days', when the leading Bolsheviks were under arrest or in hiding and the struggle between 'defencists' and 'internationalists' had set up a sharp dividing-line — though even then Martov and his Menshevik Internationalist group stayed unhappily poised between the contestants. At no time was there any real possibility of an all-Socialist Provisional Government representative of all the Socialist factions. Lenin was the arch-traitor in the eyes of the 'defencists'; and the 'defencists' were, in Lenin's eyes, one and all traitors and betrayers of the revolutionary cause.

Unhappiest among the Socialists were the relatively small groups who were neither Bolsheviks nor 'defencists', such as Martov, Sukhanov — who has left a vivid and unforgettable first-hand account of these fateful months — or even Chernov, who entered the Government as Minister of Agriculture, but had been at Zimmerwald and occupied a left-central position among the S.R.s. Martov — or, to give him his actual family name, Yuly Osipovich Zederbaum (1873–1923) — next to Plekhanov the outstanding theorist of Marxism among the Mensheviks and widely regarded as the leader of the Party, was in a peculiar difficulty. At the head of his group of Menshevik Internationalists he strongly opposed the 'defencist' policy of the Menshevik majority; but he remained unwilling to split his Party and entirely opposed to what he regarded as the sectarian policy of the Bolsheviks. He wanted to end the war, but dissented utterly from Lenin's view that the only way of ending it was by international Socialist revolution, in the practicability of which he had no belief. This disbelief in the near approach of World Revolution confirmed his view that the Revolution in Russia could not be carried on to a Socialist stage; but he also shared the traditional Menshevik opinion that it was no business of Socialists to enter into coalition with the bourgeois Parties in conducting a capitalist Revolution. He therefore favoured bourgeois government checked and controlled by a strong and united Socialist opposition. The effect of this attitude was to isolate him and his group from both the defencists and the Bolsheviks ; and, as such a policy was not easy to explain convincingly to a popular audience, they tended to become rather a notable band of theorists than a mass Party. Continuing to count as a fraction of the still nominally united Menshevik Party, they were continually outvoted in it, and could exercise little influence on the course of events. Moreover, Martov himself, though few excelled him in power to analyse a situation, was apt to be irresolute in action and seldom gave his followers a clear practical lead. N. Sukhanov, a former Social Revolutionary who presently joined Martov's Internationalist group, saw this weakness in its leader, and also realised the impossibility of establishing any united Socialist front. In Sukhanov's view the gulf between defencists and internationalists was too wide to be bridged : what he wanted was a coming together of all the 'Zimmerwaldians' against the defencists. This, however, was impracticable unless the Bolsheviks could be brought in ; and from the moment of Lenin's return to Russia no chance existed that this could be achieved. For though, without Lenin, the Bolsheviks might have been induced to rally to any united attempt to create a 'Zimmerwaldian' majority in the Soviets, after his return there was no prospect of their agreeing to common action except on their own terms, which were bound to involve the displacement of the Provisional Government by a Soviet Government directly responsible to the mass organisations of the workers and soldiers and of such peasant groups as would accept a clearly proletarian leadership — and in practice dominated by their own Party. This would have meant passing straight from the bourgeois to the Socialist Revolution — which seemed to Martov an impossible step to take. Doubtless, the Bolsheviks, as well as the other fractions of the left, were calling insistently for a Constituent Assembly and thus appeared to be endorsing the claim that the structure of the new Russia should be settled by the verdict of the whole people and not by the workers alone. But for the Bolsheviks the Constituent Assembly was much more a stick for beating the Provisional Government than the forerunner of a democratic parliamentary régime. What they wanted — and they made no secret of it — was a dictatorship of the workers — of the proletariat aided by the poorer peasants — and the exclusion of other classes from any share in political power. They no doubt envisaged this class-rule as the dictatorship of a majority over a discredited minority ; whereas Martov and Sukhanov were alike afraid that it would mean in practice the dictatorship of the Bolshevik minority over the main mass of the workers.

Accordingly there was no real possibility of a common policy for the Bolsheviks and the Menshevik Internationalists or others who accepted the Zimmerwaldian label but were not prepared to move straight on from the bourgeois to the Socialist Revolution or to rest all their hopes on the speedy advent of Socialist Revolution in the other belligerent countries. There was, however, another group, the Mezhrayonists, or Inter-district Organisation, with whom the Bolsheviks were able to come to terms because this group was ready to accept just these principles of action. The Mezhrayonists, equally with Martov's fraction, were a group of leaders with no considerable mass following. They included, as we saw,[1] such outstanding figures as Lunacharsky, Uritsky, and Vorovsky, and above all Trotsky, who joined them immediately on his arrival in Petrograd. This highly significant group was at first held apart from the Bolsheviks because it regarded their methods as unduly sectarian. It accepted the main Bolshevik objectives, shared the Bolshevik belief in the imminence of the World Revolution, and wished to pass on at once from the bourgeois to the Socialist stage ; and even before the July Days it had reached the point of deciding to merge its identity in the Bolshevik Party. Its leader, Trotsky, as we saw earlier in this study,[2] had been for a long time before 1914 kept apart from the Bolsheviks because he disapproved of the extreme exclusiveness of Lenin's party policy and was trying, as a 'Conciliator', to build bridges between the Bolshevik and Menshevik fractions of Social Democracy. Trotsky was also, as we saw, the principal exponent of the theory of 'Permanent Revolution', rejecting the sharp distinction drawn by Lenin between the 'bourgeois' and the 'Socialist' Revolution and insisting that, in view of the weakness of the Russian bourgeoisie, the proletariat would be forced to take the lead and the responsibility in any successful revolution in Russia. On both these issues, the differences between his view and Lenin's had by 1917

[1] See p. 74.　　　　　　　　　[2] See Vol. III, Part I, p. 462.

been largely wiped out. Lenin had virtually come round to Trotsky's opinion concerning the necessary course of the Revolution in Russia; and Trotsky's 'conciliationism' had been undermined by the cleavage between defencists and internationalists, in which he was wholly on Lenin's side. There remained, as we saw,[1] the difference that, whereas Lenin, in his plotting for the second Revolution, put the main emphasis on the rôle of the Party, Trotsky stressed rather the rôle of the Soviets as the main agents and as the prospective exercisers of the coming proletarian dictatorship. This difference, however, did not seem considerable enough to keep them any longer apart, though it came to be very important at a later stage. Both saw the imperative need to win over a majority in the Soviets for the new Revolution, whether the Soviets or the Party were to be its chief makers. The Mezhrayonists therefore threw in their lot with the Bolshevik Party, and Trotsky became in August a member of the Party's Central Committee and its outstanding popular orator.

The Bolsheviks could thus absorb; but they could not at all easily co-operate on any other terms. They could not work with Martov, who refused to break finally with the Menshevik defencists; nor could they co-operate with the followers of Maxim Gorki (1868–1936), grouped round his newspaper, *Novaya Zhizn*. Even more difficult was it for them to come to any real understanding even with the extreme left of the Social Revolutionary Party — though they did for a few months actually share power with them in a coalition Government after the October Revolution and did in effect adopt, in dealing with the land question, the traditional S.R. policy, to the exclusion for the time being of their own. There was a deep unbridgeable gulf between the S.R.s and the Social Democrats — Bolsheviks and Mensheviks alike — because the Social Democrats believed that it was necessary for industrialisation to precede and prepare the way for Socialism, whereas the S.R.s were either against industrialisation or at least regarded it as quite unnecessary as a means to a Socialist order. The old controversy between Narodniks and Marxists was still very much alive in 1917. Whereas all the Social Democrats held fast to the idea of two distinct Revolutions, bourgeois and

[1] See p. 88.

Socialist — even if some of them had come to believe that the two might turn out to be rapidly successive stages of a single movement — the S.R.s had no use or place for the notion of a bourgeois Revolution, but thought of a single people's Revolution that would make the peasants the dominant force in the new society. No doubt, different groups of S.R.s conceived of this single Revolution in widely different terms. As early as 1906 they had divided into Maximalist and Minimalist fractions,[1] and the latter, who constituted the majority, had envisaged the Revolution as taking place by stages, of which the earlier would fall a long way short of setting up a Socialist society. But the Minimalist stage of the S.R.s was entirely different from the bourgeois Revolution contemplated by the Social Democrats : it was essentially agrarian, and had nothing to do with the development of capitalism or with bourgeois rule. The Maximalist stage, too, had little or nothing in common with the Socialist Revolution envisaged by the Marxists ; for though a majority of the 1906 S.R. Congress envisaged the possibility of a transitional period of peasants' and workers' dictatorship for the purpose of establishing a Socialist society, the transitory character of such a dictatorship was strongly emphasised, and it was taken for granted that after the new society had been set up, there would be a highly decentralised system of government resting on a foundation of universal democracy.

Among the S.R.s, Maximalists and Minimalists had not been at the outset rival factions. At their Congress of 1906 they had been in agreement that their goal was a completely Socialist society, resting mainly on agrarian foundations and on common ownership of land. Both administration of the land and the general control of the State were to be entrusted primarily to the local communes, in which the basic authority was to reside. The State was to be a loosely organised federal agency built up on this communal foundation, and the whole administration was to be carefully guarded against the dangers of bureaucracy and centralisation. The S.R.s, in their ideal objectives, were essentially the heirs of Bakunin and of the Narodniks, and not of Marx ; and this applied as much to their left as to their right wing. Their Minimum Programme, which was worked

[1] See Vol. III, Part I, p. 471.

out in considerably greater detail, was not an alternative to the Maximum Programme but an instalment of it — a statement of priorities rather than the expression of a rival doctrine. Both programmes were essentially revolutionary : no section of the S.R. Party believed in the possibility of worth-while reforms as long as the Czarist system remained. Their agreed first objective was a social revolution that would overthrow the Czar and make it possible to convene a Constituent Assembly, chosen by universal suffrage, to enact a new, democratic, federal constitution and to put the peasants in full possession of the land. This constitution was to embody recognition of full rights of self-government for all the nationalities included in the Russian empire, and was to provide for complete separation of Church and State. Besides these structural changes, the Minimum Programme provided for the establishment of complete freedom of expression of political opinion and for no less complete freedom of organisation — rights which were to be guaranteed by the Constitution as inviolable. In the economic field the Programme provided for encouragement to Trade Union development, and for Trade Union participation in working out plans for the democratic control of industry. It also required the general establishment of the eight-hours day and the enactment of protective industrial and social legislation ; but the Minimum Programme excluded the nationalisation of industry, on the ground that this could be acceptable only when the power of the State had been transformed from a reactionary into a democratic form of authority. State Capitalism and State Socialism were to be opposed as long as the State remained in the hands of reaction.

Most important of all were the parts of the Minimum Programme that dealt with the question of the land. All privately owned land was to be expropriated, without compensation to the previous owners. The land, including land already owned by the State, was to be put under the collective management of popularly elected local authorities, which were to parcel it out, either to individual tenants or to Co-operative groups, in such a way as to ensure that every peasant household should have enough to provide for its means of living. In order to help the tenants to put the land to the best use, Co-operative credit agencies were to be developed and the fullest encouragement was to be given to other forms of Co-operative activity — in marketing and purchasing of requisites as well as in actual cultivation. Consumers' Co-operation also was to be developed. A further feature of the Programme was the prohibition of all dealing in land, so as to prevent the emergence of a class of wealthy, labour-employing peasants hiring land from their neighbours and thus undermining the equality of village life. Further, to safeguard this equality, the local authorities were to impose rents or taxes on the occupants of the better holdings, and were to apply the proceeds to communal uses, such as land improvement.

This was a far-reaching Minimum Programme, clearly incapable of realisation except as the outcome of a comprehensive social revolution. It was not, however, Socialist in any ordinary sense of the term in that it contemplated the continuance of individual peasant cultivation, supplemented by a network of Co-operative agencies that were expected to lay the foundations for a fully socialised system. The Maximalist fraction dissented from the Minimum Programme, not so much because its adherents stood for more far-reaching immediate socialisation as because they demanded a more intensive policy of struggle by terroristic methods against the existing régime, and insisted on the necessity of a transitional system of peasants' and workers' dictatorship for the complete eradication of the old social structure. At the 1906 Congress a majority endorsed the view that such a dictatorship *might* prove to be necessary ; but a substantial minority voted against this concession, and the majority did not go beyond this conditional assent.

Soon after the Congress, which had resulted in the adoption of a common Programme including both the Minimum and the Maximum demands, the more extreme groups began to gather together in a Maximalist fraction. This fraction urged the need to maintain an active terrorist policy in face of the reaction which followed the defeat of the 1905 Revolution ; and it also rejected the alleged 'parliamentarism' of the leading members of the Party as expressed in the demand for a democratically elected Constituent Assembly. The Party leadership retorted in November 1906 by expelling those Maximalists who refused to accept the full verdict of the Congress. Thereafter, the excluded Maximalists constituted a small, extremist

Party of their own ; and this Party remained in being, though without much influence, in 1917. In the Second Revolution of that year the Maximalists sided with the Bolsheviks, but immediately afterwards appeared as advocates of democratic workers' control in industry through factory groups, in opposition to the centralised control which they regarded as being favoured by the Bolshevik Party. Tolerated during the early days of Bolshevik rule, they were able to publish a journal, *The Maximalist*, and to get a few of their members elected to the Soviets in Petrograd and elsewhere. But before long they were quarrelling hard among themselves ; and in April 1920 they decided by a majority to merge their organisation in the Communist Party. The principal dissidents then either left Russia or were arrested ; and the movement died out.

The Maximalists were not at any time more than a small fraction of the Social Revolutionary movement. At its other extreme stood another group, the Populists, whose best-known leaders were the exiles, Nicholas Chaikovsky and Felix Volkhovsky, who died in 1914. The Populists formed a distinct group in the pre-war Duma, and there represented the most moderate section of the broad Social Revolutionary movement. From 1914 onwards they strongly supported the war ; and under Chaikovsky they were later to take the lead in the Archangel Government set up under British auspices in 1918. The Populists, however, stood well outside the main stream of the S.R. movement, and never commanded any large body of support. At the head of the main central group of S.R.s stood, after the death of the chemist G. A. Gershuni (1870–1908), the intellectual Victor M. Chernov (1873–1952), son of a Czarist official and an active Socialist from his student days. Chernov, unlike most of the S.R. leaders, was a keen student of Marxism and well acquainted with the Socialist movements of the West. Before the Revolution he had lived long in exile, mainly in Switzerland, where he had edited the chief S.R. organ before the Revolution of 1905. In exile he had learnt to regard as obsolete the old Narodnik doctrine which looked to the building of a peasant Socialism on the basis of the ancient communes. He had also shed his opposition to industrial development, while retaining a strong objection to the extension of capitalistic large-scale methods to the countryside. He had even learnt to look to the industrial proletariat to play the part of vanguard in the coming Revolution, in which, in his view, it would supply most of the direction, with the peasants forming the main body of the army of progress. He had learnt, too, to reject the Narodnik way of thinking of the entire peasantry as constituting a single revolutionary class. In the Revolution, he said, the poorer peasants would contend against the rural bourgeoisie, while the urban proletariat dealt with the bourgeoisie of the towns. As for the bourgeois Revolution, to which the Social Democrats looked forward as a future event, Chernov placed it in the past, as having taken place already when the serfs were emancipated and supplies of workers for industry were thus made available from the country districts. Accordingly, there could be no place for a further bourgeois Revolution. Nevertheless, Chernov believed that the coming Revolution would have two stages, of which the first would establish a democratic Republic and give the land to the peasants, whereas the second would establish Socialism on the basis of a socialised agriculture in accordance with the S.R. Maximum Programme. Chernov believed that his 'Constructive Socialism' combined what was good in Marxism with what was good in Utopian Socialism. His thought was largely 'Western' and owed much to his contacts with Western Socialists ; but he remained convinced that the way to Socialism lay through the victory of the poorer peasants and was wholly antagonistic to the idea that Russian agriculture ought to go over to capitalistic methods of production.

Most of the S.R. leaders were primarily men of action, with whom a little theory had to go a long way. Chernov, on the other hand, was essentially a theorist rather than a man of action. He was also, because of his Western contacts, much more internationalist than most of them in his political outlook. Far from rallying to the side of the 'defencists' at the outbreak of war, he not only clung to the Stuttgart line but participated actively in the Zimmerwald Conference of 1915 and endorsed its demand for a people's peace. He adhered, however, to the side of the pacifist majority and not to Lenin's minority group which called for the ending of the war by universal proletarian revolution. At the time of the February Revolution he was still abroad. Returning to Petrograd early in April, he found the

S.R. Party at sixes and sevens, with its defencist right wing tending to rally to the support of Kerensky, and its left wing in lively opposition to the Government, while a vast mass of politically inexperienced recruits from the army and the intelligentsia wandered leaderless in the confusions of the time. He attempted to put himself at the head of this central group and to imbue it with some of his internationalist ideas. There was some surprise when, after the fall of Milyukov, he accepted the position of Minister of Agriculture in the new coalition Government, doubtless in the hope of influencing it both to make urgent peace proposals to the Allies and to take early steps to call a Constituent Assembly that would take the land problem in hand. As a Minister, however, he appears to have made no effective impression on his colleagues ; and his position in the Government was fatal to his prospects of gaining popular support. Wishing for peace, he found himself committed to a continuance of the war ; sincerely eager to get the land for the peasants, he had as Minister to do what he could to prevent them from taking it for themselves without waiting for the Constituent Assembly to give it them. He found himself under attack from the right because of his Zimmerwaldian record, and from the left as a hanger-on of the bourgeoisie and an opponent of Soviet influence. He was indeed evidently at a loss what to do, and unable to give his Party any effective leadership. During the July disturbances, he was actually seized and held captive by demonstrators against the Government, and was rescued by Trotsky, who ventured into the crowd to save him and brought him safely away. When, after the 'July Days', Kerensky constituted the third Coalition Government, Chernov was once again a member of it, and was thus involved in the great anti-Bolshevik witch-hunt of the ensuing weeks. He remained, however, the recognised leader of the S.R. Party, in which he still kept his central position and something of his old prestige as the outstanding inspirer of the Party's social doctrines. During the October Revolution, to which of course he was opposed, he had no opportunity of taking any significant action. When it was over, he continued to express his views without being molested until the Constituent Assembly met on January 16th, 1918. The Assembly chose him as its President against Marie Spiridonova, the candidate of the Left S.R.s : and he proceeded to deliver an opening address in which he recited his Socialist faith. Bukharin, for the Bolsheviks, answered him rudely, asking what sort of Socialism he had in mind and saying that 'a Socialism that would come about in two hundred years time' was pretty much the same as no Socialism at all. The Socialism the workers wanted, said Bucharin, was a Socialism that showed them how to act in the present, not the mere promise of an ideal future. Chernov had no chance to argue the question at the Assembly ; for next day the Bolsheviks locked it out of its meeting-place and told its members to go home. Chernov, called on by some of his colleagues to summon his supporters to its aid, refused, saying that he would be no party to the shedding of blood in internecine Socialist conflict.

After the dispersal of the Assembly Chernov stayed on in Russia. We find him next in Samara, where many leading S.R.s had come together, with a few Mensheviks, and were attempting to set up a new Provisional Government made up of members of the dispersed Constituent Assembly. Hardly had this Government been set up when the Czech legionaries captured Omsk, Samara, and a number of other towns, and so cut the Bolshevik Government off from contact with Siberia and a large part of East European Russia. Amid these confusions, other Provisional Governments made their appearance in Siberia and in the Urals. The new Siberian Government, dominated at the outset by the S.R.s, was speedily captured by right-wing counter-revolutionary elements ; and the Government of the Urals, established in July, was from the first mainly Populist and Cadet, though it had some small Menshevik support. In September, at a Conference held at Ufa, in the Urals region, it was decided to establish an All-Russian Provisional Government, with instructions to reconvene the Constituent Assembly early the following year. The Ufa Conference was presided over by the right-wing S.R., N. Avksentiev (1878–1943), who became head of the new Government, with another right-wing S.R., V. M. Zenzinov (1881–1953), as his principal colleague. Chernov, with the support of the Central S.R. Committee, opposed the formation of the Ufa Government, which included Cadets as well as Socialists and was plainly dependent on the counter-revolutionary forces under Admiral

Kolchak's command. Soon after its formation, the Red Army recaptured Samara. The Ufa Government remained in nominal existence till November 1918, when Kolchak overthrew it and proclaimed himself Supreme Ruler of All Russia. Avksentiev, Zenzinov, and other right-wing S.R.s fled abroad and settled down in Paris, where they continued to conduct a violent propaganda campaign against the Bolshevik Government and in favour of Allied intervention. The remaining S.R. leaders stayed on in the Volga area, but for the most part gave up armed resistance to the Bolsheviks. Chernov declared his intention of continuing an unarmed struggle against both extremes ; but the S.R. Party continued to melt rapidly away. Early in 1919 a group headed by V. K. Volsky and N. I. Rakitnikov went to Moscow and made its peace with the Government ; and in February of that year the Petrograd S.R.s held a conference at which they formally renounced all armed resistance. In response to these overtures, the Soviet Government re-legalised the S.R. Party, which had been banned the previous June. Chernov, who for the most part agreed neither with Avksentiev nor with Volsky, but did agree with the latter about the renunciation of armed force, was then able to resume his activities as a propagandist. In June he got together in Moscow a Congress of the rump of the Party, which proceeded to condemn both Volsky and Avksentiev. The Volsky faction thereupon left the Party, which was thereafter of little account and suffered increasing persecution. Chernov stayed on in Russia some time longer, and then escaped abroad, where he wrote an account of his experiences. His last appearance in Russia seems to have been in May 1920, when he arrived in disguise and made a speech at a meeting organised by the mainly Menshevik Printers' Union to meet the British Labour Delegation, then visiting Russia. F. I. Dan (1871–1947), the Menshevik leader, also spoke at the meeting. The end of the S.R. Party came in 1922, when its remaining leaders in Russia were tried for treason and condemned to death, after the Belgian Socialist leader, Émile Vandervelde, had been sent to Russia to act as counsel for the defence. Vandervelde and his Russian co-counsel, Muraviev, both protested against the conduct of the trial, and withdrew from the court before the verdict was given. The victims, though condemned, were not

executed, because the Government had given a promise to the
Western Socialist leaders that their lives should be spared.
Their fate in captivity remains, I think, for the most part
unknown. A number of them were produced from time to
time as witnesses at the great treason trials of the 1930s and
were required to give incriminating evidence against the victims
of these prosecutions — which some of them did, but others
had the courage to refuse to do. Of the leading figures, Abram
Raffailovich Gots (1882–1937) was at length shot in 1937, and
V. A. Karelin died or was killed at about the same time. Another,
the formerly prominent critic Ivanov-Razumnik, survived to
be made a prisoner in Lithuania by the Germans in 1941 and
died in Berlin two years later, leaving behind him Memoirs that
were subsequently published in New York. These contain a
vivid account of his experiences in prison and of the fate of
a number of his fellow Socialist Revolutionaries condemned
in 1922.

During the trial the prosecution made many attempts to
convict the leading S.R.s of complicity with the 'Whites' and
with the Allied interventionists during the civil war ; but no
real evidence of this was produced against the persons who
were being tried — though it was, of course, easy to show that
many S.R.s who were not on trial — such as Avksentiev and
Zenzinov — had been guilty of this crime.

Thus the once great Social Revolutionary Party passed
finally out of existence. Always an amalgam of many groups
and tendencies, it had owed what theoretical coherence it ever
had almost entirely to Chernov, who had been almost the sole
architect of its Programme in 1906 and had retained his leadership, despite his evident practical incapacity, because there was
nobody to take his place. There were, of course, other leaders ;
but none of them ever formulated a coherent policy. The S.R.
Party had been built up at the beginning as the champion of a
host of local peasant movements, each mainly concerned with
its own local problems. It had given expression to the common
elements of rural discontent — above all, to land hunger and
to sheer hatred of the whole Czarist system of landlordism
and repression. After its enormous expansion in 1905–6, it
had shrunk rapidly, and had been sharply divided over the
question of terrorist policy. This problem had been solved

after a fashion by the setting up of an autonomous secret terrorist organisation, which was allowed to go its own way without deeply implicating the main body of the Party ; but, after the exposure of Azev's [1] connection with the Czarist police, terrorism had fallen into discredit and had been officially renounced by the party leadership. Already, well before 1914, the Party was beginning to fall apart, as its right wing became more deeply involved in fostering Co-operative ventures, while the main body kept its essentially revolutionary outlook. As we have seen, the war issue divided it further, causing a deepening cleavage between the 'patriots' and the anti-war left wing. In 1917, during and after the February Revolution, it experienced an enormous growth, serving as the main focus of attraction both for the local peasant movements and for the mainly peasant soldiers. It also attracted a large body of hitherto unattached intellectuals and professional people, who knew little of Socialism and saw in it the most Russian of all the Parties supporting the Revolution. Thus overrun with newcomers, and short in any case of responsible leaders, the S.R. Party was unable to arrive at any coherent attitude. On the whole, it supported the successive Provisional Governments and especially Kerensky, who actually joined it after the Revolution had broken out. But this support, which was never solid, waned rapidly when it appeared that these Governments were giving the people neither bread nor peace, and were not even authorising the peasants to take possession of the land. In effect, well before October 1917, the S.R.s had ceased to be a single Party, and a large part of their following had gone over to a left wing which, though still nominally attached to the older Party, was already acting in alliance with the Bolsheviks to carry out a second, definitely Socialist, Revolution.

The Left Social Revolutionaries, who became fully organised as a Party only on the morrow of the October Revolution, were entirely distinct from the Maximalists, already discussed, who had split away from the main S.R. Party eleven years before. They were a new group born of the Revolution, at first as an undefined left wing of the widely embracing S.R. movement, but were sharply differentiated in attitude not only from its right wing but also from Chernov's central group. Chernov's

[1] See Vol. III, Part I, p. 449.

entry into the Provisional Government on his return to Russia was an important factor in causing them to organise as an independent fraction, though still without formal separation from the S.R.s as a Party.

Among the outstanding personalities in this new movement was the veteran Narodnik leader Mark A. Natanson (1850–1919), also known as Bobrov, who had long-standing connections with the S.R. Party and had been active in the 1905 Revolution. Natanson stood in 1917 on the extreme left of the S.R.s, as an opponent of all forms of co-operation with the bourgeoisie and of all support for the war effort. He was on the far left of the Zimmerwaldians, and looked to the ending of the war by universal Socialist revolution. He was not a Marxist, however, but a peasant leader of the school of Peter Lavrov — hostile to capitalist industrialisation and a believer in mass peasant revolt as the way to the new social order. The second outstanding figure was Marie Spiridonova (1885– ?), an immensely popular agitator who had made her great name in 1906 by assassinating an unpopular provincial governor. Other prominent leaders included B. Kamkov (alias Katz) and V. A. Karelin, who were on the movement's extreme left, and Isaac Nachman Steinberg (1888–1957), who became Commissar of Justice in the short-lived coalition Government of Bolsheviks and Left S.R.s set up after the October Revolution, and devoted the rest of his life, after the destruction of the Party, mainly to working for the resettlement of Jewish refugees in the West. Yet another was Alexandrovich, who represented the Left S.R.s in the Petrograd Cheka. He was shot in July 1918, after the disturbances that followed the assassination of the German Ambassador, von Mirbach, by another Left S.R., Jacob Blumkin (b. 1898), who survived to work for the Soviet régime under Trotsky, and was shot as a Trotskyist in 1929.

At any rate from May 1917, when the Social Revolutionaries held their Third Congress, this left wing was demanding an all-Socialist Government, an immediate peace, and the immediate handing over of the land to the peasants ; and during the ensuing months its members put themselves at the head of the local peasants who seized the land for themselves without waiting for the Government to give it them. Their numbers grew very fast, as Chernov's hold on the S.R. movement grew weaker ; and they won a large amount of support, not only in the countryside, but also among the sailors in the Baltic and Black Sea fleets and to some extent among the industrial workers. Their opposition to all compromise with the bourgeoisie and their attitude on the land question, as well as their opposition to defencism, brought them steadily closer to the Bolsheviks, from whom they differed chiefly in objecting to a centralised, closely disciplined Party and in their hope of winning over as many as possible of the Socialist Parties and fractions to support of a broad-based, all-Socialist revolutionary crusade. By August the S.R. party organisation in Petrograd itself had gone over almost solidly to their side, leaving the official S.R. leadership nearly isolated in the capital ; and they had also a large body of support in many of the local and provincial Soviets elsewhere. A definite break with the main S.R. Party followed in October, at the first meeting of Kerensky's pre-Parliament, when the Left S.R.s walked out, refusing to give any countenance to the defencist policy of the majority. They were strongly represented on the Petrograd Soviet's Military Revolutionary Committee, which Trotsky organised, but seem, even in October, to have been still opposed to an immediate insurrection. At all events they were not consulted by the Bolsheviks in planning the *coup* ; and such part as they took in it was arranged through the Soviet's Military Committee, as far as it was arranged at all. But on the day that followed the *coup* the Left S.R.s finally broke with the S.R. Party, by refusing to follow it when it seceded from the second Congress of Soviets as a protest against the Bolshevik seizure of power. A fortnight later they held their own first Congress, with numerous delegates from the provinces, and formally constituted themselves as a separate Party. At the outset they rejected Lenin's offer to form a coalition Government with the Bolsheviks, and made some attempt to negotiate for a broader Socialist coalition. But when nothing came of this they joined forces with the Bolsheviks, at the second National Congress of Peasant Soviets held early in December, to exclude the hostile S.R. elements and to elect a new pro-Bolshevik Peasant Executive. This action was immediately followed by their decision to join the Council of People's Commissars, with A. Kolegaev, their principal agricultural expert, as Commissar of Agriculture

— a key position — and with Steinberg in the hardly less important office of Commissar of Justice, and Alexandrovich in a leading post in the newly established Cheka.

The Bolshevik-Left S.R. coalition was short-lived. What brought it to an end was the Bolshevik decision to accept the Brest-Litovsk Treaty, which the Left S.R.s denounced as a betrayal of the revolutionary cause. They were not alone in this ; but, unlike the Bolshevik minority, they refused to accept the majority verdict and voted solidly against the Treaty at the fourth All-Russian Soviet Congress of March 1918. This involved their withdrawal from the Government and drove them into sharp opposition to the Bolshevik Party. What they demanded was that the Russian Government, instead of accepting the German terms, should set on foot a mass resistance to the Germans in the form of a revolutionary guerrilla war. The peasants and workers, they urged, should be called on to rise wherever the Germans came, to interrupt communications, and to commit acts of sabotage and terrorism which would make it impossible for the German armies to enjoy a moment's security. When this heroic policy was rejected, they did not give way. In June 1918 they publicly announced their intention of organising terroristic acts against the Germans, and they did their best to stimulate revolt in the German-occupied districts. On July 6th the youthful Jacob Blumkin, one of their members attached to the Cheka, succeeded in assassinating von Mirbach, the new German Ambassador, in his own embassy. F. E. Dzherzhinsky (1877–1926) and other Cheka leaders were held prisoners in their headquarters by a body of soldiers under Left S.R. orders ; and there were a few hours of fighting before they were evicted and the revolt suppressed. As no attempt seems to have been made to occupy other public buildings or to bring about a general rising, it is by no means clear what the Left S.R.s implicated in this affair were setting out to do. Marie Spiridonova and others flatly denied that any plans had been made for a rising ; and it seems most likely that a small group took action on its own, without the general support of the Party. Marie Spiridonova did, however, accept responsibility for authorising Mirbach's assassination ; and there is no doubt that the Left S.R.s' Central Committee was behind the policy of terrorism against the Germans.

What is surprising, in the light of later Bolshevik behaviour, is that after this affair the Left S.R.s were for the most part treated with singular mildness. Alexandrovich, indeed, was shot for his part in the Cheka affray ; but Blumkin, after escaping for the moment, was allowed to resume service under Trotsky, and Marie Spiridonova was left free to carry on her agitation. No doubt this was mainly because the Bolshevik leaders were well aware of the extreme unpopularity of the Germans, and of the great popularity both of Spiridonova herself and of the Left S.R. opposition to the Brest-Litovsk Treaty and to the further exactions which the Germans were enforcing during the ensuing months. It was also no doubt a factor that the Bolsheviks were hoping, with good chances of success, to win over the bulk of the Left S.R. following to their side, and could not afford, in the precarious conditions of mid-1918, to make further enemies. For the Left S.R. troubles coincided in time with the occupation of Omsk, Samara, and other cities by the Czech forces, with the setting up of rival Provisional Governments by the Right S.R.s and others in Siberia and the Urals, with the emergence of Admiral Kolchak as the formidable leader of the counter-revolution in arms, with the beginnings of serious armed intervention by the Allies, and with a grave decline in the popularity of the Bolsheviks themselves. The loyalty of the Left S.R.s to the revolutionary cause was beyond question, and the Government could not afford at that stage to drive their rank and file into mass revolt. What the Bolsheviks did was only to set on foot a process of weeding out the more active Left S.R. representatives from positions of influence and from the local Soviets, without definitely outlawing the Left S.R. Party. It was widely believed that, although the Central Committee of the Party, or at any rate a part of it, was deeply involved in the Mirbach assassination and in the Cheka affray, the main body of the membership had not been a party to these events, and may even have disapproved of them ; and despite strong German pressure for action against those responsible, the Bolsheviks were reluctant, for the reasons given, to resort to drastic measures. The Left S.R. leaders who were put on trial in November 1918 received only mild sentences : Marie Spiridonova, though sentenced to a year's imprisonment, was actually set free at once under an amnesty.

Despite the mildness of the action taken against the Left S.R.s, their Party soon began to break up. Small groups acted on the instruction to organise guerrilla warfare against the Germans and thus contributed to the difficulties of the occupation as the German armed forces began to crack later in the year. Many Left S.R.s joined the Communist Party and took part in the Civil War on the side of the Soviet Government. A residue of the Party carried on as best as it could a campaign of propaganda for democratic control of industry and against the requisition of peasant supplies organised by the Government. In the spring of 1920 a group, headed by Steinberg, was even allowed for a time to publish its own journal, *Znamya*, which demanded industrial control by the Trade Unions, the control of agriculture by peasant Unions, control of distribution by the Co-operatives, and a decentralised structure of government, and also discussed the question of the permissible limits to the use of violence and terrorism as political weapons. But *Znamya* was finally closed down in May 1921, and in the following year the remaining Left S.R. leaders were either liquidated or managed, like Steinberg, to escape abroad. Natanson, nearing 70, was allowed to go abroad after the troubles of 1918, and died the following year. Marie Spiridonova, rearrested early in 1919, was sent to a sanatorium, from which she soon escaped. She remained free, in hiding, until October 1920, when she was rearrested. What happened to her thereafter is unknown. Kamkov was sent to prison, to be brought out in 1938 to give evidence against Bukharin, with whom he was alleged to have conspired twenty years before to kill Lenin, Stalin, and others, in order to form a Trotskyite Government — an absurd allegation which Kamkov refused to corroborate.

Of all the Russian Socialist Parties of 1917 the Left S.R.s were the most idealistic and in some respects the most attractive. They were essentially a peasant Party, descended from the Narodniks and convinced that there was no need for Russia, on its way to Socialism, to pass through an intervening phase of capitalist industrialisation. They were not planners, and were keenly hostile to every kind of centralisation and bureaucracy: like Rosa Luxemburg in Germany, they believed, above all, in the creative force inherent in the masses and in the capacity of these masses to throw up their own leaders and build a new society of their own choosing. Their mission, as they saw it, was to rouse the masses by every means in their power, not stopping short of peasant risings or of terrorist assassination when it could help the cause, but hostile to such other forms of terrorism as served all too often to cloak acts of sheer banditry or wanton violence. Until the war came, they did not differ sharply from the main body of S.R.s, whom they sought to stimulate to greater activity rather than to oppose. They were, however, no compromisers ; and when the right wing and centre of the S.R. Party allowed themselves to become entangled in coalitions with the bourgeois Parties in the cause of national defence, they reacted sharply and found themselves allied with the Bolsheviks in opposition to the successive coalition Governments and to their war policy. The State they saw as the enemy of freedom no less after the February Revolution than before ; and they set out to fight it by every means open to them. Their faults, from the standpoint of successful revolutionary action, were an inability to distinguish between the possible and the impracticable, and an incapacity either to compromise or to pretend, or to organise action on more than a local scale. They were not, for the most part, outright Anarchists, but had much in common with them, in method if not in theory. The Bolsheviks quite naturally found them impossible as colleagues after the seizure of power, but could not at once do without them because of the extent of their influence among the peasants, whom they alone seemed capable of bringing over in substantial numbers to the side of the second Revolution. It was their policy in relation to the land that Lenin induced his Party to adopt in the critical period during and after 1917, when the Bolsheviks joined the Left S.R.s in telling the peasants to seize the land without waiting for anybody's consent and acquiesced in the establishment of an individualist peasant economy against their own doctrine, well knowing that any attempt at immediate collectivisation would destroy the Revolution by setting the mass of the peasants against it. The Bolsheviks, however, in borrowing the policy of the Left S.R.s for dealing with the immediate emergency, did not at all become converts to it or prepared really to share power with its exponents. They only took rather longer to liquidate the Left S.R. Party, and readily accepted from it converts who were prepared to join their ranks and help them in destroying the influence of the old S.R. Party, whose leaders were either ranged against them in the Civil War or, at best, not prepared to make common cause with them against the 'Whites'.

During his brief tenure of office as Commissar of Agriculture in the Bolshevik-Left S.R. coalition, Kolegaev was largely responsible for drawing up the definitive law on land policy. Under this law the redistribution of the land was taken out of the hands of the special Land Committees to which it had been entrusted before the coalition was formed, and was handed over to the peasant sections of the local Soviets. This was an important change because the Land Committees had been dominated by the old S.R. Party, whereas the new system gave the final authority to the general Soviets controlled by the Bolsheviks and Left S.R.s. The Land Law itself was based largely on the old S.R. Programme and provided for distribution on a basis designed to assure the means of living to every peasant household. But it also laid great emphasis on the need to introduce improved methods of production and to give encouragement to collective cultivation as economically superior to individual peasant farming. The earlier Bolshevik decree had contained no reference to the matter of collective cultivation, which had been shelved at a moment when the Bolsheviks were aiming, above all, at securing a maximum of peasant support for their assumption of power. The inclusion of a declaration in favour of collective farming, under the auspices of a Commissar belonging not to the Bolshevik but to the Left S.R. Party, was a very significant sign that the Bolshevik Party, though ready to make very large immediate concessions to the peasants, was by no means prepared to abandon its intention of socialising not only the land but the peasants as well, at the earliest convenient opportunity. Nor does it seem that the Left S.R.s were against this on principle, though they would undoubtedly have offered strong opposition to *enforced* collectivisation. The Left S.R.s, unlike many of the members of the old S.R. Party, were definitely Socialists and were by no means unaware of the danger that under a system of individual cultivation the peasants might easily turn into a very conservative force. They hoped to prevent this largely by the fullest possible development of Co-operative methods, as against enforced collectivisation. The Bolsheviks objected to this, on the ground that voluntary Co-operatives were apt to be most to the advantage of the better-off peasants ; and on this ground they often accused the Left S.R.s of taking the side of the richer peasants against the poor. But in fact the main support of the Left S.R.s came from the poorer peasants, and the last thing they wanted was to encourage the growth of inequality in the new structure of rural life. The issue between them and the Bolsheviks was not that of collective versus individual farming, but rather that of enforced as against voluntary development of collective methods.

The real strength of the Left S.R.s at the height of their influence is difficult to estimate. In the Constituent Assembly of January 1918 they had a mere 40 delegates, as against 370 from the old S.R. Party. This, however, gave no indication of their real influence, as the elections took place before the definitive split. They were very much more strongly repre-sented in the Peasant Congress, from which they were able, with Bolshevik help, to oust the old S.R.-controlled Executive and replace it with their own nominees. By the beginning of 1918 they were certainly well ahead of the old S.R.s in popular influence in the countryside in the areas under Soviet control ; but this was partly because so many of the old leaders had already been thrust out of their positions of authority. They were also, as we saw, very influential among the sailors ; and in the towns they were able to work in well with the rapidly developing Trade Unions because of their stand in favour of democratic workers' control. If, after the events of July 1918, their following melted rapidly away, this was mainly because the exigencies of civil war and War Communism made strongly against their libertarian principles and forced many who sympathised with their aspirations into the Bolshevik ranks.

After the October Revolution, while the Social Revolu-tionaries were splitting into entirely separate rival Parties, the Mensheviks showed an opposite tendency towards reunion. Martov's Internationalist following had been virtually a separate Party during the months between the Revolutions, being cut off from the majority both by its opposition to the war and by its rejection of coalition with the bourgeois parties. Practically, the second of these issues disappeared for the time being with the October Revolution ; the first also vanished with the signing of the Brest-Litovsk Treaty. Thereafter, advocacy of co-operation with the bourgeois Parties meant open rebellion against the Soviet Government ; and opposition to the Treaty meant nothing unless it carried with it either advocacy of a revolutionary war against the Germans or an appeal for Allied intervention. But only a very few Mensheviks were prepared to adopt any of these courses. Consequently, the rival Menshevik factions found themselves drawn together again by a common opposition to the Bolsheviks, but restrained from carrying their opposition to extremes. In Petrograd and Moscow Martov's Internationalists had already become the predominant group ; and in the Soviet-controlled parts of Russia what remained of the old right-wing majority soon came to accept his leadership.

The policy followed by the Mensheviks in these areas after the Bolshevik *coup* was essentially one of peaceful, constitutional opposition. They would not, said Martov and Dan, engage in any attempt to overthrow the Bolshevik régime by force ; but they would use such opportunities as were left to them to demand freedom of speech and organisation, freedom and independence for the Trade Unions and the Co-operatives, and the maintenance of the effective power of freely elected Soviets as against the autocratic practices of the Bolshevik Party. Some of them demanded the convening of a new, freely elected Constituent Assembly ; but most of them had no objection to Soviet rule, or to the exclusion of the non-producers from voting rights, provided that the Soviets were chosen by really free elections, with a full right for opposition Parties to organise and run candidates. They insisted that the workers' and peasants' dictatorship was being undermined and perverted by the Bolshevik Party's assumption of power to enact enforceable decrees without Soviet agreement and consent, that the Soviets themselves were being hand-picked and not freely elected, and that, even so, they were being forced to renounce their real authority to still more hand-picked Executives and Committees, which the Bolsheviks found it easier to control. They were also very insistent on the need for autonomous

Trade Unions, untrammelled by party control and authorised to play a major part in the shaping of industrial policy ; and they demanded a limited freedom for private enterprise, subject to an overriding system of planned state control that closely resembled the New Economic Policy actually introduced on Lenin's initiative in 1921.

In effect, within a few months of the October Revolution, the reunited Menshevik Party was doing its best to play the part of a constitutional opposition within the Soviet system. It was, moreover, allowed for a time a considerable amount of freedom to act in this way. Up to the middle of 1918 it enjoyed a substantial representation on the Soviets in most of the bigger towns and was able to publish a large number of party journals and newspapers, in which it vigorously criticised the Government for its offences against democracy. Then, in June 1918, the Bolsheviks, faced with growing difficulties arising out of renewed German aggression, Left S.R. discontents, and the beginnings of counter-revolutionary civil war, suddenly changed their line. The Menshevik papers were closed down, and orders went out to expel their representatives from the Executive Committees of the Soviets and from other public positions. At the same time, the Menshevik and S.R. Parties were both declared illegal, and arrests of active Mensheviks began to be made in considerable numbers, though most of those arrested were fairly soon set free. The following month the ban was extended to Maxim Gorki's group, *Novaya Zhizn* being closed down.

This policy, however, was partly reversed in November 1918, when the decree banning the Menshevik Party was repealed, and the Party regained a limited freedom of action, which lasted until the following spring. Then there were again numerous arrests of Mensheviks ; but the general ban was not re-enforced. During the summer of 1919 the Mensheviks issued a party Manifesto reaffirming their main political and economic demands, and also an appeal to their followers to join and support the Red Army in the civil war. Their exclusion from the Soviet Executive Committees had not driven them out of the Trade Unions ; and in April 1920 they still mustered a significant number of delegates (70 out of about 1000) at the Third All-Russian Trade Union Congress, and had a much more considerable following in many individual Trade Unions. The rope was, however, already being tightened ; and it was drawn tighter still when, in the course of 1920, Martov delivered a series of attacks on the policy of the Comintern in splitting the Socialist movements of the Western countries. Martov, despite these attacks, was allowed to go to Germany in the autumn of 1920 to attend the Halle Congress, at which the U.S.P.D. debated the question of joining the Third International. He there made a speech attacking the Twenty-one Points, but, having got out of Russia and being in failing health, decided not to go back. Instead, he founded in Berlin a Menshevik journal, of which many copies were smuggled into Russia during the ensuing year or so. Dan replaced him as leader of the Mensheviks inside Russia, and was able to carry on some propaganda during the next few months. Then, early in 1921, a fresh round of arrests began ; and in February of that year Dan too decided to emigrate and, with a number of his colleagues, was allowed to leave the country unmolested. Against the Mensheviks who remained in Russia an increasing persecution set in at the time of the Kronstadt Rising — in which they had no part — and of the introduction of the New Economic Policy — which as we saw bore a considerable resemblance to what they had been advocating for some years. The N.E.P., even more than the Kronstadt Rising or the industrial troubles which preceded and accompanied it, was probably the chief reason for the final liquidation of the Menshevik Party during the first half of 1921. The more concessions the Bolsheviks had to make in order to save the situation of the Russian economy, the less could they afford to allow open criticism of their doings.

The Menshevik Party thus came to an end within about four years of the opening of the Revolution. It had, however, during the period between 1917 and 1921, contributed many individual recruits to the Bolshevik Party, including not a few who came to occupy high official positions. During 1917 there had been a steady drift of left-wing Mensheviks into the Bolshevik ranks ; and this drift continued after the second Revolution. No doubt, in subsequent purges of the Communist Party these recruits always ran a more than average risk of being weeded out — and a high proportion of them were actually liquidated in the course of Stalin's great purges during the 1930s ; but quite a number of them remained for a long while to serve the Soviet Government in official positions, especially in diplomacy. Many went over to the Bolsheviks, and very few to the counter-revolution, during the civil war ; and many more, without becoming Communists, renounced their opposition and were employed in minor non-political administrative posts, especially in economic work. All this meant a continuous erosion of the organised Menshevik opposition, which nevertheless kept a considerable hold in some of the Trade Unions — notably the Printers — almost to the end. In the Trade Unions the Mensheviks often joined forces with discontented elements in the Bolshevik Party to demand greater autonomy and a larger measure of workers' control. When they could not be got rid of by other means, the Bolsheviks, during the period of War Communism, learnt the way of shutting down the recalcitrant Unions or branches and setting up new ones in their place. But this took time ; and the Mensheviks were able to keep their position in the Unions for some time after they had been driven out of any positions of influence in the Soviets.

The Bolshevik attitude to the Mensheviks differed from their attitude to the Social Revolutionaries, even of the left wing. For the Mensheviks claimed to be Marxists — indeed to be better Marxists than the Bolsheviks, whom they accused of perverting the Marxist doctrine ; and many of them were old comrades in the revolutionary struggle — for example, Martov had worked very closely with Lenin. Moreover, there was not even in 1917 an entirely clear line of separation between the Bolshevik and Menshevik fractions of the Social Democratic Party. Outside Russia there had been, right up to the Revolution, 'Conciliators', who were trying to bring the rival fractions together — for example, Trotsky ; and inside Russia there were still in some places Social Democratic groups which had never accepted the division. In addition, the war issue had divided the Mensheviks. Plekhanov and his 'patriotic' group had broken away from them on the right ; and on the left Martov's Internationalists were acting more and more as a distinct Party in opposition to the group that had become associated with Kerensky and the successive Provisional Governments.

What was common to the Mensheviks was the view that backward Russia was not yet ripe for the Socialist Revolution and could not become ripe for it for some time to come. The Mensheviks had very little following among the peasants and put few hopes in the revolutionary capacity of the peasantry, save in a destructive sense. The peasants might help to overthrow the old order ; but in the Menshevik opinion they could do little or nothing towards creating the new order that was needed — nothing either towards establishing Socialism or towards the development of capitalism as an instrument of economic progress. Socialism, they thought, would have to be the creation of the industrial proletariat ; but the industrial proletariat could not become strong enough for this task until it had undergone much more extensive growth under capitalist conditions. Accordingly it was indispensable that the overthrow of the Czarist autocracy should be followed by the establishment of a democratic political structure under which capitalism could develop freely, and thus bring the proletariat to the degree of maturity needed for its emergence as the ruling class. The Mensheviks were united in wishing to halt the Revolution at the bourgeois state and in holding that a premature attempt to move on to the Socialist stage would of necessity lead to disastrous betrayal of the revolutionary cause, to civil war, to despotism, and to famine and economic breakdown.

In February 1917 this need to stop short for the time being at the bourgeois stage of the Revolution was still the official view of the Bolsheviks as well as of the Mensheviks. The difference between them was that the Mensheviks drew the conclusion that the Socialists, while helping on the bourgeois Revolution, should keep out of any form of coalition with the bourgeoisie and should form an opposition which should press working-class claims for improved conditions under capitalism without carrying these claims to such lengths as would render capitalism unworkable ; whereas the Bolsheviks, more conscious of the weakness of the Russian bourgeoisie, were prepared, if the necessity arose in order to defend the Revolution, even to enter into temporary coalition with it against the autocracy — though only, of course, with the intention of turning on it later, when the conditions for Socialist Revolution had become ripe. There was also the further difference that most Mensheviks envisaged a longish period of economic development under bourgeois rule as needed to prepare the way for a Socialist assumption of power ; whereas most Bolsheviks envisaged this period of transition as relatively short. Up to 1914, however, hardly anyone except Trotsky, who was neither Bolshevik nor Menshevik, had reached the conclusion that the two Revolutions might turn out to be merely successive, or even overlapping, stages in a single, continuous revolutionary process.

This Trotskyite view rested, as we saw,[1] on an appreciation of the weakness of the Russian bourgeoisie and on a belief that the industrial proletariat, because of this weakness, would find itself compelled to take the leadership of the Revolution even in its 'bourgeois' phase. It was also Lenin's sense of the feebleness of the bourgeoisie that had led him to the view that the Socialists might need to assume a share in government responsibility in order to ensure the victory of the bourgeois Revolution over the autocracy. Lenin, however, held fast, up to 1914, to the belief that there would have to be two distinct Revolutions — bourgeois and Socialist — separated by an interval of time, and rejected the idea of a single Revolution in which both would be combined. But after 1914 Lenin was convinced that the way was clear for World Socialist Revolution, irrespective of the ripeness or unripeness of any particular country. This brought him into *de facto* agreement with Trotsky, though they argued on different bases. But it left the Mensheviks, who by no means shared Lenin's belief in the imminence of World Socialist Revolution, undisturbed in their opinion that Russia's immediate task was to replace autocratic by bourgeois-democratic rule, and that only countries already well advanced in capitalism could be ripe for Socialist Revolution.

The Mensheviks were, in effect, Westernisers who accepted in full, as a pattern for action in Russia as well as elsewhere, the German Social Democratic conception of Socialism as destined to be reached by way of a democratic conquest of political power made possible by the high development of industrial capitalism. They made, in applying this doctrine to Russian

[1] See Vol. III, Part II, p. 955.

conditions, altogether too little allowance for the sheer incapacity of the Russian bourgeoisie either to defeat Czarism or to govern the country if Czarism were successfully overthrown. The situation that arose after the February Revolution plainly showed how far astray they had gone in estimating the powers of the Russian bourgeoisie, which neither played any real part in bringing that Revolution about nor showed any capacity of riding the storm when the autocracy had lost its power. It also appeared plainly that the Mensheviks had not only grossly overestimated bourgeois capacity, but also no less grossly underestimated the rôle of the peasants ; whereas Lenin had seen clearly both the incapacity of the bourgeoisie and the vitally important part the peasants would inevitably play. Thus, after February 1917, the Mensheviks had to choose between rallying to the side of the bourgeoisie in the successive coalitions and standing aside from the immediate struggle — unless they were prepared to give up their conviction that it was premature to make any attempt to give the Revolution a Socialist character. As, for most of their leaders, this conviction was fundamental, they were forced to choose between backing first Milyukov and then Kerensky and having no clear policy at all. Some of them, headed by Tseretelli, chose the first alternative : the Internationalists, under Martov's leadership, chose the second, and in doing so forfeited all ability to put themselves at the head of the Revolution.

Under these circumstances, it was inevitable that there should be a drift of unhappy Mensheviks towards the Bolshevik camp ; and it was also inevitable that the Bolsheviks should look hopefully, if also with suspicion, for converts from Menshevism as the dissolution of the bourgeois-democratic régime became more and more apparent. That more Mensheviks did not go over to the Bolsheviks before the October Revolution was, I think, mainly due to the extreme suspiciousness with which Lenin and most of the old Bolsheviks received potential converts and to the already highly disciplined organisation of the Bolshevik Party. This sectarianism left many Menshevik waverers hovering on the brink, and made it impossible, for personal as well as ideological reasons, for the left-wing Menshevik leaders to take the plunge. But the Martov wing at any rate was far too deeply Socialist and Internationalist to entertain any thought of going over to the counter-revolution after the Bolshevik seizure of power. Its adherents either followed their leader into the attempt to build up a constitutional democratic opposition to the Bolsheviks, while taking their side in the civil war, or went over individually to take service under the Bolshevik order and become absorbed into the Bolshevik administrative machine, in which they were, for the most part, treated ever afterwards with deep suspicion by the Bolshevik leaders, and in many cases ultimately weeded out or liquidated under charges of treason.

So far, in this consideration of the Menshevik attitude, I have left aside the very special case of the Transcaucasian Mensheviks, whose history followed a different course largely because they were cut off for a time from the area of the new Russian Soviet Republic, and thus became the victims both of their own dissensions and of the power politics first of Germany and Turkey and then of Great Britain. At the time of the October Revolution the Bolsheviks had little following in Transcaucasia except at Baku — an old storm-centre of revolution. In Georgia the Mensheviks had a considerable following : in Armenia and also in Azerbaijan, outside Baku, Socialism of all sorts was weak and undeveloped, and national antagonisms were strong. There were a good many smaller national groups besides the Georgians, Armenians, and Azerbaijanians ; and there were also sharp religious differences between Christians and Moslems. Immediately after the October Revolution a Transcaucasian Commissariat was set up at Tiflis, mainly under Georgian control, and recognising a rather vague allegiance to the new Russian State to be established by the forthcoming Constituent Assembly. This Commissariat was not Socialist, and functioned side by side with a regional Workers', Peasants', and Soldiers' Soviet dominated by the Georgian Mensheviks. It signed an armistice with the Turks in December 1917. Then came the Brest-Litovsk Treaty, about which the Transcaucasian authorities were not consulted, though under it the Russians agreed to surrender certain areas — Kars and Erzerum to Georgia, and the Abadan district of Armenia to Turkey. Objecting strongly to this, the Commissariat retaliated by proclaiming an independent Transcaucasian Federal Republic, which fell to pieces almost at once and was replaced in May

1918 by three separate Republics — Georgia, Armenia, and Azerbaijan. Baku, under Bolshevik control, proclaimed a Soviet Republic of its own. The Turkish armies speedily overran Armenia and Azerbaijan ; and their separate Republics collapsed. Georgia saved itself only by signing a treaty with the Germans, giving Germany control of its resources for the period of the war, and by concluding with German aid a treaty of peace with Turkey. The Germans then forced Russia to recognise Georgia's independence in a treaty supplementing that of Brest-Litovsk. At this point the Georgian Mensheviks felt strong enough to displace the previous Government and take power themselves, with Noah Jordania (1869–1953), hitherto President of the Georgian Soviet, as Prime Minister.

Meanwhile, the British had advanced from Persia into Azerbaijan, and had overthrown the Baku Soviet Republic ; and in the collapse of Germany and Turkey in the autumn of 1918 British forces occupied all the chief Transcaucasian towns, but left the Georgian Menshevik Government in office under their supervision. The British Government undertook to support Georgia's claim to independence at the Paris Peace Conference ; but the Russian Whites — Kolchak and Denikin — refused to agree to this. By the end of the following year the British forces had evacuated Transcaucasia (except Batum, where they remained until July 1920) ; and, left to themselves, the Transcaucasian Republics had to face the growing power of the Bolsheviks after their victory in the Civil War. The Azerbaijan Government left in power by the British was overthrown in April 1920 by a Communist rising in Baku, and an Azerbaijan Socialist Republic was proclaimed. But the Russians, busy with the Polish War, had no forces to spare as yet for establishing their authority over the rest of Transcaucasia. Instead, they signed a treaty with the Georgian Republic confirming the recognition of its independence. In Armenia the Communists attempted to seize power, but were defeated. The Sèvres Treaty of August 1920 recognised Armenia's independence ; but Kemal's forces invaded the country, and the Armenian Government collapsed. Only then, in November 1920, did the Russians advance into Armenia and proclaim an Armenian Soviet Socialist Republic, which proved unable to maintain itself without Russian aid. There was a revolt, which was put down by the Red Army, and the Soviet Government was restored to power.

Thus, only Georgia still kept its precarious independence. The Georgian Mensheviks tried to save themselves by getting the support of the Western Socialists ; and a Socialist delegation, including Ramsay MacDonald, Vandervelde, and Kautsky, visited Georgia in September 1920 and brought back a very favourable report. The Georgian Government then applied for admission to the League of Nations. It was not accepted ; but the Allied Supreme Council recognised Georgia's independence in January 1921. Meanwhile in September 1920, at the Soviet-inspired Baku Congress of Eastern Peoples, the Georgians were charged with violent acts of repression against national minorities in Georgia, and there was a rapid deterioration of relations with the Russian Soviet Republic. Finally, in February 1921, the Red Army, accompanied by a force of Georgian Bolsheviks, marched in and captured Tiflis. The Menshevik Government was overthrown, and a Georgian Socialist Soviet Republic was proclaimed. Lenin gave special instructions that the Georgian Mensheviks were to be leniently treated ; and an amnesty was announced in their favour, but was ignored by Stalin, who conducted a ruthless campaign of repression against them. Most of the Menshevik leaders, however, escaped abroad and established themselves in Paris. Some remained and came to terms with the new Bolshevik régime.

The Georgians, who alone — apart from the mixed population of Baku — really counted for anything in this confusing sequence of events, thus became the puppets successively of the Germans, the British, and the Russians, only to fall under Bolshevik rule as soon as the Russians were free to attend to their affairs after the conclusion of the Civil and Polish Wars. Numbering no more than two millions, the Georgians were evidently incapable of maintaining themselves as an independent State without external aid, and were bound to fall victims to one or other of their more powerful neighbours. True, nationalities no more numerous had been able to secure Russian recognition of their right to independence under bourgeois régimes in Latvia and Estonia ; but these small States owed their success partly to Allied support and partly to Russia's need for a 'window in the West', through which trading relations could be opened up. Georgia had no such advantage and survived only as long as the Russians had their hands full elsewhere. The Russians, however, were in a difficulty because they could hardly deny that the Georgians, equally with the Finns, the Poles, the Latvians, and the Estonians, had a claim to national self-determination if they wanted it. Their qualms on this account — and also perhaps the Georgian origin of Stalin and other leaders—help to explain both the Russian preparedness to recognise the Georgian Republic in 1918 and in 1920, and Lenin's plea for leniency in the handling of the Georgian Mensheviks in 1921.

The Georgian Mensheviks, during their troublous tenure of power, followed out the approved Menshevik policy. They made no attempt to turn backward Georgia into a thoroughly Socialist country. On the contrary, they did their best to encourage capitalist development and to establish a bourgeois-democratic, rather than an outright Socialist régime. There was, in effect, nothing else for them to do, in view of the country's economic backwardness and of its dependence, through most of the Mensheviks' tenure of power, on the support of countries which would certainly not have tolerated a fully socialised régime.

Closely associated with the Mensheviks was the Jewish Bund, a Social Democratic organisation which claimed to be recognised as the representative of the Jewish workers throughout the old Russian empire, but had its main strength in Poland and Lithuania. The Bund, as we saw,[1] had been in and out of the Russian Social Democratic Party during the years up to 1914, mainly on this issue, on which it was opposed by both Lenin and Rosa Luxemburg. In social doctrine it was, broadly speaking, Menshevik ; and some of its leaders, including Rafael Abramovich (1879–?), were active in the Menshevik Party during 1917. Mikhail Lieber (1880–1937), a violent opponent of the Bolsheviks, who was finally executed by them in 1937, was its principal spokesman in the Petrograd Soviet. It remained in existence as a separate organisation until 1921, when its surviving members were finally absorbed into the Communist Party as the result of an arbitration award made by

[1] See Vol. III, Part I, pp. 471 and 483.

the Comintern. A year earlier the Bund had agreed by a majority vote to join the Communists ; but its leaders tried to hold out for the preservation of a status of partial autonomy, which ran directly counter to the centralism of the Communist Party. In default of agreement, the issue was referred to the Comintern, which, of course, settled it in favour of the complete dissolution of the Bund as a distinct organisation. The Bundists in exile, who rejected this going over to the Communists, continued their activities mainly as Mensheviks, as long as any remnant of Menshevism survived.

It remains only, in order to complete the tale of the Russian opposition groups, to add a few words about the Anarchists. By far the greatest of the Russian Anarchists was, of course, Prince Peter Kropotkin, with whose ideas and career I have dealt in previous volumes of this History.[1] Kropotkin, after many years of exile, chiefly in Switzerland and in England, returned to Russia in 1917 and spent there the closing years of his long life in a mood of growing disillusionment as the Revolution took a course entirely contrary to his hopes. He died in February 1921, just before the Kronstadt Rising ; and his funeral provided the last occasion on which the Russian Anarchists were able to make a public appearance. Kropotkin, the great libertarian advocate of 'mutual aid', was left unmolested in Russia because of his age and his immense prestige, though he did not conceal his complete disapproval of Bolshevik theory and practice. Too old and ill to play any part in public affairs, he lived on into his seventy-ninth year as a 'grand old man' belonging to a past epoch. He had no direct following in the new Russia, though many of the Left Social Revolutionaries as well as the Anarchists owed much to his ideas. With Kropotkin out of the picture, Russian Anarchism, in any ideological sense of the word, was not at any stage of the Revolution a powerful independent force. There were small Anarchist groups in Petrograd and in other cities during the critical months of 1917 ; but they were too weak to count as a major element in the Revolution. Sukhanov gives some account of the Anarchist headquarters at the Durnovo villa in Petrograd in June 1917, whither he was sent by the Soviet to appeal to them not to appear armed at the demonstration of the 18th of

[1] See Vol. II, Chapter XII, and many references in Vol. III.

that month. He was told by their spokesman in the Soviet — Bleichman — that they did not recognise the Soviet's authority — it was the servant of the landlords and the bourgeoisie — that they admitted no authority outside themselves, and that they proposed to demonstrate armed or unarmed as the spirit moved them. Sukhanov tells later of the bloodless capture of the Durnovo villa, which the Anarchists had evacuated in good time, during the 'July Days'. He appears at the outset to have regarded them as a somewhat formidable group, but to have been greatly reassured by meeting them on their home ground and to have thereafter dismissed them as harmless.

But, though the professed Anarchists did not count for much as an organised group, Anarchist and Anarcho-Syndicalist tendencies were of greater account, especially inside the Left Social Revolutionary Party and the Trade Unions. The Anarchists themselves were not, of course, a Party : that would have been against their principles. They were a sect, and Anarchistic notions extended far beyond their ranks, manifesting themselves both in the more extreme demands for workers' control in industry, and, on a much greater scale, on the extreme left of the peasant movement. Yaroslavsky's very unsatisfactory and dishonest *History of Anarchism in Russia* has practically nothing to say about them except in the latter aspect. For him, the arch-Anarchist was the Ukrainian peasant leader Nestor Makhno (1889–1934), whose forces ran amok in the countryside, and even captured substantial towns, during the German occupation and the subsequent Civil War.

In the Revolution of 1917, Yaroslavsky says, the Anarchists played no significant part. They became of any importance at all only after the October Revolution, when they began to penetrate some of the Trade Unions — notably the Bakers — and to agitate for Trade Union independence of the Government. Even then, they counted, except in the Ukraine, only as far as they came to be allied with the Bolshevik Workers' Opposition and with the urban section of the Left S.R.s. Later, in 1921, they appeared as one of the agencies supporting the industrial troubles which culminated in the Kronstadt Rising. The Anarcho-Syndicalists, he says, held their first conference in August 1918, and set up their League of Anarcho-Syndicalist Communists in Moscow only in 1920 — when it was quickly liquidated. During the Civil War some of the Anarchist groups managed to procure arms and established fortified strongholds in Moscow, Petrograd, and other cities, as bases for raids on bourgeois property, which they seized and divided up. This sounds more like mere brigandage by criminal elements than like the work of any ideological Anarchist movement.

There were, however, real ideological Anarchist groups in Russia, as distinct from those it was merely convenient to brand with the name. Among these probably the most important was the *Nabat* (Alarm) group, which included Voline (Vselvolod Mikhailovich Eichenbaum, 1882–1945), and the Ukrainians Fanis and Aaron Baron and P. Archinov (1887–?), who rallied round Makhno in his earlier exploits, when he was leading the anti-German revolt in the Southern Ukraine. Makhno himself,[1] originally a school-teacher, was not of much account as a theorist, though he was imbued with Anarchist ideas and has been credited in some Anarchist quarters with much greater theoretical importance than he really had. He was essentially a leader of peasant revolt and a 'man of blood', who conducted marauding bands about the countryside, and carried out a series of appalling massacres including terrible anti-Jewish pogroms, but achieved no stable organisation in the areas he controlled. Intermittently, he fought against the Whites after the Germans had gone, and for a time he was recognised as a commandant in the Red Army until, refusing to merge his bands in it, he was excluded and treated as an enemy. Finally, after losing most of his following, he crossed the border into Rumania and disappeared from history. But right on into 1920 he was still a force to be reckoned with, though, despite pressure from the Nabat group, he made no real attempt to put his Anarchist theories of free, non-governmental society into practice.

Two other Anarchists deserve a mention — Alexander Berkman (1870–1936) and Emma Goldman (1869–1940), though their main activities took place outside Russia, to which they came back only in 1920 and in which they stayed for less than two years. Berkman, Russian-born, had lived in the United States for about thirty years before his return to Russia,

[1] For Makhno, see further, p. 608.

where he at once became active in the Anarchist movement.
He was prominent in connection with the Kronstadt Revolt of
1921, and subsequently wrote a history of it, proclaiming it as
the beginning of the Fourth (Anarchist) Revolution. Emma
Goldman had long been the leader of the American Anarchist-
Communists and a prominent figure in the Anarchist International. She had suffered repeated imprisonments in the
United States. She soon found, on her return to Russia, that
she liked the new Soviet system as little as the capitalist Governments she had left behind ; and she joined in the agitation for
a 'Fourth Revolution' to be based on freely elected Soviets
which would make an end of the authoritarian Bolshevik-
Communist State. Both she and Berkman, surviving the
Kronstadt affair, left Russia in 1922 and became leading
figures in the Anarchist wing of the anti-Bolshevik movement.
In Russia itself, neither played a significant part.

CHAPTER VII

THE REVOLUTION IN AUSTRIA-HUNGARY: AUSTRIA, HUNGARY, CZECHOSLOVAKIA

THE Austro-Hungarian empire, as we saw in the preceding volume of this study,[1] was already threatened with dissolution well before 1914. In 1910, of its 51 million inhabitants, no one national group accounted for as much as a quarter. The two most numerous language groups — Germans and Magyars — numbered respectively about 12 and about 10 millions — a long way short of a majority, even taken together. There were about $8\frac{1}{2}$ million Czechs and Slovaks, divided between the Austrian and Hungarian sections of the Dual Monarchy — roughly $6\frac{1}{2}$ millions under Austria and 2 millions under Hungary. Serbs, Croats, and Slovenes together accounted for about 7 millions, also partly in the Austrian and partly in the Hungarian section. The 5 million Poles were almost all under Austrian rule, as were the great majority of the 4 million Ukrainians or Ruthenians. There were more than 3 million Rumanians, mostly under Hungarian rule, and more than three-quarters of a million Italians, under Austria. Finally there were about a quarter of a million Vlachs and gipsies — two quite distinct racial and linguistic groups, both widely scattered, mostly in the Hungarian part of the Dual Kingdom.

These national groups were at widely different stages of development and of national consciousness. The Austrian Socialists, as we saw,[2] had for a long time been trying to work out ways of recognising the cultural claims of the various nationalities without disrupting the unity of the empire, not because they felt any loyalty to it in its existing form but because it was necessary to find ways in which workers belonging to different nationalities that were greatly mixed up territorially could co-operate as members of a common movement, both politically and, even more, in Trade Union affairs. The

[1] See Vol. III, Part II, Ch. XII.   [2] See Vol. III, Part II, p. 520.

pre-war Austrian Social Democratic Party, at any rate up to the Czech dispute of 1907, even prided itself on being a 'Little International' — the forerunner of a wider international Socialist community to be established by the efforts of a united working class. It was indeed a federation of Parties, each representing a particular nationality and autonomous in its own affairs, but all linked together in a Reichspartei which held periodic conferences of the federated Parties and acted together as a single Party in the Austrian Reichsrath.

Austrian Socialism, however, had no unity of organisation with Hungarian Socialism ; and the Austrian 'Little International' was in fact made up mainly of Germans, Czechs, and Poles, with other nationalities playing only a minor part. The relatively weak Hungarian Socialist Party had its main strength at Budapest, and was dominated largely by Jewish intellectuals. Its rank and file was very mixed, consisting of Magyars, Slovaks, and many other elements ; but it played little or no part in the working out of any particular theory of the place of nationality in the working-class struggle. The important theorising on this issue was done mainly by German Austrians who had to face the developing influence of Czech nationalism and its threat to disrupt the unity of the Socialist and Trade Union movements of the Austrian, as distinct from the Hungarian, part of the Dual Monarchy.

The Czech Social Democratic Party, in opposition to the largely middle-class Czech National Socialist Party, formed part of the Austrian Social Democratic Reichspartei ; but the majority of the Czech Trade Unions in Bohemia had broken away from the Austrian Trade Union Centre in 1907, and had aligned themselves with the Czech national movement. This breakaway was supported and fostered by the Czech Social Democratic Party under Antonín Nemec (1858–1926), despite that Party's continued membership of the federal Austrian S.D.P. In Moravia, however, and in other parts of Austria, the Czech workers remained attached to the All-Austrian Trade Union Centre in Vienna. The Trade Union split was debated at the Amsterdam International Socialist Congress of 1910, which decided against the Czech separatists ; but the dissidents refused to accept the verdict of the International and insisted on maintaining their separate Trade Union organisation. Their contention was that, whereas politically the need for autonomous national Parties and for a federal structure was recognised, the Austrian Trade Unions were highly centralised, and refused to agree to any system of regional autonomy. The Trade Union Centre retorted that, as Czech, German, and other workers were often employed side by side in the same establishments, it was impracticable to split up the Trade Unions on national lines without destroying their effectiveness in serving the common interests of the working class.[1]

The Polish problem caused much less trouble because, as we saw, the Austrian Poles of Galicia felt themselves to be considerably better off under Austrian rule than their co-nationals in Russian and German Poland. In Galicia the main problem facing the Austrian Socialists was that of the large Ukrainian minority which, oppressed by the Poles, had a fellow-feeling with the Ukrainians under Russian rule. But the Ukrainians in Galicia were largely a primitive peasant people, among whom Social Democracy had only a small following. The Russian Social Revolutionary movement, or rather its Ukrainian section, had an easier appeal to them than the Marxist Social Democracy of the Austrian Party.

The relations between Germans and Czechs thus constituted the heart of the problem for the Austrian Social Democratic Party ; and, as we saw, the pressure of Czech nationalism — itself mainly in its origins a bourgeois movement — had been great enough to lead to a split in the Trade Union ranks. The old-established Czech Social Democratic Party, though affiliated to the federal Reichspartei of Austrian Socialism, had insisted on establishing a separate Trade Union movement of its own ; and although the Austrian Social Democratic Party had tried to deal with the situation by constituting itself as a federation of a number of national Parties, all accepting a common direction, and had succeeded on this basis in keeping the political adherence of the majority of organised workers in Bohemia and Moravia as well as of the large Czech contingents of workers employed in Vienna and elsewhere, it had not been able to prevent the development of a considerable separatist tendency in the Czech Social Democratic movement, quite apart from the Czech National Socialist

[1] For a further account of this dispute, see Vol. III, Part II, p. 533.

Party, which was only mildly socialistic and acted in fairly close collaboration with the Czech bourgeois nationalists led by Masaryk. The strong preponderance of German elements in the leadership of the Austrian Social Democratic Party made these conflicts unavoidable — the more so because the German Austrians could not help being greatly influenced by the powerful Social Democratic Party of Germany, which held so dominant a position in European Socialism and in the Second International up to 1914. There were indeed in the ranks of Austrian Socialism not a few, such as Engelbert Pernerstorfer (1850–1918), who foresaw the collapse of the Austrian State and looked forward to the absorption of German Austria into the German empire. This pan-Germanism, however, involved a head-on conflict with Czech nationalism ; for in Bohemia and Moravia Czechs and Germans were so intermingled that it was impracticable to unite the Austrian Germans with Germany without at the same time bringing the Czechs under German rule and perpetuating their separation from the Slovaks of Hungary — which neither were the Czechs prepared to accept nor most of the Germans among the Austrian Socialists prepared to force upon them. Accordingly, the majority of the Austrian Socialists clung to the notion of a reformed Austrian State within which there could be complete equality of national groups together with a large measure of cultural autonomy, but were at the same time anxious to preserve the essentially German intellectual quality of the Austrian Social Democratic Party and to keep on the best possible terms with the increasingly powerful German Social Democracy. This was the attitude of the unquestioned leader of the pre-1914 Party — Victor Adler (1851–1918) — who had begun his career with pan-German leanings, but had modified his views when he came to be the chief organiser and inspirer of the Austrian 'Little International'. The closeness of contact between German and Austrian Social Democracy also appeared in the considerable places occupied in the S.P.D. by Socialists of Austrian birth. Both Kautsky and Rudolf Hilferding (1877–1942) were Austrians, and a good many other Austrians, among them Adolf Braun and Friedrich Stampfer, held important positions in the extensive German Social Democratic press.

We have seen that, when war actually broke out in 1914,

the Austrian Social Democratic Party — but not its counter-part in Hungary — rallied to the patriotic side. It did indeed protest strongly, before the actual outburst, against the terms of the Austrian Government's ultimatum to Serbia ; and it would have been heartily glad of both Russian and German agreement to stand aside, so as to localise the conflict and give mediation a better chance of settling it without war. But Victor Adler reported to the International Socialist Bureau at Brussels that the state of patriotic feeling in Austria was too excited to allow the Austrian Socialists to come out decisively against the Serbian war ; and when the Russians and Germans came in, he and nearly all the other leaders instinctively took the German side. A few of the younger Socialists, including Adler's son, Friedrich (b. 1879), were against the Party's decision ; but for the time being they were helpless and dismayed.

Most of the Slav adherents of Socialism within the Austro-Hungarian empire could not be expected to take the same line, in relation to a war against Slavic peoples. Many of the Southern Slavs were bound to sympathise with Serbia and to look on Russia as a possible source of succour for their national causes ; and many Czechs were bound to see in the war a possible chance of national liberation. The Poles, because of their hatred of Russia and their fear of a Ukrainian uprising, were likely to take the Austrian side ; but hardly anyone could help realising that the war, unless it ended in a speedy victory, might lead to the break-up of the multi-national empire. None of the national groups was strong enough in 1914 to attempt positive rebellion, even if it had wished to do so. The conscripts obeyed the summons to join the Austro-Hungarian armed forces, and the workers throughout the country remained at work to keep the army and the population supplied. But many of the conscripts went unwillingly ; and as soon as it became plain that there would be no runaway victory of the Central Powers, the Czech nationalists went systematically to work abroad to prepare the way for an Allied recognition of Czechoslovak independence and thus aligned themselves de-cisively on the side of the Allies, carrying with them the separate Czech Socialist Party, but not, at the outset, the Czech section of the Austrian S.D.P., which, under the leadership of Bohumil

Smeral (1880–1941), followed the German section in its policy of supporting the war.

As the struggle was prolonged, the peoples of Austria-Hungary suffered severe and increasing privations which brought into being a growingly intense desire for peace. Before long Czechs began to desert from the armed forces in increasing numbers ; and Masaryk and his lieutenants, who had gone abroad on the outbreak of war in order to press the Czech claim to independence on the Allies, began to build up, mainly out of war prisoners, armed Czechoslovak units for service with the Allied armies. The Czechs who had settled in the United States were drawn in to provide finance for the exiled nationalist movement ; and Masaryk managed to win promises of recognition for an independent Czechoslovak State from one Allied Government after another.

Up to the autumn of 1916, however, there had been no really serious internal threat to Austria-Hungary, except from the Czechs. Then three events in rapid succession greatly altered the situation. In October 1916 Friedrich Adler shot dead Count Stürgkh, the Austrian Prime Minister, as a demonstration against the war ; and the deed was widely popular.[1] The following month the old emperor, Francis Joseph, died and was succeeeed by Karl, who was known as an advocate of reforms that would give the subject nationalities greater rights within a federal Hapsburg empire. On top of this came, in February 1917, the Russian Revolution, which was acclaimed by all the Socialists and naturally raised high hopes among the Slav subjects of Austria-Hungary. Friedrich Adler at his trial delivered in defence of his action a challenging speech which was a fierce accusation of the empire and its war policy and did much to wean even the German Austrians from support of the war. Karl meanwhile called on the Hungarian Government to reform the narrow Hungarian franchise by extending the vote to persons with army service. The Tisza Government refused to do this, and resigned ; and a new Government, pledged to the reform, replaced it. The Austrian Reichsrath, which had been in abeyance since 1914, was summoned to meet at the end of May 1917, and at once showed its changed temper when the Poles demanded a united, wholly

[1] See p. 38.

independent Poland, the Czechs a self-governing Czech State as part of a new federal Austria-Hungary based on freedom and equality of all national groups, and the Slovenes the union of all the Southern Slavs within the empire into a single independent State still under the Hapsburgs, but completely self-governing in its own affairs.

Before this, in March 1917, the new Emperor had attempted to open negotiations secretly with the Allied countries for a separate peace. The negotiations broke down mainly because Italy refused to make any concessions from the territorial claims which the Allies had accepted in the secret treaties arrived at in order to bring the Italians into the war. The Austrian Government then approached Germany and tried to persuade the Germans to join it in an attempt at a negotiated peace ; but the German Government refused and even threatened to turn its arms on Austria if the Austrians made a separate peace. Meanwhile the new Hungarian Government failed to induce the Magyar-controlled Hungarian Parliament to accept the franchise reform ; and it was even feared that, if the Emperor attempted to force it through, Hungary would secede from the empire and continue the war with the Germans as allies.

Then came the Bolshevik Revolution in Russia, followed a few months later by the Brest-Litovsk Treaty, which included the recognition of an independent Ukraine At Brest-Litovsk the Ukrainian delegation pressed for the inclusion, in their new State, of the Ukrainian parts of Austrian Poland ; and the Austrian negotiators were forced to agree, not to this, but to the cession of a small area and to the recognition of an autonomous Austrian-Ukrainian State in East Galicia and Bukovina. This infuriated the Galician Poles, who were determined to keep their hold on the Ukrainian part of Austrian Poland, as well as to share in the just-recognised independence of Russian Poland. The Austrian Government had been forced to accept Ukrainian independence largely by the hope of getting supplies from the Ukraine to remedy the disastrous food shortage in Austria, which had already led to widespread strikes in the cities in January 1918. But few supplies arrived ; and in effect the Ukrainian districts, as well as Polish Galicia, almost broke away from Austrian rule. These districts were destined later to become a prey to Petlyura, who, after appearing on the scene as a Ukrainian leader, proceeded later, as we shall see,[1] to do a deal with the Poles.

Meanwhile, in 1917, America's entry into the war and President Wilson's Fourteen Points had aroused fresh hopes of peace in Austria. The Government, however, could not sue for peace on the basis of the Fourteen Points because the Hungarian Parliament still refused to make any concession to the claims of the Hungarian national minorities. Austria-Hungary, therefore, remained in the war under the ever-increasing threat of sheer dissolution, and the Government was compelled to set its hopes on the success of the great German offensive of early 1918. When this failed, the break-up of the Austro-Hungarian empire became inevitable. Then, in September, the Bulgarian front broke and the armistice between the Allies and Bulgaria laid Hungary open to direct Allied attack. The Magyar units in the army clamoured to be sent home to defend their native land. The Austrian Government, at the end of its tether, announced that Austria was to be refashioned as a federation of free States and, two days later, on October 3rd, joined the Germans in asking President Wilson for an armistice. The Poles promptly proclaimed their independence in Warsaw ; and the Czechs, who had already been recognised as co-belligerents on the Allied side, formed a Czechoslovak Provisional Government in Paris, while in Prague the Czechs in Bohemia-Moravia independently displaced the Austrian authorities and assumed power without fighting. The Ukrainians convened a National Council to settle their country's future. Other Provisional Governments established themselves at Sarajevo, Trieste, Laibach, and elsewhere. The old empire, despite continued Magyar insistence on the integrity of the Hungarian subject lands, was definitely at an end. In Austria itself, the Germans set up their own national State, and Victor Adler, on behalf of the Social Democratic Party, called for its adoption as a federal State into the German Reich.

AUSTRIA

In Austria itself the process of disintegration had gone a long way before the final collapse of October 1918. The two

[1] See p. 609.

Revolutions in Russia had produced a deep effect in stimulating anti-war feeling and in arousing hopes of national independence. Friedrich Adler's speech at his trial had also done a great deal to influence the attitude of Austrian Germans who had supported the war in its earlier stages. In January 1918, while the peace negotiations were proceeding at Brest-Litovsk, a great wave of strikes, beginning at Wiener-Neustadt, had spread over Austria and had even extended into Hungary, paralysing the munition factories and giving rise to huge demonstrations which demanded peace as well as bread and less tyrannous conditions of employment. These great strikes were in part a hunger-movement, provoked by a reduction in the already inadequate bread ration ; but they took on everywhere a political character. They failed to develop into an insurrection mainly because the soldiers who were moved into the industrial districts to repress them were mostly peasants from the Slav areas, whose political consciousness was low, and of whom many did not speak the language of the strikers. There could be no successful insurrection as long as most of the army was prepared to obey orders to shoot at the insurgent workers ; and under severe military repression the strikers were forced back to work. They had barely gone back when the strike movement spread to Germany, there to be similarly defeated by military force. But in both countries, though the strikers were beaten, their action began the process of internal disintegration which prepared the way for the subsequent Revolutions. Moreover, in Austria the great strikes were followed, on February 1st, 1918, by the mutiny of 40 vessels of the Austrian fleet in the Bay of Cattaro. The mutineers arrested their officers and hoisted red flags, but remained in the Bay, exposed to the fire of powerful shore batteries and also to the danger of attack from a numerous fleet of German submarines in the vicinity. Threatened with bombardment and submarine attack and not knowing what to do next, the mutineers were finally induced to surrender. Their leaders were then arrested, four of them shot out of hand, and a much larger number imprisoned pending trial. The Austrian Government did all it could to keep the affair secret ; but Julius Braunthal (b. 1891), then an artillery officer stationed at Cattaro, managed to get the news of what had happened through to Victor Adler in

Vienna, and Adler, by threatening mass action if further executions were ordered, induced the authorities to limit further sentences to periods of imprisonment. This mutiny, though unsuccessful, also played its part in the disintegration of Austria-Hungary, and helped to prepare the way for the subsequent collapse.

The new Austrian State set up by the German members of the Austrian Reichsrath on October 21st, 1918, was still in form part of the Austrian Kaiserreich, though that Reich had in fact dissolved. Only on November 12th, the day following the Emperor's abdication, was a German-Austrian Democratic Republic formally proclaimed, as the sequel to a revolutionary movement in Vienna. At the same time as the Republic was set up, the Assembly declared it to be 'a component part of the German Republic', which had just been proclaimed by Scheidemann in Berlin. The new Austrian Republic claimed jurisdiction not only over the old lands of the Austrian Crown, except those peopled by non-German national groups, but also over the predominantly German districts in Bohemia and Moravia, which were also claimed by the new Czechoslovak Republic. The Allies, however, promptly prohibited the *Anschluss* with Germany and recognised the Czechoslovak claims to the whole of Bohemia and Moravia, and also to Slovakia, the Ukrainian area of Sub-Carpathian Ruthenia, and a part of Silesia. They also decreed that the new Austrian State should bear the name of Austria, instead of Austrian Democratic Republic. As against the loss of the German areas in what became Czechoslovakia, Austria was enlarged in the east, at the expense of Hungary, by the acquisition of the Burgenland; but nearly three years passed before the new frontiers were finally defined and occupied. When they were, Austria became a small State of about 6½ million persons, of whom nearly 2 millions were in Vienna and its immediate environs. Vienna, which had been the capital of an empire of more than 50 million persons, was suddenly turned into the grossly over-populated centre of a small, largely agricultural State, surrounded by other States which were soon busy raising tariffs against its exports and replacing the imperial civil, banking, and commercial services of the erstwhile capital with new national services under their exclusive control. Economically, the new Austria was an almost unworkable unit ; and it was also subject to serious political disabilities because, whereas the Socialists controlled Vienna and a few other towns, the rest of the country was dominated by the Catholic Christian Social Party, the traditional anti-semitic enemy of Social Democracy, or by the pan-German Nationalist Party. The elections for a Constituent Assembly, held under proportional representation and adult suffrage in February 1919, gave the Social Democrats 69 deputies, the Christian Socials 63, and the Nationalists 26. These three Parties, deep though their antagonisms were, formed a coalition, with the Socialist Karl Renner (1871–1950) as Chancellor, and the leader of the left-wing of the Socialist Party, Otto Bauer (1881–1935), who was but newly returned from imprisonment in Russia, as Minister of Foreign Affairs. Yet another Social Democrat, Karl Seitz (1870–1950) was chosen as President of the new Parliament and, as such, became acting President of the Austrian Republic.

The Austrian Social Democrats, though without a majority, were the dominant force in the Republic in its early days, and were in unquestioned control of Vienna, its disproportionately populous centre. They had been carried to power on a wave of mass unrest and rebellion against the old order throughout the Austrian empire, and had found themselves masters of what was left after that empire had dissolved. Immediately, their control of the Government was the outcome of the Revolution in Vienna itself ; and, in Vienna, it was in their hands to set up, for the time being, whatever régime they wished. Some of the working-class leaders looked to them to follow the Russian example by establishing a Workers' and Soldiers' Republic resting on the authority of the Councils which had sprung up everywhere, in the factories and in the armed forces. The Austrian Socialists, however, made no attempt to do this, though they did set to work to ensure that the small army allowed to them should be loyal to the Republic. They granted the soldiers full civil rights, including the right to have Trade Unions ; they carefully chose officers on whose loyalty they thought they could rely ; and they tried to make sure of a politically educated army. They also made haste to proclaim the eight hours' day for industry, and to give the factory committees an assured legal status. But instead of trying to create a Soviet Republic, they set to work to build the new order on foundations of parliamentary democracy ; and despite the strength of revolutionary feeling among the workers, they were able to secure the support of this policy by the great majority. A small left wing broke away and set up an Austrian Communist Party ; but this got only a scanty following and was never able to win even a single seat in the Austrian Parliament. The most critical moment for the new Republic in its early days came when the Hungarian Communists, having amalgamated temporarily with the Social Democrats, established the Soviet Republic in Budapest and summoned the Austrians to follow their example and come to their aid.[1] But the small group which then attempted a Communist rising in Vienna got no mass support and was easily put down without any resort to the employment of counter-revolutionary forces, such as Noske was using in Germany, and without there being left behind the legacy of hatred between Socialists which Noske's methods involved.

The reasons for this difference, and also the reasons against setting up a Soviet régime in Austria, are clear enough. The Austrian Social Democratic Party, as it existed in 1918–19, was definitely a left-wing Party, in the sense that its most active and influential leaders, Otto Bauer and Friedrich Adler, were well on the left, and even its moderate leaders, after Victor Adler's death in 1918, such as Karl Renner, Karl Seitz, and Friedrich Austerlitz (1862–1931), the formidable editor of the celebrated *Arbeiter Zeitung*, stood far to the left of those of the German Majority Socialists. In Vienna especially the hold of the Social Democratic Party on the workers was immensely strong, not only politically, but also culturally and in every aspect of social life. Viennese Socialism, much more than German, was an entire way of living : the activities of the Party penetrated into everything — into music, drama, travel and holidays, education and sport, no less than into political and Trade Union affairs. The workers' concerts organised by David Bach were world-famous ; and the great Vienna daily, the *Arbeiter Zeitung*, edited by Austerlitz, was much less a newspaper than a daily journal of opinion in which every sort of issue, cultural as well as political or economic, was freely

[1] See p. 246.

discussed at an astonishingly high cultural and literary level. The culture was indeed essentially German-Austrian, and the roots of the Party were in the German-Austrian section of the people. But that, after the dissolution of the old empire, was a source of strength rather than of weakness. Above all, in Vienna, as the Communists soon discovered, the hold of Social Democracy on the workers was much too strong to be shaken off.

There were also very strong reasons of expediency against any attempt to turn the new Austria into a Soviet Republic. The truncated Austrian Republic could not exist without help from outside ; and the only possible sources of immediate help were the States with which the Austrians had been at war. Even in the long run the new Republic could hardly hope to be able to feed its citizens adequately out of their own products ; and there were no resources that could be used to pay for imports, even if the Allies would allow them to be brought in. The Republic depended for its very existence on Allied recognition and on Allied help in the reconstruction needed to put the country back on its feet. Accordingly, as in Germany, fear of what the Allied Governments might do acted as a powerful deterrent from any measures likely to offend them. Moreover, there were strong internal reasons against any action calculated to antagonise the non-Socialist part of the nation. Vienna had to be fed ; and the peasants of rural Austria were by no means likely to consent even to be drawn along in the wake of an urban proletarian Revolution. The Social Democrats had little support in the countryside, in which the Roman Catholic Church and its political ally, the Christian Social Party, were very strongly entrenched. The Austrian peasants, moreover, had been accustomed to much less oppressive and tyrannous exploitation than the peasants of Hungary, and would certainly not have submitted to having their produce requisitioned by Socialist or Communist detachments from the towns. Austria was mainly a country of small and middle-sized agricultural holdings, rather than of great estates, and was given over to dairying and cattle-breeding rather than to cultivation of cereals. It is true that, in 1918 and 1919, the power of the Church was for the time being greatly reduced, and the Christian Social Party, under the leadership

of the peasant Jodol Fink, much less under clerical and reactionary influences than it came to be as soon as the Church
and the petty bourgeoisie had recovered from the state of scare
into which the Revolution had thrown them. Nevertheless,
even in 1918–19, a Viennese Soviet Republic would have meant
civil war and sheer starvation for the townsmen ; and even
if the products of Austrian agriculture could have been gained
for urban consumption, Vienna would still have not been able
to be fed from that source without imported supplies. The
new Republic was simply not viable without Allied aid ; and
the Social Democratic leaders were correctly convinced that
the Allied Governments would not tolerate a Soviet Republic,
but would promptly starve it into submission.

In these circumstances, Sovietism would have been sheerly
impracticable even if the main body of the Viennese Socialists
had wished for it. But, deeply loyal to the Austrian Social
Democratic Party, most of them had no such wish and were
prepared to follow their leaders in seeking to build up the new
Austria as a parliamentary Republic, even though this was soon
seen to involve sharing power with their old enemies, the
Christian Socials, and even with the reactionary Nationalists.
No doubt many Social Democrats hoped at the outset that
their Party would prove strong enough to win a parliamentary
majority and to take the government of the whole country into
its hands, with the other Parties in constitutional opposition.
But when the General Election left them, though the strongest
single Party, in a minority in the new Assembly, most of them
reluctantly acquiesced in coalition government as the only alternative to a civil war in which, even if they were victorious at
home, the fruits of victory were bound to be snatched from
them by Allied intervention.

Even apart from these considerations, most of the leaders
of Austrian Social Democracy, and many of the rank and file,
were themselves believers in parliamentary democracy, for
which they had been struggling so long under the old order,
and wanted to set up a parliamentary, rather than a Soviet,
Republic. Indeed, they wanted this the more because most of
them did not believe that the Austrian Republic could be
strong enough to stand alone, and looked forward to its incorporation as an autonomous State within the new German

Federal Republic. It soon became plain, after November 1918, that what was being set up in Germany was, in form at any rate, a parliamentary democratic Republic, and that Austria could not be united with Germany except under a similar régime. For the moment, union on any terms was excluded by the veto of the Allies ; but it was widely hoped that this veto would soon be lifted.

Accordingly, the Austrian Socialists preferred coalition with the Christian Socials in an attempt to save the new State from dissolution, to running into the acute perils that would have beset a Soviet Vienna ringed round with enemies, both at home and abroad. This does not mean that they liked the coalition, or found it easy to work. But it provided a means of securing some sort of co-operation between town and country, and of getting Allied assistance in the immediate tasks of feeding the people and reorganising the economic life of the sadly truncated State.

This compromise, which alienated only small groups on the extreme left, provided an opportunity for the anti-Socialists, who had been in disarray immediately after the Revolution, to reassert themselves and to regain a good deal of support at the expense of the Social Democratic Party. Before long the Christian Social Party was able to insist on 'proportional government' — that is, on a sharing out of Cabinet posts in proportion to the numerical strength of the three main Parties ; and under this arrangement the new Constitution was drafted and put into force, in October 1920. At the ensuing election the Social Democrats lost their parliamentary lead, returning only 66 deputies as against 82 Christian Socials, 20 German Nationalists, and 6 for the new Peasant Party. The Socialists thereupon left the Government, which was reconstructed under Christian Social leadership, and became increasingly reactionary as the Church and the middle classes took control of it out of the hands of its peasant leaders. The Socialists kept, however, their firm hold on Vienna, for which they had been able to secure the status of a Province, as well as a city, under the new federal Constitution ; and they were thus able to carry on in Vienna the advanced social policy, especially in relation to housing and unemployment relief, which they were no longer able to pursue for the country as a whole. They were indeed able, despite the extreme difficulty of the economic situation, to carry through in Vienna itself a constructive policy which made 'Red' Vienna the admiration of democratic Socialists throughout the world. After the Socialists had withdrawn from the government of the Republic Austria had in effect two Governments — one in Vienna and another in the rest of the country. In the former, in order to pay for a really big programme of housing, education, and other social services, including the maintenance of a very large number of unemployed workers, a system of local taxation bearing with unexampled severity on the wealthier classes was introduced ; rents were kept down to a very low level ; and the great blocks of workers' flats, which became one of the most famous sights of the new Vienna, were erected at public cost. The cultural work of the Social Democratic Party also underwent a big development with municipal support ; and the city, despite its immense economic handicaps, carried through a profound social transformation which merits all the praise it has received.

In achieving these results, the Austrian Socialists were to some extent able to build on foundations that had been laid by their opponents, the Christian Socials, under Karl Lueger, in the days of the empire. For Lueger's régime, despite its antisemitism, had been, in some respects, progressive in social affairs. The Socialists advanced, however, thanks to their success in making Vienna an autonomous Province with wide powers, far beyond anything that had been attempted before ; and their ability to do this affected their attitude to the question of Austrian government in general. Originally the Social Democrats had stood for a strongly centralised Republic, against the Christian Social wish for a federal system. But, having secured their control over Vienna, they became less concerned over this matter, and in the main the Christian Socials got their way.

Thus Austria came in many respects to harbour a dual system of government, with the Social Democrats controlling the top-heavy capital and the Christian Socials most of the rest of the country. Austria, indeed, however it had been governed, could scarcely have survived at all through the postwar years without help from outside, in view of the mass unemployment of its industrial workers and of the unwillingness of the peasants to supply them with foodstuffs for which they could give little in exchange. Austrian industries, under the empire, had been concerned largely with the production of luxury and artistic goods, the markets for which were now lost ; and shortage of capital, as well as of the necessary techniques and materials, made it difficult to shift over to types of production more suitable for the narrowed and impoverished internal market. Under the empire, Hungary had supplied foodstuffs in exchange for Austrian manufactures ; but this trade was now cut off. The tasks of feeding the towns and maintaining the unemployed were very onerous ; and before long Austria had to be rescued from sheer collapse, first by American famine relief and then by reconstruction loans floated under the auspices of the League of Nations. Even so, the problem was never solved, and could not be solved ; for Vienna was much too populous a city to be adequately maintained as a capital for only a few million people, and its neighbours were by no means prepared to allow it to regain its position as a centre of economic and financial services for the whole group of Succession States. From time to time ambitious projects of Danubian Federation were put forward, especially by Aristide Briand ; but they never stood any real chance of acceptance.

The conditions under which the Socialists in Austria agreed at the beginning of the Republic to share power with the other Parties, in preference to attempting to set up a Socialist State, precluded any drastic legislation of a socialist kind, and limited their achievement to the eight hours' day, the establishment of works councils, the granting of workers' representation in the direction of the major industrial enterprises, and the enactment of a fairly advanced code of social legislation. From 1920 onwards they were outside the Government as a parliamentary opposition, first to Dr. Mayr's Christian Social Cabinet and then to the non-political Ministry of officials headed by Dr. Schober, which lasted till 1922 and was then replaced by a further and much more reactionary anti-Socialist Ministry under the Christian Social, Monsignore Ignatz Seipel, and, after his retirement, under Dr. Ramek.

During the years which followed the constitution of the Austrian Republic, relations between the Socialists and their political opponents grew almost continuously worse. At the outset, as we have seen, the Socialists had for a time the upper hand, within the limitations placed on them by their imperative need for Allied recognition and financial help. But before long, with the Socialist predominance almost restricted to Vienna, the anti-Socialists were able to re-group their forces and not only to oust the Socialists from the central Government, but also to begin building up, mainly in the rural areas, powerful reactionary movements that were presently in a position to resort to methods of violence against the Socialists with the connivance, and even the support, of the Christian Social Government. The most dangerous of these forces was the landlord-inspired Heimwehr, led by Prince Ernst Starhemberg, which set to work to build up para-military formations in opposition to the Socialist 'Republican Schutzbund'. This latter hardly existed outside the major towns and could be used only for local defence ; whereas the Heimwehr, with large money resources behind it and with the backing of many persons in high official positions, was much more mobile and better able to concentrate its forces on any area in which it had decided to resort to violent measures. The Heimwehr was not, indeed, always at one with the Government, which did sometimes make half-hearted efforts to keep its violence within bounds ; nor were the Heimwehr leaders always prepared to pay due deference to the wishes of the Catholic Church. But when Seipel became Chancellor and set to work with the definite object of destroying the Socialists' power, the Heimwehr became his most important auxiliary in the increasingly violent conflicts between Socialists and anti-Socialists, both in the country areas and in the smaller towns ; whereas in Vienna itself the Socialists were still for some time too strong to be openly challenged by violent methods.

It was under Seipel, in July 1927, that Austrian Socialism suffered what proved to be a most serious defeat. This arose out of the steadily worsening relations between the armed irregular forces which had been set up both by the reactionaries in the countryside — the landlord-led 'Heimwehr' — and, in self-defence, by the urban workers — the Socialist 'Republican Schutzbund'. The crisis developed out of an affray in which a number of workers belonging to the Schutzbund were killed by reactionary bands. The killers, arrested and put on trial, were acquitted by a reactionary jury in plain defiance of the facts. The following morning the Viennese workers spontaneously left the factories and marched in procession to a demonstration before the Parliament House. There was a riot : the Palace of Justice was stormed and set ablaze, and the police fired on the demonstrators and killed no fewer than 94 of them.

These events brought Vienna to the verge of revolution. It had been shown that the police were prepared, at the Government's call, to shoot the workers down ; and there were not a few Socialists who called on the Social Democratic Party to summon the Schutzbund to arms and to overthrow the reactionary Government by force. But the Socialist leaders felt that, even if they could make themselves masters of Vienna, as they might have been able to do, they would be unable to maintain their power in view of their weakness in the rest of the country. Accordingly, they restricted their action to the calling of a general strike, which met with a virtually complete response. The Government, however, realising that the strike could not last, refused to make any concessions ; and the Socialist Party, still unprepared to issue a call for insurrection, was compelled to bring the stoppage to an end. The Socialists, despite their assured control of the Vienna administration, had to accept defeat unless they were prepared to stake everything on a rising for which they could see no prospect of lasting success. They could have risen only as a proletariat asserting its class right against a democratically elected parliamentary majority ; and some of them would have rejected such a course even if they had held victory to be within their grasp. At all events, after 1927 the violence of the reactionaries steadily increased, and the Socialists, though they held on as best they could, were definitely in retreat, in face of the mounting power of the clerical reaction, even before the world economic crisis of the years after 1929 struck them a further heavy blow. The democratic Republic, though it lasted in form for some years longer — until Dollfuss's *coup* of 1934 — was in effect doomed to destruction from the moment when the Socialists drew back from open rebellion in July 1927. Right up to the destruction of their power by Dollfuss in 1934 and to Hitler's invasion in 1937, the Austrian Socialists remained in opposition through the successive phases of inflation, painful stabilisation, and endemic economic crisis after 1929. Outside Vienna they had no chance after 1920 of constructive Socialist action ; for they never came near to winning a parliamentary majority. In Vienna, on the other hand, they were able to accomplish a great deal, and to keep the spirit of Socialism alive, and, by doing so, to prevent the Communists from winning any large amount of working-class support, despite the very adverse economic conditions. In opposition to the Christian Socials they did their best to work out a land policy as the basis for an appeal for peasant support. In 1925 Otto Bauer produced on their behalf a scheme for the setting up of local communities based on the system of common land (*gemein*), to consist of small dairying and cattle-owning farmers dependent largely on use of the common land and on Co-operative credit and marketing, but with grain-dealing as a state monopoly. They never had the chance, however, of putting this plan into operation ; nor did it win them any substantial peasant support. They remained an urban Party, closely allied with the Trade Unions, which succeeded in enrolling almost all the industrial and black-coated workers of the towns, but did not provide a sufficient foundation for winning a parliamentary majority over the country as a whole.

Austro-Marxism, of which the theoretical aspects were discussed in the preceding volume,[1] underwent only secondary further developments as a theory after 1918. The problem of nationalities, which had been a principal concern of many of its leading exponents, such as Karl Renner and Otto Bauer, no longer existed in its pre-war form after the break-up of the Austro-Hungarian empire ; and in the new situation dominated by the independent Succession States, Bauer's conception of cultural autonomy no longer had much relevance.

Bauer did, however, make substantial contributions to Socialist thought both in his booklet on *Bolshevism and Social Democracy* and his various writings in the Austrian Socialist journal, *Der Kampf*, and in his drafts for the Party's agrarian programme of 1925 and for the general programme which it adopted at its Linz Congress the following year. His book on *The Austrian Revolution* (1923) was a penetrating study of the situation the Austrian Socialists had to face in and after 1918 ;

[1] See Vol. III, Part II, p. 546.

and the Linz Programme embodied one of the best expositions of democratic Socialist ideas of the process of transition from capitalism to a Socialist economy, with a strong emphasis on the need for industrial democracy, and for the avoidance of bureaucratic over-centralisation.

Of the other leading theorists of the Austrian movement, Rudolf Hilferding had transferred his activities to Germany and had become a citizen of the Weimar Republic, Max Adler — no relation of Victor or Friedrich Adler — had been greatly influenced by Russian ideas and had become the principal theoretical exponent of left-wing conceptions, and Friedrich Adler devoted his energies first to the attempt to rebuild a united Socialist International and later, when this failed, to the revived Second (or Labour and Socialist) International.[1] The Austrian Socialists, under the Republic, gave a remarkable display of practical achievement under very difficult conditions and also produced well-devised and imaginative policies which their minority position in the country did not allow them to carry into effect.

In their position of continuous opposition to successive anti-Socialist and increasingly reactionary Governments they were able to remain well to the left of the German Majority Socialists and thereafter of the reunited S.P.D. There was always within the Austrian Party a left wing which criticised its moderate courses and tried at times to co-operate with the small Austrian Communist Party ; but this left was never strong enough, while political freedom lasted, effectively to challenge the leadership in face of the extreme economic difficulties from which the country suffered continuously between the wars, and of the remarkable record of the Vienna provincial administration under Karl Seitz. Up to the coming to power of Hitler in Germany the Austrian Socialists continued to favour the *Anschluss*, but had no power to bring it about. After the Nazis had taken power in Germany they lost some followers to the Austrian Nazis, but not very many. Nevertheless, their power was being steadily eroded from the early 'twenties onwards by their apparent condemnation to the permanent status of a minority Party ; and the Christian Socials, who had begun in social matters as a relatively enlightened Party, moved

[1] For the new post-war Internationals see Chapter IX.

further and further rightwards under both ecclesiastical and bourgeois pressure. Socialist insistence on *laicité*, popular with the urban workers, brought them into increasing conflict with the dominant Catholic Church, which became, both spiritually and politically, more and more aggressive and industrially reactionary, till at length it attempted to rebuild a sort of mediaeval class-transcending industrial structure based on the conceptions of Karl von Vogelsang,[1] and including a revived system of *Zünfte*, or trade guilds, enrolling both masters and men, and set out to destroy the Trade Unions. To follow these developments, would, however, take me a long way beyond the period with which the present chapter is intended to deal.

CZECHOSLOVAKIA

The Republic of Czechoslovakia was set up in October 1918, while the Austro-Hungarian empire was finally dissolving in ruins. It was indeed proclaimed twice over, once in Paris by the National Council that had been in operation abroad during the war, and a second time in Prague by the National Committee headed by the Young Czech leader Karel Kramarc, who became its first Prime Minister, with the support of the Czech section of the Austrian Social Democratic Party — then led by František Soukup (1871–1940). Two days later the Slovak National Council pronounced itself in favour of Czechoslovak unity. The national movements on the spot sent delegations to meet those of Masaryk's National Council at Geneva ; and the two joined forces to establish the new Republic. The Social Democrats had to face the question whether to co-operate with the bourgeois Parties in this task or to endeavour to give the Revolution a Socialist character. The position was complicated by the fact that Germans made up about one-third of the total population of Bohemia, about one-quarter of that of Moravia and Silesia, and well over one-fifth in the country as a whole. Only about two-thirds of the total were of Czech or Slovak nationality. In 1918 the German Social Democrats in Bohemia and Moravia, in common with the other German Parties, were refusing to recognise the Czecho-slovak Republic and were demanding the inclusion of the

[1] For Vogelsang, see Vol. II, p. 259.

German districts in the new Austria and the admission of German Austria as an autonomous State into the new German Federal Republic that was already on the way. The situation was further complicated by the existence, side by side with the Czech and German sections of the Austrian Social Democrats, of a Czech National Socialist Party closely associated with the bourgeois nationalists and drawing its chief support from the black-coated and professional classes. This was the Party with which Dr. Edward Beneš, the chief associate of Masaryk in the Czechoslovak National Council, had some connection. It had been founded in 1897 by J. F. Klovač, who was still its leader in Czechoslovakia in 1918, and attached to it was a Czech national Trade Union movement separate from the main Austrian Trade Union Commission, which covered workers of all nationalities.

A further complicating factor was the weakness of Socialism in Slovakia, which was dominated by Monseigneur Andrej Hlinka's Populist Catholic Party and would certainly have refused to accept absorption into a definitely Socialist Czecho-slovak State. Moreover, nationalist feeling was strong in 1918 even among the Czech Social Democrats, who were impelled by it into a willingness to co-operate with bourgeois nationalism in laying the foundations of the new order. In these cir-cumstances the Czech Social Democrats, who had played a large part in the revolutionary assumption of power in the industrial areas, did not feel strong enough to take full authority into their own hands or to attempt to move straight on to a Socialist Revolution. Despite strong pressure from their left wing they agreed to enter Dr. František Kramarc's Provisional Government, though they were given only 3 Cabinet posts out of 17, as against 4 for the Agrarian Party, 3 apart from Dr. Beneš for the Czechoslovak National Socialists, 3 for the National Democrats, and 2 for minor Parties, with 2 non-party members, including Beneš, who was counted on this occasion as a non-party representative of Masaryk's National Council. Masaryk himself became President of the Republic : the German Parties, including the German Social Democrats, per-sisted in their refusal to co-operate or to recognise the new State.

It was, however, recognised from the first that the Social Democrats, who were at this time by far the strongest single force, were grossly under-represented in the Kramarc Ministry and in the Provisional National Assembly that had been set up. In the municipal elections of June 1919 the Czechoslovak Social Democratic Party secured by far the biggest vote — 935,000, as against 637,000 for the Agrarians, 485,000 for the National Socialists, and only 256,000 for the National Democrats, the main Party of the urban bourgeoisie. The Kramarc Government thereupon resigned, and a new Coalition Ministry presided over by the Social Democrat Vlastimil Tusar (?-1924), took its place. The new Ministry was made up of 4 Social Democrats, 4 National Socialists, 4 Agrarians, and 2 Slovaks, with Dr. Beneš retaining his position as non-party Foreign Secretary. This Government, sustained by the first General Election under the new Constitution in April 1920, remained in office till September of that year, when it resigned and was replaced by a temporary Ministry of officials under Jan Černý, mainly because of serious dissensions inside the Social Democratic Party which had made its continuance impossible. The German Parties, throughout this period, maintained their refusal to co-operate.

Under the Kramarc and Tusar Governments the Czechoslovak State was endowed with a democratic parliamentary constitution ; and a substantial body of social legislation was enacted. This included the eight-hours' day, health and unemployment insurance, protection for tenants, and a capital levy ; and the Tusar Government also enacted a Land Law providing for the distribution of expropriated land taken from large proprietors, partly to individual farmers and partly to Co-operative bodies. The Tusar Government also passed a law setting up works councils in the mines and giving the miners a share in the control of the mining industry, as well as laws for the regulation of industrial wages and employment in domestic industries. It was, however, hampered by the opposition both of the non-Socialist Parties represented in the Government and of Hlinka's Catholic Slovak Party, which clamoured loudly for autonomy for Slovakia within a loosely federal State, as well as by the continued non-co-operation of the German Social Democrats and the growing dissatisfaction of its own left wing which stood for an attempt to establish a Socialist Soviet Republic on the Russian model.

The Czechoslovak Agrarian Party, which held an important place in both the Kramarc and the Tusar Governments, was at this period a real farmers' and peasants' Party, with a substantial following among the rural labourers as well. It was an active promoter of land reform and of agricultural Co-operation and credit banks. It was, however, strongly anti-Socialist ; and before long it began on the one hand to lose ground among the poorer peasants and agricultural workers, many of whom went over to Socialism, and on the other to be infiltrated by members of the urban middle classes who regarded it as a better bulwark against Socialism than the conservative National Democratic Party. It thus tended to move rightwards and to come into increasing conflict with the Social Democratic left wing. Its chief leaders were its President, Rudolf Beran, Jan Malypetr (1873-?) — a Co-operative leader who became President of the National Assembly in 1925 — and Milan Hodža (1878-?), a Slovak professor who became Prime Minister in the later 1930s.

The crisis in the Social Democratic Party came to a head in the summer of 1920, while the recently elected Parliament was in recess. The left wing, headed by Bohumil Smeral, who had recently returned from a visit to Russia, started a campaign with the object of capturing the Party Conference, due to meet in September. Of the 74 Social Democratic deputies, 23, reinforced later by a few more, took up a stand against the party leadership and demanded affiliation to the Communist International. The Tusar Government, deprived of a third of its Social Democratic parliamentary following, thereupon resigned in order to devote its energies to the party struggle. The leaders postponed the Party Conference ; but the left wing refused to wait and, at a Conference of its own, broke away and, under Smeral's leadership, formed itself into a Communist Party. Its adherents took forcible possession of the People's House in Prague, the Social Democratic headquarters, and stirred up widespread disturbances in the industrial districts. These were vigorously combated by the Černý Government of officials, advised by an inter-party junta, the Petka, or Council of Five, representing the five main Czechoslovak Parties, including the Social Democratic majority. The Communists were driven out of the People's House, and thereupon called for a general strike, which was defeated with great severity — in some places, only after an armed struggle. The new Communist Party, meanwhile, joined the Third International ; and the Social Democrats set to work to reorganise their Party in preparation for taking their place in a new and broader coalition Government. The German Parties, during this period of disturbed conditions, intensified their opposition to the Czechoslovak State and in 1921 announced their secession from Parliament and thereafter refused to take any part in its affairs.

In September 1921 Beneš became Prime Minister at the head of a broad coalition of all five non-Communist Czechoslovak Parties, and with the support of Hlinka's Slovak Catholics. The Social Democrats and the National Socialists were both represented ; but the influence of the former was much decreased by the split, and effective power now rested with the bourgeois elements and the Czechoslovak National Socialists. The Germans returned to Parliament, but remained in opposition. The Beneš Government made some attempt to conciliate the Germans by concessions of greater toleration of their cultural claims ; and the German bloc began to break up, with the different German Parties beginning to align themselves more on social issues. But no real settlement of the German problem was reached. Only in 1925 did the German *bloc*, exclusive of the German Social Democrats, agree to take part in the working of the Czechoslovak State ; and the German Social Democrats persisted three years longer in their policy of non-co-operation. The separate German Trade Unions, however, amalgamated with the Czechoslovak Trade Union Centre in 1925. The Slovak Catholics, who at first supported the Beneš Ministry, soon passed into opposition over the issue of help for Catholic schools.

The Beneš Ministry lasted till October 1922, when it was replaced by a new broad coalition under the Agrarian Antonin Svehla, as Prime Minister, with much the same party composition ; and this Government continued till 1926, when it finally broke down as the result of a dispute between Agrarians and Social Democrats on the question of agricultural tariff protection. Throughout its existence the Government was engaged in an acrimonious struggle with the Communist Party, especially in connection with its economic policy of deflation in the interests of currency stabilisation and of reductions in wages and salaries, particularly in the case of public employees. In January 1923 the right-wing Finance Minister, Alois Rašin, was assassinated by an Anarchist ; and in the ensuing outcry the Government enacted a special law for the protection of the Republic. The Communists continued their anti-government agitation ; and the following year the Government carried a new law stiffening the punishment for libel. There were, however, increasing difficulties inside the coalition ; and finally in 1925 the Parliament was dissolved.

In the ensuing General Election — the first since the Communists had broken away from the Social Democrats — the Czechoslovak Social Democratic Party was reduced to 29 deputies, as against the 74 of 1920, whereas the Communists won 41 seats and the Czechoslovak National Socialists 28. The German Social Democratic Party had a further 17 seats. Thereafter, however, the Communist strength fell away — to 30 at the General Election of 1929, whereas the Social Democrats regained some of the ground they had lost, though never enough to reinstate them in their position as the largest Party. The successive coalition Governments, in which the Social Democrats sometimes took part, were increasingly dominated by the Agrarian Party ; but no single Party stood any chance of gaining an independent majority, even if the German and other minorities were left out of account. The German Social Democrats, led by Ludwig Czech (1870–?), entered the Government in 1928, reversing their previous policy of opposition. The Czechoslovak National Socialists, though they had nothing in common with Hitler's German Party of the same name, were hardly to be regarded as Socialists. They were mildly radical progressives, with a sensible and moderate attitude in international affairs, and were well served by a widely circulated party press ; but apart from Beneš, who was no more than loosely associated with them, they produced no outstanding leaders.

During the years after 1918, Czechoslovakia's nearness to Russia and its position as a Slav State with a considerably developed industrial population in its Czech and German areas made it a storm centre in the struggle between Communism and Social Democracy. The Czech Social Democrats, however, were too much preoccupied with their national problems to be in a position to concentrate on Socialism, of any kind, as their central objective. The German workers, who included a considerable part of the industrial proletariat, were fighting a rearguard action against incorporation in a predominantly Slav State, and were in no mood to co-operate with the Czech or Slovak Socialists, who were themselves divided into the three Parties of Communists, Social Democrats, and National Socialists. The Czechoslovak Social Democrats, though they remained outside Masaryk's National Front during the war, were prepared to co-operate with it in establishing the Czechoslovak Republic, and were thus led into a policy of coalition with the National Socialists and the Agrarians, and even with Parties still further to the right. They were able to come to terms with the Agrarians on the land question ; and they were strong supporters of the policy of *laïcité* which was followed by the bourgeois left and centre in opposition to the Slovak Catholics. They were, moreover, centralisers, anxious to avoid a federal system that would foster Slovak separatism and might also strengthen German claims for some measure of autonomy. They therefore continued to give general support to a succession of coalition Governments even when they had ceased to be the predominant partners in them, or even to be partners at all — for after 1925 the Social Democrats ceased to be represented in the Ministry.

As against this, from the moment of the split in 1920 the Czechoslovak Communist Party was mainly governed in its changes of policy by the influence of the Comintern. Its first leader, Bohumil Smeral, was in some respects a very curious Communist. During the war he had been on the right wing of the Austrian Social Democratic Party, and had been opposed to the break-up of the Austrian territories into separate national States. He had thus found himself isolated from the national Czech movement for independence ; and after the war he remained in opposition to the party leadership and, after visiting Moscow, came back a convert to the Third International and became the leader of the secessionist movement in the Social Democratic Party. When the split took place, he became the leading figure in the Czechoslovak Communist Party and obediently followed the Moscow line. The left wing of the German S.D.P. in Czechoslovakia also seceded and joined up with the Communists, who thus became the one Party in which Czechs, Slovaks, and Germans were united on equal terms. A split followed in the Trade Unions, which then came to be divided into three rival groups, Communist, Social Democratic, and National Socialist, with the Communists holding for a while the leading place among the industrial workers. Their influence, however, was considerably shaken by the defeat of the general strike they called in December 1920, though they fairly soon recovered and, as we saw, gained large successes at the General Election of 1925. During the later 'twenties they lost ground again, but remained strong in the mining areas and were able to build up a following among the poorer peasants and rural labourers, especially those belonging to the national minorities hostile to Czech nationalism. Before the 'twenties ended, however, their leaders had fallen into disgrace at Moscow for their failure to pursue a sufficiently revolutionary policy. Smeral and others were removed from the leadership ; and the Party was left under new leaders, among whom Klement Gottwald (1896–1953) soon became the outstanding figure, to face the world depression of the early 'thirties.

During the years after 1918 Czechoslovakia was often extolled in the West as a 'model democracy'. It had indeed a thoroughly democratic parliamentary constitution, under which full voting rights were extended to its national minorities ; and its Parliament enacted a fairly advanced code of social legislation. The great estates were broken up and the land distributed mainly to peasant cultivators, among whom Co-operative organisations developed on a very considerable scale. But the very conditions that made these successes possible also prevented the establishment of a Socialist system. Czechoslovakia was a country both of advanced industries, which were greatly developed under the Republic, and of widespread peasant agriculture, which needed protection in order to hold its own in a world of low and fluctuating food prices ; and the peasant sector was large enough to prevent the Socialists from winning a clear majority under the parliamentary system, at any rate while proportional representation was in force. The Agrarian Party was strongly entrenched in the rural parts of Bohemia and Moravia ; and the country could not be governed on parliamentary lines without its participation. Moreover, though voting rights were equal, the large German element in the population deeply resented the loss of its former superiority and the inevitable preponderance of the Czech elements in the new State ; the Slovaks, too, were discontented and demanded more complete autonomy than the Czech centralisers were willing to concede ; and there were also considerable national minorities — Ukrainians in Sub-Carpathian Ruthenia, Magyars in Slovakia, and Poles in the Czechoslovak area of Silesia — who cherished aspirations of reunion with their fellow-nationals in the Soviet Union, Hungary, and Poland. Through the early years of the Republic the German Parties, by their refusal to recognise its legitimacy or to play any constructive part in its affairs, made the position of the predominant Czechoslovak Parties very difficult, and especially weakened the Socialist movement because they included a considerable section of the industrial workers. Relations between Germans and Czechs improved in the later 'twenties, and the boycott was withdrawn ; but they were soon to become much worse again after the Nazis had come to power in Germany and had set to work to build up Henlein's Sudeten Nazi Party among the Germans of Czechoslovakia. There were also continual difficulties with the Magyars in Slovakia and with the Ukrainians in the economically backward area of Ruthenia ; and it was in these districts that Communism, as the only party grouping that transcended national differences, was able to build up a substantial rural following. There was, however, even less prospect of a successful Communist Revolution in Czechoslovakia as a whole during the inter-war period than of a Socialist parliamentary victory. The Communists, even when they won for a time the support of a majority of the industrial workers, remained much too weak to have any real chance of seizing power against the combined opposition of all the other groups. They could at times create considerable disturbances ; but there was never any doubt of the power of the Government to defeat them when it came to a trial of strength. These struggles, however, inevitably involved the Socialists in common action with the bourgeois Parties against the Communists, and thus set up very bitter divisions within the working-class movement — divisions which went right back to the old quarrels between the pre-war Austrian Socialist Party and the Czech groups which had become estranged from it in the days of the Second International. The old differences between Social Democrats and Czechoslovak National Socialists remained unresolved, leaving the Social Democrats a middle group between the two fires of Czechoslovak National Socialism and international Communism. This accounts for the diminished influence of the Social Democratic Party after the first few years of the Republic and for the greatly increased influence of the Agrarian Party in the successive Governments. As a progressive bourgeois democracy Czechoslovakia did meet its many difficulties with considerable success until the rise of Nazism undermined it, and until the failure of the Western countries to come to its aid in 1938 left it wholly at Hitler's mercy. But in the matter of Socialism, as distinct from moderate bourgeois social reform, its Socialist Parties were never in a position to win the day.

HUNGARY

I come now to the ill-fated Hungarian Revolution of 1918, which ended less than a year later in the 'White Terror'. Up to 1918 there had been no country in Europe — not even Russia — where national minorities were more oppressed than they were in Hungary. Nor did most of the poorer Magyars in the country areas fare much better than their Slav fellow-subjects. The Hungarian Parliament was both an aristocratic and a nationalistic preserve, into which only a tiny group even of the urban bourgeoisie and one or two isolated Socialists had been able to penetrate ; and none of these isolated figures had belonged to the Social Democratic Party, the main representative of the urban workers. Hungarian industry was not strongly developed outside Budapest and a few mining districts ; and for the most part those engaged in it, whether as employers or workers, were not of Magyar nationality. Jews, with some Germans, predominated among both employers and skilled workers : a considerable proportion of the less skilled workers were immigrants from Slovakia or other Slav areas. The skilled workers were quite strongly organised in Trade Unions, which were tolerated as long as they made no attempt to organise the rural workers ; and these Unions worked closely with the Social Democratic Party. Among the aristocracy there were many small as well as large landowners, certain great families owning enormous estates : the landless members of aristocratic families crowded mainly into the Civil Service, regarding trade and industry as beneath their attention. In some areas unimproved lands had been bought up on a large scale by speculators, who had developed them for leasing or resale. Most of the peasants and landless labourers were very poor and lived under wretched conditions of oppression, especially on the great estates. There had, however, been some development of agricultural Co-operation ; and a few aristocrats, notable among them members of the great Károlyi family, had been active in the Co-operative movement. In many areas rural discontents had been endemic for many years, but had been savagely repressed. Liberal movements were very weak, and nationalist feeling among the Magyars was quite exceptionally strong.

In the Hungarian Parliament the Magyar aristocrats, who made up almost its entire membership, had been traditionally divided into two Parties, the one, broadly speaking, content with the 'Compromise of 1867' which had established the Dual Monarchy and given Hungary a large measure of self-government, and the other, descended from Kossuth's nationalists of 1848, demanding complete independence without necessarily wishing to get rid of Hapsburg rule. Union with Austria had indeed evident advantages, both as providing markets for Hungary's surplus foodstuffs and because the 'Compromise of 1867' gave the Magyars the assurance of Austrian support for their rule over their subject peoples. Within the 'Independence' Party, however, there had grown up before 1914 a left wing, headed by Count Mikhail Károlyi (1887–1955), which showed sympathy for the plight of the oppressed Magyar peasants and at times took sides with the Radicals and Social Democrats against the dominant Magyar aristocratic groups.

During the war the Hungarian ruling classes, in the main, supported the imperial Government's war effort, and the Hungarian regiments fought well. But as Austria-Hungary's difficulties increased, serious discontents began to appear, especially in the Slav districts. When, after the death of the old emperor, Franz Josef, in November 1916, his successor

Karl began to press for concessions to the subject nationalities, in the hope of saving the empire from dissolution, the Hungarian Government under Count Stefan Tisza flatly refused to agree to any interference with Magyar supremacy, or to any extension of the franchise such as had been conceded in Austria well before 1914. A more amenable Government took office, but was unable to persuade the Hungarian Parliament to give way. Even during the closing stages of the war, in the summer and autumn of 1918, when military collapse was evidently near at hand and Karl was making a desperate attempt to reconstruct his tottering empire as a federation of self-governing national States under Hapsburg sovereignty, the attempt had to be restricted to the Austrian provinces, because even then the Hungarian Parliament still refused to have anything to do with projects of reform that would upset Magyar aristocratic predominance. When Hungary's neighbours began to advance into Hungarian territory, with the declared purpose of liberating their fellow-nationals from Magyar rule, the Hungarian aristocrats could think of nothing better than to demand that the Hungarian armies should be sent home to fight the invaders and defend the historical frontiers against the enemy.

By this time, however, popular discontent inside Hungary was growing fast. There had been big strikes among the munition workers in Hungary as well as in Austria in January 1918; and from March onwards, after the signing of the Treaty of Brest-Litovsk, war prisoners began to return from Russia in considerable numbers, not unaffected by their experiences of the Russian Revolution. After the collapse of Bulgaria in September 1918 the Hungarian frontier lay wide open to attack from Rumania and from the South; and as soon as it became known that both Germany and Austria-Hungary had asked President Wilson for an armistice on October 4th the home front began to break down. Workers' and Soldiers' Councils, mainly under Socialist leadership, began to be formed in Budapest and a few other places, and threats of revolutionary action began to be heard. While negotiations for an armistice were still going on, on October 25th, a National Council was set up in Budapest under the presidency of Count Károlyi, and the previous Government was, in effect, displaced. The new authority proclaimed a general amnesty for political offenders and released the many who had been in gaol ; and it also promised a new electoral law and the breaking-up of the great estates. On October 30th several regiments in the capital mutinied, joined the demonstrators who were thronging the streets, and seized the military headquarters, the general post office, and other public buildings. On the following day all Budapest was in the hands of the Revolution. The old Government resigned, and Károlyi was appointed by the King to form a new one with himself as Prime Minister. This he did, supported by his own followers together with Oscar Jaszy's Radicals and the Social Democrats, who provided his principal backing. The strong man of the old Hungary, Count Tisza, was murdered during the disturbances. Károlyi, faced with the sheer eclipse of the Austro-Hungarian empire and with the country surrounded by hostile armies bent on breaking it up, had to embark on the exceedingly difficult task of making peace and of attempting to build up the new Hungarian State without at all knowing where its boundaries would be. In the north the Slovaks were demanding admission to the new Czech State : in the east, the Rumanians were advancing into Transylvania : in the south the Allies were threatening to take away Croatia, Slovenia, and all the other predominantly Slav areas. Nor could there be any assurance that the hostile armies would stop even at the ethnic frontiers of Magyar Hungary. It could not be a simple matter to negotiate armistices with so many triumphant enemies ; and it was certain to be very difficult indeed to induce the proud Magyar rulers to accept the immensity of their defeat.

Indeed, during the next few months the Hungarian Government and High Command found themselves faced with one demand after another for the re-fixing of the armistice lines closer and closer in upon the central Hungarian plain. Károlyi tried, by appealing from the generals on the spot to the Allied High Command under General Franchet d'Esperey and to the Allied Governments, to obtain a general settlement that would halt all his enemies at once ; but he got no satisfaction. President Wilson had insisted from the first on the complete liberation of both the Czechoslovaks and the Southern Slavs ; but there was still no definition of the areas that Hungary was to lose, and each moving forward of the armistice lines was in effect the staking out of a further territorial claim. Meanwhile there was chaos at home, with the old machinery of government broken down and nothing ready to take its place; for the old Civil Service was mostly useless for the new tasks and bitterly hostile to the Revolution. Even the form of government was unsettled until November 16th, when Károlyi proclaimed the Republic and the old Parliament was finally dismissed, new democratic elections being promised as soon as conditions made them possible — which clearly they could not be until the frontiers had been at any rate approximately settled. For the time being the self-appointed National Council had to carry on as best as it could, though it had no generally representative character.

So matters went on until the New Year, when Károlyi took office as President of the Hungarian Republic and a new Cabinet was appointed under the Socialist, Desirer Berinkey (1871–1948), still with the Social Democrats as its most solid backers. By this time a fresh factor had been introduced into the situation by the arrival from Russia of a number of specially trained revolutionaries, headed by Béla Kun, with orders to bring about a proletarian Revolution. Béla Kun (1886–1936) had been before the war a journalist working for Socialist and other papers and also an official of a workers' friendly society in Transylvania, where he had played some part in the Socialist movement. On his return to Budapest he gathered a group of left-wingers round him and set on foot an agitation among the workers for improved wages and conditions, vigorously denouncing the supineness of the Trade Union leaders, and seeking to build up a following among the discontented soldiers and the unemployed, who were suffering serious hardships. There were indeed plenty of grievances to exploit; but for the most part the Government was powerless to remedy them because of the shortage of supplies reaching the towns and of the dislocation of industry after the munition factories had come to a stop. Markets too were everywhere disrupted; and it was difficult to administer food rationing at all fairly with the Civil Service mainly hostile.

Kun's propaganda therefore made considerable headway and drew a good deal of support away from the Social Democrats, who were tied up with the Government and were therefore held responsible for its shortcomings. Nor did Kun and his supporters refrain from exploiting the outraged nationalistic feelings that were widely prevalent in the armed forces as well as among civilians. In this way Kun was able to gain some support from among officers as well as from the Soldiers' and Workers' Councils, and to make the position of the Government increasingly difficult. At this point, on March 20th, 1919, the Allied Armistice Commission at Budapest, headed by Colonel Vix, delivered to the Hungarian Government yet another ultimatum, requiring the evacuation of still more territory, including Hungary's second town, Debreczin, which lay well within the Magyar area. This demand roused a fury of indignation. Károlyi felt it to be hopeless to resist; but he was also aware that, if he gave way, a rising against the Government would be certain to follow. His Cabinet was in a like dilemma; but the Vix ultimatum did not allow any delay. The Cabinet was at this time a coalition, in which the Socialists formed the most coherent element. Its bourgeois members, unwilling either to accept or to reject the ultimatum, resigned. Károlyi, left entirely dependent on Socialist support, thereupon advised the Socialists, headed by Kunfi, to endeavour to come to terms with the Communists with a view to setting up a Socialist-Communist Cabinet able to command united working-class support; for he realised that the Socialists were not strong enough to take power alone, even if he continued, as President, to give them his support. Károlyi did not, as has been so often claimed, resign his office and hand power over to the Communists. He makes it clear in his memoirs that he expected, and intended, to remain at the head of the State, in conjunction with the new Cabinet. He did, however, advise the Socialists to try to come to terms with the Communists, though he had no notion of the terms at which they did in fact arrive.

At this time, as the sequel to disturbances in the capital, Kun and a number of his associates were in prison. A group of Socialist leaders, headed by the former school-teacher Zaigmond Kunfi (1879–?), a member of the outgoing Government and the outstanding figure in the Hungarian Social Democratic movement, visited them in the prison and, after only half an hour's discussion, agreed to fuse the Social Democratic and Communist Parties into a single Party and to take power into their joint hands under the auspices of the Workers' and Soldiers' Council. The following day the prisoners were set free. A Trade Union leader, the stonemason Alexander Garbai (1879–1947), became President of the new Government, with Kun as Foreign Commissar, with Josef Pogany, the President of the Soldiers' Council, and Kunfi as other leading members. The Socialist Vilmos Boehm (1880–?), who had been a Minister under Károlyi, became head of the Red Army which the new Government at once began to form ; and another Socialist, Josef Haubrich, the leader of the metal-workers, was appointed as Commandant of Budapest. Other notable figures included the economist Eugen Varga (b. 1879), as Commissar responsible for nationalisation, the lawyer Eugen Landler (1875–1928), Matyas Rakosi in charge of trade, and Tibor Szamuely (1890–1919), a journalist and close associate of Kun, as Commissar of the Interior.

As for Károlyi, he did not resign, but was simply pushed out. He was presented with a paper tendering his resignation, which he refused to sign ; but even before it was shown to him it had been sent to the press with his signature added to it, and he found himself faced with the choice between accepting the accomplished fact and repudiating the forgery with the probable result of a civil war in which he would, contrary to his convictions, be ranged on the side of the reactionaries against the Republic. He decided, in face of this dire alternative, to remain silent and to renounce the power he was no longer in a position to wield as the Socialists' ally. He knew indeed that not a few of the Socialist leaders would be bitterly opposed to the fusion of the Socialist and Communist Parties ; but he realised that they were as helpless as he, because they could stand out against it only at the cost of making common cause with the reactionaries. What in fact happened was that the right-wing Socialists, such as Erno Garami and Julius Peidl, were for the moment isolated and unable to stand out effectively against the Communists, but remained sullenly in opposition or fled out of the country in order to escape from the calamity they saw to be on its way.

The new Soviet Government proceeded immediately to drastic action at home. It decreed the comprehensive abolition of private property in the means of production, and went to the length of commandeering all stocks of goods and ordering the temporary closure of all shops except grocers, tobacconists, and chemists, until arrangements could be made for taking them over. It also abolished private property in land ; but instead of distributing the great estates among the landless peasants and rural workers, it ordered them to be carried on undivided under managers appointed by the Government — who had in most cases to be those who had operated them for the dispossessed landlords. Both the Communists and the Social Democrats were strongly hostile to the peasants and regarded the parcelling out of the estates as an essentially anti-Socialist measure that would serve only to entrench reaction. Because of this, nothing had been done under Károlyi to distribute the land to the peasants, with the exception of Károlyi's own great estates, which he had put freely at the public disposal. Peasant land-hunger accordingly remained unappeased ; and soon peasant discontent was made much worse by the sending of punitive expeditions into the countryside to requisition food for the towns.

Under these conditions more and more of industry closed down ; and a great inflation began. The old Austro-Hungarian 'blue' notes continued to circulate, but were not nearly enough. The Soviet Government was forced to meet its expenses by printing a new 'white' currency of its own, which depreciated at a great rate. Peasants, wage-earners — indeed, all who could — demanded payment in the old 'blue' notes ; and serious strikes broke out over this question.

Simultaneously there was the matter of national defence against the Rumanians, who were threatening to march into the disputed area. General Smuts, on behalf of the Allies, came to Budapest to negotiate and offered to set back the 'Vix' line provided the Hungarians refrained from mobilising their army and undertook to abstain from propaganda abroad. Béla Kun did not accept the offer : despite the evident weakness of his position he decided to go to war. The Hungarian army was easily defeated, and the Rumanians began to advance on Budapest. Already the Hungarian 'Whites' had set up a counter-revolutionary Government in Szeged, in the south, under the protection of French forces. It seemed as if the fall of the Budapest dictatorship was imminent. At this point, however, the people of Budapest rose and improvised a new army, which was joined by many officers of the old one, for a war of national self-preservation. Vilmos Boehm was made Commander-in-Chief, with the assistance of a regular officer, Colonel Aurel Stromfeld (1878–1927), who became a member of the Communist Party. This new army defeated the advancing Rumanians and drove them back across the Theiss during May. No sooner had this startling victory been won than the Czechs began to march through Slovakia towards Budapest. The Hungarians counter-attacked and defeated them, and recaptured most of Slovakia, which had been formally made part of the new Czechoslovak State. But at this point a serious revolt broke out in Western Hungary, beginning on June 8th with a widespread railway strike for improved rations and payment in 'blue' money. The strike reached Western Budapest, and had to be met by conceding the railwaymen's terms and by taking strong measures against the peasants, who were refusing to deliver supplies. Punitive expeditions under Szamuely were sent into the affected districts and behaved with great brutality, shooting many peasants and hanging some who had been taken as hostages. The revolt was stamped out ; but it badly shook the Government's standing, even among its own supporters.

At this point the Allies peremptorily ordered the Hungarians to quit Slovakia, stating that in return the Rumanians would withdraw from the Magyar areas they still held. The Hungarian Government reluctantly obeyed ; but the Rumanians did not withdraw. By this time, however, there was among the Hungarian workers an insistent demand for peace. Many of the Socialists strongly disliked Kun's dictatorship ; and this section began to win back much of the support it had lost to the Communists. At the June Conference of the combined Party — known as the Socialist Party of Hungary — an attempt was made to get rid of the Communist leadership, and there was even talk of a Socialist rising against Kun and his group. The rising failed to develop mainly because the Socialist Commandant of Budapest — Josef Haubricht — refused to support it, much to the annoyance of the Socialist Commander-in-Chief, Vilmos Boehm, who had quarrelled bitterly with Kun.

Meanwhile Kun's partisans, headed by Ernst Bettelheim (b. 1889), whom he had dispatched to Vienna, were trying to stir up a Communist Revolution there. In Austria, however, they had to face a well-organised Socialist Party, firmly entrenched in the capital, and by no means minded to countenance an irresponsible *putsch*. Ahead of the day fixed for the rising — June 15th — almost all the leaders were arrested, though Bettelheim himself evaded capture. A body of demonstrators made an attempt to storm the prison where they were confined, but were beaten off with twenty or so killed ; and the whole affair collapsed. Bettelheim was captured a few weeks later, but was soon set free, the Communist danger having completely disappeared. Kun's hopes of finding help in 'Red' Vienna had evaporated ; and ten days after the Vienna fiasco he had to face rebellion at home. The naval monitors in the Danube revolted and shelled the Government headquarters ; and in the city the cadets of the officer training school rose to join them. The revolt was put down in blood ; but it was followed by considerable uprisings in the countryside, which Szamuely's armed police were again sent out to quell. There were more executions, at any rate several hundreds ; and in the midst of this the Hungarian army — or what was left of it — was dispatched once more against the Rumanians. The army was, however, a mere shadow of itself. Boehm and Stromfeld had resigned their commands, and most of the worker-recruits to the Red Army had gone home. The regiments that remained either had no will to fight or were commanded by officers who were only waiting their chance to carry them over to the Whites. When it came to actual fighting, some regiments actually deserted to the enemy, while others refused to do battle or physically dispersed. The Rumanians broke right through the lines and again advanced on Budapest.

This time there was nothing to stop them. On August 1st, Béla Kun's Government admitted defeat and resigned. Kun and some of his companions commandeered a train and escaped across the frontier to Vienna. Others remained behind : among them Szamuely, who committed suicide. A Government of moderate Socialists, with Julius Peidl as Prime Minister, assumed office, but found itself entirely without authority. On August 4th the Rumanian forces entered Budapest without resistance ; and the Whites in the capital seized their chance to overthrow the Socialist Government. The Archduke Joseph attempted to take over authority, but was forced by the Allies to leave. A so-called 'all-party', White Government was formed under Charles Huszár and remained in possession under the Rumanian occupation. When the Rumanians at length withdrew, in November, Admiral Horthy marched in at the head of the main White forces. By this time the Hungarian Revolution had been completely liquidated : the right-wing Socialists who had been most hostile to the dictatorship were hardly safer under the ensuing White Terror than the Communists themselves. The Red Terror of Szamuely was avenged many times over : only a few even of the right-wing leaders, such as the respected Erno Garami (1876–1935), managed to escape abroad. The Radical leader, Oscar Jaszi (1875–1957), well known as a historian, also escaped, to write his account of the Revolution and presently to settle down as a professor at Oberlin College in the United States. Not only the Hungarian working-class movement, but also Hungarian Liberalism was torn up by the roots. Kun survived to carry on his career as a professional revolutionary under the aegis of the Comintern: we have seen him in a previous chapter seeking to foment Communist Revolution in Germany in 1921. In Hungary itself, after the final defeat, nothing was left save a very small body of underground workers. The counter-revolution set to work to undo the entire work of the Revolution. All the laws passed under Károlyi and his successors were declared invalid : the old constitution was brought back into force and a new right-wing Parliament elected under it in January 1920. All that was missing was a monarch to reign over the diminished Hungarian State. This presented a difficulty ; for the Magyar aristocrats were strongly monarchist, but felt no love for the Hapsburg emperor who, they felt, had attempted to betray them to the Slavs in order to save his throne. They resorted to the expedient of a monarchy without a king — Admiral Horthy being chosen as Regent to fill the vacant place. In June 1920 the Hungarian Government, with many complaints, signed the Peace Treaty ; and the Parliament, after much debate, was finally persuaded to ratify it in November. Hungary had finally lost all its subject peoples, and had been forced to accept the incorporation of substantial Magyar minorities into both Rumania and Czechoslovakia.

This was not quite the end. In March 1921, and again in October, the ex-emperor Karl made a bid for restoration to the Hungarian throne. On the first of these occasions he made an unarmed dash for the capital, but was persuaded to leave. On the second occasion, Karl managed to assemble a few troops and marched on Budapest, refusing to give way when the Government informed him that any attempt to restore his authority would be ruinous to the country. The Allied powers made it clear that they would refuse to recognise any Hapsburg on the throne ; and Yugoslavia began to mobilise. Karl continued to advance until his soldiers, when they met the troops sent out against them by the Government, melted away almost without fighting. He and his wife were captured and were presently sent out of the country on a British vessel of war. The Hungarian Parliament, at Allied insistence, declared his deposition by law. After this episode the White Terror began to subside ; and the following year a small group of moderate Socialists was able to secure election to the Hungarian Parliament, but not to exercise any real power. Later the same year, Hungary was admitted to the League of Nations. Limited measures of land reform were introduced between 1921 and 1925 ; but Hungary remained for another twenty years a prey to extreme forms of landlordism and aristocratic control.

As one looks back on the events in Hungary in 1918 and 1919, it is easy enough to see that Béla Kun's Communist Revolution never stood any chance of lasting success, but much less easy to see what would have been the right course for the Revolution to follow. Károlyi, however excellent his intentions, had quite inadequate forces at his command to bring about a democratic Revolution, such as took place in Austria. The Hungarian Socialists, on whom he had largely to rely, had neither influence in the country districts nor any understanding of rural problems or sympathy with peasant claims. The intellectuals were few, unstable, and largely Jewish, and there was only a small middle class, also largely Jewish, and a Civil Service, Magyar indeed, but utterly out of sympathy with the Revolution. The forces of counter-revolution, though badly disorganised at the outset, were always strong, and were bound to regain the upper hand unless the land question was settled to the peasants' satisfaction. But how could it be dealt with effectively, with war repeatedly breaking out afresh and the towns and armies in continual need of food, even though they had little except worthless paper to give in exchange for it? Károlyi had to try to make peace, which the people wanted but would not endure at the expense of the terms on which alone it could be made. Accordingly both patriotic anger and economic discontent arising out of sheer privation turned against Károlyi ; and the left became a curious mingling of these discrepant elements, blended together by the demagogy of Kun's lieutenants, who were out to make a Communist Revolution on any terms. Pressed again and again by the Allies for further concessions, which he could not make without provoking revolution against himself, Károlyi ended by being thrust out of office by the Communists with the acquiescence of most of those who had been his Socialist supporters.

The Socialists, with their influence already eroded by the propaganda of the Communists, well knew that they were much too weak to bear power alone. The Radicals having already left the Government, there was no-one to whom they could look for help except the Communists, who would clearly come in only on their own terms. These were the circumstances in which Zaigmond Kunfi patched up his party alliance with Béla Kun, and induced Social Democrats and Communists to join forces in a United Socialist Party, which accepted the gospel of proletarian dictatorship because there seemed to be no other course open. A good many Social Democrats, however, remained hostile to the fusion and to the dictatorship, and stood aside, hoping that it would speedily collapse and the Socialist supporters of it come back to sanity. As we saw, by June this was already happening, as quarrels developed between the Communist and Social Democratic wings. But the dictatorship managed to last on till, by the beginning of August, it had not only lost its Red Army and was on the point of losing its capital, but was also confronted with increasingly powerful White forces built up with Allied support. Only then did it attempt, at the eleventh hour, to put the moderate Socialists into power as against the Whites ; and by that time the Socialist Government under Peidl had not even the ghost of a chance of saving anything from the wreck.

So much abuse has been poured on Béla Kun's dictatorship

that I feel no impulse to add to it. It is, however, of some importance to try to understand why it happened as it did. When Kun and his colleagues came to power they were not without hope that help might come from the Russians, who were beating back Petlyura's forces in the Western Ukraine ; but this hope, such as it was, speedily disappeared when it became plain that the Russians had their hands all too full elsewhere. It has, however, to be borne in mind that in 1919 the Communist leaders were still convinced of the early arrival of Revolution over the greater part of Europe, and were doing all they could to stir it up wherever they saw a chance. The deeply disturbed conditions in Hungary and the severe repression practised on its peoples made that country seem to them eminently ripe for revolution ; and they had no hesitation in sending in their Russian-trained professional revolutionaries to bring it about. Either they did not appreciate, or Kun and his co-workers did not, that an indispensable condition of revolution in Hungary was an alliance of some sort between the peasants and the urban workers. Lenin had seen clearly enough that in Russia success involved telling the peasants to take the land for themselves, and actually helping them to do so, even at the price of making Socialism immediately impossible in the rural areas. The Hungarian revolutionaries appear never to have understood this necessity and to have been driven to violent measures against the peasants, in order to get food for the towns, without giving them the land as a *quid pro quo*. Their writ, therefore, never ran outside the towns, except to the accompaniment of acts of violence which utterly estranged the peasants and thus prepared the way for the counter-revolution.

Even, however, if the Communists had shown much more sagacity in handling the peasant problem, their chance of lasting success would have been practically none. The Hungarian working class, even had it been united, was too weak and too alien from the rest of the country to be able to establish itself as a ruling class, especially in face of the certain hostility both of the Allied great powers and of Hungary's ring of hostile neighbours. Given peace, Károlyi might conceivably have succeeded in stabilising the country under some sort of democratic rule and in destroying the power of the aristocracy by breaking up the great estates. That he could have done so is unlikely : at any rate he was not given the chance. When he was reduced to relying mainly on the Socialists and to advising them to come to terms with Kun, he was in effect throwing up the sponge ; for he was putting into office a Government which could have no hold on most of the country and was bound to be destroyed before long by its enemies within and without. To Kun that prospect was not sufficiently deterrent : it was his professional mission to make revolutions, even if they were bound to fail. That so many of the Socialists and Trade Unionists followed him into his adventure was a sign of the intensity of the nation's disturbance and of the immaturity of its working-class movement, which had neither tasted power or responsibility before 1918, nor become in any way integrated with the main body of the people. After 1919 the Hungarian working-class movement was knocked flat : it made no real recovery till the Russians marched in to set up the 'People's Democracy' of 1945, and, as we have reason to know to-day, that was by no means the final chapter in Hungary's tragic history.

CHAPTER VIII

THE BALKANS—BULGARIA, RUMANIA, YUGOSLAVIA, GREECE

FOR the purpose of this chapter, the 'Balkans' signify the area stretching from Greece, Albania, Croatia, and Slovenia in the west to the Asiatic frontier and from Transylvania and Old Rumania in the north to the Mediterranean. They thus include the pre-1914 States of Greece, Albania, Serbia, Montenegro, Bulgaria, Rumania, and Turkey in Europe, together with considerable tracts of the pre-war Austro-Hungarian empire, but exclude Hungary proper, the territories which were assigned to Poland after the war, and, of course, the whole of what became Czechoslovakia on the break-up of the Dual Monarchy. All the countries included in this 'Balkan' region were overwhelmingly agricultural in population; and in most of them the greater part of the land was already in the hands of small or medium peasants. The exception was Rumania, which in 1914 was still, like Hungary and Poland, a country of big landed estates with a large population of landless labourers heavily oppressed by the landowning class. There were also big estates elsewhere, especially in some of the areas previously under Austrian or Hungarian rule; but, generally speaking, there was not a great deal of scope for land settlement through the dispossession of great landowners. In Bulgaria, particularly, the social structure was already largely equalitarian, with most of the land owned by small cultivators and hardly any development of industry to serve as the basis for a business middle class. But even where the peasants possessed the land, political power was not in their hands. There were only a few areas, notably Bulgaria and Croatia, in which peasant organisations had made any substantial headway; and even in these areas they had not attained to any considerable political power or influence, though both the Radić brothers in Croatia and Stambolisky in Bulgaria had already built up considerable followings in the rural areas.

The peasants, even where they had land, were for the most part terribly poor, both because their methods of cultivation were primitive and most of their holdings too small to maintain them at a tolerable level and because the main burdens of taxation were laid on their shoulders by the classes which monopolised political power. Moreover, as population increased, holdings tended to get smaller under the prevailing system of division among the sons of the peasant household, and also to be broken up into smaller and smaller strips, which made good husbandry nearly impossible. This atomisation of peasant holdings continued during the inter-war period and was accompanied, especially after 1929, by a sharp fall in the value of agricultural in relation to industrial products — which greatly reduced peasant standards of living and much more than offset any benefits derived from land distribution, even in the areas in which there were considerable quantities of land available for this purpose. The Balkan region was already suffering badly from rural over-population in 1914; and after 1918 this over-population grew steadily and rapidly worse, aggravated by the obstacles put in the way of emigration, which had afforded a large measure of relief before the war. Though there was some development of industry, it was nowhere on a scale to afford substantial relief; and the large reserves of labour in the countryside continually provided to the towns a supply of unskilled immigrant workers, whose competition for jobs kept industrial wages down to sheer subsistence level, except for the small minorities of skilled workers. These skilled workers enjoyed a relatively favourable situation and were able to maintain fairly strong Trade Unions in some areas; but they were too few to serve as a foundation for really powerful Labour or Socialist movements, and in most cases were forcibly prevented from making any attempt to extend their organisation or their propaganda into the rural districts.

Each Balkan country had its 'intellectuals', who played a leading part in the growth of the various Socialist movements and groups. But the main body of intellectuals was associated with nationalism rather than with Socialism and, even where it was affected at the outset by Socialist ideas, tended to forget its socialistic tendencies under pressure of nationalist preoccupations. The Universities, which provided the main road of access to higher education, played a large part in the development of the intellectual *élites* ; and, in the absence of extensive openings for industrial or commercial positions, they sent a high proportion of their graduates into the public services, which were in many cases much inflated in order to provide careers thought suitable for educated men. There was very little technical education ; and schools of law occupied a disproportionate position in university studies. A substantial number of children of better-off peasant families found their way to the Universities, where they mostly became divorced from village life and joined the ranks of the urban middle class. Some of them became leaders or supporters of Peasant or Agrarian Parties ; but these Parties, under their influence, tended for the most part to move rapidly to the right and to become mere groupings of politicians who wooed peasant support with high-sounding phrases but showed less and less practical zeal in the pursuit of peasant interests that threatened the established régime. The great exceptions were Stambolisky's Agrarian League in Bulgaria and, to a smaller extent, the Peasant Party of the Radić brothers in Croatia. Even before 1914 the Serbian Radical Party, which had been at one time a real exponent of popular radicalism, had shed its radical characteristics and become in effect the conservative champion of bourgeois nationalism ; and after the setting up of the enlarged Yugoslav State it turned into the principal upholder of Serbian domination and centralised government against the advocates of a federal state based on the autonomy of the various branches of the new Yugoslav society. After the defeat of the revolutionary movements of the early post-war years the Balkan intelligentsia went over more and more to the support of the various dictatorships which destroyed parliamentary government in country after country ; and in the 1930s a large part of it was greatly influenced by Nazi ideas : so that in many cases the university students, organised in Fascist or quasi-Fascist gangs, became important auxiliaries of the repressive public régimes in beating up left-wingers, in helping to put down strike movements, and, not least, in organising brutal anti-Semitic agitations in the name of nationalist awakening.

The politicians of all parties, except those which were driven underground, favoured industrialisation and took the side of capitalism, both against the industrial workers and at the peasants' expense ; for it was in the main the peasant who paid for industrial development both in taxes and through the high prices of such industrial goods as he had to buy. Protection for native industries raised the prices of such goods, the more so because the industries chosen for development were in many cases highly unsuitable and involved very high production costs. Protection went largely by favour, and often by sheer bribery : there was no attempt to plan for the development of those types of production that would best serve the needs of the main body of poor consumers. There was, no doubt, a strong case for industrialisation as a means of drawing off surplus labour from the over-populated countryside ; but sound industrial development was impracticable unless it was accompanied by a real improvement in agricultural productivity, and such an improvement was out of the reach of all but a small minority of larger farmers. Something could have been done if the Governments had been prepared to give real encouragement to the right forms of agricultural Co-operation ; but in most cases the only forms Governments did encourage — chiefly marketing Co-operatives or certain kinds of Credit Unions — were of use only to the more prosperous farmers, and brought no benefit to the small-holders who lived chiefly on their own produce. Other forms of Co-operation, which might have led to joint use of implements and machinery and even to Co-operative tillage, were frowned upon and even forcibly put down as savouring of Bolshevism. It was indeed the case that a good many so-called Co-operative Societies were in fact no more than political associations attached to the Peasant Parties, and did little to apply Co-operative methods in practice. But this was largely because they were given less than no encouragement to do so. Only in one or two areas of relatively prosperous farming — e.g. in Slovenia — was Co-operation given freer scope because it was mainly under clerical influence and control and was not feared as a potentially subversive political force. After the overthrow of Stambolisky's Agrarian Government in Bulgaria in 1923 the peasant movement stood no further chance. Revolutionary feeling remained strong among the mass of poor peasants in many areas ; but there was no concerted leadership and no link between the discontented and oppressed peasants and the urban workers. The latter were both far too weak to be able to take any effective action without agrarian support and divided into a small minority of skilled workers, who were relatively well-off in an economic sense, and a much larger urban proletariat of unskilled workers continually exposed to the competition of starving refugees to the towns from the overcrowded rural areas.

Yet in Rumania, the one Balkan country which in 1918 was still dominated by big landed estates, most of these estates were in fact broken up and distributed among peasant holders. There was in Rumania a real agrarian revolution, though it was carried through on terms of compensation very onerous to the peasants and there was a great deal of favouritism and discrimination in the parcelling out of the land. Why did the great Rumanian land reform do so little to improve the condition of the Rumanian peasants ? Partly because of its terms, but mainly because the peasants were left without means of increasing productivity by the adoption of better farming methods. They were mostly too poor and their holdings too small and dispersed for them to be in a position to advance beyond the most primitive methods of cultivation ; and almost nothing was done by the State to help them or to enable them to help themselves. They would in any case have become victims of the great fall in agricultural prices that took place after 1929 ; but they could have been better placed to meet this fall had they been given more help during the 1920s. It is a disputed question whether the parcelling out of the land actually decreased agricultural output as a whole ; but it is indisputable that productivity was much greater on the surviving large and middle-sized holdings than on the exiguous holdings of the great majority, and that it was sheerly impossible to introduce more advanced methods without Co-operative credit and Co-operative supply of improved implements, or without a great campaign for technical education to accompany Co-operative effort. In the absence of these, the Rumanian peasants, after the land reform, continued for the most part to fare as ill as their neighbours who had been accustomed to the cultivation of exiguous peasant holdings over a longer period.

The suffering and the positive deterioration of peasant conditions were indeed common to all the Balkan countries.

Population rose fast, as the outlets for emigration were more and more cut off. The openings for industrial employment remained very small in relation to the size of the rural surplus ; and peasant holdings got smaller and smaller as they were divided up at the holders' deaths. But the peasants were helpless in face of police repression and denial of even a minimum of civil rights ; and in effect the entire governing class and the bulk of the middle classes were against them and all too ready to denounce any protest as 'Bolshevism' — the more so because they were conscious of living by a volcano that might at any moment erupt and sweep them away unless it were firmly bottled up. The urban proletariat, preoccupied with its own troubles, did nothing to help them : even the Socialists, at best barely tolerated, found it prudent to keep out of the villages in order to avoid provoking yet greater police repression. The Communists, who did try to stir up rural unrest when it was too late, failed to give support to Stambolisky at the critical moment, on the plea that his peasant movement was essentially bourgeois and that they had no interest in the faction fights of the bourgeoisie ; and when they did attempt to reverse this ostrich policy, they were already proscribed and confined to underground action which severely limited their effectiveness. They were, in fact, temperamentally and by conviction so hostile to the peasant attitude as to be incapable of sympathising with anything in the peasant except his discontent and potential revolutionism ; and this sympathy was not sufficient foundation for a concerted movement under the prevailing conditions.

Yet there was, at any rate in Bulgaria and over a large part of Yugoslavia, a deep current of pro-Russian feeling which made the unhappy peasants look eagerly to the Soviet Union as a source of liberation, and thus laid them open to Communist propaganda, not because they were Communists but because they were fellow-Slavs suffering under an oppression from which they believed the Russian peasants to have been set free. In Bulgaria a large part of the following of Stambolisky went over to the Communists after his death ; and in Yugoslavia too the Communist Party made much more headway than its Social Democratic rival in the rural districts, especially in Old Serbia and in the Yugoslav part of Macedonia. Communism became the rallying point for revolutionary feeling, not as Communism in any theoretical sense, but because there was no effective alternative when the Peasant Parties had gone over in practice to no more than half-hearted criticism of the existing order. The consequences were seen only after the second world war, when the dissolution of that order laid the road open to the 'People's Democracies' under Communist leadership and control. In the 1920s and 1930s, after the first revolutionary wave had been beaten back, Fascism and military-royal dictatorship had matters all their own way.

In the Balkan countries, when the European war broke out in 1914, only Bulgaria had a Socialist movement of a highly developed kind; and Bulgarian Socialism was notable for the ferocity of its internal controversies between the rival Parties of the 'Narrows' and the 'Broads'. In Rumania, where the chief intellectual influence was that of Christian Rakovsky, Socialism had only begun to recover from the drastic repression that had followed the agrarian revolt of 1905, and was still mainly an underground movement, with little or no following outside the towns. In Serbia the Socialist Party and the Trade Union movement associated with it were still inchoate, and had little influence; and the same can be said of both Greece and Turkey.[1]

All these countries were, as we saw, overwhelmingly agricultural, only Rumania having any considerable industrial development, centred mainly on its oil wells. But agricultural conditions differed sharply. Both Bulgaria and Serbia were predominantly cultivated by small peasant farmers, and had few great landed estates and relatively few landless peasants except refugees from the areas still under Turkish rule; whereas Rumania was still dominated by great landlords, and its peasants suffered under much heavier oppression than the Bulgarians or Serbs, but had been so beaten down after the revolt of 1905 as to be able to offer little resistance to their oppressors. The comparatively favourable conditions of the peasantry in Bulgaria and Serbia were due mainly to the fact that the land had been in the hands of Turks, who had been driven out when these countries won their position as independent States. The comparative immunity of the peasants from

[1] See Vol. III, Part II, pp. 603 and 605.

oppressive landlordism did not mean that they enjoyed a good standard of living; for agricultural methods remained largely primitive, especially in Serbia, though in Bulgaria there had been a rapid growth of the cultivation of tobacco for the market during the years before 1914.

Between 1912 and 1914 the economies of these countries had suffered serious upsets because of the Balkan Wars, which had involved considerable territorial changes, especially at Bulgaria's expense. The Socialists, under the influence of the Second International, had played their part in the struggle for peace and had espoused the idea of a Balkan Federation designed to check interference by the great powers in Balkan affairs; but the war atmosphere had adversely affected their influence, which was in any case small. When the European War came, with Serbia directly involved in it from the outset, the Serbian Socialists, despite the threat to their country's independence, refused to vote for the war credits. Bulgaria and Rumania became involved only later; but from the first the Socialists worked to keep their countries out of the war, and, when they had become belligerents, took up an anti-war line. The Bulgarian Narrow Socialists and the Rumanian Socialists were represented at the Zimmerwald Congress of 1915; and the Balkan Revolutionary Socialist Federation was one of the participating bodies at the inaugural Congress of the Third International in 1919.

BULGARIA

Balkan Socialism was throughout greatly influenced by the development of Socialism in Russia. Dimiter Blagoev (1856–1924), the leader of the Bulgarian 'Narrow' Socialists, and the Rumanian leader, Christian Rakovsky (1877–?), both had intimate connections with Russia. Blagoev had lived and worked there before his return to Bulgaria in 1886, and had taken part in the Russian Social Democratic movement; [1] and he was largely responsible for the split of 1903, which finally divided the Bulgarian movement into two hostile Parties. There was indeed some resemblance between the Bulgarian split and the dispute between Bolsheviks and Mensheviks in the Russian

[1] See Vol. III, Part I, p. 418.

Social Democratic Party ; but whereas the Russian factions maintained a sort of unity up to 1917, the Bulgarians split finally and decisively in 1903 and firmly resisted the attempts of the International to reunite them. Blagoev was much more fiercely sectarian than Lenin. On the other hand, the leader of the 'Broad' Socialists, Ianko Sakosov (1860–1941) had studied and worked in London, and was greatly under the influence of Western Socialist ideas. He was on intimate terms with the Western leaders of the Second International and supported the International's peace policy during the Balkan Wars, becoming the best-known advocate of a policy of Balkan federation. His influence and that of his Party were deeply undermined after Bulgaria's entry into the European War ; and the 'Narrows' emerged after the war as much the stronger party and became the outstanding champions of Communism modelled on the Russian example. Both wings of the Socialist movement, however, were for the time being overshadowed by the growth of Stambolisky's Agrarian Party, which won immense support among the Bulgarian peasant farmers and seemed for a time likely to become the point of focus for a 'Green' or Peasant International powerful enough to direct the course of Revolution in the Balkan region.

Alexander Stambolisky (1879–1923) was the most considerable figure among the leaders thrown up by the peasant movement in Eastern Europe. The son of a peasant farmer who owned his own land, he was educated first in Bulgaria and then in Germany, at the Halle agricultural college. Returning to Bulgaria, he became in 1902 editor of the journal of the newly formed Agrarian League, and set to work to organise the peasants into a nation-wide structure of agricultural associations. Returned to the Sobranje in 1908, he soon became leader of the Agrarian Party, which developed rapidly under his masterful impulsion. He came into conflict with King Ferdinand in 1911 over the issue of constitutional reform. During and after the Balkan Wars he bitterly attacked Ferdinand's policies ; and on the outbreak of the European War he strongly opposed the King's attempt to bring about Bulgaria's entry into it on the side of the Central Powers. Summoned to the King's presence, he threatened him with the loss of his crown in the event of such intervention ; and Ferdinand thereupon ordered his arrest. He was tried by court-martial and sentenced to imprisonment for life ; and he remained a prisoner until Bulgaria's military collapse in September 1918.

Stambolisky, though a thorough-going Radical, was no Socialist. He believed in a peasant society based on individual property and cultivation, but reinforced by Co-operative organisation and led by actual peasants and not by town politicians or intellectuals out of contact with village life. When he was released from prison in September 1918 he was sent to pacify the soldiers, who were returning towards their homes in mutinous mood ; but instead he put himself at their head and marched on Sofia. The Government, however, sent agains them Macedonian units from districts threatened with separation from Bulgaria ; and Stambolisky's forces suffered a reverse. Nevertheless, King Ferdinand's unpopularity was so great that he was forced to abdicate and to flee from Sofia, leaving the crown to his son, Boris. Stambolisky then came to terms with the new King and, in January 1919, joined the new Government, to which fell the unpleasant task of making peace on behalf of a defeated country. He was sent to Paris to conduct the peace negotiations, and was presently confronted with an ultimatum from the Allies involving the acceptance of frontiers that condemned great numbers of Bulgars to Greek or Yugoslav rule and were certain to be strongly resented both in the areas affected and among the numerous refugees from them in Bulgaria itself. Realising resistance to be impracticable, Stambolisky favoured acceptance under protest and attempted only to secure guarantees of fair treatment and cultural autonomy for the minorities concerned. In October 1919 he became Prime Minister ; and the Treaty of Neuilly was signed the following month. He next proceeded, early in 1920, to dissolve the Sobranje and carry through a General Election, which gave his Agrarian Party a clear majority in the new Parliament. From February 1920 to June 1923 Stambolisky governed Bulgaria virtually as an absolute ruler, with the support of the main body of the peasants but in face of strong opposition both from the bourgeoisie and from those nationalistic elements powerful among army officers and refugees from 'Greater Bulgaria', which refused to acquiesce in the hard terms of the treaty of peace.

At the time of the Revolution in 1918 Stambolisky had appealed for the support of the Socialists against King Ferdinand and his reactionary clique, and had made overtures to the 'Narrow' Socialists, who represented the only other powerful left-wing force. The 'Narrows', however, intent on a proletarian Revolution on the Russian model, would have nothing to do with him. In their view the peasant Revolution at which he aimed was essentially a petit-bourgeois movement, with which they had nothing in common ; and they denounced his attempted *coup* as no more than a quarrel between rival factions of the bourgeoisie. Stambolisky himself, when he came to power, made no attempt to attack the monarchy, now that his old antagonist, Ferdinand, was out of the way ; and the 'Narrow' Socialists, who had meantime joined the Third International and changed their name to Communist Party, took this as confirming the correctness of their refusal to give him their support. They did, however, under his régime enjoy a freedom to organise and agitate openly which had no parallel in other relatively backward countries not under Soviet control ; and they were able considerably to increase their membership and influence.

Stambolisky, having won power under very difficult international conditions, took the greatest care not to fall foul of the Allies who had dictated the terms of peace, and not to quarrel with the neighbours who had profited by them at Bulgaria's expense. By his moderate and conciliatory policy in international negotiations he won the good opinion of the statesmen of the great Allied powers and succeeded in extracting considerable concessions from them, including a very big reduction in the amount claimed as reparations from the badly disorganised Bulgarian economy. But his policy of conciliation, involving the abandonment of territorial claims based on national self-determination, also made him implacable enemies, especially among the Macedonians, who constituted a substantial and influential element in the population. The Nish Agreement, which he concluded with Yugoslavia in 1922, was loudly denounced by these irredentist groups and was among the main causes of his overthrow the following year.

With this conciliatory international policy, based on recognising Bulgaria's weakness as a defeated State, Stambolisky combined a by no means conciliatory policy in home affairs. He set out, in particular, to administer condign punishment to those who had been responsible for bringing Bulgaria into the war on the German side, throwing the leading war-time politicians into prison and putting many influential and wealthy persons on trial for offences against the State. As a peasant leader he was violently hostile to lawyers and financiers, whom he accused of exploiting the peasants ; and he demanded the complete exclusion of such persons from the Sobranje and from all official posts. In a country already mainly in the hands of peasant cultivators owning their own land, there were few big landowners to be dispossessed ; but Stambolisky introduced an agrarian law providing for the breaking-up of such large estates as there were and also for the expropriation of church lands and for the distribution of these and of publicly owned lands among the landless peasants and among those who had too little land to be able to maintain their families at a tolerable standard. The army having been reduced within very narrow limits by the Peace Treaty, he took the opportunity to enact a law providing for a year's compulsory labour service by all male citizens ; and he also attempted to solve the housing problem by what amounted to confiscation of big houses and capitalist-owned dwellings. His social policy was thus very advanced and earned him the solid hostility of the bourgeois elements ; but in his agricultural policy he was accused, hardly with justice, of favouring the better-to-do peasants by consolidating private land-ownership. This was naturally one of the charges levelled against him by the Communists, who disregarded the beneficent aspects of his social policy in their hostility to its effects in consolidating the peasant-ownership structure and thus standing in the way of proletarian Revolution.

Through his period of power Stambolisky did what he could, within the limits of the Neuilly Treaty and the powers of the League of Nations, to stand up for the claims of the Bulgars who were under foreign rule. There were, however, narrow limits to what could be done in this way, in face of the hostile attitude of the Greek and Yugoslav Governments, which could not be compelled to observe the spirit of the clauses of the League Charter or of the Neuilly Treaty designed to safeguard minority rights : nor were the Macedonians and the other irredentist elements at all disposed to acquiesce in the frontiers established by the treaty. Accordingly, Stambolisky's enemies were irreconcilable ; and in June 1923 a combination of bourgeois politicians and business interests with nationalist army officers largely inspired by Macedonian irredentists was able to organise in Sofia a *coup* which overthrew the Government. Most of the Ministers were arrested and thrown into prison. Stambolisky was absent at the time, at his native village of Slavovitsa, where an attempt was made to seize his person. He escaped for the moment and fled into the mountains in an attempt to get away across the frontier ; but a few days later he was overtaken and captured, and then shot, tortured, mutilated, and finally killed — it was said, in attempting to escape — by Macedonian terrorists. Meanwhile, in Sofia, a reactionary Government headed by Professor Z. Tsankov assumed power without serious opposition, the Communists once more refusing to come to Stambolisky's help. There was sporadic resistance from agrarian groups in a number of villages ; but there was no concerted leadership, and it was speedily put down. Only in September, three months after Stambolisky's death, did the Bulgarian Communists, under pressure from the Comintern, attempt to translate their principles into action by organising their own rebellion against the Tsankov Government. The Government got advance information of their plans and arrested about a thousand Communists. This did not prevent the rising, but reduced it to a number of unco-ordinated local movements, in the suppression of which about 5000 of the insurgents were killed.

Upon these events followed a 'White Terror', in the course of which there were mass arrests of persons suspected of Communist tendencies, many quite innocent persons being held in prison without trial for many months.

During the following year, 1924, the troubles continued, despite these ruthless measures. But they were complicated by the outbreak of serious disturbances in Macedonia. Todor Aleksandrov, the able leader of the Internal Macedonian Revolutionary Organisation, was murdered by his opponents, and there followed a series of reprisals and counter-reprisals, which sent many Macedonians fleeing as refugees into Bulgaria and aggravated nationalist feelings among the Macedonian elements in Bulgaria. Thus, a third source of internal trouble was added to the conflicts between the Government and the Communists and between the Government and the Agrarian followers of Stambolisky. There were a number of assassinations and other acts of violence, variously attributed to one or another of the dissatisfied groups. In April 1924 the troubles came to a head with two nearly simultaneous outrages — an unsuccessful attempt to assassinate King Boris and a highly successful bomb outrage in Sofia Cathedral during the funeral of General Gheorghiev, who had been murdered just before. The explosion killed no fewer than 123 persons, and injured many more ; and the victims included many notables who were attending the funeral ceremony. It never became fully clear who was behind this outrage, though in government circles it was widely attributed to Agrarians. It provided the excuse for yet another reign of terror, in the course of which more than 5000 persons were arrested, and large numbers of persons accused of anti-government activities were brought to trial, some being sentenced to death, some to banishment, loss of civil rights, imprisonment or fines, while some were acquitted for lack of any evidence at all to justify their arrest.

After this climax the disturbances gradually died down, though they continued on a smaller scale. The Agrarian and Communist Parties both continued to be officially proscribed, and remained in being only underground. Only some years later was a new Labour Party allowed to come into existence — in effect, mainly as a disguised form of Communist Party ; and before this body had been able to achieve any substantial following, one of its leaders, M. Traikov, was murdered by terrorists in 1933, and it was soon driven underground in its turn by the Zvenov military *coup* of 1934, which was followed by the Fascist *coup* organised by King Boris the following year.

Meanwhile, the pre-war leader of the 'Broad' Socialists, Ianko Sakosov, remained at the head of the non-Communist Socialist Party till its dissolution in 1933. This Party belonged to the Labour and Socialist International and continued to advocate Western Social Democratic ideas ; but it had only a small following, almost confined to the towns. A few of its members, without formal party sanction, took some part in collaborating with the Tsankov Government after the *coup* of

1923, and were subsequently expelled. In the General Election of 1927 the Party, by then called the Social Democratic Labour Party, formed a coalition with the remaining Agrarians, organised in a Smallholders' Party ; and their so-called 'Iron Bloc' got nearly one-third of the total vote, and 62 seats. Of these, however, the Social Democrats got only 10. The communistic Labour Party, working under severe repression, won only four seats at this election, though it undoubtedly had in reality much the bigger following.

Thus Bulgaria, after Stambolisky's death, passed through a sequence of violent outbreaks and White Terrors fully as ferocious as those in Finland and Hungary a few years earlier ; and the outcome was a Fascist dictatorship which, though it was able to sustain its authority until the Russians marched in in 1944, was always confronted with powerful underground forces which only awaited their chance.

The Tsankov Government of 1923 and its successors, despite their reactionary composition, could not undo the most important part of Stambolisky's achievement — the land reform — or alter the fundamentally democratic basis of Bulgarian society. Nor could they unmake the Neuilly Treaty or satisfy the aspirations of the Macedonian Bulgars who had taken a large part in bringing in the new régime after Stambolisky's fall. What they could and did do was to destroy, for the time being, the Communist-dominated working-class movement and to reinstate the capitalist elements which Stambolisky had sought to subdue, while leaving in existence a large body of social discontent that continued to break out from time to time in local revolts.

The overthrow of Stambolisky was a heavy blow to the cause of peasant radicalism not only in Bulgaria but over a large part of Europe. Of all the peasant leaders he was by far the most forthright and effective and also the most intelligent ; and he had seemed for a time destined to become the leader of a more than national peasant movement, to be given expression and means of influence through the 'Green' International which it was his ambition to create. Stambolisky, though no sort of a Socialist, was prepared to accept Socialist, or Communist, help in his struggle against the detested bourgeois politicians and their capitalist supporters. He was a thorough-going Radical with a deep belief in the virtues of a system of peasant democracy that would set the countryside free from the domination and exploitation of the town-dwellers. He believed in a peasant society resting on individual ownership of the land by those who actually tilled it, and in the capacity of free peasants thus owning their lands to make the State serve their ends, as well as to improve their position by using Co-operation as an instrument. His mind was not subtle ; but he was an intellectual as well as a peasant and wrote cogently in support of his policies. His best-known works are *Authority, Anarchy and Democracy* and, still more rewarding, *What a Politician Ought to Be*. Though he cannot be regarded as a profound theorist, he wrote with evident sincerity and conviction ; and it was as a journalist that he originally made his mark. In personal contacts he was undoubtedly impressive — witness the impact he made on the seasoned Western politicians with whom he had to negotiate. Physically, he was big and broad, black-haired and rugged of countenance and of speech, but capable of conciliatory behaviour and with a power of making himself liked as well as feared. Perhaps the Communists were right in refusing to come to terms with him ; for if they had, at any rate in 1918 or 1919, he would have swallowed them up, and not they him, and the success of his policy in Bulgaria would have given a fillip to the peasant movements in many other countries, and would have put formidable barriers in the way of Communist attempts to take the leadership in peasant revolts. Stambolisky's fall was the end of the Green International as a serious factor in European affairs and therewith of the peasant revolutionism which, in its Russian manifestation, the Bolsheviks had already subdued to their centralising, industrialist control. This peasant revolutionism never had, I think, much chance of constructive success ; but if it had any chance, Stambolisky was the man to lead it.

YUGOSLAVIA

The establishment of the new State of Yugoslavia — the Kingdom of the Serbs, Croats, and Slovenes — on the morrow of the European War involved the coming together into a single movement of the Socialist Parties of the areas incorporated in the new State. None of these Parties had been strong in 1914 ; but the ferment of the war years — above all the events of the Russian Revolution — had brought a great access of potential strength. The various Parties had, however, different traditions. The Serbian Socialist Party was a left-wing Marxist Party, resembling the 'Narrow' Socialist Party in Bulgaria, but rather less doctrinaire. As we saw, it had refused to vote the war credits in 1914 ; and it had consequently undergone persecution and developed along revolutionary lines. As against this, the Croatian Socialist Party and the small Party in Bosnia-Hercegovina included substantial elements more closely akin to Western, and especially to Austrian, Social Democracy ; and these elements did not combine easily with the Serbs, who formed part of the Balkan Socialist Federation and took part in the initial Congress of the Communist International in March 1919. The following month, the Serbian Socialist Party united with the left-wing groups in Croatia, Bosnia, and Dalmatia to form the Socialist Labour Party of Yugoslavia, which changed its name to Communist Party the following year. The right-wing groups refused to join the new Socialist Labour Party and set up a rival Social Democratic Party. In the General Election of December 1920 the Communists won 58 seats, and the Social Democrats 10, in an Assembly of 414 members. The Trade Unions mainly followed the Communist Party, a rival Federation under Social Democratic auspices having only a very small membership.

The main immediate issue confronting Yugoslavia after 1918 was the drawing up of a Constitution for the new State, in face of sharp differences of opinion not only on social and economic issues but also on the question of federalism or centralisation. The Serbs represented on the whole a centralising force, desiring a unitary State in which they hoped to make their influence predominant ; whereas the Croats and Slovenes were for the most part strongly insistent on autonomy, and in Macedonia a bitter struggle was developing between rival nationalist factions, and between Macedonian Bulgars who resented incorporation in Yugoslavia and pro-Serb advocates of Yugoslav unity. The strongest party in the post-war Yugoslav Parliament was the Radical Party, led by Nicolas Pasić, who regarded the new State as simply an enlargement of pre-war

Serbia, and strongly insisted on centralisation. The Serbian Radicals, in the early years of the century, had been a really radical party, resting largely on peasant support and taking a strongly democratic line. But even before 1914 they had been developing into a conservative party, standing for industrial development and largely controlled by leaders drawn from the urbanised bourgeoisie; and after 1918 their great desire was to unify the much enlarged kingdom under predominantly Serb control. This was keenly resented by the Croats and by other peoples who had been under Hungarian or Austrian rule and regarded themselves as superior to the Serbs in culture and economic development.

Nearly as numerous in Parliament as the Radicals were the adherents of the Democratic Party, made up of a mixture of the Serbian opposition with a number of groups drawn from other parts of the enlarged Kingdom. The Serb Democrats were rather more advanced in social policy than the Radicals, but were for the most part equally insistent on Serb predominance; whereas many of the other elements in the Democratic Party were more disposed to preserve some measure of regional autonomy, but were not agreed about the precise form it should take, or even about the units into which the country should be subdivided. These two Parties — Radicals and Democrats — were very nearly equal, each with between 90 and 100 deputies. Next strongest were the Communists, with 58, and Stjepan Radić's Croatian Peasant Party, with 53.

The Croatian Peasant Party had been founded before 1914 by the Radić brothers — Anté and Stjepan (1871–1928); but Anté Radić, who had been its chief theorist and intellectual inspirer, died during the war, and the surviving brother, though immensely popular as an orator, had no very clear policy and preferred the rôle of agitator to that of a negotiator prepared to state his terms and reach an agreement. In the post-war situation he demanded not only a federal Constitution but also a Republic, to which the main Serbian parties were not at all likely to agree; and after his success in the elections, he called on his followers to boycott the new Parliament by refusing to take any part in its proceedings. He thus left the making of the new Constitution to the Radicals and Democrats, neither of whom could make it without the other's support. These two Parties were thus driven into an uneasy coalition Government, which forced through a mainly centralising Constitution against the bitter opposition of the main body of Croat and Slovene opinion. The new Constitution was formally inaugurated in June 1921 ; but during the ceremony a bomb was thrown in an attempt to kill the Prime Minister and the Prince Regent. This outrage was attributed to the Communists ; and the Government proceeded to pass a number of emergency decrees for the suppression of an alleged widespread terrorist conspiracy. The Minister of the Interior, M. Drašković, was thereupon murdered by a Bosnian Communist ; and Parliament retaliated with a series of emergency laws of great severity, including the annulment of the mandates of the 58 Communist deputies. The Communist Party was driven underground.

Meanwhile, Radić's Peasant Party continued its policy of abstention and passive resistance ; and in the Parliament, shorn of any effective opposition, the two coalition Parties quarrelled among themselves with increasing violence. Late in 1922 the Democrats resigned from the Government ; and the Radicals formed a rump Government, which decided to hold new elections. The result of these, in March 1923, was that the Radicals slightly increased their strength, whereas the Democrats lost heavily ; and Radić's Croat Peasants rose from 50 to 70, but still refused to take their seats. Attempts by the Radicals to negotiate with Radić broke down ; and after conducting a violent campaign against the Government Radić fled abroad and, first in London and then in Vienna, tried to induce the Western powers to intervene on the side of Croat autonomy. At length, early in 1925, he came to terms with the Democratic opposition and, himself remaining abroad, instructed his followers to take their seats in the Shupskina, for the purpose of ejecting the Radical Government. A prolonged political crisis followed, until in July the Democrats took office with support, but not participation, from the followers of Radić. Radić, after visiting Moscow and discussing, not very seriously, the entry of his group into a projected Peasant International under Russian influence, returned to Croatia and resumed his campaign for autonomy. His activities led to demands, from the Crown, the army, and the centralisers, for his arrest ; and the Democratic Government fell and was replaced by a predominantly Radical

Cabinet, supported by Democratic dissidents who favoured centralisation. Radić was arrested and his Peasant Party declared to be dissolved. The Government held new elections, at which it secured a small majority ; Radić reorganised his Party under a new name and, from prison, came to an agreement with the Democrats and other opposition groups. The Government, meanwhile, annulled the mandates of most of the Peasant deputies.

Then came a sudden change of front. Radić's nephew, Paul, on behalf of the Croat Peasant Party, issued a declaration accepting the Constitution ; and Radić himself came to terms with the Radicals, abandoned his alliance with the Democrats, and took office as Minister of Education in a coalition Cabinet of Radicals and Croat Peasants. But this peculiar alliance did not last long. After the death of the old Radical leader, Nicholas Pasić, in 1926, the rival Serbian Parties came to an agreement, and the Croats were forced back into sharp opposition. Then in June 1928 a Montenegrin Radical deputy, in the parliament chamber itself, shot and killed two Croat deputies and mortally wounded Radić, who died a few weeks later. This brought on a sharp crisis. The Croats under Radić's successor, Vladimir Maček, seceded from Parliament and set up an extra-legal Parliament of their own at Zagreb ; and after a few months King Alexander, in January 1929, declared the Constitution abolished and took power into his own hands. Yugoslavia thus passed under dictatorial rule, which lasted until Alexander's assassination by a Croat agent at Marseilles in 1934, and thereafter in a modified form until 1939, when Croatian autonomy was at length recognised on the eve of the second world war.

In the conditions that prevailed in Yugoslavia after 1923 there was little scope for successful Socialist activity. The dissolved Communist Party resumed legal activity under the title of Independent Workers' Party, but was subjected to continual persecution and was not able to achieve much. It obtained only 13,000 votes at the elections of 1925, and 25,000 two years later, and did not win even a single seat. The rival Socialist Party, in which Zivko Topalović was the outstanding figure, did little better. In 1925 it received 25,000 votes, but won no seat ; in 1927 it got 23,000 votes, and won a single seat.

It also managed to win over some of the Trade Unions which had previously followed the Communist lead ; but the Trade Union movement remained weak and divided into rival factions adhering to Amsterdam and Moscow. In the elections, especially in 1925, both Parties fought under very severe handicaps : there was a great deal of violence and intimidation, and not a few Socialists and Communists were seriously injured, and a few killed. The Socialist Party joined the Labour and Socialist International on its formation, but was too small to be allowed more than a single vote, whereas the Rumanians had 4 votes and the Bulgarians 3. It had no following among the peasants, who in Croatia continued to follow Radić and his successors, though his Party became steadily less active in the interests of its peasant supporters. Outside Croatia after 1923 the peasants played little part in politics.

RUMANIA

In 'Old Rumania' — that is, in Rumania as it existed before the war of 1914 — Socialism was weak and heavily repressed. The Socialist Party had been almost wiped out in the troubles of 1907, and had only reconstituted itself, under severe police conditions, in 1911. The Party opposed Rumanian intervention in the European War and was represented at the Zimmerwald Conference of 1915. After Rumania had become a belligerent in August 1916 the Party maintained its opposition ; and it suffered intensified persecution after the Germans had occupied most of the country. Its best-known leader, Christian Rakovsky, was in Russia and took an active part in the Russian Revolution, especially in the Ukraine, and in the establishment of the Communist International. After the outbreak of revolution in Russia there was a rapid spread of unrest. Rumania, unlike Bulgaria and Serbia, was a country of great landed estates, with few independent peasant farmers and an exceedingly repressive policy towards the impoverished and landless rural population. Under stress of war conditions the suffrage, hitherto restricted to a tiny minority, was widely extended in 1917 ; and a considerable redistribution of land was promised, with full compensation to the owners of the estates that were to be broken up. At this point, however, the collapse of the

Russian armies allowed the Germans to complete the destruction of the Rumanian forces ; and the Central Powers proceeded to impose peace terms which involved both territorial losses and the subjection of the Rumanian economy to German control. A period of enforced inflation followed, involving very severe hardships for the people ; and revolutionary feeling grew rapidly as the defeat of Germany was seen to be near at hand.

The end of the war brought with it not a diminution of Rumanian territory but a great enlargement, largely at Hungary's expense but including also the incorporation of Bessarabia — till then under Russian rule — and of areas previously disputed with Bulgaria. An interim Government under General Coandă was set up to take steps for the consolidation of the new State, and this Government introduced manhood suffrage, and then gave place to a so-called Liberal Cabinet under Ionel Bratianu. In December 1918 the unrest culminated in a general strike, which was defeated after the Government had arrested the entire executives of both the Socialist Party and the Central Trade Union Commission, and had acted with ruthless severity against the strikers. Such was the reign of terror introduced for the preservation of 'order' that at the General Election of 1919, held under the auspices of a temporary 'Ministry of Generals', the Socialist Party withdrew its candidates in protest. The election resulted in the defeat of the Liberals by a coalition of the Peasant Party and the National Democrats ; and a comparatively mild Government under Alexander Vaida-Voevod took office and embarked on a fairly ambitious plan of land reform. This, however, was too much for the reactionaries to stomach ; Vaida-Voevod was forced to resign, and in March 1920 General Averescu, the 'strong man' of post-war Rumania, and one whose prestige among the soldiers gave him a big popular following, replaced him, with the support of a so-called People's League with markedly Fascist tendencies. New elections were held in June 1920, and gave Averescu a large majority, though the Socialists, reversing their policy of abstention, succeeded in electing 20 deputies.

The Socialist Party, which was stronger in the territories newly joined to Rumania than in the old provinces, was at this time sharply divided on questions of policy. In February 1921 its Executive voted in favour of joining the Communist International ; but against 18 votes for doing so, 12 were cast in favour of joining the 'Two-and-a-Half' Vienna Union and 8 for the Berne Second International, the opponents of Communism coming chiefly from the new provinces. A split followed : the dissidents formed a Social Democratic Party, which proceeded to join the Vienna Union.

In May 1921 the majority, in process of reorganising themselves as a Communist Party, held a Congress at Bucharest. The Government, declaring that an insurrection was being prepared, arrested all the delegates and put them on trial for treason, and introduced a new law subjecting the Trade Unions to a state system of mediation in industrial disputes and forced the measure through in face of strong Socialist and working-class protests. While, however, it took strong steps against the working-class movement, it was forced by popular pressure to implement the promises of land reform that had been made during the war ; but the landowners were powerful enough to ensure that land distribution should be made only on a basis of generous compensation to the dispossessed proprietors and to defeat the proposal to make the subsoil — that is, in the main, the oil resources — the property of the State. Nevertheless, vicious though the land reform law was in many respects, it did change Rumania from a country of great estates into one cultivated predominantly by peasant farmers, and did thus bring about a fundamental social revolution. The land redistribution was particularly effective in Bessarabia and in other newly acquired areas in which it could be made largely at the expense of foreign (*e.g.* Hungarian) owners.

Meanwhile, in 1920, there had been a second general strike, mainly under Communist control. It was broken by the Government, which recalled the railway workers to the colours, and embarked on a savage policy of repression. After the troubles of 1921 the Communist Party was outlawed and was unable to present candidates at the General Election of 1922, at which the Social Democrats managed to secure the election of a single deputy, Jacob Pistiner (?–1930), who became their representative on the Labour and Socialist International. Pistiner held his seat until 1926, when he was ousted under the terms of an electoral law which denied representation to any Party polling less than 2 per cent of the total votes cast over the whole country. But elections in Rumania had little meaning : they could be manipulated by the Government actually in office so as to produce startling changes in the apparent views of the electors. In the country areas opposition candidates were frequently prevented from even offering themselves to the electors ; and even in the towns there was continual interference with the right of meeting and discussion. Then, in 1926, the 'Liberal' leader, Ionel Bratianu, forced through a new electoral law under which the Party securing the largest aggregate vote, provided it polled 40 per cent of the total votes, got 50 per cent of the total number of seats, over and above those falling to it in proportion to its voting strength. This peculiar system, together with the intimidation regularly practised by the Government in power, made sheer nonsense of the constitutional democracy on which the State was supposed to be based, and rendered it impossible for any Socialist Party to contest a general election with hope of winning more than, at most, a very few seats.

Ionel Bratianu died the year after this system was introduced, and after his death a Peasant Party Government came to power under Julius Maniu. Bratianu's Liberal Party, based mainly on the commercial classes, had been trying to develop Rumanian industries on nationalist lines without bringing in capitalists from abroad. The Maniu Government reversed this policy, and for the next few years there was an inrush of investment by foreign capitalists, resulting in a boom which came to an abrupt end, at the beginning of the 1930s, with the onset of the world depression. Maniu's Government, though rather more favourable to the peasants than the Liberals, showed itself no less hostile to the industrial working class, whose attempts to win concessions during the boom were relentlessly put down.

In effect, Rumania, throughout the period between the wars, lived under conditions of political dictatorship, whatever the name of the Party or coalition in office might be. It made little difference to the Socialists whether the Liberal, Bratianu, or the Peasant, Maniu, or the Conservative Democrat, Take Jonescu, or the leader of the People's League, General Averescu, was at the Government's head. Under them all, almost equally, Communism was proscribed, and moderate Socialism, and even Trade Unionism, persecuted and rendered ineffective as a political force.

GREECE

In no country of Europe were the conditions for the development of a Socialist movement, during and after the first world war, more unfavourable than in Greece, where social issues were overshadowed both by the conflict between the pro-German King Constantine and the liberal nationalist movement headed by Eleftherios Venizelos, and by the problems of territorial adjustment and absorption of transferred populations which arose out of the war. The Balkan Wars of 1912 and 1913 had added largely to Greek territory, both on the mainland, in Epirus and Macedonia, and by the acquisition of Crete and most of the Aegean islands, the population of 'Old Greece' being nearly doubled by these accessions. The world war brought further gains in Macedonia and Thrace and also, momentarily, a footing in Asia Minor at and round Smyrna. But the Greeks were driven out of Asia Minor by Kemal's forces in 1921 ; and an immense refugee problem was added to that of the large-scale exchanges of populations in Macedonia and Thrace, designed to resettle these areas of mixed population in such a way as to achieve greater homogeneity. These exchanges and the settlement of the Greek refugees from Asia Minor would have been impracticable without international financial help, provided under the auspices of the League of Nations. They had, moreover, to be effected under conditions of the utmost political instability in Greece itself, to the accompaniment of a sequence of fundamental upsets and revolutionary changes in political structure.

At the outbreak of the European War in 1914 Venizelos was at the head of the Greek Government and favoured intervention on the Allied side, at any rate to the extent of coming to Serbia's help in the event of an attack by Bulgaria. The King, on the other hand, was pro-German and was determined to keep Greece neutral in the German interest. In April 1915, when Great Britain wanted Greek help for its attack on the Dardanelles, the King dismissed Venizelos from office. After winning a General Election, Venizelos came back to office in August and authorised the Allied landing at Salonika ; but in October he was again dismissed, and a new General Election was ordered. This time the Venizelists boycotted the election ; and a succession of weak Cabinets carried on at the King's bidding. In September 1916 Venizelos seceded to Salonika, where he set up a rival Provisional Government under Allied protection and organised a rival State, whose soldiers fought on the Allied side. The Allied powers nevertheless refused to recognise his Government ; and Constantine remained in control at Athens until June 1917, when the powers at length forced him to abdicate in favour of his son, Alexander. Venizelos went back to Athens as head of a new Government, recalled the Chamber which the King had unconstitutionally dissolved in 1915, and declared war on the Central Powers. Thereafter, Greece officially took part in the war as an Allied power, and received its reward at the Peace Conference under the Treaties of Neuilly and Sèvres. But Venizelos, when he returned to Athens in August 1920 after these treaties had been signed, found himself faced with strong opposition at home. In October 1920 King Alexander died ; and there arose a demand that Constantine should be recalled to the throne. At the General Election of the following month Venizelos was heavily defeated. He resigned from office and, with many of his Ministers, left the country ; and after a plebiscite had been held Constantine was reinstated as King.

Then came the disastrous war in Asia Minor, in which the great powers, hostile to Constantine, gave the Greeks no support. The Greeks were driven out of Asia Minor ; and the retreating forces, gathering at Chios, proclaimed a Revolution. Constantine fled from Athens, and died abroad a few months later ; and the leading members of the Cabinet were tried by court-martial and shot. Then followed a confused period, during which the revolutionary Government vainly attempted to establish a constitutional régime, while Venizelos, still abroad, represented Greece in the negotiations that led to the signing of peace with Turkey at Lausanne in July 1923.

The question of Monarchy versus Republic was meanwhile still unsettled. In October 1923 General Metaxas attempted to make a royalist counter-revolution, but was easily defeated. In

December the King, under pressure, left the country while a National Assembly debated the future of the régime. The following month Venizelos returned to Greece and again became Prime Minister, but resigned almost at once when the Republicans objected to his plan for a plebiscite on the question of the Monarchy. The Officers' League was revived, and demanded the immediate establishment of a Republic. Venizelos again left the country ; and the Republic was proclaimed in March 1924 and subsequently ratified by a plebiscite. Prolonged debates followed about the new Constitution ; and these were still in progress when, in June 1925, General Pangalos organised a *coup d'état* and proceeded to set up a military dictatorship. But he was speedily overthrown, and after a confused interval Venizelos returned and headed the Government from 1928 to 1932. Then came further confusions, culminating in the return of King George in 1935 and in the dictatorship set up by General Metaxas in 1936.

In all these events the Socialist movement played only an insignificant part. During the European War the small Greek Socialist Party — founded in 1911 by a group which included Nicolaos Yiannios (b. 1885), now the doyen of Greek democratic Socialism — supported Venizelos against King Constantine ; and it paid the penalty by sharing in his defeat in 1920. Its old leader, Platon Drakoulis (1860–1941), had been expelled from it in 1915, and it found no outstanding leader to replace him. There was, however, as we saw, a rival centre of Socialist activity in Salonika, which had been annexed to Greece as a result of the Balkan Wars ; and the Salonika Labour Federation, which belonged to the Balkan Socialist Federation, took an anti-war line, and in 1915 was the chief promoter of a new pan-Hellenic Socialist Labour Party, which joined the Communist International on its formation in 1919. A General Confederation of Labour, based on the inchoate Trade Union movement, was set up in 1918, and joined the Red International of Labour Unions in 1920 ; but it was seriously weakened by the arrest and deportation of its leading members, and was not strong enough to play any significant rôle. The presence in Greece of vast numbers of starving refugees, from Asia Minor and elsewhere, provided a limitless supply of strike-breakers and rendered effective Trade Union action almost impossible.

The old Greek Socialist Party, led by A. Sideris, remained in being, but shrank up to almost nothing. In the elections of 1923 it was able to contest only 3 seats, none of which was won. But a group of 6 deputies, elected as Radicals, thereafter joined the Party and constituted a Socialist fraction in the Chamber. The rival Communist Party had a substantially larger vote, but also failed in 1923 to win a single seat. In 1926, however, it nearly doubled its vote, and won 10 seats. Meanwhile, the Socialist group in the Chamber had disappeared ; and in 1928 a General Labour Congress was convened to discuss the re-organisation of the Socialist forces. This Congress resulted in a split between the Communist and Socialist elements ; and the anti-Communist Socialists set up a new Socialist Labour Party with an orthodox Social Democratic programme.

This attempt at unity, however, had no better fate than its predecessors ; and a renewed attempt in 1931, when the Socialist organisations of Athens (Piraeus) and Salonika issued a joint manifesto and summoned a Unity Congress, was also unsuccessful in setting up an effective Party, though in that year the General Confederation of Workers, the main Trade Union body, was reorganised. The Socialist, D. Stratis (b. 1889), who had been General Secretary of the Railway Workers' Union from 1919 to 1925 and thereafter of the General Trade Union Federation prior to the reorganisation, remained in office as Secretary, and N. Yiannios, who had been among those principally active in the cause of Socialist unity, served as correspondent in maintaining relations with the Labour and Socialist International. In general, the situation was that, as long as the internal situation continued to be dominated by Venizelos, there was little chance of a powerful Socialist movement developing, especially because there was always tension between the Athenians and the groups centred on Salonika, which had traditions of association with the other Balkan countries rather than with the West. There were, moreover, even in Athens, deep divisions between right and left. From 1929, when Venizelos established a Senate largely representing vocational groups, the General Federation of Workers accepted seats on this body, despite the opposition of the Socialist Party and of the Trade Union left wing — and, of course, of the Communists, who, though by this time proscribed as a Party, continued to have some influence. Professor Alexandros J. Svolos (1892–1957), who later became the leader of the Greek Socialists, was in the 1920s a lawyer and teacher of law without political connections, though already of known radical tendencies. From 1917 to 1920 he had been Director of Labour Problems at the Finance Ministry, but had then returned to legal practice and teaching. In 1929 he became Professor of Constitutional Law at the University of Athens, and thereafter he became deeply engaged in the struggle for political decentralisation and for civil liberties. His activities cost him dismissal from his chair in 1935, and the following year he was arrested and deported to an island, whence he was set free and reinstated as Professor in 1940, on the outbreak of the Greek-Italian War. In 1944 he was again driven from his University post, and became for a short time President of the partisan Government which attempted to liberate Greece from the occupying forces. He then became Minister of Finance in the Papandreou Government and carried out the first attempt to stabilise the drachma. In December 1944, however, he resigned from the Government, and a few months later became Chairman of the Popular Democratic Union (E.L.D.), leaving his University position once again in 1946. In 1950, Svolos was elected to Parliament in both Athens and Salonika, choosing the latter seat, and thereafter leading the E.L.D. group and, from 1953, the new Socialist Party which arose out of the fusion between the E.L.D. and the Socialist League of which Stratis and Yiannios were outstanding figures. In addition to his political work he wrote extensively on questions of constitutional law and practice.

CHAPTER IX

THE RIVAL INTERNATIONALS, 1919–1921

THE projected Stockholm Conference of 1917 originated, as we saw,[1] not with the Russians, but with the Dutch-Scandinavian Committee set up by the West European neutrals in the hope both of hastening the end of the fighting and of bringing international Socialist influence to bear on the terms of peace. When the Russians came in after the first Russian Revolution of 1917, the initiative was in the hands, not of the Bolsheviks, but of a Petrograd Soviet still dominated by Mensheviks and Social Revolutionaries and still at an early stage of its contest for power with the Provisional Government : so that the Russians, in appealing for world-wide support for the Conference, spoke not as a Government but as the representatives of a working class that was still only feeling its way to power. The Russian delegates, who went to Stockholm to join the enlarged Russian-Dutch-Scandinavian Committee and presently toured the West European Allied countries in search of support for the projected Conference, suffered from a double weakness : they were never safe either from being repudiated by the Provisional Government or from the danger of ceasing to represent aright the attitude of the Soviet that had sent them on their mission. In the event, the Petrograd Soviet was too powerful a body for the Provisional Government ever to dare quite to disown its emissaries, or to come out openly against the Stockholm project ; but its attitude was ambiguous enough to be made much of by the opponents of Stockholm in the Allied countries, including their Governments. Moreover, the longer the Russian delegates remained in the West, the less they actually represented the body that had sent them, and the less weight their views carried with the Western Socialists.

The Bolsheviks, while they were still out of power, did not actively oppose the Stockholm project ; but it nevertheless ran

[1] See p. 45.

directly counter to their ideas. At Zimmerwald, as we saw, there had been two quite different conceptions both about the ending of the war and about the future of Socialist international organisation. Lenin and his group, which had been outvoted at Zimmerwald but had carried the day at Kienthal, had stood for a new International that would be pledged to the cause of World Revolution and would definitely exclude all the Socialist 'patriots' and 'defencists' who had supported the war efforts of their respective countries. The Leninists had denounced the 'social pacifists' who were intent on peace between the warring Governments rather than on a 'peoples' peace', following upon their overthrow by proletarian revolution ; whereas the Zimmerwald majority had stood for a negotiated peace without any such insistence on World Revolution as a prerequisite. It was therefore natural that the conquest of power by the Bolsheviks in Russia should lead to a fundamental change in Russian policy in international as well as in home affairs, and to an attempt to take the lead in constructing a new, revolutionary International instead of doing anything to help to rebuild the old International on a basis of unity between reformists and revolutionaries or between defencists and defeatists. It was an axiom of Bolshevik thought that the imperialist war would prepare the way for World Revolution, of which the Russian Revolution was simply the opening phase. The essential task, therefore, was not to bring together all those who called themselves Socialists into a common organisation, but rather to mobilise all the real revolutionaries in every country both against their reactionary Governments and against the false Socialists who had made common cause with these Governments during the war and by doing so had betrayed the revolutionary Socialist cause. The establishment of the Third International at Moscow in March 1919 was an entirely logical implementation of this policy. The consequences — in many respects unhappy — were due to the falsity of the Bolshevik assumption that the proletariats of the advanced Western countries were ready, given the lead, to follow a revolutionary policy at all resembling what Lenin and Trotsky expected of them. In the most powerful capitalist countries — in Great Britain, France, and Germany, and, even more, in the United States — the necessary conditions for

Socialist Revolution simply did not exist ; and the attempts of Communist minorities to act as if they did brought down disaster upon them and, even where Revolutions of a sort did occur, opened the way for counter-revolution — for example, in Germany, in Italy, and, most speedily of all, in Hungary. The disaster was less where the Communists were either too weak to make any attempt at revolution — in Great Britain for example, and in the United States — or, though relatively strong, did not in fact follow a revolutionary policy — for example, in France and Norway.

The Stockholm idea had included that of an International Socialist Conference, representing all sections and tendencies, that would meet simultaneously with the inter-governmental Peace Conference and would insist that the demands of the workers of the world should be incorporated in the official terms of peace. With this in view, the Stockholm Committee met delegations from all the Socialist Parties and groups it could induce to send them to Stockholm, and endeavoured to build up out of the oral and written statements of these bodies a draft Peace Plan which the Stockholm Conference would have been asked to ratify, had it ever met. As we have seen, it was never able to meet, partly because some of the Allied Socialist Parties refused to sit down in conference with the Germans, and partly because the Allied Governments, well aware of the dissensions in the Socialist ranks, felt strong enough in certain cases to refuse passports for the delegates from their countries to attend. Indeed, the leaders of the pro-war majority Socialists in the Allied countries preferred, in 1917, to confer with each other in an attempt to arrive at agreed Allied Socialist 'War Aims' to entering into any wider discussions until they had agreed among themselves, and were mostly lukewarm about Stockholm even when they were not positively against it.

Consequently, after the second Russian Revolution the Stockholm project lost its driving force. The Russians ceased to want it ; and such support as there had been for it in the Allied countries melted away. The idea of a Socialist Conference to meet simultaneously with the Peace Conference was not given up ; but opinions were divided between those who wanted this Conference to represent the whole Socialist movement and those who thought rather in terms of an Allied

Socialist Conference designed to bring pressure on the Allied Governments alone, as the sequel to an Allied victory. After the Peace of Brest-Litovsk, such an Allied Conference would, of course, have excluded the Russians, as well as the neutrals and the Socialists of the Central Powers. During 1918, though the Dutch-Scandinavian Committee remained in being and continued to advocate a general Conference, the Stockholm project dropped right into the background and, particularly in France, the centre of the stage came to be occupied by the internal struggles between the advocates of war to the bitter end and those who stood for a negotiated peace, with lesser minorities — usually small — upholding against both the claims of an out-and-out revolutionary policy based on the Russian example.

In France, by the summer of 1918,[1] the minority, headed by Jean Longuet, had become the majority ; and this change radically altered the balance of Allied Socialist opinion. For France and Belgium had constituted, till then, the main obstacles to a Socialist Conference on the Stockholm pattern, including representatives of German Socialism ; whereas Arthur Henderson, albeit with much difficulty, had secured a bare British majority for such a meeting. When, in the autumn of 1918, the Central Powers' resistance finally cracked, and Revolution broke out in Germany and Austria-Hungary, there was no longer, except in Belgium, any serious opposition to meeting the Germans, though there was still much insistence that the German Socialists must come to an international meeting ready to admit the war guilt of the Government they had recently overthrown. With the fighting at an end, Stockholm had passed out of the picture as a meeting-place — the more so because its Russian support had been removed ; but there seemed to the leaders of the Western Parties to be a strong case for a speedy meeting in a neutral country, in order both to discuss the Socialist attitude to the peace negotiations that were in prospect and at least to prepare the ground for the reconstitution of a Socialist International.

The Berne International Conference of February 1919 was not, in form, either a revival of the pre-war Socialist International or an outcome of the Stockholm project of 1917. The

[1] See p. 466.

summons to it was issued by a Committee set up at the Inter-Allied Labour and Socialist Conference of March 1918, acting in conjunction with Camille Huysmans, the Belgian Secretary of the International Socialist Bureau. The members of this committee were Émile Vandervelde, who was also President of the I.S.B., Arthur Henderson, and Albert Thomas — a Belgian, an Englishman, and a Frenchman — who had all been Ministers in war-time coalition governments and had been active in the series of Allied Socialist discussions dealing with War Aims. The purpose of the Berne Conference was to carry out the declared intention that the representatives of world Socialism should meet simultaneously with the official Peace Conference, and should convey to it the claims of the international Socialist and working-class movement in connection with the peace settlement, and with the future structure of international relations. As these claims were industrial as well as political, including the adoption of an International Labour Charter to govern both the rights of working-class combination and the minimum conditions of employment, it seemed essential that the Berne Conference should include delegates from the Trade Union movements of the various countries as well as from the Labour or Socialist Parties ; and accordingly the invitation was extended to both, on equal terms. But whereas, in the pre-war International, representation had been open in a number of cases to several rival Parties or other bodies from a single country, the Berne invitation went in most cases only to a single Party in each country and to a single Trade Union Centre. In the case of Great Britain the effect was to exclude separate representation of the Independent Labour Party, the British Socialist Party, and the Fabian Society, which had been members of the Second International in their own right, while leaving it open to the Labour Party, to which they were all affiliated, to include members of these bodies in its own delegation if it thought fit. This exclusion, which caused considerable annoyance to the Socialist bodies affected, was in part an outcome of the insistence of the British Labour Party Conference in 1917, that they should be denied representation at the proposed Stockholm Conference of that year. The decision to invite only the principal Trade Union Centre of each country also ruled out the General Federation of Trade Unions, which, as we saw, had represented Great Britain in the pre-war Trade Union International, and put the Trade Union representation exclusively in the hands of the Trades Union Congress, which, paradoxically, had been connected with the pre-war Socialist International but not with the Trade Union International. From the United States the American Federation of Labor, which had taken an active part in formulating proposals for an International Labour Charter, was invited, but refused to come, as it was unwilling to meet with German delegates on friendly terms. The Belgian Labour Party and its affiliated Trade Union Centre rejected the invitation on similar grounds.

There were also other refusals, for different reasons. The Italian and Swiss Socialist Parties, which had been active in the Zimmerwald movement, objected to a Conference summoned under the auspices of the 'patriotic' Socialists of the Allied countries ; and the Serbian and Rumanian Socialist Parties stood aside on the same grounds. In Bulgaria the 'Broad' Socialists led by Ianko Sakosoff accepted the invitation, whereas the 'Narrow' Socialists, in process of turning themselves into the Bulgarian Communist Party, refused. The Italians, however, were represented by the minority Reformist Socialist Party of Leonida Bissolati (1857–1919) and Ivanoe Bonomi (1873–1951), who had been expelled from the main Party in 1912 and had supported Italy's participation in the war on the Allied side. In all there were at the Berne Conference delegations from 26 countries, not counting 2 delegations — from Australia and the Ukraine — which arrived too late to take part. The countries represented by full delegations included Great Britain, France, Germany, Austria, Bohemia, Holland, Denmark, Norway, Sweden, Finland, Spain, and Argentina ; and there were also delegations from Russia, Poland, Georgia, Armenia, Estonia, Latvia, Bulgaria, Hungary, Greece, Italy, the Palestinian Jews, Ireland, Canada, and Alsace-Lorraine — this last in process of transfer from German to French sovereignty. The Russian delegation represented the Mensheviks and Social Revolutionaries, but not the Bolsheviks or Left S.R.s ; and the Georgian, Armenian, Latvian, and Estonian delegations were of similar composition. The Poles represented Pilsudski's Polish Socialist Party, and not the Polish Social Democrats. There was, in effect, no representation of Communist Parties, or of Parties closely allied to Communism, except the Norwegians, whose left wing had recently gained control of the party machine.

The Berne Conference met on February 3rd and elected as its President the Swedish leader, Hjalmar Branting (1860–1925), who had been Chairman of the Stockholm Dutch-Scandinavian Committee. Albert Thomas (1878–1932), of the French right wing, which had lost its majority position in the French Party a few months before, immediately proposed that priority should be given to a discussion of the war responsibility of the Socialist Parties — that is, mainly to the question of the 'war guilt' of the German Majority Socialists, who were present in force. Thomas further proposed that the second item on the agenda should be a discussion of the place of democracy in the struggle for Socialism — that is to say, of the question of parliamentary democracy versus proletarian dictatorship. These proposals were accepted, and the debate on Socialist war responsibilities occupied the two opening days' proceedings. The question was obviously ticklish ; for it was clear both that some of the Allied delegates would refuse to go on with the Conference unless some admission of German 'war guilt' could be secured and that the German Majority could not be expected to proclaim their own guilt, whatever blame they might be prepared to assign to the German imperial régime they had just helped to overthrow. Finally a compromise was found by setting up a special commission which procured from the Germans a declaration strongly dissociating the new, revolutionary Germany from the old régime which had been responsible for the war. On the strength of this declaration it was agreed to leave over 'to a future International Congress, convened under normal conditions, the task of formulating the judgment of the International on the world-historic issue of responsibility for the war'. This left the German Majority Socialists free to participate in the rest of the Conference on equal terms ; and in practice the entire question was thereafter shelved, as it was bound to be if a new International was to be set up with the German Majority Socialists among its members.

The Berne Conference then turned to the question of 'Democracy versus Dictatorship'. The Commission to which this matter was referred produced two rival resolutions — the 'Branting' resolution of the majority, and the Adler-Longuet minority resolution. The first of these, supported by a large majority of the delegations, was an emphatic declaration of the inseparableness of Socialism and 'democracy' and a denunciation of 'dictatorship' and, by implication, of the entire policy of Bolshevism. 'Democracy' was explicitly defined in terms of parliamentary government in the following passage : 'The institutions which constitute Democracy — freedom of speech and of the press, the right of assembly, universal suffrage, a Government responsible to Parliament, with arrangements guaranteeing popular co-operation and respect for the wishes of the people, the right of association, etc. — these also provide the working classes with the means of carrying on the class struggle'. And in another passage : 'A reorganised society more and more permeated with Socialism cannot be realised, much less permanently established, unless it rests upon triumphs of Democracy and is rooted in the principles of liberty'. The resolution did indeed begin by 'hailing' the Revolutions 'which, in Russia, Austria-Hungary and Germany, have destroyed the old régimes of imperialism and militarism and overthrown their Governments'. But, having done this, it went on at once to declare that 'in full agreement with all previous Congresses of the International, the Berne Conference firmly adheres to the principles of Democracy' — which it then proceeded to define. Having made its general attitude clear, it proceeded to accept the proposal of the Russian delegates (*i.e.* of the Mensheviks and Social Revolutionaries) that a Commission 'representative of all Socialist tendencies' should be sent to Russia 'to report to the International on the political and economic situation there'. It further proposed that the question of Bolshevism should be put on the agenda for the next Conference, at which the Report of this Commission would be received and debated.

As against this outright condemnation of Bolshevism, the rival Adler-Longuet resolution was, first and foremost, a protest and a warning against 'any kind of stigma that may be applied to the Russian Soviet Republic'. It was not a defence of Bolshevism : it declared that 'we (*i.e.* the Socialists of other countries) have not sufficient material for a judgment'. 'We do not wish', the resolution continued, 'by passing premature judgment on political methods, to be the victims of the manœuvres and interested calumnies of bourgeois Governments.' Its sponsors declared themselves unable to rely solely on what was said by the Russian delegates, 'who represent only a minority of the Russian working class' — though the good faith of these delegates was not questioned. The resolution then drew attention to the less than fully representative character of the Berne Conference, in view of the absence of the Italian, Swiss, Serbian, and Rumanian Parties, and warned the Conference against doing anything that would make it more difficult to bring about a meeting of the working classes of all countries. 'We desire to reserve free entry into the International for the Socialist and Revolutionary Parties of all countries conscious of their class-interests.' Accordingly, the minority declared its refusal to be bound by the terms of the Branting resolution as a whole.

This minority resolution received the support of the French majority — till a short while before, the minority — and of the Norwegian, Dutch, Spanish, and Irish delegations, and also of half the Austrian delegation, and of one Greek delegate. On the other side, in support of the Branting resolution were the British, the Germans, the Swedes, the Danes, the Finns, the Hungarians, the Russians, the Letts, the Estonians, the Georgians, the Armenians, the Bulgarian 'Broads', the Canadians, the Argentinians, the Alsace-Lorraine delegates, the French Minority, the Italian Reformists, and half the Austrian delegation. The majority was thus swollen by the votes of the delegations from Russia and the border States formerly under Russian rule ; but its central core consisted of the British, the Germans, the Swedes and Danes, and the still considerable French Minority. The Belgians, who would have voted with the majority, were absent ; but so were the Italian Majority and the Swiss, who would presumably have voted for the Adler-Longuet proposal. The essential effect of the Branting resolution was a break with the Communist left no less decisive than the break with the right which Lenin and his supporters had been calling for ever since the Zimmerwald Conference of 1915. This left in existence a middle group which wanted a reconstructed inclusive International uncommitted for the time being either for or against Dictatorship ; and the outstanding question was what this middle group would or could do in view of the intransigence of the two extremes.

The Berne Conference, however, was not quite so irrevocably committed, at any rate formally, as this summing-up suggests ; for the entire question was to be open to further debate when the proposed Commission of Enquiry got back from its visit to Russia — if indeed it was able to go there. What the Berne majority had refused to do was to defer its interim condemnation of Dictatorship and its declaration in favour of parliamentary Democracy till after the Commission had done its work.

Having disposed of these 'prior issues', the Berne Conference settled down to what had been designated as its principal task — the formulation of the Socialist and Trade Union case for presentation to the official Peace Conference. To deal with these matters it set up three Commissions — on the proposed League of Nations, on Territorial Questions, and on the proposed International Labour Charter. On the second of these groups of problems the Conference contented itself with a quite general resolution affirming the principle of national self-determination, but leaving the detailed application of this principle to be worked out later, either by a future Conference or by the Permanent Commission which the Berne Conference established to carry on its work. In the matter of the League of Nations the Conference proclaimed itself in favour of the setting-up of a permanent international body, to be based on a Peace Treaty embodying a just settlement and to include on terms of equality all nations that were, or came to be, organised on a foundation of national self-determination and self-government. The League advocated by the Conference differed deeply, however, in one essential respect from the League which actually emerged from the Paris Peace Conference ; for it was to be made up of national delegations, not from Governments, but from the Parliaments of the member-countries, and these parliamentary delegations were to be representative of all the Parties in each Parliament, in accordance with their numerical strength. The Berne Conference thus went on record as demanding, not a League of Governments or of Sovereign States, but one governed by an international assembly representative of popular opinion in all democratic countries possessing parliamentary institutions. Clearly, such an assembly, in control of the League of Nations, would have involved an undermining of national State Sovereignty and a real step in the direction of international government. It may have been fantastic to suppose that the Governments of the leading countries could be brought, under the conditions of 1919, to accept any such drastic departure from their traditions of national independence ; but it is no less clear that the League of Governments which was actually set up fell utterly short of realising the aspirations even of right-wing Socialists for an international body capable of maintaining the peace of nations or of serving as an instrument for a transition to an international Socialist order.

The third of the Berne Conference Commissions, manned by the Trade Union delegates from the various countries, succeeded in drawing up an International Labour Charter which was to be presented to the Peace Conference for inclusion in the Treaty of Peace. It included the establishment, as part of the new machinery of international government, of a permanent International Commission on Labour Legislation, which was to consist of representatives not only of the States belonging to the League, but also, in equal numbers, of the national Trade Union Centres of these countries. The principle of a guaranteed minimum standard of life for all workers, including recognition of a common right to work or maintenance, was to be embodied in the proposed Charter, and was to be recognised as binding on the Governments of all the member-States. Out of this proposal came, in the event, the International Labour Organisation set up at the Washington Conference of 1919 ; but in this case, too, what was achieved fell a long way short of what the Berne Conference demanded — for the I.L.O. was established as a tripartite body, with workers' and employers' delegates together equal in number to the government delegates, and with no power to do more than recommend Conventions for adoption by the Governments of the several member-States.

Finally, the Berne Conference, which recognised its inability to proceed at once to establish a new Socialist International, attempted to lay the foundations for such a body by choosing a Permanent Commission, consisting of two representatives from each national section, with the double function of carrying on the work of the Conference by elaborating its conclusions in detail and placing them before the Peace Conference, and of preparing the way for a further Conference at which a new International would be definitely constituted. Under this Permanent Commission there was also appointed an Acting Executive of three members — Branting, Henderson, and Huysmans — who were to be responsible for carrying on the day-to-day work between the meetings of the Commission. To these three, four further members were added at the first meeting of the Commission at Amsterdam in April 1919. Two of these — Ramsay MacDonald and G. H. Stuart-Bunning (1870–?) of the Postmen's Federation — were British, and two — Jean Longuet and Pierre Renaudel — French, representing the Majority and Minority fractions of the French Socialist Party. The Belgian Labour Party, which, as we saw, had refused to be represented at Berne, sent delegates to the Amsterdam meeting and thus rejoined the new embryo International. The Italian and Swiss Parties, however, still held aloof, as did the Americans and also the East European Parties which had rejected the Berne invitation.

While these steps towards the re-establishment of a Socialist International were being taken under the auspices of the parliamentary Socialists, mainly in Western Europe, but with the support of the anti-Bolshevik Socialists of Russia and of the countries previously subject to the Russian empire, the Bolsheviks were making haste to put into effect their rival project of an International that would firmly exclude all the 'social patriots' of the war period and all Parties and groups which stood for a reformist as against a revolutionary policy or for parliamentarism as against proletarian dictatorship. But the Russian Bolsheviks and their sympathisers in other countries were ill-placed, in the early months of 1919, for immediate action either to set up a rival International or even to bring together a widely representative International Conference. They were, to a great extent, isolated from the Western countries and unable even to communicate without great difficulty with their potential supporters abroad. Communist Parties existed in more than embryonic form in only a few countries outside the former Czarist empire, and, where they did exist, as in Germany, Austria, and Hungary, were still very weak : in most countries — for example in France, Italy, Switzerland, Spain, Norway, and Holland — the main forces of right and left were still waging internecine war within a single Party, or, as in Sweden, the Balkans, and the United States, though rival right and left wing Parties already existed, the left wing was still not explicitly Communist, at any rate in name. Besides Soviet Russia, the only countries with substantial Communist Parties were Poland and perhaps the Ukraine and Germany, though Communist Parties of a sort existed also in Hungary, Finland, Latvia, Estonia, and Lithuania, and also, on a very small scale, in Austria and Armenia, while in Bulgaria the long-established 'Narrow' Socialist Party could be relied on to rally to the Soviet side. Elsewhere only scattered groups were in being, though steps were already on foot for the establishment of Communist Parties in a number of other countries.

In these circumstances there were many, even among the Russian Bolsheviks, who regarded any immediate attempt to set up a rival Communist International as premature. There were, however, strong considerations on the other side. If, as the principal Bolshevik leaders continued to believe, World Revolution was well on the way, and the proletariats of the advanced countries needed only a properly organised revolutionary leadership to precipitate the crisis, clearly no time should be lost in providing this leadership and no effort be spared to break the workers away from the reformist leaders who were doing their best to prevent the Revolutions. Clearly, it seemed, the Bolsheviks ought to do their utmost to prevent the re-establishment of the old International under the leadership of the very men who had played it false in 1914 and, having fought one another for four years, were now busily making friends again on a basis of common hostility to Bolshevism and Revolution. The Berne Conference could not be left unchallenged ; and how could it be challenged except by proceeding at once to rally against it the international forces of revolutionary Socialism under the leadership of the one great country which had actually carried Socialist Revolution into effect ?

These arguments prevailed ; and on January 24th, 1919, a wireless message addressed to the revolutionary Socialists of all countries went out from Moscow, calling on them to send delegates to an International Congress to be held there in March for the purpose of forming a 'Third', or Communist, International. The invitation was issued in the name of the Russian Communist Party, with the support of the Communist Parties of Poland, Latvia, Finland, Austria and Hungary, and of the Balkan Revolutionary Socialist Federation — and the American Socialist Labor Party was also named in the invitation, though it had had no opportunity of approving it except through its representative, Reinstein, who was living in Russia. It was further stated that the proposed Platform for the Third International, which was sent out with the invitation, had been drawn up 'in agreement with the programme of the Spartakusbund in Germany, and of the Communist Party (Bolshevik) in Russia'. This Platform included fifteen points, covering both the principles on which the new International was to be based and the form of organisation proposed. The aim was to be the immediate and universal establishment of the dictatorship of the proletariat in view of the actual or impending dissolution of capitalism throughout the world. This was held to involve : (a) the seizure of governmental power in order to replace it everywhere by the apparatus of proletarian power ; (b) the disarming of the bourgeoisie and the general arming of the proletariat in order to make the Revolution secure ; and (c) the use of the dictatorship for the purpose of suppressing private property in the means of production and of transferring these means to 'the proletarian State under the Socialist administration of the working class'. The method proposed was 'mass action by the proletariat to the extent of open conflict in arms against the governmental power of capitalism'. Then came seven points dealing with the relation of the new International to other Socialist Parties. The projected 'Berne International' was condemned as an opportunist combination of a number of disparate groups and tendencies, of which three were distinguished separately. There were, first, the old 'social patriots', who were to be fought relentlessly, on the ground that at moments of crisis they always opposed the Revolution. Secondly, the 'Centre', consisting chiefly of the war-time Minority groups, such as Longuet and his followers in France, Kautsky and the U.S.P.D. in Germany, and the Independent Labour Party in Great Britain : these were characterised as made up of 'hesitant' elements and as incapable of adopting a determined attitude. Their leaders were to be mercilessly criticised, and every effort was to be made to divide and break them up, so as to bring over the revolutionary elements to the Communist side. Thirdly, there were the revolutionary groups, which were to be persuaded to throw in their lot with Communism. These last were held to include not only the embryonic Communist Parties and groups, but also the revolutionary Industrial Unionists and Syndicalists — indeed, all working-class groups and organisations which, without having openly joined the Left Revolutionary movement, nevertheless showed in their development a clear tendency towards the left. Finally, the Platform laid down that the new International should be named 'The Communist International' and should be set up as a fighting organ for directing the international Communist movement, on the fundamental principle of 'subordinating the interests of the movement in each country to the general interests of the International Revolution as a whole'. It was thus proposed to establish the Communist International, not as a loose federation of independent national Parties on the model of the old International, but as a centralised controlling authority for the whole world-wide revolutionary movement. The battle between the fundamentally conflicting conceptions both of Socialism and of international activity was thus fairly joined.

In view of the prevailing conditions, it was impracticable for the Congress which met at Moscow in March 1919 to be at all widely representative. Not only was Communist organisation in most countries still in an embryonic state : it was also very difficult for the delegates of such bodies as did exist to make their way to Moscow, and in many cases these bodies were unable to hold conferences of their own to mandate their delegates, some of whom were unable even to start, while others were stopped or arrested *en route*. In the event, 19 Parties or groups were given voting rights at the Moscow Congress ; but in some cases the standing of their representatives was by no means certain. For example, the American Socialist Labour Party, which was given the maximum voting power (5 votes), had given no authorisation to its supposed representative ; and this was also the case of the Swiss Social Democratic Party, which was allowed 3 votes. There were in

all 11 explicitly Communist Parties, with a total of 29 votes —
5 each for Russia and Germany, 3 each for the Ukraine, Finland,
Austria, Hungary, and Poland, and 1 each for Armenia,
Estonia, Latvia, and Lithuania. The Norwegian Social Demo-
cratic Labour Party, the Swiss Social Democratic Party, the
Swedish Left Socialist Party, and the Balkan Revolutionary
Socialist Federation were given each 3 votes, and the American
S.L.P., as we saw, 5 votes. Finally, the Communist Party of
the German Colonies in Russia and the Group of Oriental
Nationalities in Russia were given each 1 vote, and 5 votes were
assigned to the Left Zimmerwaldian organisation set up at the
Kienthal Conference of 1916. This provisional Zimmerwaldian
organisation was wound up at the Moscow Congress, its
functions being transferred to the new Communist International.

In addition to these delegates with voting rights, the Moscow Congress included a considerable number of persons admitted as advisory representatives without voting rights. These
came from a large number of countries not formally represented, including Great Britain (J. Fineberg), France (Jacques
Sadoul), Holland, Czechoslovakia, Turkey, Persia, Korea, and
China, and there were also persons from the separate Balkan
countries — Bulgaria and Yugoslavia, and from countries
which had formed part of the Czarist empire — Azerbaijan,
Georgia, and Turkestan, and also a few additional individuals
from Switzerland and the United States. In addition, Angelica
Balabanova attended in her capacity as secretary of the Zimmerwald International Socialist Commission.

There was some doubt among the delegates at Moscow
whether it was wise to announce at once the launching of a new
International in view of the necessarily unrepresentative character of the Congress and of the confused condition of affairs
inside many of the existing Socialist Parties — for example, in
France, Italy, Switzerland, and the United States. It seemed
possible that in these Parties a majority might be won for Communism and the machinery of the existing Parties thus fall into
Communist hands — clearly an enormous advantage for the
revolutionary wing of the movement. It was, however, an
open question whether the immediate establishment of a Communist International would prejudice the chance of such
victories or positively help towards them. The Germans were,

at the outset, the principal advocates of delay, largely because the existing German Communist Party — the Spartakusbund under a new name — needed to take account of its position in relation to the German Independent Social Democratic Party (U.S.P.D.), which was a mixture of revolutionary and parliamentarian elements and contained a high proportion of those whose help was essential for the creation of an effectively unified German Communist movement. The Spartacists wanted to split the U.S.P.D. in such a way as to bring a majority of its members over to Communism, while getting rid of its parliamentarian elements, and to take over its press and its central and local organisation. They were afraid that, if the new International were set up in Germany with no more than Spartacist membership, the effect might be to alienate the U.S.P.D. membership and thus help the parliamentarian leaders, such as Kautsky, to retain control. The Russians, however, were quite determined to go ahead and, with the control of the Congress practically in their hands, swept aside the objections raised by one Albrecht, the chief German delegate. In the Appeal sent out from Moscow in January, together with the invitation to the Congress, there had been included a list of the 39 Parties and groups which it was proposed should 'take part in the Third International with full rights' as 'accepting its point of view in its entirety'. This list included 11 duly constituted Communist Parties (Russia, Ukraine, White Russia, Latvia, Estonia, Lithuania, Finland, Poland, Hungary, Austria, and Holland), the German Spartakusbund, the Bulgarian Narrow Socialist Party, the entire Italian, Norwegian, and Rumanian Socialist Parties, the Swedish Left Socialist Party, the 'Class-struggle' group in Denmark, the American S.L.P., the British Socialist Party and the S.L.P. in Great Britain, the Left Social Democrats of Switzerland (not yet a formally constituted separate Party), the 'revolutionary elements' in Czech Social Democracy, in the Belgian Labour Party, in the Spanish and Portuguese Socialist Parties, and in Ireland, the Left Wing of the Serbian S.D.P., the 'left elements' in the American Socialist Party, especially those headed by Eugene Debs, the Socialist groups in Japan headed by Sen Katayama, the French Socialist and Trade Union groups 'which agree on fundamental questions with Loriot', and also the

I.W.W., the I.W.G.B. and 'the revolutionary elements of the Shop Stewards' movement in Great Britain, and finally the Young Socialist International under the leadership of Willi Muenzenberg.

This was a sufficiently heterogeneous collection of 'revolutionary' groups, wide enough to include Syndicalists hostile to parliamentary political action (while excluding Anarchists), but at the same time narrow enough to exclude all reference to such important groups as the German U.S.D.P., the new Longuet Majority in France, and the I.L.P. in Great Britain. The exclusions were not, of course, meant to rule out negotiations with these bodies with the object of winning majorities in them over to Communism ; but the list was designed to give a clear recognition to the Communist status of the bodies included in it, though in some cases — for example, in that of the Italian Socialist Party — it was clearly contemplated that the left-wing majorities would need to expel the right-wing elements in order to play their appointed part in the promotion of World Revolution. As we shall see, this question of expulsions was destined to play a most important part in deciding the issue of adhesion to the Third International by a number of the Parties concerned.

Though the decision at Moscow was in favour of setting up the new International at once, it was deemed inexpedient to proceed there and then to endow it with a formal constitution. In this respect no more was done than to provide the Communist International with an Executive Committee made up of one representative from the Communist Party of 'each of the most important countries', defined for this purpose in the first instance as Russia, Germany, Austria, Hungary, and Switzerland, together with Scandinavia and the Balkan Federation. This Executive Committee was to elect a Bureau of five persons, and, pending the arrival of the representatives from other countries, the Communists 'of the country in which the Executive Committee is located' (*i.e.* Russia) were to take charge of the International's affairs. These agencies were given, from the outset, full powers of action : the Executive was to draw up a full draft Constitution for submission to the next Congress, for which no date was fixed.

Apart from these questions of membership and organisation

the main work of the Moscow Congress of 1919 was to approve the text of a new *Communist Manifesto*, successor to that of 1848, for publication to the whole world as the challenge of international Communism both to capitalism and to the rival Socialist schools — above all, to the Parties which had met shortly before at the Berne Socialist Conference. This *Manifesto* soon became a world-famous historical document ; but at the outset there was much doubt concerning its exact text. It was issued on March 10th, 1919, four days after the ending of the Moscow Congress, and was signed by five persons — Lenin, Trotsky, and Zinoviev from Russia, Christian Rakovsky from the Balkan Federation, and Fritz Platten from Switzerland — the same five as had signed the *Declaration of Participants in the Zimmerwald Conference* presented to the Moscow Congress and proclaiming the liquidation of the Zimmerwald Union. These five thus became the first public sponsors of the Third International.

To any student of Communism who reads to-day the *Communist Manifesto* of 1919, what is likely to stand out as most remarkable is the absence of any explicit reference to the rôle of the Communist Party in carrying through the Revolution in each country or in relation to the dictatorship of the proletariat to which the Revolution was to give rise. This omission was, no doubt, due mainly to the emphasis that was put on the essentially international character of the Revolution and on the rôle of the International itself as a central controlling agency of the revolutionary proletariat. The national Communist Parties were clearly intended to be entirely subject to the controlling authority of the International, which was contrasted in this respect with the Second International as having been a mere federal grouping of independent national Parties. It remains, however, remarkable that in the account given of the institutions of the proletarian dictatorship the entire stress was laid on the Soviets as mass organs of the revolutionary workers, and that nothing at all was said about the Communist Parties, despite the actual differences over this matter between Lenin and Trotsky in the course of the Bolshevik Revolution in Russia and of Lenin's insistence on assigning the chief place to the Party in organising the revolutionary *coup*.[1] In the words of

[1] See p. 89.

the *Manifesto*: 'Wherever the masses are awakened to consciousness, Workers', Soldiers' and Peasants' Councils (Soviets) will be formed', and 'By means of these Soviets the working class will win power in all countries most readily and most certainly when these Soviets gain the support of the majority of the labouring population. By means of these Soviets the working class, when it has once attained power, will control all the fields of economic and cultural life, as in Soviet Russia.' There was no hint here that in any country the Communist Party, as distinct from the Soviets, would have a special part to play. It was laid down that: 'In the Soviet system the mass organisations rule and through them the mass itself, inasmuch as the Councils or Soviets draw continually increasing numbers of workers into the state administration; and only by this process will the entire working population gradually become part of the Government. The Soviet system, moreover, builds itself directly, as the mass organisation of the proletariat, on the Councils themselves, on the revolutionary Trade Unions, the Co-operatives, etc. . . . In this way, the Soviet system brings true proletarian democracy.'

Indeed, the only passage in which the rôle of the Party in the coming Revolution was referred to specifically, spoke, not of Communist Parties in the plural, but, most significantly, of 'the International Communist Party', whose task was to overthrow the capitalist order and 'to erect in its place the structure of the Socialist world order'. The working men and women of all countries were urged 'to unite under the Communist banner, the emblem under which the first great victories have already been won'. And then the *Manifesto* went on to say: 'Under the standard of the Workers' Councils, under the banner of the Third International, in the revolutionary struggle for power and the Dictatorship of the Proletariat, proletarians of all countries, UNITE!' The entire emphasis was put on the one hand on the Soviets, which were to develop everywhere as direct instruments of proletarian power and self-government, and, on the other hand, on the Communist International, as the central and centralised directing agency first in carrying out the Revolution and subsequently in 'transforming the whole world into one Co-operative Commonwealth, and bringing about real human brotherhood and freedom'. The final words of the *Manifesto* were : 'Long live the International Republic of the Workers' Soviets'.

Thus the entire *Manifesto* was cast into the form of an appeal for world-wide Revolution, conceived as a single vast movement transcending national frontiers. It was maintained that 'the national State, which was given a tremendous impulse by capitalist evolution, has become too narrow for the development of the powers of production'. The illusions of the independence of small nations under the capitalist system and the 'hypocritical character' of the 'Wilsonian programme' of national self-determination were insisted on ; and it was laid down that : 'Only the proletarian Revolution can secure the existence of the small nations, a Revolution which frees the productive powers of all countries from the restrictions of the national States, which unites all peoples in the closest economic co-operation on the basis of a universal economic plan, and enables the smallest and weakest peoples freely and independently to carry on their national culture without detriment to the united and centralised economy of Europe and of the whole world'.

Despite this sustained insistence on the singleness of World Revolution and on the need to transcend the limitations of merely national action, the *Manifesto*, when it came to the defining of the concrete Programme of Communism, was unable to avoid recommendations which were largely national in content, or at any rate directly related to the action to be taken for the establishment of the new order in the individual States falling under proletarian power. 'The organised power of the bourgeoisie', it was said, 'is in the civil State, with its capitalist army under control of bourgeois-junker officers, its police and gendarmes, gaolers and judges, its priests, government officials, etc.' The conquest of political power, it was argued, 'means not merely a change in the personnel of ministries but annihilation of the enemy's machinery of government ; disarmament of the bourgeoisie, of the counter-revolutionary officers, of the White Guard ; arming of the proletariat, the revolutionary soldiers, the Red Guard of workmen ; displacement of all bourgeois judges and organisation of all-proletarian courts ; elimination of control by reactionary government officials and substitution of new management organs of the proletariat. The victory of the proletariat consists in shattering the enemy's organisation and in organising the proletarian power ; in the destruction of the bourgeois and the building up of the proletarian State machine.' This is, of course, the doctrine that had been already set forth in Lenin's famous booklet, *The State and Revolution*, written shortly before the Bolshevik Revolution. It clearly envisages the replacement of capitalist States by new, proletarian States based on the principle of dictatorship ; and presumably such States, even if they were destined to merge in due course into an 'International Workers' Republic', would need to be set up in the first instance on the ruins of the separate capitalist States.

Similarly, the measures envisaged in the *Manifesto* for 'the expropriation of the bourgeoisie and the socialisation of production' were set out in terms of what was to be brought about in the first instance country by country, or State by State. It was laid down that 'the dictatorship of the proletariat does not in any way call for partition of the means of production and exchange ; rather, on the contrary, its aim is further to centralise the powers of production and to subject all production to a systematic plan'. The *Manifesto* went on to urge, 'as first steps', socialisation of the great banks, of all government-controlled economic utilities and communal enterprises, and of 'the syndicated and trustified units of production, as well as of all other branches of production in which the degree of concentration and centralisation of capital makes this technically practicable' ; and, further, the conversion into Co-operatives of large agricultural estates, the abolition of 'the exploitation of the people by capitalistic landlords, the transfer of large mansions to the local Soviets, and the moving of working families into bourgeois dwellings'. It was, at the same time, careful to disclaim any intention of expropriating small properties or of dispossessing 'property owners who are not exploiters of labour'. In the field of distribution it was cautious and said only that 'the following methods are to be considered — the socialisation of wholesale establishments ; the taking over of all bourgeois State and municipal apparatus of distribution ; control of the great Co-operative Societies, which will still have an important rôle' ; and 'the gradual centralisation of all these organisations and their conversion into a systematic unit for the national distribution of products'. It was added by way of summary that 'During this great period of transition the power of the Soviets must constantly be building up the entire administrative organisation into a more centralised structure, but, on the other hand, be constantly drawing ever-increasing elements of the working people into the immediate control of government'.

Thus, the *Manifesto* fully reaffirmed the emphasis which the Erfurt Programme of the pre-war German Social Democratic Party had placed on economic centralisation and centralised public planning of production and distribution, while urging the need to democratise the new State apparatus by enlisting the mass organisations of the workers in the tasks of control and by bringing about a larger and larger participation in this control by persons belonging to the working class. 'The task of the proletarian dictatorship', it laid down, 'can be fulfilled only to the extent to which the proletariat is enabled to create centralised organs of management and to institute workers' control.' The phrase, 'workers' control', in this connection, clearly has no reference to proposals for industrial self-government by the workers in particular industries or establishments : it signifies control by the workers as a class over the entire apparatus of production. One of the resolutions adopted at the Berne Conference had declared that : 'True socialisation implies methodical development in the different branches of economic activity under the control of the democracy : the arbitrary taking over of a few concerns by small groups of workers is not Socialism ; it is merely Capitalism with numerous shareholders'. But this had been directed not against the Communists but against Syndicalists and other industrialist groups that were accused of demanding 'the mines for the miners' or of putting forward similar claims to 'the whole product of labour' for particular working groups. For the Communists, not the entire 'people' but the entire working class was the fundamentally important unit, and the whole problem was looked at in terms of proletarian class power.

The dictatorship of the proletariat, however, was declared in the *Manifesto* to be 'only a provisional institution'. 'As the opposition of the bourgeoisie is broken, as it is expropriated and gradually absorbed into the working groups, the proletarian dictatorship disappears, until finally the State dies and there is no more class distinction.' And again : 'The proletariat, as the overwhelming majority of the people, openly exercises its class power by means of its mass organisation and through its Soviets, in order to wipe out the privileges of the bourgeoisie and to secure the transition, or rather the transformation, into a classless Communist Commonwealth.'

In what sense, it can fairly be asked, is the proletariat 'the overwhelming majority of the people' which it is here asserted to be. Evidently, this cannot be true of the *industrial* proletariat, save in a very few countries, if indeed in any at all. In most countries a large proportion of the population consists either of peasants or of workers and dependants on large landed estates or plantations, and there is usually also a considerable body of self-employed artisans and other non-employers in various 'white collar' jobs ; and in the most advanced countries, in an economic sense, the middle classes and 'blackcoats' make up a very substantial minority, for the most part quite unconnected with the organised working-class movement. Accordingly, the word 'proletariat' must here be understood in an extended sense, as including all groups that are potentially on the working-class side in the class-struggle — peasants, or at any rate poor peasants, as well as agricultural wage-labourers, most blackcoats as well as manual workers, and self-employed artisans and craftsmen as well as industrial wage-earners. Elsewhere in the *Manifesto* the *industrial* proletariat is specifically distinguished from the proletariat in this larger sense.

'The proletariat', it is said, 'created a new institution which embraces the entire working class, without distinction of vocation or political maturity — an elastic form of organisation which is capable of continually renewing itself, of expanding and of drawing into itself ever new elements, ready to open its doors to the working groups of city and village which are near to the proletariat.' The word 'proletariat' seems here to be used to designate, at least in the main, the *industrial* workers, to whom the other groups are described as near or akin. The Soviet begins mainly as the instrument of the industrial workers, but is regarded as having in itself the capacity for adaptation to meet the needs of the entire labouring population. The *Manifesto* says later on that 'the Soviet system brings true

proletarian democracy', and adds that 'the *industrial* proletariat '[1] is favoured in this system because it is the most
aggressive, best organised and politically ripest class, under
whose leadership the semi-proletarians and small farmers will
be gradually raised up. These temporary privileges of the
industrial proletariat must be utilised to draw the small farmers
away from the control of the big landowners and the bourgeoisie,
and to train them as helpers in the building of the Communist
structure.' Thus, it appears that the proletariat comes to be
'the overwhelming majority' only when this process of training
has been carried through under the tutelage of the industrial
workers. Be it observed that in this passage the industrial
proletariat, rather than the enlarged proletariat of the future,
is described as a 'class'.

In all this there is some ambiguous use of words ; but the
essential ideas are plain enough. The organised industrial
wage-earners form the spearhead of the revolutionary movement, and the whole body of such workers forms the proletariat
proper and provides the basis for the initial creation of Soviets.
But this very elastic form of organisation speedily shows its
appropriateness to serve as a vehicle for the grievances and
demands of other discontented groups, especially for the
soldiers, who are drawn largely from the rural population, and
for the peasants and landless rural workers. Thus comes about
the alliance of Workers', Soldiers', and Peasants' Councils or
Soviets, which serves as the basis for the new Workers' State ;
and this form of State, once established, can draw into itself yet
other elements too backward, or too divided in allegiance, to
play any constructive rôle in the Revolution itself. The door
is left open to differing views concerning the relative rôles in
the Revolution of industrial workers, of soldiers, and of peasants
(or of 'poor' as against 'rich' peasants) — a question on which
Lenin and Trotsky, for example, had held divergent opinions.
There is, however, no doubt that the rôle of ideological leaders
and of shock troopers of the Revolution is assigned mainly to
the *industrial* proletariat. As for the artisans and small-scale
industrial producers, they, together with the small farmers and
the rest of the urban petty bourgeoisie, 'will be gradually drawn
into the Socialist organisation through the force of example,

[1] Italics mine.

through practical demonstration of the superiority of the new order of things, and through the regulation by which (they) . . . will be set free from economic bondage to usurious capitalism and landlordism and from tax burdens — especially by the annulment of the national debts'.

At what point in the process of transition to the new society the existing boundaries of nations and States were to disappear the *Manifesto* nowhere made clear : nor could it have attempted to do so without more profession of foreknowledge of the course of the Revolution than its authors ever pretended to. But a passing reference to 'countries where the conditions for a workers' Revolution are not yet ripe' make it clear that the Revolution was not expected to take place simultaneously in all parts of the world, though in all the same processes would be at work preparing the way for it. In spite of any differences in timing it would be essentially a single Revolution because it was a matter of replacing a world capitalist order which had been fundamentally undermined and could not possibly be reconstructed to provide the basis for a workable system for the future.

This assumption that the war had undermined capitalism beyond all possibility of restoration loomed very large in the general argument put forward in the *Manifesto*. The opening paragraphs, after recalling the *Communist Manifesto* of seventy-one years before and after saying that 'the epoch of the last decisive battle came later than the apostles of the Social Revolution expected and wished', went on to state unequivocally that it had now arrived and that the immediate task of the Communists was 'to sum up the practical revolutionary experiences of the working class, to cleanse the movement of its admixture of opportunism and social patriotism, and to unite the forces of all the true revolutionary proletarian Parties in order to further and hasten the complete victory of the Communist Revolution'. Then came a paragraph recalling the predictions of the Second International that capitalist imperialism was leading the world into war, and therewith the threat of the International that war would lead to Revolution, 'the retaliation of the proletariat for the crimes of militarism'. The *Manifesto* went on to accuse the German 'social patriots', after making themselves the accomplices of the Kaiser, of joining with the Socialists of the

Allied countries in 'vulgar sycophancy', 'in the hope of erasing the memory of their own guilt and of gaining the goodwill of the victors'. It then turned to a no less vehement attack on the 'immemorable vileness' of the rulers of France, England, Italy, and the United States, as revealed by the disclosures concerning the diplomatic antecedents of the outbreak of war in 1914. 'London', it was said, 'wanted war', in the hope that in addition to crushing Germany it would so exhaust France and Russia as to leave Great Britain with all the advantages of the situation; and when Germany proved too powerful to be crushed, 'the United States assumed, in respect of Europe, the same part that England had played in former wars and had intended to play in 1914'. The British were accused of deliberately misleading the Germans into a belief that they would stay out of the war, in the hope of preventing Germany from drawing back at the moment of crisis.

The *Manifesto* next proceeded to give a highly coloured account of the devastation that had been wrought in Europe, arguing that the effect had been to vindicate the much-disputed doctrine of 'increasing misery' by wiping out all the apparent gains of the workers under developing capitalism and by laying bare the irreconcilable contradictions of the capitalist order. It pointed to the catastrophic experiences which finance capital itself had undergone through inflation and 'the complete deterioration of paper money', which 'now reflects the general deadly crisis of capitalist commodity exchange'. It went on to argue that the control previously exercised to an ever-increasing extent by capitalist trusts and monopolies had been replaced, under the exigencies of war, by military control of supplies and production. 'All these basic matters of the world's economic life are no longer regulated by free competition, nor yet by combinations of national and international trusts, but through direct application of military force. Just as the complete subordination of the State's power to the purposes of finance capital has, through the mass slaughter, entirely militarised not only the State but also finance capital itself, so it (finance capital) can no longer carry on its essential economic functions except by means of blood and ruin.'

Yet, said the authors of the *Manifesto*, 'the opportunists who before the war exhorted the workers, in the name of a gradual transition to Socialism, to be moderate ; who during the war called for submission in the name of "civil peace" and defence of the Fatherland, now again demand of the workers self-abnegation in order to overcome the terrible consequences of the war. If this preaching were listened to by the workers, Capitalism would build "out of the bones of successive generations a new and still more formidable structure, leading to a new and inevitable world war. Fortunately for humanity, this is no longer possible." '

Why was such an outcome deemed impossible ? The answer of the *Manifesto* was none too clear. It amounted to saying that 'the only question is what shall be the future mainstay of State production, the imperialist State or the State of the victorious proletariat', and to arguing that only the latter could 'in a few years heal the open wounds caused by the war and raise humanity to heights now undreamed of '. Then came the passage about the inadequacy of the national State as an economic entity, about the falsity of the Wilsonian conception of national self-determination, and about the proletarian Revolution as 'the only means of securing the existence of the small nations' within the 'united and centralised economy of Europe and of the whole world'.

The *Manifesto* then turned to the colonial question. It pointed out how the imperialist powers had forcibly drawn their colonies into the war, with the consequence of 'a series of open rebellions and revolutionary ferment in all colonies'. Ireland, Madagascar, Annam, and India were cited as outstanding examples. The *Manifesto* pointed out that 'already in the more advanced colonies the battle goes on not only under the flag of national liberation, but also takes on an open and outspoken social character'. It proclaimed that 'Liberation of the colonies can come only through liberation of the working class of the oppressing nations', and that 'Socialist Europe will come to the aid of the liberated colonies with its technique, its organisation, its spiritual influence, in order to facilitate the transition to the orderly system of Socialist economy'.

All this, however, comes to no more than unproven assertion of the impossibility of capitalist reconstruction. The Communists, indeed, did not regard this assertion as needing to be proved anew. They held its evidence to be an integral part of the Marxist theory of historical determinism, and the success of the Revolution in Russia to be sufficient demonstration that the 'final crisis' of capitalism had already begun. They were so confident that the World Revolution had already started and could not be held back, as to see no need for further argument, except the final argument of proletarian insurrection.

From this point the *Manifesto* proceeded to an exposure of the unreality of the liberty and the political democracy alleged to exist in the bourgeois State. 'The whole bourgeois world accuses the Communists of destroying liberties and political democracy'; but in truth 'the proletariat, having come into power (*i.e.* in Russia) only asserts the sheer impossibility of applying the methods of bourgeois democracy and creates the conditions and forms of a higher working-class democracy. . . . In a realm of destruction, where not only the means of production and transport but also the institutions of political democracy are shattered and bleeding, the proletariat must create its own forms, to serve above all as a bond of unity for the working class, and to enable it to accomplish a revolutionary intervention in the further development of mankind.' This new form is the Soviet, an instrument capable of embracing the entire working class.[1] Moreover, the development of proletarian consciousness carries with it the disintegration of the vast conscript armies which imperialism has mobilised. 'The imperialist war which pitted nation against nation has passed and is passing into the civil war which lines up class against class.' This civil war 'is forced upon the labouring classes by their arch-enemies . . . it has become an iron necessity'. The task of the Communists is not to 'conjure it up', but to 'shorten its duration as much as possible, to minimise the numbers of its victims, and above all to secure victory for the proletariat'. This makes necessary 'the disarming of the bourgeoisie . . . and the formation of a Communist army to protect the rule of the proletariat and the inviolability of the social structure. Such is the Red Army of Soviet Russia which . . . is inseparable from the Soviet State.'

Civil war, then, the *Manifesto* argues, is a necessary part of the Revolution; and it follows that relentless struggle must be waged not only against the 'Labour Parties which have converted themselves into servile organs of the bourgeois State'

[1] See p. 79.

but also against the 'hazy, fickle and irresolute Socialist "Centre" which is at present trying to revive the Second International'. This 'Centre' includes the German Independents (U.S.P.D.), the present Majority of the Socialist Party in France, the Menshevik group in Russia, the Independent Labour Party in England, and similar groups, which 'appear with proposals for compromise and conciliation and thereby paralyse the energy of the proletariat, lengthening the period of crisis and consequently increasing the wretchedness of Europe'. 'War against the Socialist Centre is a necessary condition of successful war against imperialism.' 'The Third International is the International of overt mass-action, of revolutionary realisation, the INTERNATIONAL OF DEEDS. Socialist criticism has sufficiently stigmatised the bourgeois world order. The task of the International Communist Party is now to overthrow this order and to erect in its place the structure of the Socialist world order. . . . Proletarians of all countries, UNITE.'

So far the *Manifesto* itself : appended to it is the Programme, of which the greater part has already been described. It deals chiefly with the conquest of political power, with the methods of expropriating the bourgeoisie and of socialising production, and, in its concluding paragraphs, with 'the way of victory'. It reiterates the pledge 'to support the plundered colonial peoples in their fight against imperialism, in order to hasten the final collapse of the imperialistic world system', in contrast to the attitude of 'the Yellow International of the social patriots ' ; and it asserts that 'the revolutionary era compels the proletariat to make use of the means of battle that will concentrate its entire energies — namely, mass action, with its logical resultant, direct conflict with the governmental machinery in open combat'. It adds that 'all other methods, such as the revolutionary use of bourgeois parliamentarism, will be of no more than secondary significance'.

This forthright challenge, sent out to the world at a moment when the statesmen of the Allied countries were meeting in Paris to formulate their dictated terms of peace, and when the parliamentarian Socialists of France and Great Britain had just met the German Majority Socialists in conference and taken the first step towards the establishment of a definitely parliamentarian and reformist International, initiated a tremendous struggle for the control of the world-wide Socialist and working-class movement. It was based, as events were soon to show, both on a gross under-estimation of the recuperative powers of capitalism and on a no less mistaken over-estimate of the immediate revolutionary potential of the working classes in the Western capitalist countries ; and before long the new Communist International was compelled to recognise, in practice, that it had miscalculated in both respects. The fundamental diagnosis, however, remained unaltered ; for it was a great deal easier for the leaders of Communism to admit that, like Marx and Engels before them, they had got the timing of the 'final crisis' of world capitalism wrong, and therewith that of the World Revolution, than to entertain at all the notion that neither of these great events was scientifically predictable as a certainty or destined necessarily to come about in the fairly near future. Over the entire period between the wars the continuing *malaise* of world capitalism — the economic and monetary instability of the 1920s, followed by the depression and unemployment of the 1930s in all the capitalist countries — seemed to warrant the belief that stable reconstruction of the old order was impracticable, and that capitalism had reached the limits of its potential development and would be less and less able to recover from each ensuing cyclical crisis, especially in face of increasing discontent in the colonies and dependencies of the leading countries, of the growth of nationalism in China and India and also in Latin America, and of the increased strength of Trade Unionism and of Labour movements generally as compared with conditions before 1914. The coming of Fascism, first in Italy and then in Germany, might have done something to disturb this confidence in the inevitability of Socialism as the successor to capitalism in decline ; but the Communists, to their own satisfaction, explained Fascism away as merely the 'last throw' of capitalism in decline and as lacking the means to resolve any of the fundamental contradictions of the capitalist-imperialist system. The belief in the necessary breakdown of capitalism because of its developing contradictions and in the necessity of Socialism succeeding to its inheritance were elements of the Marxist doctrine too fundamental to be questioned, even when it had become clearly requisite to admit that the 'final crisis' might take a considerable time to mature, and that meanwhile the Russians had no alternative to attempting to build up 'Socialism in a single country', despite the certainty most of them had felt at the outset that such a task would be beyond their powers.

In 1919 the Russians, at any rate, entertained no doubt that capitalism was doomed to speedy overthrow and World Revolution well on the way ; and their confidence was shared by many of their supporters in other countries — above all in Southern and Eastern Europe. In Germany, as we saw,[1] there were more doubts, even among the Communists themselves and still more among the left-wing members of the U.S.P.D. ; and in France, and much more in Great Britain and the United States, there were few, even among the supporters of Communism, who seriously believed, at any rate for long, in their power speedily to achieve a Communist Revolution, or even to overthrow the capitalist order. In such countries, however, Communists, who knew perfectly well their impotence for the time being to bring about the Revolution and the sheer futility of attempting to act on the Third International's precepts about armed insurrection, were not deterred by this knowledge from holding to their faith in Communism, or from believing that the World Revolution was bound to come in its own time. They were only induced by their knowledge of conditions in their own countries to put above everything else their duty to defend the Russian Revolution against its enemies, to await the day when it would become possible for them to act on the precepts of Moscow, and in the meantime to do all they could to disturb and weaken the capitalist order and to undermine the workers' confidence in their reformist leaders and in the 'waverers' who attempted to sustain a Centrist position and to bring back reformists and revolutionaries into an inclusive International.

This Communist hostility to the Centrists was, indeed, in practice the key issue at the Moscow Congress of 1919. The Communist leaders were well aware that the Revolution they were planning could not be brought about without mass working-class support, and that it was indispensable to win over the main body of those who were, for the time being, following the lead of such 'waverers' as Longuet in France,

[1] See p. 135.

Friedrich Adler in Austria, Serrati in Italy, the I.L.P. in Great Britain, and the Socialist Party in the United States. But they were also aware that these Centrist leaders were for the most part divided from them by an impassable doctrinal gulf. Most of them were definitely parliamentarians, to the extent of believing that parliamentary action could and should be used for purposes of constructive socialistic reform and not merely as a platform for revolutionary propaganda. Most of them, even if they favoured Soviets, and did not exclude the possible need for revolutionary action, rejected the notion of civil war as the necessary road to Socialism in countries possessing the institutions of parliamentary democracy and repudiated the view that bourgeois democracy could be dismissed as a mere sham — a façade behind which the great imperialist capitalists could be sure of having matters all their own way. Most of them, even if they regarded themselves as good internationalists, believed in the nation State as the necessary instrument of popular government and stood for the development, through some sort of League of Nations, of pacific means of settling international disputes. Most of them supported the Wilsonian concept of national self-determination, and wished to see it more generally applied, in colonial areas as well as in Europe. Finally, most of them shrank back appalled at the call to universal civil war as the necessary road to Socialism and were, if not absolute pacifists, at all events most averse from the notion of war in any form.

Accordingly, the Communists had no expectation of being able to convert most of the Centrist leaders to the philosophy of action proclaimed in the Moscow *Manifesto*, and the task, as they saw it, was to detach the main body of workers who were following Centrist leadership from their misguided or muddled misleaders, and to bring them over decisively to the Communist side. Of course, the Communists hoped to bring over also many of the workers who were following, not Centrist, but right-wing leadership ; but the Centrist groups offered for the time being much the most hopeful target for attack. It therefore seemed expedient to make the most violent onslaught, not on the out-and-out reformists, but on the 'conciliators' who were seeking to uphold a middle position ; and these persons found themselves subjected to a campaign of most violent abuse both from the Comintern and from the Communist supporters within their own Parties and groups. Just as Lenin had attacked most violently the 'conciliators' who had attempted before the Bolshevik Revolution to build a bridge between the Bolshevik and Menshevik factions of Russian Social Democracy, so now the Comintern showed the most inveterate hostility to the 'pretended left' that would not follow it the whole way. The Comintern, however, did not immediately show the whole of its hand ; for one of its important immediate objectives was to secure the adhesion of those Socialist Parties which had either refused to take part in the Berne Conference or, even if they had taken part in it, contained large elements that were hostile to its outright condemnation of the whole notion of dictatorship and to its emphatic adhesion to the cause of parliamentary democracy. Among these discontented Parties the most important were the French, the Italian, the Norwegian, the Swiss, the Austrian, the Spanish, and the American, and also, in Great Britain, the I.L.P. The Moscow Congress was immediately followed by an intensive campaign to secure the majority backing of these Parties, as well as by efforts to constitute Communist Parties in countries where they did not yet exist. The first favourable response came from the Italians, whose Executive voted, in March 1919, by 10 votes to 3 in favour of joining the Third International. The first set-back came the following month, when the Easter Conference of the French Socialist Party followed the lead of Longuet's group by voting in favour of remaining within the Berne International, but of working for a single, united International including the Communists as well as the Right and Centre. The vote in favour of this course was 894, whereas 757 voted for unqualified adherence to the Berne International, and only 270 for affiliation to the Third. Then, in May, the Norwegian Labour Party voted in favour of joining the Moscow International, and the Bulgarian 'Narrow' Socialists, who were already attached to it, changed their name to Communist Party. In June the Greek Socialist Labour Party left the Berne International and decided to take steps to join the Third ; and during the same month the Hungarian Social Democrats amalgamated with the Hungarian Communists and attached themselves to the Third International. In addition, the Swedish Left Socialist Party and the Dutch Social Democratic left wing adopted the name of Communist Party. In August the Swiss Social Democratic Party Conference voted overwhelmingly against the Berne International and by a substantial majority in favour of the Third, but made its adhesion to the latter subject to a referendum of the whole membership. The result, declared in September, showed a substantial majority against joining the Communist International. Meanwhile, in August, on the fall of the Béla Kun Soviet Goverment, the Hungarian Social Democrats had separated from the Communists and re-attached themselves to the Berne body. In October the American Socialist Party decided to take a referendum on the question of affiliation to Moscow, and meanwhile to remain apart from both Internationals. In January 1920 it was announced that the referendum vote had gone in favour of the Third. Further, in October 1919 the Austrian Socialists, while dissatisfied with both Internationals, decided to send delegates to the Geneva Congress convened by the Committee appointed at Berne ; and a branch referendum of the British Socialist Party resulted in an overwhelming majority for the Moscow International. The Italian Syndicalist Union also rallied to Moscow during this month. In December the Spanish General Confederation of Labour joined the Third International, whereas the Spanish Socialist Party by a small majority rejected affiliation to Moscow in favour of a resolution demanding purification of the Berne International and union between it and the Third. During the same month the German Independents (U.S.P.D.), after a great debate, rejected the Berne International and decided to attempt to take common action with other revolutionary Parties with a view to the formation of a united International including the Communists.

Thus, by the end of 1919, the Communist International appeared to have won the allegiance of the Italian Socialist Party, of the Swedish Left Socialists, of the Norwegian Labour Party, and of the British Socialist Party, but to have lost the Swiss and the Hungarian Social Democrats, and to have failed to win over either the French or the Austrian Socialists. The position of the German U.S.P., of the American Socialist Party, and of the Spanish Socialist Party, as well as of some others, remained doubtful. The Czechs, the British I.L.P., and a number of other Parties were sharply divided. The British Labour Party, the German Majority Socialists, the Belgian Labour Party, and the Swedish, Danish, and Dutch majority Parties formed a solid block of supporters of the reformist International, which the Berne Committee was preparing to endow with a formal constitution at a Congress to be held in Geneva in February 1920. In December, however, it was decided to postpone the Geneva Congress to June 1920, in order to allow more time for the doubtful Parties to determine their policy.

In the meantime the Permanent Commission set up at the Berne Conference had held four meetings, the first at Berne in February 1919, immediately after the full Conference, the second at Amsterdam in April, the third at Lucerne in August, and the fourth in London in December 1919. The first of these meetings appointed a delegation to present the Berne resolutions to the Paris Peace Conference and set up the Committee of Action already referred to.[1] The second, attended by delegates from 17 countries, including Belgium, was mainly concerned with passing a large number of resolutions dealing with the territorial and national questions which the Berne Conference had been unable to discuss in detail. It also re-iterated and amplified the Berne conclusions concerning the structure of the proposed League of Nations, and sent its Committee of Action to Paris to interview the 'Big Four' and protest against the course taken by the Peace Conference on a number of matters ; and it decided to convene the constituent Congress of the new Socialist International at Geneva in February 1920, and instructed the Committee of Action to prepare draft statutes. This was before the Allied Peace Terms were handed to the Germans in May : when they were issued, the Committee of Action at once published a Manifesto criticising them in detail and declaring roundly that 'this peace is not our peace'.

At Lucerne in August the Permanent Commission, repre-senting 19 countries, followed up this Manifesto with a detailed criticism of the Peace Terms, for the most part agreed upon by both the main groups — that is, by the Branting-German-British majority group and by the minority which had followed,

[1] See p. 297.

at Berne, the Adler-Longuet line. These two groups, however, were more sharply divided than ever on the question of the new Socialist International and on the attitude to be taken up towards Soviet Russia and the Communist movement as a whole. The minority still wanted, despite the terms of the Moscow Congress *Manifesto*, to work for the creation of an inclusive International and to refrain from outright condemnation of the Russian Communist régime. The majority, no less than the minority, was prepared to condemn Allied intervention in Russia ; but it insisted on its absolute opposition to all forms of dictatorship, whereas the minority wished the forthcoming Geneva Congress to consider, without pre-judgment, 'general questions of Socialist tactics, the respective value of democracy and dictatorship, and the relations between the political and economic organisation of the working classes', and insisted that 'only on the solid basis of the permanent principles of the International — that is to say, the class-struggle pursued without compromise with the bourgeois Parties' — could an understanding capable of bearing real fruit be established among all Socialists throughout the world.

The Lucerne meeting also approved the draft statutes drawn up by the Committee of Action for submission to the Geneva Congress and the draft agenda for it, and decided to convene simultaneously with it an International Conference of Labour and Socialist Members of Parliament, such as had existed in conjunction with the pre-war International. The London meeting in December was chiefly occupied with the question of postponing the Geneva Congress, which, as we saw, was put off from February to the end of July 1920.

By the time the Geneva Congress actually met, the basis of the projected new International had been substantially narrowed since the Berne meeting. The French Socialist Party had decided in February 1920, by an overwhelming vote, to leave the Berne-Geneva body, and to attempt to build a broadly based revolutionary International, while rejecting immediate affiliation to Moscow by a majority of almost two to one. The German Independents also had decided against Geneva ; and several of the Parties which did send delegates, including the Austrians and the Spaniards, had announced their strong dissatisfaction with the basis on which the Geneva Congress had been convened. In effect, the Geneva Congress was to a great extent a British-German Majority affair, supported by the Belgians, Swedes, Danes, and a few lesser Parties and groups, but evidently falling a long way short of providing an adequate foundation for an effective International. Almost as much as Moscow dominated the Third International, Great Britain and the German Majority dominated its rival. Nevertheless, the promoters went ahead with their plans and, when the Congress actually met, carried through a series of resolutions which unequivocally embodied the reformist philosophy of the Socialist right wing, with no concessions to Communism or dictatorship, though not without some attempt to appeal to the middle groups which stood nearest to them on the key issues of parliamentarism and a gradualist interpretation of the Socialist gospel.

The Geneva resolution on the 'Political System of Socialism' so clearly embodies this point of view as to merit quotation in full. Its fundamental standpoint is that of complete acceptance of parliamentary democracy as the basic institution of a Socialist society, involving the complete rejection of every sort of dictatorship. Although it gives qualified approval to the idea that some sort of National Industrial Council, representative of the various trades and professions, '*may* be desirable', it makes plain that such a body is to be no more than advisory or at most endowed by Parliament with subordinate, delegated powers. It insists more than once — following therein the line of the British Labour Party's manifesto on *Labour and the New Social Order* — on the essential partnership of the workers 'by hand and brain', and it defines the term 'Labour' as including 'not merely the manual working wage-earners, but also the intellectual workers of all kinds, the independent handicraftsmen and peasant cultivators, and, in short, all those who co-operate by their exertions in the production of utilities of any kind' — a definition wide enough to bring in not only all professional workers but even all employers and managers who take an active part in production in the widest sense.

Here, then, is the text of the resolution :

The progressive disintegration of the Capitalist System, which has been increasingly taking place during the years of war, and not less during the years of peace following the war, makes it ever more urgent that Labour should assume power in society. In the term Labour we include not merely the manual working wage-earners, but also the intellectual workers of all kinds, the independent handicraftsmen and peasant cultivators, and, in short, all those who co-operate by their exertions in the production of utilities of any kind.

(1) It is an essential condition of this assumption of power by Labour that its ranks should be sufficiently united, and that it should understand how to make use of the power in its hands.

(2) Whilst the Congress repudiates methods of violence and all terrorism it recognises that the object cannot be achieved without the utilisation by Labour of its industrial as well as its political power ; and direct action in certain decisive conflicts cannot be entirely abandoned. At the same time, the Congress considers that any tendency to convert an industrial strike automatically into political revolution cannot be too strongly condemned.

(3) The Socialist Commonwealth can come into existence only by the conquest by Labour of Governmental power. The main work of a Labour Government will be to adopt, as the fundamental basis of its legislation and administration, both Democracy and Socialism.

Socialism will not base its political organisation upon dictatorship. It cannot seek to suppress Democracy : its historic mission, on the contrary, is to carry Democracy to completion. The whole efforts of Labour, its Trade Union and Co-operative activities equally with its action in the political field, tend constantly towards the establishment of Democratic institutions more and more adapted to the needs of industrial society, becoming ever more perfect and of higher social value.

It is to-day the forces of Labour that, in the main, ensure the maintenance of Democracy. Socialists will not allow factious minorities, taking advantage of their privileged positions, to bring to naught popular liberty. Inspired by the great traditions of past revolutions, Socialists will be ready, without weakness, to resist any such attacks.

(4) The franchise for a Socialist Parliament must be universal, applying with absolute equality to both sexes, without exclusions on grounds of race, religion, occupation, or political opinions. The supreme function of Parliament is to represent all the popular aspirations and desires from the standpoint of the community as a whole. It will deal with defence against aggression from without or within. It will be in charge of the property and also of the finances of the community.

It will make the laws, and administer the public business. The Ministers in charge of the various departments will be chosen from among its members ; and the government of the nation will be its Executive Committee.

But it will be free to delegate particular powers and duties to any of the other organs of the community hereinafter mentioned, in order to secure the greatest possible participation of those personally engaged in each branch of social life. It will be for Parliament to safeguard not only the interests of the general public of consumers, for whose representation on special Boards and Councils it will provide, but also the interests of the community as a whole in future generations.

(5) It will be for Parliament to determine the general lines of social policy and to make the laws ; it will decide to what industries and services the principle of socialisation shall be applied under what conditions ; it will exercise supreme financial control, and will decide upon the allocation of new and additional capital. In the last resort, it will exercise the power of fixing prices.

(6) In the development and expansion of the productive life of the community, a large part will be played by the various organisations formed according to the productive occupations in which every healthy person will be engaged. Thus, provision must be made, in the manner hereinafter described, for the participation in the administration of each industry or service of representatives of all the different grades of workers, by hand or by brain, engaged in that particular industry or service. At the same time, each vocation, whether of workers by hand or of workers by brain, desires to regulate the conditions of its own vocational life, whatever may be the industries or services among which its membership will find itself dispersed. Each distinct vocation may therefore group itself in a professional association, to which functions of regulation, of investigation, or of professional education, may be entrusted by Parliament.

(7) The organisations into which those engaged in the various industries and services will group themselves, whether Trade Unions or Professional Associations, may be made the basis of a further organ of social and economic life.

Alongside Parliament it may be desirable that there should be a National Industrial Council composed of representatives of the various organisations of Trades and Professions into which the persons belonging to each occupation may voluntarily group themselves. Such a National Industrial Council would be free to discuss and criticise, to investigate and to suggest, and to present to Parliament any reports on which it may decide. Parliament may, from time to time, delegate to the National Industrial Council the drafting of measures applicable to industry as a whole, or of the regulations to be made under the authority of a State.

The other main resolution adopted by the Geneva Congress dealt with Socialisation. This opened with a general declaration in favour of 'ownership and control by the community' of all the industries and services essential for the satisfaction of the people's needs, and went on to declare for 'the transformation from the economic servitude of the great mass of the actual producers under private ownership to a general participation in management by the persons engaged in the work'. This general socialisation, however, was to be brought in, not all at once, but by stages. 'Socialisation will proceed, step by step, from one industry to another, according as circumstances in each country may permit. Objectionable as private-profit-making enterprise is to Socialists, they will refrain from destroying it in any industry until they are in a position to replace it by a more efficient form of organisation. Such a gradual process of socialisation excludes, in general, expropriation of private ownership without compensation ; not only because it would be inequitable to cause suffering to selected individuals, but also because a process of confiscation would disturb capitalist enterprise in industries in which socialisation was not immediately practicable. The funds required for compensation will be derived from taxation of private property, including capital levies, income tax and death duties, and the limitation of inheritance for the benefit of the State.'

Socialisation is then described as taking three main forms — national, municipal, and co-operative. Land is to be nationalised, with provision for the security of peasant cultivators, wherever they exist. Other industries of supreme national importance, such as transport, electrical generation, and mines, are also to be nationally owned ; but many other industries are to be placed in the hands of local public authorities, or federations of such authorities, while the production and distribution of household supplies are to be entrusted mainly to the consumers' Co-operative Societies. Industries left for the time being in private hands are to be subjected to public control, including the fixing of prices and of minimum conditions of employment.

The resolution then goes on to state that the adoption of the principle of socialisation is not intended to exclude either individual peasant cultivation or the independent activities of working craftsmen or of professional persons — 'provided always they do not exploit the labour of other persons'. 'On the other hand, the principle of socialisation does exclude the ownership of natural resources or of the instruments of production in the large-scale primary industries by individuals or associations of persons of any kind ; together with the dictatorship of any person or group over the industry in which they work.' This is clearly a cut at Syndicalism. It is added that 'it is the function of the community as a whole to exercise control over the prices of commodities and to provide whatever new or additional capital is required from time to time for socialised industries'.

The resolution then enlarges on the question of 'administration of socialised industries'. It stresses the vital difference between 'control', which 'will be exercised by the popularly elected national assembly', and 'administration', which 'must be entirely separate and distinct from the organs of the political government'. Subject to variations from industry to industry, it suggests as a general type of administration for each national industry a board made up of three elements — representatives of the workers concerned, of the management, including the technicians, and of the consumers and the community as a whole, with similarly composed district councils where needed, and with works committees for the separate establishments. It then says that for purposes of collective bargaining there should be distinct machinery of joint boards representing managements on the one side and Trade Unions or professional associations on the other, and that the right to strike needs to be maintained, but that, when and where capitalist exploitation has been done away with, 'it may be expected that the public opinion of the community as a whole will be accepted as decisive'.

Finally, for the wide range of industries and services which it is proposed to place under the control of local public authorities, administration under these authorities, 'with participation in the management of their own services by representatives of the workers by hand and brain, and with distinct provision for collective bargaining', is put forward as the correct solution.

This highly specific resolution was evidently designed, while entirely repudiating Syndicalism and maintaining fully the general principle of democratic parliamentary and municipal control, to make concessions to the numerous and active advocates of various forms of 'workers' control', from Guild Socialists in Great Britain to French advocates of '*la nationalisation industrialisée*' and to German supporters of *Mitbestimmungsrecht*, and such American industrial reformers as the authors of the 'Plumb Plan'. Its acceptance with these provisions is evidence of the extent to which even the right-wing Socialists were feeling the pressure of these diverse advocates of various forms of industrial self-government — a pressure which was particularly strong during the period immediately after the war. When the pressure lost most of its force in consequence of the post-war slump, most of the parliamentary Socialists soon showed a disposition to whittle down these concessions, or even to go back on them altogether ; but in 1920 they were mostly anxious to placate those supporters of Guild Socialism and similar movements who were not suspect of Communist sympathies. The Communists, on their side, were quite unprepared to make similar concessions : they wooed the revolutionary Syndicalists and the I.W.W. because they were revolutionary, but insisted that legitimate 'workers' control' was control by the proletariat *as a class*, and showed no sympathy for the claims to industrial self-government of the workers in particular industries or establishments.

On the basis of these resolutions the Geneva Congress set up a definitely reformist International on the very narrow foundation of the Parties that were prepared not only to repudiate Communism but also to renounce all hope of a reunited working-class movement. Of the 17 countries represented at Geneva, 5 had sent only observers without authority to commit their Parties ; and in a majority of cases the delegations could not claim to represent united national movements. In effect, the Geneva International was made up of the British Labour Party, the German Majority Socialists, the Belgians, the Swedish Majority, the Dutch Majority, the Danes, and a few oddments. The headquarters were placed in London, and in effect the British Labour Party took charge of its affairs.

Well before the Geneva Congress formally established the new Socialist International, the Trade Unions had set up a Federation of their own to replace the loosely organised International Trade Union Secretariat of the pre-war period. There was much to-ing and fro-ing before this was achieved, as several different attempts were being made, and there was the same reluctance on the part of some of the movements in the Allied countries to meet German delegates on equal terms. The International Secretariat, of which Karl Legien was secretary, with his headquarters in Germany, had practically ceased to operate after the outbreak of war. In early July 1916 an Allied Trade Union Conference was held at Leeds, with delegates from Great Britain, France, Belgium, and Italy. This Conference rejected a proposal from Samuel Gompers, of the American Federation of Labor, that a general International Trade Union Conference should be held simultaneously with the Peace Conference, the ground of the rejection being unwillingness so soon to meet the Germans on friendly terms. At Leeds the delegates adopted a resolution, moved by Léon Jouhaux of the French C.G.T., demanding the inclusion in the Peace Treaty of special clauses protecting the rights of Labour and covering such matters as the rights of combination and migration, the provision of social insurance, and the regulation of the hours and conditions of employment and of industrial hygiene.

The Leeds Conference aroused Legien to action, and in October 1916 he issued from the International Secretariat a call for a General Trade Union Conference to be held at Berne in December. When the Scandinavian Trade Unions objected to this as premature, Legien cancelled the proposed meeting, but agreed with the Swiss Unions that they should issue a similar invitation to a Conference to be held the following year. While negotiations regarding this project were proceeding, the call for an International Socialist Conference at Stockholm was sent out, and it was proposed that the Trade Union meeting should be transferred from Berne to Stockholm. The Swiss refused to accept this ; and the Dutch Trade Unions thereupon, as a section of the pre-war International Secretariat, issued their own call to a Conference to be held at Stockholm in June 1917. This Conference actually met, but was attended only by delegates from Holland, the Scandinavian countries, Finland, Germany, Austria, Hungary, and Bulgaria. The Swiss and Belgian Trade Unions refused to take part : the French and British made no answer at all ; and the American Federation of Labor, though it had been the first to propose an international meeting, now rejected the invitation as premature. Recognising its inadequate composition, the Stockholm Conference limited its activity to inviting the Swiss Trade Unions to make a further attempt. The Swiss thereupon sent out a summons to an International Trade Union Conference to be held in Berne in October 1917.

This too was a failure : the Swiss and Czechs were the only new-comers, the French, who had intended to be represented, being refused passports by the French Government. The British, Belgians, and Americans again declined to come. Jouhaux sent a message from France urging that the headquarters of the International Trade Union Secretariat should be moved from Germany to a neutral country ; but Legien strongly opposed this, as constituting in effect 'a vote of censure on Germany'. In view of his opposition, the proposal was not carried ; but authority was given to the Dutch to act for the time being as intermediaries for the purpose of international relations. For the rest, the Berne Conference adopted most of the demands endorsed by the Leeds Allied Conference of the previous year and added demands that Trade Union representatives should be admitted to take part in framing the economic and social clauses of the Peace Treaty, and that the international Trade Union movement should be recognised by Governments as the spokesman of Labour in matters of international labour legislation.

The next step made towards the re-establishment of the Trade Union International was the participation of the Trade Unions, jointly with the Labour and Socialist Parties, in the Berne Labour and Socialist Conference of February 1919, where the Trade Union delegates held separate sessions and drew up the draft of an International Labour Charter for incorporation in the treaty of peace. But the American Federation of Labor, which was independently pushing the same idea, refused to attend either the Berne meeting or the International Trade Union Conference which the Dutch were again attempting to bring together, this time at Amsterdam. Instead, Gompers demanded a purely Allied Conference, which was in fact never held because only French and American delegates presented themselves on the appointed day. The Berne Conference, however, broke the ice ; and in July 1919 a general Trade Union Conference, preceded by a preliminary conference demanded by the Belgian Trade Unions for the purpose of 'squaring accounts' with the Germans, was held at Amsterdam and gave birth to the International Federation of Trade Unions, known thereafter as the 'Amsterdam International'. These gatherings, which represented most of the important Trade Union movements of Western Europe and also the American Federation of Labor, opened with violent recriminations against the Germans by Camille Mertens of Belgium and by Gompers, brought to an end by the acceptance of the 'Sassenbach' resolution in which the Germans admitted that Germany had been the aggressor in the war and expressed regret for the wrong done to Belgium, but laid the blame on the deception practised on the workers by the Imperial German Government. The Germans accepted this resolution only with great difficulty, first agreeing to it, then withdrawing their agreement, and finally again endorsing it when they realised that it wouldbe impossible to establish the new Trade Union International without it.

This matter having been disposed of, it became possible to proceed to the constitution of the I.F.T.U. But there were many angry disputes between Gompers and the European delegates concerning the provisions of the Labour clauses of the Peace Treaty, which had been drawn up by a committee of the Peace Conference with Gompers as chairman and were regarded as seriously defective by most of the European leaders. Only the British delegates sided with the Americans on this issue ; and the Trade Unions agreed to take part in the forthcoming Washington Conference, designed to constitute the International Labour Organisation, only on condition that invitations should be issued to Germany and Austria and that workers' representation should be reserved exclusively for Trade Union bodies affiliated to the newly formed I.F.T.U.

There were other clashes over the proposed League of Nations constitution and over questions of I.F.T.U. organisation ; but the Conference did not quite break down, though in the end Gompers refused to commit the Americans to join the new International, pending the decision of the A.F. of L. Convention.

Next came the Washington Conference of the I.L.O. — a tripartite affair of government, Trade Union, and employers' representatives, including delegations from 41 countries, of which 14 were represented only by government delegates. The Germans and Austrians were not present because their invitations had been issued too late for the obstacles in their way to be surmounted ; and the Americans, too, were absent because the United States had not ratified the Treaty of Peace. Nevertheless, the Washington Conference formulated a number of Labour Conventions, of which the most important proposed the general adoption in the more advanced countries of the forty-eight-hour week. Though much difficulty was to be encountered in attempts to get this Convention ratified by the leading countries, its adoption at Washington was widely acclaimed by Socialists as a big step towards the acceptance of the long-standing working-class demand for the eight hours' day. It was received very differently by the Comintern, which roundly denounced both the I.L.O. and the Amsterdam International as counter-revolutionary agencies.

This was the situation when the Communist International held its second Congress at Petrograd and Moscow in July and August 1920. This was a very much bigger affair than the small, unrepresentative and hurried gathering of March 1919. There were now several hundred delegates purporting to represent 37 countries and including a substantial contingent from Asian countries, from Egypt and from Turkey, as well as from the European Parties which had applied, conditionally or unconditionally, for admission to the Third International. By no means all these delegates had voting rights : in a number of cases they were present only as observers, whose claims had still to be pronounced on by the Comintern Executive, over which Zinoviev presided. This, for example, was the position of the French, represented by L. O. Frossard (1889-1958) and Marcel Cachin (1869-1958), of the Italians, and of the German Independents. Only the Russians and a few other delegations from Eastern Europe represented solidly organised Communist Parties : the rest were mainly from splinter Parties which had broken, or were in process of breaking, away from the Socialist Parties of their several countries, or were from Syndicalist or similar movements such as the I.W.W.

This second Moscow Congress met at a moment when, despite the failure of the World Revolution to spread into Western Europe, the Russian Communists were in fine fettle because of their recent victories over the counter-revolutionary forces of Kolchak and other generals and of their success in repelling Allied military intervention. These successes more than made up for the eclipse of the Hungarian and Bavarian Revolutions and for the Communist defeats in Germany as a whole. Moreover, the war against Poland seemed to be going well ; and the Russians, though greatly exhausted by war and famine, were becoming more confident of their ability to maintain their Revolution even if its spread to the Western countries were delayed and the impending collapse of capitalism unhappily deferred. This did not make them the less eager to promote Revolution in the rest of the world, and above all in Germany, or to do all they could to disorganise the attempts of the capitalist States, with the aid of the reformist leaders of Labour, to achieve recovery and stabilisation. On the contrary, it led them to redouble their efforts to bring into being everywhere Communist Parties prepared to accept the full rigour of the doctrine proclaimed in the *Manifesto* of the previous year and to conform exactly to the requirements of orthodoxy laid down through the Russian-dominated Comintern.

In this spirit, the second Congress of the Third International formulated the 'Twenty-one Points', complete acceptance of which was to be a condition of admittance to the International — a much more stringent and deterrent set of conditions that the Fifteen Points of 1919. 'We are living', the Congress declared, 'in an epoch of civil war : the critical hour has struck.' The appalling state of affairs which the war had left behind it was proclaimed to be driving the workers everywhere into 'revolutionary warfare destroying objectively the foundations of the capitalist State'. In pursuance of this warfare, the revolutionary workers of all countries were called upon to break away from the Socialist Parties and to form distinct Communist Parties accepting the centralised discipline of the Comintern. All such Parties were required to be ready to take illegal as well as legal action, including active propaganda among the armed forces, and to do their utmost to 'accelerate the Revolution', though without artifiically promoting it by attempting Blanquist *coups*. In particular, a new requirement was that all Parties wishing to join the Third International should remove all reformists from responsible positions and should expel all such persons as the Comintern might designate as open or hidden enemies of the revolutionary cause. Another 'Point' committed all adherents of the Third International to a 'stubborn struggle against the Amsterdam International of the Yellow Labour Unions' and against the International Labour Organisation of the League of Nations. In pursuance of this struggle, a number of Trade Union delegates from Great Britain, France, Italy, Bulgaria, and Yugoslavia met Alexander Solomon Lozovsky (1878-194?) and Zinoviev and set up a Provisional Council of a new Red International of Labour Unions in competition with the I.F.T.U. This body had, indeed, no considerable mass support except in Russia : elsewhere its adherents represented no more than small minority fractions. These groups, however, set to work actively at their appointed task of undermining the authority of the established Trade Union leaders, in the same way as the Communist Parties and groups were attempting to discredit the reformist political leaders. The question whether the R.I.L.U. and its national affiliates were or were not to encourage the formation of rival Trade Unions, at the cost of the economic unity of the working class in relation to collective bargaining, was soon to become of great importance. If the World Revolution was coming almost at once, the bargaining strength of the Trade Unions did not greatly matter, as the power of the capitalists would in any case speedily vanish. On the other hand, if there was to be considerable delay, it would clearly matter a great deal to the workers that their bargaining strength should be maintained and increased during the remaining years of capitalist supremacy, and division in the Trade Union ranks might positively worsen the Revolution's prospects of early success. As against this, it was felt to be clearly the task of Communists to develop the class-war spirit in the Trade

Unions, and, as their efforts to do this might easily lead to expulsion, they had to be prepared at least to set up rival Unions where they were unable to carry on their work of agitation within those already in being. The struggle over this issue came, as we saw,[1] very early in Germany, especially in the Ruhr mining area and in parts of Saxony. For the most part it came later elsewhere because, in most countries, the Communists' position in the Trade Unions was at the outset relatively weak.

Thus, the issue between the two extremes — Communism and reformist parliamentarian Socialism — was fairly joined in the industrial as well as in the political field. There was, however, a difference. In the Trade Union field the Communists, in declaring war on 'Amsterdam', were challenging an International which had the support not only of the right wing but also of such relatively militant Trade Union movements as the French Confédération Générale du Travail and the Italian C.G.L. ; whereas in the Socialist field the only rival International — the Berne-Geneva body — was essentially a right-wing agency, and the considerable body of Centrist opinion had kept the Parties in which it was strong from committing themselves finally to either International. The French, the Italian, the Swiss, the Austrian, and a number of other Parties, as well as the German Independents and the British I.L.P., were still in the midst of their own internal struggles over the question of their international allegiance. Some of them — for example, the Italians — had voted in principle for the Comintern, but were now facing the consequences as made plain in the Twenty-one Points. Others — for example, the French — were still predominantly Centrist, but were engaged in intense internal battles. Yet others — for example, the Austrians — were firmly and almost unitedly Centrist, and showed no sign of a willingness to be torn apart by the struggle between right and left — a struggle which, in their highly precarious national and international position, they could evidently not afford. The Communists, in face of this situation, had made up their minds to treat as enemies all bodies — or at all events all leaders — that were not one hundred per cent on their side ; but they could not wage this war merely by personifying the

[1] See p. 137.

Berne-Geneva International as the enemy, in the same way as they could in the case of the Amsterdam Trade Union International. They needed to make war separately on the right wing — the Berne-Geneva grouping — and on each national Party in which the Centrist tendency was either predominant or powerful enough to obstruct complete submission to the exactions of the Twenty-one Points.

This situation was changed when, in February 1921, a Conference representing Socialist Parties and groups from 13 countries met in Vienna and set up the International Working Union of Socialist Parties, which came to be known as the 'Vienna Union', or, more familiarly, the 'Two-and-a-Half' International, because of its intermediate position between Berne-Geneva, as the successor of the 'Second', and Moscow, as the progenitor of the 'Third'. The Vienna Union itself disclaimed the status of an 'International', proclaiming that its purpose was merely to prepare the way for an International wide enough to include both parliamentarians and Sovietists, and thus to restore Socialist unity. It could not, however, avoid being a point of focus for those Parties and groups which were dissatisfied both with the out-and-out reformism of the Berne-Geneva Parties and with the intransigent Sovietism of the Comintern.

The principal Parties represented at the Vienna Conference, besides the Austrians, were the French, the German Independents, the British I.L.P., the Czechs, the Hungarians, the Swiss, and the Russian Mensheviks and Social Revolutionaries ; and there were also groups from Latvia and Lithuania, and from Yugoslavia and Rumania. The Finnish and Argentinian Socialist Parties, though not represented, sent messages of adhesion. In the cases of France and Germany, however, the Parties represented were not those within which the struggle between the rival tendencies had previously been carried on, but fragments of them, resulting from recent splits. In France the old Socialist Party had finally decided, in December 1920, to affiliate unconditionally to the Third International, and had become the French Communist Party. The old Right and Centre, headed respectively by Pierre Renaudel and Jean Longuet, had thereupon broken away and re-established the Socialist Party (S.F.I.O.) with the support of a majority of the sitting Socialist M.P.s. The once bitter quarrel between Majoritaires and Minoritaires had been driven into the background by the rise of Communism ; and the Longuet fraction, enjoying much greater support than the old Majority led by Renaudel, was able to bring the new Party into the Vienna orbit. Similarly, in Germany, the Independents (U.S.P.D.) had voted at their Halle Congress of October 1920 in favour of joining the Third International on the basis of the Twenty-one Points. The Halle Congress had then broken up into two separate Congresses, each claiming to be the inheritor of the U.S.P.D. The majority fraction, led by Däumig and Helene Stöcker, thereafter, in December 1920, amalgamated with the existing German Communist Party — the former Spartakus-bund — at a Unity Congress held in Berlin, which set up the United Communist Party of Germany. The minority had decided to continue as the U.S.P.D. under the leadership of Ledebour, Crispien, and Hilferding ; and it was this minority that attached itself to the Vienna Union.

In Czechoslovakia, too, there had been a split, as a result of which the Communists had been cast out of the Social Democratic Party to the accompaniment of violent conflict.[1] At the time of the Vienna Conference, the Czech left wing was still in process of reorganising itself as a Communist Party, with a view to adhesion to the Third International. The body represented at Vienna was the Czechoslovak Social Democratic Party, shorn of its Communist elements. In Hungary, as we have seen,[2] the Social Democrats, after fusing with the Communists to support the Béla Kun régime, had re-formed their Party, apart from the Communists, on the fall of Kun's Soviet Government ; and it was this re-formed Party, then suffering under the White Terror, that sent its delegates to the Vienna meeting. In Switzerland, as we saw,[3] the Socialist Party Conference had voted by a majority, in August 1919, in favour of joining the Third International, but this decision had been reversed by a referendum vote. A second referendum, in January 1921, confirmed this reversal by a vote of almost three to one ; and the Communists in the Party thereupon broke away and amalgamated with the small existing Swiss Communist Party. The Swiss delegates at Vienna represented the

[1] See p. 237.   [2] See p. 248.   [3] See p. 321.

Social Democratic Party, without the Communists. Finally, the British I.L.P., which, after negotiations with the Comintern, had refused to accept the Twenty-one Points, had suffered a secession of its not very considerable Communist fraction. It remained in affiliation with the British Labour Party, the mainstay of the Berne-Geneva International, but maintained its right to follow an independent international policy, and sent its delegates to the Vienna meeting.

The Vienna Union declared itself to be 'a Union of such Socialist Parties as aim at realising Socialism by the conquest of political and economic power along the lines of the revolutionary class struggle'. It 'has the task of unifying the activities of the affiliated Parties, arranging common action, and promoting the establishment of an International which will embrace the whole revolutionary working class of the world'. Membership was to be open to all Parties which accepted these principles and were not affiliated to either the Second or the Third International. 'The resolutions of the Working Union are binding on all its members : in particular all Parties belonging to the Union engage not to enter into any separate negotiations for joining with other international organisations, and, for the rest, to determine their international policy by mutual agreement.'

Out of the Vienna Conference emerged a remarkably sensible and penetrating 'Statement on the Methods and Organisation of the Class Struggle', defining the Vienna Union's position in relation to the rival Internationals already in being. In this Statement, great stress was laid on the error of prescribing a single course for the attainment of Socialism in all countries, irrespective of the widely differing economic and political conditions — for example, as between predominantly agricultural and industrial countries, as between countries of large landed estates and of small-scale peasant holdings, and as between countries possessing and not possessing the institutions of parliamentary democracy, and those dominated and not dominated by militarist influences. It was absurd, the Union argued, for international Socialism to bind itself to the exclusive use of parliamentary democratic methods, which in some countries there was no opportunity at all to use, and which, in others, might be rendered nugatory by the possible suppression of democratic institutions at the hands of the reactionary and capitalist classes. But it was no less absurd to bind the workers of all countries by prescribing 'the mechanical imitation of the Russian peasants' and workers' revolution, as the Communist International would like to do'. The struggle of the workers for political power would of necessity take different forms in different countries. 'Only in those countries where the capitalist class does not command the power required, and in particular is bereft of military power, and therefore cannot venture to replace the fight of political democracy by open civil war, only in such countries will the working class be able to gain political power by means of democracy. But even where this happens, the capitalist class will as a general rule use its economic power to neutralise the effects of the democratic State power gained by the working class. In that case too the working class, after arriving at political power, will have to use dictatorial means in order to break the resistance of the capitalist class. Proletarian dictatorship will take the form of the dictatorial exercise of the State power achieved by the working class.' This was the course of events foreseen where the Revolution was carried through under the favourable conditions of a democratic parliamentary system.

'But where the capitalist class is strong enough to maintain by violent means its rule against the revolting masses of the working people, it will break democracy, keep control of the means of coercion, and challenge the working class to an open fight. In this fight it will not be the vote that will decide the battle, but the economic and military strength of the opposing classes. In these circumstances the working class will be able to become the ruling power only by direct action of the masses (mass strikes, armed rebellions, etc.), and it will have to maintain its power by suppressing the conquered capitalist class. The dictatorship of the working class must in this case be based on Workmen's, Peasants' and Soldiers' Councils, on Trade Unions, or on other working-class organisations.' Thus, the word 'dictatorship' is given two different meanings in different situations. In the one type of situation, it can take the form of 'a dictatorial exercise of the State power achieved by the working class'; in the other it requires the exercise of dictatorial power by specifically working-class bodies, such as

'Soviets or Councils of Workers, Peasants and Soldiers.'
Whereas the Communists proclaimed the universal necessity of
shattering the old State and of building up an entirely new
proletarian State in its place, the Vienna Union, though
recognising that this might be necessary in certain cases, maintained that in others the existing State, captured by the workers
by constitutional means, might be usable as the instrument of
Socialist defence and revolutionary construction.

The Vienna Union's Statement went on to recognise the
essentially international character of capitalist power, and concluded that 'the final liberation of the working class can therefore not be achieved within the national boundaries, but can
only be the outcome of international action. To organise this
action is the proper task of the Working-class International.'
This, however, requires that the International must take into
account the variety of objective conditions of the struggle in
the various countries. It must not tie all the Parties down to a
rigidly uniform way of action, as both the existing Internationals, in their opposite ways, were seeking to do. 'But
with all the variety of methods in various countries, the International must unite all the resources of the international working
class in concerted action against international capitalism.' This,
however, is impracticable unless there can be a comprehensive
class organisation of the world's working class — that is, a
really inclusive International. 'For, however important the
agitation and action of the Parties on the basis of their theory,
it is no less important that, in the last instance, not party
doctrine but the self-determination of the working class should
be the deciding factor. This self-determination can only be
exercised within an organisation in which all class-conscious
workers are united. But such an international organisation is
an actual reality only if its resolutions are binding on all its
parts. Every resolution, therefore, of the international organisation means a self-imposed limitation on the autonomy of the
Parties of all countries.' The Vienna Union is here insisting,
on the one hand, on the need for variety of method and action
from country to country, as against the uniform patterns pre-
scribed by both Internationals, but also, on the other hand, on
the need for common discipline, as against the loose federation
favoured by the Parties of the Berne-Geneva International.

What was wrong with the Vienna Union's Statement, from the standpoint of its practical influence, was that it was much too sensible. Though, in comparison with the Berne-Geneva declarations, it leant over a long way to the left, it failed to capture the imagination of the leftists because of its failure to enlist on its side the strong emotions aroused by the Bolshevik Revolution. It antagonised the reformists, but failed to attract the revolutionaries : so that the Vienna Union was left high and dry, talking what was, for the most part, good sense to a working class that wanted, for the most part, not to listen to good sense but to have its emotional sympathies appealed to. In a logical sense, the demand for a united International, for unity of working-class action for the overthrow of capitalism, was unassailable. But the united International, under the conditions prevailing in the post-1918 world, was quite impracticable. The gulf between Communists and parliamentarian reformists was much too wide to be bridged, not only because the ideologies were so far apart, but also because the two extremes hated each other much too passionately to be capable of working together in any common organisation.

CHAPTER X

SOCIALISM AND INTERNATIONALISM IN THE 1920s: COLONIALISM, PEACE AND DISARMAMENT

IN the foregoing account of the conflict between the rival Internationals in 1919 and the following years I have concentrated attention mainly on the issue of 'democracy versus dictatorship', and in doing so may appear to have done less than justice to the contestants, by leaving out of account other issues that divided them no less deeply. Of all these other issues, by far the most important in its effects on general policy was that of colonialism, or imperialism — that is to say, of the policy to be followed in dealing with the problems of the dependent territories of the great powers, and of some lesser countries, such as Belgium and Holland, and also of the less developed areas not directly subject to colonial rule — for example, China and the Republics of Latin America. Something was said in the preceding volume [1] about the discussions on colonial policy that took place at the Congresses of the Second International and about the views of the Socialist leaders on the connection between imperialist rivalries and the danger of world war. We saw that the leaders of the Second International were at one in regarding the war danger as arising mainly, if not exclusively, out of economic factors and as becoming rapidly greater as the great powers came into sharper conflict over 'spheres of influence' and openings for imperialist exploitation. We noted the partition of the African continent among the European powers, the rivalries of Russia, Germany, and Austria-Hungary in South-Eastern Europe and the Near East, the conflict between Russian and Japanese expansionism in the Far East, the tortuous course of great power policies in relation to China, the earlier phases of American penetration into Central and South America — especially in relation to

[1] See Vol. III, Part I, pp. 42 and 57.

Mexico — and a good many more manifestations of the working of finance-capital as an international disturbing force. We noted, too, the disputes over colonialism at the Congresses of the Second International, at which a general attitude of hostility to imperialism was complicated by differences of attitude between those who took a firm stand against colonial exploitation in all its forms and those who were prepared to defend some forms of colonial development as making for the better use of the natural resources of the under-developed countries, while insisting that an obligation to protect native interests and to improve living standards in these countries must rest upon the advanced countries that claimed the right to rule them as the champions of civilisation and general human progress.

Indeed, we saw that at any rate one world-famous Socialist thinker, Bernard Shaw, took the extreme line, in *Fabianism and the Empire*, of asserting that in the twentieth century the die was cast in favour of the imperialist powers and that no backward people had any right to stand in the way of economic progress by holding its potential productive resources out of effective use with the aid of modern techniques and capital investment such as only the wealthier areas could supply.[1] This was, to be sure, a doctrine which very few Socialists, even in Great Britain, were prepared to endorse. But there were not a few, especially among the German Socialists, who claimed that the powers which had been left behind in the race for colonial annexations had a right to do as others did, and to create for themselves such colonial empires as were within their reach. Among the Dutch Socialists too there were indications of a desire to justify the workings of colonialism in Java and in other Dutch overseas possessions. The Belgians were differently placed, because the assumption of responsibility for the government of the Congo State was forced on them against their will as the only way open to them of bringing the abominable régime of King Leopold to an end. Nevertheless, having for very good reasons assumed this responsibility, they found themselves in a position in which it was difficult not to defend the partly reformed colonialism of which they had become the exponents. On the whole, however, the sentiment of the Second International was strongly anti-imperialist, because its leaders

[1] See Vol. III, Part I, p. 190.

saw in imperialism the most powerful force making for war, which they were bent on preventing if they could in order to clear the road for advances in social policy in their own countries and for the peaceful conquest of political power by parliamentary means. Whatever reservations might be made by right-wing German or British or Dutch delegates, the anti-imperialists were always certain of carrying the day at a Socialist Congress if the question came to a vote — which, broadly speaking, it seldom did except in connection with the great debates on the means of preventing war.

Of course, whenever colonial policy was debated, the Socialists were at one in insisting that every colonial power was under an obligation to govern its possessions and dependencies in the interest of their inhabitants, to refrain from brutal exploitation or suppression of the native peoples, and to direct its attention to measures for improving their standards of life. They were also at one in demanding that foreign investment should be so regulated as to protect native interests, in protesting against the abuses of forced labour, and in urging that self-government should be accepted as the goal to be aimed at, and therefore in giving general support to national emancipation movements where they existed, as in India and Egypt. But in the period up to 1914 colonial nationalism was still in most areas no more than embryonic, and in most tribal societies had hardly begun to take shape on any considerable scale : so that the Socialist demands for colonial self-government had, save in a few areas, a good deal of a utopian flavour ; and even in relation to India the matter did not occupy a great deal of the International's attention or assume a very practical form. On one or two occasions, Socialist Congresses loudly cheered Indian nationalist visitors who were invited to address them fraternally in the Indian people's cause ; but when the cheering was over nothing happened beyond general resolutions supporting anti-imperialist claims. Indeed, nothing more could happen until the foundations of imperialism were shaken by the first world war and by the impact of the Russian Revolution on popular sentiment over a large part of the colonial world — above all, in Asia and the Middle East.

The war and the Russian Revolution between them profoundly transformed the entire situation. Pre-war Russia had been a vast empire covering a wide range of subject peoples at many different levels of social and economic development, but had differed from other empires in that its territory consisted of a single, continuous land mass. It had been an integral part of the programme of all the Russian Socialist Parties to demand self-government and equality for all the peoples of the Czarist empire, including, at any rate for some of them — those which had strong national traditions and developed cultures of their own — the right, should they wish, to secede and set up as independent States. Lenin was among those who most firmly upheld this right and, as we saw, had fallen foul in this matter of Rosa Luxemburg, who had insisted on the need for the peoples of the Czarist empire to work together for a Revolution that should lead to the setting-up, not of nationalist States, but of an international Workers' Republic transcending national frontiers, and had fiercely opposed the separatist nationalism of Pilsudski and the Polish Socialist Party. This, of course, does not mean that Lenin had wished the Russian empire to break up into a large number of separate national sovereignties, but only that he had been prepared to admit the claim of certain national groups to break away should their peoples so desire. In relation to most parts of the Russian empire the issue had never been really faced before 1917, when it arose in drastic form with the severance of the Ukraine under German occupation and with the disintegration of the Czarist military and administrative structure. After the Bolshevik Revolution the Bolsheviks were cut off from a large part of the old empire by the German occupation and by the civil war, and the Red Army could only fight its way gradually back to control over the Asiatic territories and over the South. Not only Finland and Poland but also Estonia, Latvia, and Lithuania in the north established themselves as separate States : the Ukraine and the Caucasian Republics came under Soviet rule only as the outcome of a sequence of aggressive wars, in which the Soviet forces did their best to appear as liberators of their peoples from counter-revolutionary rule : [1] the Japanese and the Whites were gradually driven back in the Far East. What emerged was a federal structure, the U.S.S.R., made up of a number of nominally equal Sovereign States, among

[1] For the fate of Georgia and the other Caucasian Republics see p. 205.

which the R.S.F.S.R. was immensely the biggest and most populous and included a high proportion of the lesser nationalities and national or tribal groups. The whole mass, except the areas which had broken away, was held together tightly by the large powers of the central federation — the U.S.S.R. — and by the strongly centralised authority of the Communist Party, which spread over the entire area. Economic power in relation to all major industries and services, including agriculture, was strongly centralised ; whereas large efforts were made to develop cultural autonomy, in matters outside the political and major economic fields, for the lesser as well as for the greater national communities. All the inhabitants, irrespective of nationality or level or type of culture, became in form equal citizens — men and women alike — of the Soviet Union : so that in place of a vast empire made up of many peoples subject to Russian rule and russifying pressure there appeared an only rather less vast Union of Socialist Soviet Republics resting on foundations of common citizenship over its entire area. In the Bolshevik view, Russia ceased to be an empire, and the entire problem of imperialism was liquidated once and for all. Westerners might still accuse the Soviet Union of being the old Czarist empire in a new guise : the Bolsheviks scornfully rejected the charge and pointed with pride to their achievement in reconciling the unity and solidarity of the new order with the generous recognition of legitimate cultural claims.

Mentally, the establishment of the Soviet Union exerted a powerful influence on its neighbours, above all in Asia ; and the Bolsheviks, in their hot pursuit of the cause of World Revolution, made haste to do all they could to stir up revolutionary feeling both in the colonies and dependencies of the imperialist powers and in the countries subject to various forms of feudal or autocratic rule. The Baku Congress of Peoples of the East, held in September 1920 with Zinoviev as President, and Radek and Béla Kun supporting him as delegates from the Comintern, was their first large-scale attempt to bring together under their leadership the varied movements of revolt among the peoples of Asia and the Near East. To the Baku Conference came delegates or self-appointed persons from a great number of disturbed areas, standing for a wide variety of opinions, but all in some sort of nationalistic or social revolt against the established order. From that time onwards it was part of the task of the Comintern and of the Soviet Union to provide refuge and revolutionary training for potential rebels from all parts of the world, and especially from the Asiatic countries, and to send back the trainees to their own countries to act as missionaries for Communism and sometimes to displace those local Communist leaders who were not sufficiently responsive to directions from the Comintern. The alliance between the Chinese Communist leaders and the Kuomintang was part of the same policy ; and, as we shall see, many Chinese were trained in Moscow at the Sun Yat Sen College, of which Radek was for a time director.[1]

The Communist attitude to imperialism and colonialism was essentially simple : its inspiring purpose was to make as much trouble as possible for the imperialist powers in their dependent territories, and to support every movement of colonial nationalism that could be used to serve this end. It was also, in areas not directly subject to colonial rule, to make trouble for the ruling classes, to do whatever could be done to link nationalist movements to movements of social unrest, and to persuade the local nationalists everywhere to look upon the Soviet Union as the great liberating power that was eager to come to their aid as far as its strength allowed. As we shall see, Communist Parties made their appearance in India and in other Asian countries in which no Socialist Parties as yet existed, though there were socialistic tendencies in the left wings of the various nationalist movements. Much the same methods were used to spread Communism in Latin America, except that in the American republics the Communists appeared not as the allies but as the enemies of nationalism, which was then, during the years after 1918, predominantly a right-wing force ; for the popular nationalism, later associated with the name of Perón, did not make its appearance on any considerable scale until the 1930s.

It is not surprising that in India, with its already considerable movement of popular nationalism and anti-imperialism, Communist propaganda had, in the years after 1918, a considerable success among the more left-wing adherents of the national movement. There, M. N. Roy[2] was for a time the

[1] See p. 785.   [2] For Roy, see p. 811.

outstanding exponent of the new doctrine; and Roy was also sent by the Comintern to both China and Latin America as an emissary.[1] In most of the colonial territories, however, both political nationalism and working-class organisations were still too undeveloped to offer much scope for successful Communist agitation, though in Java the group of propagandists led by Sneevliet were able to infiltrate with substantial success into the nationalist movement.[2] For a time the outstanding example of Communist infiltration appeared to be China, until Chiang Kai-shek turned on his erstwhile associates and brought the Chinese Communist movement down in ruins, leaving to Mao Tse-tung the long and arduous task of building it up again on utterly different foundations of rural revolt.[3]

It would be tedious to recite the complex story of Communist activities during the 1920s in the colonial areas and in other countries suffering the effects of imperialist penetration. All that I need emphasise here is that the policy of the Comintern and of the Soviet Government was essentially that of making things as awkward as possible for the imperialist powers, at first in the hope of a speedy spread of the Revolution over the entire world and of the immediate ruin of imperialist capitalism in all its forms, and later, when these hopes had to be deferred, of keeping the imperialist powers too busy dealing with colonial and other disturbances and problems to be able to direct all their forces against the Soviet Union. This policy, of course, involved urging on the Communist Parties in the imperialist countries to constant denunciations of imperialist exploitation; and these Parties steadily put forward the argument that the advanced countries were living on the results of colonial exploitation and that the workers in them — or at any rate the better-off workers — owed their standards of living to the exploitation of colonial labour and thus made themselves partisans of the exploiting capitalists unless they ranged themselves firmly on the side of the colonial peoples. World capitalism, it was argued, was saving itself from its inherent contradictions only by making itself the master of the markets and raw materials of the less advanced countries : so that the best way of ensuring its downfall was to strike at it at this, its most vulnerable, point. It was not always easy to

[1] See pp. 752 and 786.   [2] See p. 823.   [3] See p. 800.

present this argument to the workers of the advanced countries without it suggesting to them that, if they owed their higher standards of living to colonial exploitation, they would be foolish to forgo it, and had better, in their own interests, leave it to continue undisturbed. But the Communists argued that the main body of the workers in the advanced countries did not get the benefits of colonialism, which accrued mainly to the capitalists, though some small share filtered down to a minority of skilled workers, and that the benefits of Socialism to the whole working class would far outweigh any loss a few might suffer through forfeiture of their status of semi-bourgeois privilege.

The Socialists of the right wing, who regarded parliamentary democracy as the necessary prerequisite of Socialism and envisaged the coming of Socialism as a process of gradual development through the reform and improvement of existing social and political institutions, and not as the outcome of a sudden revolutionary upheaval, were in much greater difficulty than the Communists in defining their post-war policies in relation to colonialism and imperialism. For the prevention of future wars and for the stimulation of international co-operation in the promotion of the general welfare, they wanted to bring into being an international authority powerful enough to hold aggression and inter-power rivalries in check, and, suspicious of the intentions of the post-war Governments of the great powers, they wanted this international agency to be so constituted as to represent peoples rather than Governments, and saw the best hope of this in a body representing the Parliaments of the constituent countries rather than their executive Governments. As for colonies and dependencies, they wished those they thought capable of managing their own affairs to be advanced as speedily as possible towards self-government, but envisaged this as being brought about, not by colonial revolutions, but by concessions of increasing self-government by the imperialist powers under pressure of the proposed international authority. With a view to making this pressure effective, they wanted the imperial powers to agree to place their colonial administrations under some form of international trusteeship to be exercised by the new supra-national authority, which would be committed to securing that they should be administered primarily with a view to the well-being of their inhabitants, rather than in the interests of the imperial powers or their investing classes. More generally, they wanted all countries to pledge themselves to submit all international disputes to arbitration either by an International Court of Justice backed by the new world authority or by that authority itself. Finally, as we saw, they demanded that the Peace Treaty and the constitution of the international authority should embody a comprehensive charter of the rights of labour, which each member-country would be required to pledge itself to observe. By these means they hoped to establish a world-wide code of minimum economic rights for all workers and to create an instrument for the continuous raising of the minimum thus initially laid down.

The League of Nations actually established by the terms of the Peace Treaty fell in every respect a very long way short of these aspirations. In the first place, it was essentially a a League, not of peoples or even of Parliaments, but of Sovereign States represented by their executive Governments. Secondly, the League Covenant, though it did establish an International Court of Justice and did equip the League Council with certain limited powers to check aggressive action by member-States, embodied no general provision for arbitration in international disputes and no general outlawing of war as a means of deciding disputed issues. Thirdly, the Labour Charter, under which the International Labour Organisation was set up as an independent League agency, laid down no enforceable code of minimum rights ; and the I.L.O. itself, with its tripartite constitution, gave half the seats to the constituent Governments and divided the other half between representatives of Capital and Labour. Nor had the I.L.O. any authority to legislate : it could only propose international labour conventions, which each State remained free to accept or reject as it pleased. Fourthly, the victorious powers which dominated the League entirely refused to put their several empires under any sort of international authority, though, in depriving Germany of its colonial empire and distributing its territories among themselves, they did agree to hold the transferred territories under mandate from the League, but not to put them under any form of international administration. This meant that, in practice, the mandated areas became, subject to a few safeguards, such as the 'open door' for trade, virtually parts of the dependent empires of the powers which took them over.

On all these, and on a number of other points, the representatives appointed under the authority of the Berne Socialist and Labour Conference of 1919 did what they could to bring pressure on the official negotiators at Paris, but did so with very little, if any, success. The post-war Governments of the victorious countries were not at all minded to surrender any real part of their sovereignty into the League's hands or take any action that might undermine the power of capitalism, or to throw their dependent empires into a pool which would involve giving the non-imperialistic countries a voice in deciding their future ; and the parliamentary Socialists, when their demands were rejected, found themselves disabled from attempting any action because they did not control either the Governments or the Parliaments of the imperialist countries, and had therefore to choose between accepting the League, with all its shortcomings, and refusing to recognise it — which would have meant renouncing such advantages as it did possess and the hope of transforming it gradually into a more effective agency. Making their dissatisfaction clear, the parliamentary Socialists accepted the League as better than nothing, whereas the Communists denounced it as a barefaced capitalist conspiracy. The former continued to press for the League's amendment — especially for the strengthening of its powers for the prevention of future wars ; but they could do no more than pass resolutions until they succeeded in becoming the Governments of the major countries, and thus got the power to amend the League Covenant into their hands. The British minority Labour Government of 1924, under the leadership of Ramsay MacDonald, did what it could to secure the reinforcement of the Covenant by strengthening the provisions for arbitration in international disputes, but fell from office before it had had the chance to achieve any really significant results.

The Socialist Parties of the imperial countries — British, French, Dutch, Belgian, etc. — had thus to shape their post-war policies in imperial and colonial affairs within the framework of a system in no respect essentially different from that of the years before 1914, except that for the time being Germany had dropped out of the running as a competitor for territorial possessions. This meant that, in order to achieve any immediate results, they had to work for the improvement of the colonial and imperial policies of their countries by demanding better treatment of the native peoples and limited advances towards self-government where these seemed to be practicable within this general framework. In this spirit the British Socialists gave their support to the more moderate demands of Indian Nationalism, did a little to urge the British Government towards more liberal policies of colonial democratic self-government and economic and social development designed to promote colonial welfare, and continued to pass resolutions in favour of some form of international trusteeship. Such matters, however, were of little interest to the main body of electors, and could not have been made an important factor in election contests even if the leaders had wished to make them so — which most of them did not. Moreover, there were not a few among the moderate Socialists who held that the break-up of the British empire would be a misfortune for the world as well as for Great Britain, and that the proper line of advance was that of a gradual development of self-governing institutions in the colonies, of such a sort as to lead by stages towards Dominion status for the more advanced colonial areas as well as for such great dependent countries as India and Burma — a solution which would leave the emancipated areas to continue their connection with Great Britain and would convert the empire by stages into a commonwealth of internally self-governing nations following in essentials a common policy in its relations with the rest of the world. From this standpoint, and even from that of the general body of parliamentary Socialists, the attempts of the Communists to stir up colonial rebellion and to make trouble for the imperial powers at every possible opportunity were to be resisted by all means as a threat to orderly development of the new, liberalised forms of the imperial connection ; while to the Communists the policies of the imperial gradualists were yet another example of the treason of the Social Democrats to the revolutionary cause. Thus, the battle between the rival Socialist factions was joined in relation to India and to other dependencies and colonies no less fiercely than over the general issue of 'democracy versus dictatorship' in the more advanced countries.

Outside India, which is discussed in a later chapter,[1] the troubles in the colonies were most acute wherever there were substantial bodies of white colonists settled in countries mainly inhabited by native peoples — for example, in East as against West Africa. For in these areas the claim to self-government was put forward by the white settlers on their own behalf even before it had begun to be seriously advanced on behalf of the native majorities. In relation to such areas the Socialists found themselves forced to rally to the defence of colonial rule from Great Britain as a bulwark against white settler rule — above all in Kenya — not because they were content with the policy of the Colonial Office or of the British Governors on the spot, but because they could, at any rate, bring some pressure to bear upon these authorities, whereas white settler rule would leave the native inhabitants altogether defenceless. Thus the British Socialists worked out for themselves by stages a moderate, evolutionary colonial policy which enabled them to reconcile their progressive principles with a temporary continuance of colonial rule, and largely removed them out of the anti-imperialist camp.

In this matter of colonial policy, the British Socialists had, within these limitations, on the whole a good record of consistent protest against the abuse of imperial power and of exposure of the maltreatment of native populations by white settlers in those colonial areas in which such settlers were present in substantial numbers. E. D. Morel followed up his successful struggle against King Leopold's monstrous régime in the Congo with further campaigns directed against imperialist policies practised by Great Britain in Africa and elsewhere; and Dr. Norman Leys, by his long and devoted studies of white rule and exploitation of the native peoples in Kenya, gave precision to the more general conclusions that emerged from L. S. Woolf's comprehensive survey, *Empire and Commerce in Africa* (1920), which was originally sponsored by the Fabian Society. H. N. Brailsford, too, took a leading part in the struggle against British imperialism; and he and Morel, together with Woolf, were largely responsible for the advanced policy laid down in the British War Aims Memorandum of 1917–18, which provided the basis for the Allied Socialist

[1] See p. 809.

Statement on War Aims and for the policy approved at the Berne International Socialist Conference of 1919.[1] The proposal to pool dependent empires under a system of international trusteeship in the hands of the proposed democratic League of Nations, as a League of Peoples rather than of Governments, came to nothing in face of the refusal of the Governments to abandon or modify their several sovereignties by admitting any sort of international control ; but the project was seriously meant, and made nonsense of the Communist allegations that the parliamentary Socialists were mere abetters of the imperialist policies of their several countries.

Other colonial powers had their own problems to face — the French, at this stage, mainly in Morocco and to a less extent in Tunisia — both dependencies with considerable European settler populations living side by side with large majorities of Arabs and other non-European inhabitants relegated to positions of economic, social, and political inferiority. The official French policy in dealing with these areas was, broadly speaking, one of selective assimilation. The colour bar was much less rigid than in territories under British control, and the official aim was to bring the wealthier and more educated members of the native communities under the influence of French culture and to an acceptance of the French hegemony, while keeping political power firmly in the hands of the settler minorities and rejecting all demands for self-government of the native majorities. Algeria, as distinct from Morocco and Tunisia, was legally a part of the French Republic, and was at this period relatively free from political troubles, of which Morocco was the storm-centre. Up to 1914 the French Socialist Party, with Jaurès as its principal spokesman, had a goodish record in its support of the claims of the colonial peoples ; but after the split, in the course of which the Communists gained a majority, a sharp opposition developed between the Communist Party, which, of course, followed the Comintern lead, and the re-formed S.F.I.O., which took up a more equivocal attitude in relation to the settlers' claims and, on the whole, stood for the maintenance of French supremacy, while urging a more liberal and progressive policy in respect of the social and economic claims of the African peoples. These issues,

[1] See p. 293.

however, did not become really acute, except in Morocco, during the period covered in the present volume.

Meanwhile in Indonesia the Dutch Government — though it operated no colour bar and a substantial mixture of races actually occurred in parts of Java — maintained a firm front against all claims to self-government by the native inhabitants, and did its best to suppress both the rather inchoate nationalist movement and the small but active Communist Party which obtained some influence in its left wing. In Holland the Socialists were sharply divided on this, as in most other, issues. The Dutch Communist Party was small but lively; and within the Social Democratic Party there were strong dissensions between the right and left wings, leading before long, as we shall see, to an actual split.[1]

The Belgians, after taking over the Congo from Leopold's corrupt and brutal administration, brought about great improvements in the treatment of the native population, unaccompanied by any advance at all in the direction of self-government, for which there appears to have been hardly any organised demand. The Belgian Socialists, in or out of office, gave their support to the reform of the old abuses, but were under no pressure from any colonial nationalist movement — for none existed as yet. Under the Peace Treaty, Belgium acquired a mandate over the populous neighbouring territory of Ruanda-Urundi, formerly part of German East Africa, and important as a source of supply of migrant labourers for the mines of Katanga and other areas adjacent to it. From 1925 Ruanda-Urundi was administered as a province of the Belgian Congo, while remaining under League of Nations mandate. As in the Congo, no important nationalist movement developed; and the Belgian administration was untroubled by claims to self-government from the Bantu peoples of the area.

The remaining European empires were those of Spain and Portugal; and of these little need be said for the purpose of the present chapter. From 1920 onwards there was heavy fighting in Morocco in both the French and the Spanish zones. The Riffi rebellion led by Abd-el-Krim began in the Spanish zone in 1920, and reached its culmination in the defeat of the Spaniards at Anual the following year.[2] The French and

[1] See p. 517.   [2] See p. 541.

Spaniards thereafter joined forces to crush the nationalists in 1926 ; but strong rivalries continued between the two colonial powers, and the Spanish zone provided a centre for anti-French propaganda directed against the French policy of colonisation followed by Lyautey and his successors. General Franco's long unfulfilled promises of self-government, made when he was seeking the aid of Moroccan troops in the Spanish civil war, fall outside the period covered in the present volume. Meanwhile in Portugal the period of entire instability following the republican revolution of October 1910 lasted until 1926, when Generals Gomes da Costa and Carmona established a military dictatorship, of which Carmona soon assumed the sole leadership. Carmona then brought in Professor Salazar as his Finance Minister ; and in 1932 Salazar, having become Prime Minister and virtual dictator, secured the acceptance by a referendum of the new corporate constitution by which Portugal is still governed to-day. Salazar's principal achievement was the balancing of the Portuguese budget by rigid economies and improved tax collections ; and he applied the same policy to the budgets of the Portuguese colonies, in which he reformed the administration, but made no concessions at all to demands for self-government — demands which, of course, he also rejected in relation to Portugal's domestic affairs.

The only colonial power of importance outside Europe was the United States, which had annexed Puerto Rico and the Philippines after the Spanish-American War of 1898, and had also assumed far-reaching powers of intervention in Cuba. American imperialism, however, manifested itself in the main, not in these areas, but in relation to Mexico and Central and South America, in the form of increasing invasion by United States investment agencies and big business concerns, against which, as we shall see,[1] the left-wing nationalist movements of these areas came to be directed with growing vehemence, with the Communists doing all they could to put themselves at the head of the anti-American agitations.

In relation both to colonialism and the rights of national self-determination and protection of the native peoples from the more extreme forms of capitalist exploitation, and also to ideas of world government and the prevention of war by the

[1] See p. 173.

acceptance of arbitration in international disputes, the Socialists of the post-war Labour and Socialist International took up again the policies of the old Second International and displayed much activity in pressing for the adoption of remedies that could be applied peacefully, without war either between States or between conflicting forces within them. They started out, as we saw, with ambitious projects for the setting up of a League of Nations with wide powers, constituted as a league, not of Governments or even of sovereign States, but of free peoples enjoying the practice of democratic parliamentary government. With projects for the renunciation of war as an instrument of State policy they sought to combine projects of co-operative world development resting on a pooling of dependent territories under League control and on a combined use of the resources of the more advanced countries for the raising of standards of living in the less advanced. It was, however, made manifest at once that there was no immediate prospect of such a League being established, and that even the liberal principles advocated by President Wilson in his Fourteen Points were regarded as having served their purpose in helping to hasten the collapse of the Central Powers and would have but little influence on the terms of peace or on the actual structure of the League and its associated agencies. The decision of the United States to stand aloof from the League and to dissociate itself as far as possible from the affairs of Europe was also a factor in bringing even the profession of Wilsonian principles into disuse. The parliamentary Socialists had accordingly to adapt their policies to the actual situation that confronted them ; and this meant putting most of their idealistic aspirations into cold storage, and making the best of a bad job. They remained free to press for a strengthening of the League Covenant in order to enlarge its powers for the prevention of war, to advocate disarmament, to urge the modification of the immediate demands for Reparations and the bringing back of Germany and the other defeated countries into the comity of nations ; but it was impossible immediately to work for these ends by the methods of parliamentary democracy except within the general framework of a restored capitalist system and of a structure of independent nation States dominated by the victorious powers. In these circumstances, projects for a world-wide crusade against poverty, to take the form of a concerted programme of development of the backward countries, were evidently ruled out. All that seemed practicable was pressure in each advanced country for better treatment of its subject peoples and for some gradual concession of self-government within the general structure of imperialist rule.

Such a policy involved at one and the same time a great sacrifice of idealism and a sharp opposition to the Communist policy of support everywhere for anti-imperialist revolt and for the stirring up of civil war wherever an opportunity occurred, or could be artificially contrived. This Communist programme of action underwent, indeed, very substantial modification when its failures had become obvious ; and the general emphasis then shifted from promoting immediate World Revolution to using the Communist Parties of other countries as agencies for the defence of the Soviet Union. In the colonies and under-developed countries, however, the modification did not make a great deal of difference ; for the more disturbed conditions were in the dependent empires and spheres of influence of the great imperialist powers, the less able would these powers be to direct their resources against the Soviet Union. Thus, the Communist attitude in relation to the colonies and dependencies of the great powers remained essentially subversive, and involved increasingly sharp conflict with the parliamentary Socialists as these latter turned their attention to the gradual amendment of colonial conditions and régimes, and sought in the colonies allies prepared to work with them for gradual improvements in opposition to the militant advocates of anti-imperialist revolt. The struggle in the colonial areas between Communist 'sub-verters' and progressive 'gradualists' was taken up on a much bigger scale after the second world war, especially in Malaya, Indo-China, and North Africa ; but it was already afoot in the 1920s as a strong barrier in the way of united Socialist action through a common International widely enough based to include both Communists and adherents of democratic parliamentary methods.

In relation to the question of war and peace, the Second International had again and again asserted that wars were due almost if not quite entirely to capitalism — to the rivalries of national capitalist groups, to the common drive of the capitalist powers towards the opening up and exploitation of the less developed areas and their consequent scrambles for spheres of influence and economic monopoly, and to the inner contradictions of a system that could escape from crises of ever-growing severity only by enlarging the markets open to capitalist exploitation. These being regarded as the root causes of war, it was believed that wars would cease to trouble the peoples as soon as capitalism had been overthrown, and the peoples had taken power into their own hands. Doubtless it was admitted that, even after capitalism had been superseded, disputes between States might still arise ; but it was thought that the obstacles to the adjustment of such disputes by peaceful legal adjudication, or by arbitration, would have been removed. The struggle against imperialist capitalism was regarded as, in effect, including the struggle against war, and international conciliation and arbitration as methods that would be readily accepted as soon as capitalism had been got out of the way. Norman Angell, in his *The Great Illusion* (1910), had set out to discredit the notion that even victorious nations could hope to profit by resorting to war, and had in the main proved his point, but had not succeeded in showing that even the general recognition of this would suffice to make wars unlikely. For even if no nation, as a nation, could expect to profit by modern war, it did not at all follow that no *interest* within a nation could do so, or that such interests might not be powerful enough to bring wars about even to the general detriment of the countries involved in them. Powerful capitalist groups, with great influence over the Governments of their countries, could still lead their States into war for their private advantage ; and such influences had been actually behind the policies pursued by the great powers in the years before 1914.

It did not, however, follow that, even if capitalist interests were fully capable of leading the nations into war, the causes of war could truly be stated in purely economic terms. The expansionist policies of the great imperialist powers had undoubtedly a large element of economic motivation ; but there were other forces also at work — especially a desire of ruling classes for power, of which economic power was only one, though a most important, aspect. This drive for power, simply as power carrying with it prestige, was, I think, particularly strong in Germany, where it rested on an assertion of German 'cultural' superiority over other peoples and on a jealousy of nations which had got ahead of Germany in the conquest of colonial possessions and on exaltation of military prowess as the highest manifestation of national superiority. Japan showed, in many respects, similar tendencies, with economic and more general 'power' motives intricately combined into a pattern of aggressiveness by no means fully explicable in purely economic terms. The Second International, with its mainly Marxist theoretical foundations, under-estimated the importance of the non-economic factors in international tensions, and accordingly formulated a theory by which capitalism was represented as the sole real force making for war. The Bolsheviks, of course, were as firm as the Social Democrats in upholding this theory, and much firmer in following it through to the conclusion that war, when it had broken out, should be used as an opportunity for the complete destruction of capitalism by World Revolution. This insistence did indeed square with what had been laid down in the well-known final paragraph of the Stuttgart resolution adopted by the Second International in 1907 on the insistence of Lenin and Rosa Luxemburg against the initial opposition of the German Social Democrats, who had accepted it only under pressure.[1] But the policy there nominally accepted had never been really part of the policy of the International's constituent Parties ; and the breakdown of the International in 1914 had effectively made an end of it as far as the majorities in the main Parties of the belligerent countries were concerned. The Germans, in their Revolution of 1918, had made no attempt to destroy capitalism along with militarist autocracy. Nor had even the Austrians, who were even more dependent for the sheer survival of their new Republic on Allied help which they knew would be withheld if they went to such lengths. In Great Britain and in France, where no Revolutions had occurred, or even been contemplated save by small minorities, the question of immediate destruction of capitalism did not even arise. It came much nearer in Italy ; but even there the main body of the Socialists drew back after challenging capitalism by occupying the factories — and the outcome of the Italian Revolution was not Socialism but Fascism.

[1] See Vol. III, Part I, p. 62.

Thus, if the Socialists had been correct, before 1914, in regarding capitalism as the essential cause of war, that cause remained operative after 1918, since capitalism, except in Russia, had succeeded in maintaining its authority and, despite the establishment of a League of Nations, each capitalist State was left free in the last resort to follow its own line, even to the point of war. Moreover, even if they had been wrong in attributing wars exclusively to economic factors, the danger of war was clearly not removed by the limited authority given to the League, which could at most only put some additional obstacles in its way. The new Labour and Socialist International, in its declarations concerning the causes of war, in the main repeated what had been said in the days of the Second International, but, despite its critical attitude towards the League of Nations as a league, not of peoples but of capitalist Governments, decided to work within it for the improvement of its machinery and methods and especially for the acceptance of arbitration as the alternative to war, and for the promotion of disarmament or at least progressive limitation of armaments. Some dispute arose over the participation of individual Socialists in League affairs as representatives of non-Socialist Governments, especially in relation to the position of J. Paul Boncour of France, who, first appointed as delegate of the Herriot Government in 1924, remained in that office under the Briand Government which succeeded it and to which the French Socialists were opposed. It was recognised that Socialist Governments, or Coalition Governments including Socialists, would necessarily be free to send Socialist delegates to take part in League affairs, but it was questioned whether Socialists ought to be free to participate unless they were so chosen. No action, however, was taken to prevent such participation, and at a later stage Arthur Henderson continued to preside over the League's Disarmament Conference after the fall of the Labour Government by which he had been appointed as a delegate. In general, the Socialist policy came to be that of using the League as an instrument for the furtherance of policies of disarmament and international arbitration, while continuing to emphasise its shortcomings and to demand an amplification of its authority.

This policy inevitably involved concentration on matters

which had little directly to do with Socialism, and raised issues on which parliamentary Socialists could agree with bourgeois Radicals and pacifists who did not accept the Socialist faith, or see in capitalism the main cause of the danger of war. There was nothing distinctively Socialist in working for the outlawing of war, the acceptance of arbitration as a final means of settling all sorts of international disputes, and the progressive disarmament by mutual agreement of the great powers, so as to relieve the peoples of the oppressive costs of intensive armament. From the Socialist standpoint, such measures were plainly desirable : the question was whether it was or was not a sheer delusion to pursue them through a League that was essentially a loose federation of capitalist Governments, which would certainly reject any proposal that attempted to strike at the roots of capitalism and of the imperialism that was regarded as inseparable from it in the modern world. For the most part the parliamentary Socialists were prepared to use the League, in the hope of gradually amending it, just as they hoped gradually to amend the practices of their own countries by increasing Socialist influence by means of electoral victories, leading in due course to the conquest of political power. The alternative — rejection of the League and of all its works — would have carried with it the implication that capitalism must be overthrown by revolution before there could come into being any League of Nations capable of giving valuable service to mankind ; and no such view could be squared with the idea of Socialism as something to be won by stages, peacefully and not by revolutionary means. Accordingly, a very large part of the activity of the L.S.I. came to be concerned with League affairs, rather than with Socialism ; and the largest and most detailed sections in the secretarial reports to its Congresses were those dealing with its efforts to promote the causes of disarmament and arbitration.

A great deal of idealism undoubtedly went into the advocacy of peace by the spokesmen of non-Communist Socialism. Socialism and pacifism were clearly linked causes in many Socialists' minds ; and the tendency of most parliamentary Socialists, in face of the restoration of capitalism over most of the world after 1918 and of the disappearance of the prospect of its overthrow by World Revolution, was to shift from the attempt to remove the causes of war by destroying capitalism — which seemed for the time impracticable — to seeking to improve the chances of an advance towards Socialism by reducing the danger of war. Thus, pacifism and social reformism seemed to go together, and were actually pursued together by the parties of the L.S.I., with almost no opposition except from the Communists and from a few other revolutionaries who had no interest in the promotion of reforms that could be carried through under capitalism, and were still set on returning to the temporarily half-suspended task of bringing World Revolution about.

One effect of this emphasis on peace, arbitration, and disarmament was that the economic aspects of potential League activity were played down, in some cases unconsciously, but in others of deliberate purpose. For in the campaign for peace it was necessary to seek allies wherever they could be found, and especially among liberal supporters of an international order ; but most of these allies would have been strongly antagonistic to the projects of a planned international economic order which had figured among the major objectives of the Socialist advocates of a League of Peoples as against a mere League of Governments. Major hopes for the pooling of the dependent empires of the various States under a democratically organised international authority, or for a world crusade to raise the living standards of the more backward peoples, simply faded away, leaving no more than a continuance of the long-standing Radical and pacifist campaign for the prevention of war and the establishment of an international authority almost restricted to this single aim. This was, for the time being, not easy to avoid for those Socialists who rejected the Communists' doctrine of universal revolution, and had to face the fact of a reconstructed capitalism that seemed likely to be able to maintain itself at any rate for a considerable time. Only when capitalism plunged into the crisis and depression of the 1930s did the situation so change as to bring the question of its impending collapse once more dramatically to the front of consciousness ; and by that time pacifism had become so ingrained an element in moderate Socialist policy that the Western Socialist Parties found great difficulty in adapting their policies to the new situation brought about by the rise of Nazism and the swift growth of the Fascist menace to peace and to democratic methods of facing world problems.

There was, indeed, in the 1920s, no effective middle way for parliamentary Socialism between accepting the existing capitalist order, while seeking to modify its working by strengthening the League of Nations and by pressing in each parliamentary country for gradual advances towards the 'Welfare State' — the policy which the Western Socialist Parties actually followed — and coming to terms with the Russians for concerted action to achieve Socialism. Socialism could not be strong enough, without positive Russian collaboration with Western Social Democracy, to overthrow capitalism or to prevent the major part of the world from continuing to be governed on capitalist lines. That was why, despite the intransigence of the Soviet Union and the Comintern, so many left-wing Socialists in the West were most unwilling to give up hope, not merely of a *détente* with the Soviet Union, but of a positive alliance with it in the realm of world affairs. Such Socialists hoped against hope that the Communists, when they realised that their expectations of World Revolution must be deferred, would be prepared to renounce their sharp hostility to other Socialists and to join with them in a common struggle to make headway against capitalism by reformist means, and that the Soviet Union would join the League of Nations and cease to behave in a merely subversive way. It is easy to say now — and it may even be true — that there was never any real prospect of the Soviet Union, under Stalin's suspicious leadership, following such a course. This was at any rate much less evident in the later 1920s, when the Russians, on the morrow of their great set-back in China, were rapidly restoring their industries and preparing to embark on the first of their Five-Year Plans ; and not only such left-wingers as H. J. Laski and H. N. Brailsford, but also ingrained gradualists such as Sidney and Beatrice Webb evidently entertained and based their policy on such hopes of a *rapprochement* and alliance between Eastern and Western Socialism. Such an alliance may have been impracticable because of intransigence on both sides, and indeed because of the sheer irreconcilability of their respective principles and basic dogmas. But what else was there for a sincere Socialist who accepted neither extreme doctrine to pursue? He could not choose either extreme view, if he did not believe in it ; and the only course left open was to keep on saying what he did believe, and to seize any chance that offered itself of working with either group in the hope, even if he could not bring them together, of accomplishing by these means some things that were worth while. In the 1920s this meant more often collaborating with the right-wing Socialists, because they were the readier to receive help and the less disposed to denounce those who tried to help them as traitors. In the 1930s, after the rise of Fascism in Germany, the Centre was led more often into joint action with the Communists, especially in connection with movements for the establishment of an anti-Fascist Popular Front. But neither orientation achieved durable success. The cleavage between reformism and revolutionism involved too deep differences — not only in matters of principle and doctrine but also in matters of day-to-day practice — for the opposition to be overcome or passed over in silence by mutual consent. The battle of the rival Internationals was a real battle of contending temperaments as well as of opposed convictions. It was, in my opinion, a battle between two wrongs which were quite unable to join forces to make a right.

CHAPTER XI

ITALY TO THE FASCIST VICTORY

As we have seen,[1] the main body of Italian Socialists
opposed Italy's entry into the first world war and maintained its opposition through the ensuing years. There
were, however, from the outset dissident groups — especially
the Reformist Socialists, headed by Leonida Bissolati (1857–
1919) and Ivanoe Bonomi (1873–1951), who had been expelled
from the Socialist Party in 1912, on a motion moved by Benito
Mussolini (1883–1945), and had thereupon set up a Party of
their own. At the same Congress, held at Reggio Emilia in
July 1912, the Socialist Party in Parliament had been made
strictly subject to the orders of the extra-parliamentary 'Direction' of the Party; and Claudio Treves (1869–1933) had been
replaced by Mussolini as editor of the Party's principal organ,
Avanti. Those were the days of the war in Libya, to which
the Socialist Party was bitterly opposed — Mussolini most
strongly of all. During the Balkan Wars the Socialists stood
for strict neutrality; and, when the European War broke out
in 1914, the Party seemed at first to be united in opposing
Italy's participation. By October 1914, however, Mussolini
had changed his mind, and had become an advocate of Italian
intervention on the Allied side. This change of front was
followed by his expulsion from the Socialist Party. Driven
from the editorial chair of *Avanti*, he started his own *Popolo
d' Italia*, and began to build up the Fasci di Combattimento,
out of which the Fascist movement developed. In April 1915
the right-wing government of Salandra signed the London
Secret Treaty under which Italy, in return for a number of
territorial concessions, agreed to enter the war on the Allied
side the following month. The old Prime Minister, Giolitti,
thereupon attempted to displace Salandra and secured the support of a majority of the Chamber of Deputies; but the King

[1] See p. 30.

367

refused to dismiss Salandra, who remained in power and, in May, declared war on Austria-Hungary, but not on Germany. Confronted with this accomplished fact, the Socialist Party sent out, through its veteran leader, Costantino Lazzari (1857–1927), a circular calling on its adherents 'neither to collaborate nor to sabotage'; and this remained for some time the official party line. In August 1916 the new Prime Minister, Paolo Boselli, declared war on Germany; and his Cabinet included Bissolati. There was already much disagreement in Italy over the London Secret Treaty, the terms of which had leaked out, though it was not published till after the Russians had discovered a copy in the Czarist archives after the Revolution. Bissolati made himself a leading advocate of what came to be known as 'Renunciation' — that is, of giving up all claims to the territories allocated to Italy under the Treaty, except those inhabited mainly by Italians. Mussolini, too, in common with the Socialist Party, was among the 'Renouncers'.

In February 1917 the Italian Socialist Party adopted a new programme, to serve as the basis of its post-war action. It declared in favour of universal suffrage, and for a Republic, and demanded an extensive development of public works, especially for the reclamation of waste lands. At this Conference, held at Rome, a sharp struggle developed between the left wing of the Party, led by Amadeo Bordiga (b. 1889), and the centre, which also received the support of the relatively weak right wing. Both groups censured the parliamentary Party for its inactivity and required it to come closer to the mass movement and to offer stronger opposition to the war. In effect, the only real difference was that the left was both definitely revolutionary and anti-parliamentarian, whereas the majority section, though it too proclaimed revolutionary intentions, supported parliamentary action for the time being, subject to the condition that the parliamentary Socialist Party should enter into no alliance of any kind with any section of the bourgeoisie and should neither participate in, nor pledge its support to, any bourgeois Government.

These events took place at a moment when the war was going badly for the Italians. With the Russian armies beginning to disintegrate after the February Revolution, the Austrians found themselves free for the first time to direct their main force against the Italians, and the Germans to give them powerful support. Within two months of the Socialist Conference Cadorna had been overwhelmingly defeated at Caporetto, and the Italian army was threatened with a disintegration equal to that which was coming upon the Russians. In this desperate situation Orlando replaced Boselli at the head of the Government, with Francesco Nitti as his leading colleague ; and Diaz, taking Cadorna's place as Commander, succeeded in restoring army discipline and in averting complete military collapse. The national crisis aggravated differences among the Socialists : the right wing of the Socialist Party, led by the veteran Filippo Turati (1857–1932) and strong among the deputies, though weak in popular backing, openly supported the war effort, whereas the left, among whom Nicola Bombacci (1879–1945) emerged as a powerful demagogic leader, saw in the general confusion an opportunity for intensified anti-war propaganda as a step towards actual revolution. Bombacci, who was later to become a leading Fascist and was finally to pay the penalty of being killed with Mussolini in 1945, stood at this time on the extreme left ; but in the main he had the support of the majority in the party organisation, headed by the veteran Costantino Lazzari. Early in 1918 both he and Lazzari were imprisoned ; but the agitation went on. The war was deeply unpopular with the Italian people ; and both the Trade Unions and the Socialist Party rapidly grew in strength. The Italian Socialists, as we saw, had been the principal promoters of the Zimmerwald and Kienthal Conferences of 1915 and 1916 ; [1] and their leaders followed with the most eager interest and sympathy the course of events in Russia in 1917. The majority of the Party gave enthusiastic support to the Bolshevik Revolution ; and left and centre alike only waited for their opportunity to follow the Russian example, even if they did not all interpret it alike. This opportunity, however, most of them felt, could not come until the war was over : there were few who felt strong enough to attempt action until, the fighting on the frontiers ended, the Government had to face the immense problems that would arise out of demobilisation and out of the promises made by the politicians of land for the peasants and social legislation in the interests of the industrial workers —

[1] See p. 31.

promises they felt sure those who had made them would not ever attempt to carry out.

Stiffened by French and British contingents, the Italian armies did not dissolve after the Caporetto disaster. Diaz, by wise clemency to deserters and defaulters, managed to hold them together ; but large bodies of deserters were abroad in the remoter areas. It was, however, Austria-Hungary and not Italy in which the decisive collapse of 1918 occurred ; and the Italians found themselves on the winning side in a war which had been unpopular from the beginning and had become more and more unpopular after the humiliation of Caporetto and the strengthening of revolutionary feeling by the events in Russia.

Revolutionary Socialism, however, was only one among a number of forces that were rising rapidly in influence after 1917. Romantic nationalism, under the influence of the poet-airman, Gabriele d' Annunzio (1863-1938), became, during the early months of 1919, a growing power among a section of the young, who were fiercely opposed to any renunciation of Italian claims under the secret treaties and to any concession to Slav claims at the expense of the Italians of Dalmatia or Trieste. Musso-lini's Fascists were also a developing group, led by a man who was determined, above all else, to have his revenge on the Socialists who had thrust him forth because of his support of Italy's intervention in the war. In the early months of 1919, however, Fascism was still a very uncertain political force. Mussolini himself was still a 'renouncer' in relation to the secret treaties. His one clear notion was that the Socialists, despite their professed revolutionary intentions, did not really mean business or have any conception of an agreed policy they would have determination enough to carry into effect. He was pre-paring to throw the weight of his Fascists against them when the right moment came ; but for the time being he was con-scious of being altogether too weak to take an independent line. Much more important for the time being seemed to be the emergence of Roman Catholicism as an organised political movement seeking parliamentary power.

Up to 1918 the Roman Catholic hierarchy, though it had abandoned its policy of calling upon good Catholics to refuse recognition of the secular Italian State, had remained hostile to the formation of any confessional Party devoted to the protection of Catholic interests. Active Catholics had played their part in parliamentary politics chiefly as members of the right-wing bourgeois Parties ; and the main body of Catholic peasants had taken no part at all. But by 1919 electoral reform had created a mass electorate under a system of proportional representation which compelled political party leaders to seek a mass following ; and in these circumstances the Papacy reversed its traditional policy and allowed the Sicilian priest, Don Luigi Sturzo (b. 1870), to establish the Popular Party as the exponent of a democratic Catholicism armed with an extensive programme of social reform as a bulwark against anti-clericalism and revolution. The Popular Party, founded at the beginning of 1919, was made up of widely different elements, from reactionary Conservatives to advanced social radicals ; but its popular appeal stressed its radical side, particularly in respect of land reform and social legislation and in its demand for decentralisation and a reduction in the bureaucratic powers of the state machine. It was thus able to take advantage of the unpopularity and discredit of the older Parties and to become a point of focus for the great mass of peasant discontent, especially in the south, which the Socialists had failed to enlist on their side. Indeed, the great weakness of the Socialists was that, in a predominantly agricultural country, they had failed, save in a few areas such as Emilia, to win any consider-able body of rural support and had shown almost no capacity to understand the problems or the attitudes of the peasantry. Among the agricultural day-labourers in certain provinces they had made substantial headway : among the Catholic peasant farmers, despite their very bad conditions and growing dis-content, almost none.

The new Popular Party was astonishingly successful in its appeal to these backward groups, and was also able rapidly to establish itself as a powerful force among the Catholics of the towns. In the General Election of 1919 it won 100 seats — almost one in every five. The Socialists and the Catholic Popolari, had they been able to come to terms, would have commanded together a small majority and, with a minimum of Radical support, could have formed a workable Government. The Fascists and the followers of d' Annunzio were alike electorally negligible in 1919. No such coalition was, however, even remotely possible. Not only were the Socialists over-whelmingly anti-clerical : they were also wholly committed to a policy, if not of immediate revolution, at any rate of revolutionary preparation which ruled out any attempt to use the Parliament as an instrument of comprehensive social reformation. In March 1919 they announced their definite secession from the Second International, or rather their refusal to take part in the Berne Conference's decision to reconstruct it. Thereafter, at their Bologna Congress of October 1919, held shortly before the election, they came out decisively in favour of revolution by violence on the Russian model, affirming that 'the proletariat must resort to the use of violence to defend itself against bourgeois violence, to conquer power, and to consolidate revolutionary conquests'. This declaration was qualified by the decision to take part in the forthcoming election and to make use of 'the organs of the bourgeois State in order to carry out the most intensive propaganda for Communist principles and to effect the overthrow of the organs of bourgeois domination'. On this basis the Bologna Congress proceeded to revise the old Programme of the Socialist Party, drawn up in 1892, and to incorporate in the revised version the assertion that 'a revolutionary period has begun in which a profound transformation of society will lead from now on to the violent overthrow of bourgeois capitalist domination'. The Programme went on to declare that 'the instruments of oppression and exploitation of the bourgeois domination, (States, Communes, and Civil Service) cannot in any way be transformed into organs of the liberation of the proletariat', and that, 'against these organs must be set up new proletarian organs, (Workers' and Peasants' Councils, Councils of Public Economy, etc.), which will function at first, during the bourgeois domination, as instruments of the violent struggle for liberation, and later as organs of social and economic transformation and of reconstruction in the Communist new order'. The Programme announced that this 'violent conquest of power' would install 'the transitional régime of the dictatorship of the whole proletariat', and that after this transition 'with the disappearance of classes will also disappear every domination of class, and the free development of each will be the condition of the free development of all'. Finally, the resolution declared the

Socialist Party's adhesion to the Third International, as 'the world-wide proletarian organisation which expounds and defends these principles', and decided to seek agreement with those Trade Unions which accepted the class-struggle in order that such Unions might 'base their action on the deepest realisation of these principles'.

What all this meant in effect was that the dominant fraction of the Italian Socialist Party, while committing itself to the pursuance of a policy of violent revolution, was aware of its unreadiness for the immediate revolutionary conquest of power and contemplated a period during which parliamentary government would continue, with the Socialist deputies in implacable opposition to the bourgeois Ministry, whatever its complexion or policy, and that outside Parliament the Socialists, aided by the Trade Unions, would do their utmost both to render this system of government unworkable and to build up their own purely proletarian institutions in readiness to replace it as soon as they had become strong enough to take power into their own hands. In thus planning for a Revolution in two stages, they were doubtless influenced not only by their own sense of unreadiness for proletarian Revolution, but also by the fact that the Russian Revolution had taken place in two stages and that the Bolshevik strategy in Russia had rested on the theory of two successive Revolutions, the first bourgeois and the second proletarian.[1] There was, of course, no real analogy between the conditions which had existed in Russia up to 1917 and those which existed in Italy in 1919 ; for in Italy the bourgeois Revolution, or at any rate the bourgeois system of government, for which the Russians had to fight in 1917, was already in being. Nevertheless, the spell cast by the events in Russia was so strong that it seemed necessary to follow out the same broad course in Italy ; and this strategy fitted in with the unreadiness of the Italian Socialists to proceed at once to attempt a complete proletarian Revolution.

This Bologna declaration of policy was arrived at on the motion of the so-called 'Maximalist Electionists', who constituted the main force of the Party. It received 48,411 votes against 14,880 for a motion of the 'Maximalist Unitarians', supported by the right wing, which was not strong enough to

[1] See p. 77.

put forward a motion of its own, and against a mere 3,417 votes for a motion of the extreme left, which was opposed to taking part in the parliamentary elections, and favoured an immediate revolutionary attempt. This left wing was led by Amadeo Bordiga, whose followers broke away from the Socialists and formed an independent Italian Communist Party. Turati and Treves, as leaders of the parliamentarian right wing, were deterred from pressing their own point of view because they clung to their belief in the paramount importance of not splitting the Party, either by breaking away from it or by getting expelled. They therefore voted with the 'Maximalist Unitarians', who shared their hostility to a split, but differed from them in admiring the Bolsheviks and in favouring a revolutionary rather than a reformist policy. As the Maximalist advocates of unity ran no risk at this stage of being expelled from the Party, this tactic saved the right wing from the immediate danger of expulsion despite its sharp opposition to the revolutionary slogans favoured by the immense majority.

The struggle inside the Socialist Party and the Trade Unions, which was thus brought to a head in October 1919, had been growing in intensity ever since the armistice of the preceding November. The first important stage in it had been reached at the Bologna Congress of the General Confederation of Labour, the principal Trade Union organisation, in January 1919. The C.G.L. had then adopted a post-war Programme, in which it called for the establishment of a Republic, for the abolition of the Senate, for proportional representation, and for the introduction of a system of popular initiative, referendum and veto in respect of legislation, as well as for the abolition of the political police and the full control of foreign policy by the Chamber of Deputies. In addition, the C.G.L. Programme included a somewhat unclear demand for the summoning of a Constituent Assembly (*Il Costituente*), which was envisaged chiefly as a body authorised to revise the basic economic institutions of Italy, to introduce comprehensive land reform, and to deal with the whole problem of the control of industry and the status of property in the proposed Republic. It was never clearly stated either how *Il Costituente* was to be elected, or what its powers and functions were to be. The words were a slogan rather than a clearly formulated project ; and the demand at once gave rise to a fiery controversy between those who held that it should be a purely proletarian body, resting on the local Chambers of Labour, and those who had in mind some sort of elected general assembly to act side by side with the regular Chamber of Deputies. The Socialist deputies in the then existing Chamber, who were mostly followers of Turati and supporters of parliamentary government, at once rejected the C.G.L. plan. It was rejected still more vehemently by the Socialist left wing, which stood for violent revolution and for the outright destruction of the existing State as an essentially bourgeois institution.

The C.G.L. indeed stood, in 1919, a considerable way to the right of the main body of Socialists. Resting mainly on the support of the local Chambers of Labour which existed in most considerable towns, it united the main body of Trade Unionists on a basis of close local cohesion rather than of national groupings by either craft or industry. It included a few strongly organised national industrial Federations, such as the Italian Federation of Metal Workers (F.I.O.M.), which was to be the central actor in the occupation of the factories in the autumn of 1920 ; but such bodies were exceptional, and the most important other industrial Union, that of the Railway Workers, was not affiliated to the C.G.L. In this latter Union Syndicalist influence was strong ; and there was also a rival grouping of Syndicalist Trade Unions, the Italian Syndicalist Union, much smaller and less influential than the C.G.L. The Catholics too had a separate Trade Union movement, the Italian Labour Union, formed before the war, but not of much account till it became, in 1919, one of the instruments of the new Popular Party. The C.G.L. itself was predominantly Socialist in its leadership, but put its main emphasis on strike action for the improvement of labour conditions and on demands for price stabilisation and social legislation, rather than on revolution. It was, however, like the French C.G.T., very much interested in workers' control and in demands for a share in the management of industry; and some of its local Chambers were actively associated with the movement of producers' Co-operation, as well as with the promotion of consumers' Co-operation on a definitely working-class basis. During 1919 both the Trade Unions and the Workers' Co-operatives were growing at a great rate ; and the Socialist Party, with all its revolutionism, was eager to keep on good terms with the C.G.L., and hopeful of bringing it over bodily to the revolutionary side.

In Italy, as in many other countries, 1919 was a year of scarcity, inflation, and rapidly rising prices. The lira, which had stood at 6·34 to the dollar at the end of 1918, had fallen in value a year later by nearly two-thirds, and stood at 18·47. There were serious difficulties over imports of coal and raw materials, on which Italian industry and transport depended for their very existence. Production had to be cut down and railway services to be curtailed ; and the returning soldiers could be found jobs only by sharing out the work, on a basis of short time, with those already in employment. Food prices rose sharply ; and the Government was forced to subsidise bread on a constantly rising scale. Strikes were very numerous, and were usually won — at any rate in the sense that wages were constantly being raised in view of the mounting cost of living. For the time being the employers had to give ground ; but the big industrialists became increasingly restive in face of the Trade Union claims not only for higher wages but also for a real share in the control of industry. By the summer of 1919 a number of big employers had begun to finance the Fascists as the force most likely to take effective action against the working-class movement.

The Fascists, indeed, had already embarked on the campaign of lawless violence that was within a few years to destroy the Socialist and Trade Union movements and put Mussolini into supreme power. Mussolini's groups of Arditi were already engaging in sporadic acts of violence against the Socialists and the Chambers of Labour during the early months of 1919 ; and in April Mussolini staged his first spectacular act of revenge against his erstwhile comrades. A force of Arditi under his orders sacked and burnt the offices of *Avanti* in Milan ; and the outrage went unpunished and unavenged. The Milan workers did, indeed, retaliate with a general strike, and a large fund was raised for rebuilding the destroyed premises. But nothing was done to break up the Fascist gangs ; and it was from this point that Mussolini began to look to the big employers for support in his anti-Socialist warfare of violence and destruction.

In June 1919 the comparatively liberal Francesco Saverio Nitti succeeded Orlando as Prime Minister. Nitti, well known as an economist and a political theorist, was a South Italian with no large Party behind him and no close knowledge, save academically, of the political and social forces with which he had to deal. He would have liked to take the lead in a moderately liberal reforming Ministry based on wide parliamentary support, and would gladly have accepted moderate Socialist help ; but there was no basis for such a Ministry in the prevailing condition of Italian politics, and Nitti was not the man to tackle effectively the appallingly difficult problems of land reform and inflation. He was indeed most concerned with matters of foreign policy, in relation to which he had to take over the situation left by Orlando's unsuccessful intransigence at the Paris Peace Conference and to do what he could to get the Allies to supply more coal and materials at not too extravagant prices, as well as to reduce the tensions between Italy and her neighbours across the Adriatic. His difficulties were immensely increased when, in September 1919, d' Annunzio led his legionaries to occupy Fiume, which was then garrisoned by Allied forces, and thus both defied the Government and precipitated a crisis in international relations. The Franco-British garrison, rather than fight the legionaries, withdrew, leaving d' Annunzio in possession ; and he proceeded to organise what was in effect an independent Government, and was able to hold the town for well over a year because the Italian Government dared not order the armed forces of the State to dislodge him.

During the ensuing months Nitti more than once resigned office, but came back to power because no alternative Government seemed to be possible in face of the combined strength of the Socialists and the Popular Party. Both strikes and inflation grew worse, and the position of the public finances continued to deteriorate fast. In March 1920 the industrialists issued a call for more vigorous government action to curb the strike movement and to reduce public expenditure ; and in May Nitti, under strong pressure from the right, issued a royal decree imposing a severe cut in the bread subsidy. The consequent rise in the cost of living led to an immense outcry on the left ; and Nitti first withdrew the decree and then, having lost his precarious parliamentary support, resigned. The 'old fox' Giolitti, who had been eagerly waiting his opportunity, came back to office at the head of a Government which included Count Sforza, the former Socialist Bonomi, and the outstanding liberal philosopher, Benedetto Croce, whose journal, *La Critica Sociale*, had a great reputation all over Europe. Giolitti, in an attempt to lessen the number of his problems, ordered the evacuation of Albania by the Italian forces, but did not feel strong enough as yet to take forcible action against d'Annunzio. Giolitti's action in Albania provoked a great outcry from the nationalist right, but did help to relieve the international tension. The domestic situation, however, became more and more acute as a great dispute developed between the big industrialists and the Federation of Metal Workers, the strongest and most vigorous section of the C.G.L. In view of the employers' refusal to agree to the demands of the workers, the F.I.O.M. in August 1920 issued orders to its members not to come out on strike, but to go slow and work strictly to rule. This exasperated the employers, and, near the end of August, the management of the big Romeo works at Milan declared a lock-out and closed down their factory. The workers retaliated by occupying the factory and by demanding that the employers should agree to grant their representatives a share in the control of the concern. The dispute spread rapidly : under the orders of F.I.O.M. factory after factory was occupied by the workers, who either coerced the managers and technicians into accepting their orders or appointed managers of their own and attempted to carry on production under Trade Union control, while demanding everywhere a new order providing for effective workers' participation in management and in the direction of industrial policy. The great metal-working establishments being concentrated in the North, especially in Turin and Milan, the movement had, for the time being, no substantial direct effect in the rest of the country ; but its immediate consequences were immense, for it clearly raised the question whether the workers intended to turn the occupation into the Revolution they had been threatening to carry out as soon as the conditions were ripe. In order to be in a position to continue production under their own control, the Trade Unions had to get materials and fuel and also money for the payment

of wages ; and they could not do this unless they could somehow market what they produced and also obtain credit to tide
them over the interval between sales and payment. Neither the
employing classes nor the bankers, nor the Government itself,
were at all likely to come to the workers' aid in any of these
respects ; and it was therefore necessary almost at once to
decide between giving up the attempt to maintain production
and converting the movement into a Revolution by seizing the
banks and the commercial enterprises which controlled the
marketing process. In these circumstances, Giolitti too had
to choose between using armed force to evict the workers from
the factories and to reinstate the capitalist managements and
allowing the occupation to continue but giving the Trade
Unions no help in meeting their difficulties, and waiting for
the movement either to turn into a Revolution or to collapse
as the workers were starved into submission. Confident that
they would not dare in fact to carry out their revolutionary
threats — or rather those of the Socialists — Giolitti chose the
waiting policy ; and the event showed that he had correctly
estimated what would happen. For the C.G.L., called upon
by the Metal Workers to define its policy, neither accepted
defeat nor declared for revolution, but attempted to carry on
the conflict by ordering the occupation to be extended from
the metal industries to others. Giolitti, meanwhile, proceeded
in person to Turin, which was the principal centre of the
Occupation movement and the great stronghold of the Socialist
and Trade Union left wing, and there made a series of speeches
in which he appeared to go a long way towards meeting the
workers' demands, including their claim to be given a share in
the control of industry. He proposed that a Mixed Commission,
representing equally the General Confederation of Industry —
the employers' central organisation — and the C.G.L., should
be set up to advise the Government by 'formulating proposals
for the Government's use in presenting a Bill to reorganise
industry on a basis of the participation of the workers in the
technical, financial and administrative control of the concerns'. In return for this, the workers were to evacuate the
factories and to resume normal work while the Commission
was sitting.

Giolitti of course, knew perfectly well that the proposed

Commission would fail to agree and that, in the end, the Government would have to make its own proposals. His purpose, as he made plain later in his memoirs, was to break the occupation movement without using force, 'so that the workers would be able to see how absurd their proposals were, and so that their bosses (*caporioni*) should be left with no excuse for putting the blame on other people'. He had not enough forces at his disposal both to evict the workers and to hold the factories against them and to keep order in the streets, in which they would have then assembled in demonstrations that would have been certain to turn to violence. If he had believed that there was a real danger of revolution, save as a response to the use of force on the government side, he would doubtless have acted differently ; but he was well aware that most of the C.G.L. leaders were opposed to a revolutionary attempt and that the Socialist leaders too were divided He was therefore confident that time was on his side, and that the occupation would soon break down, especially if at any rate a section of the participants could be induced to believe that the Government meant to do something towards meeting their claims. Things fell out as he had expected. The Socialist Party, approached by the C.G.L. for advice, offered to take over control of the movement from the Trade Unions, but shrank back from the responsibility of converting it into a revolution ; while the Socialist deputies demanded that Parliament, which was in recess, should be urgently convened to deal with the situation — which Giolitti felt he could handle much better in its absence. Consequently, after a good deal of manœuvring on both sides, the Mixed Commission was set up, spent some time bickering over the question of payment of wages for the period of occupation, disagreed utterly about the question of workers' control, and broke up. The workers returned to work with nothing gained, and were bitterly disillusioned when the Government failed to recommend the joint control Giolitti had seemed to promise. The Socialists fell into bitter recriminations among themselves over the failure to make the occupation the starting-point for the Revolution. It was felt all over Italy that the tide of revolutionary feeling among the workers had passed its peak and was beginning to recede ; and the Fascists, with rapidly increasing financial aid from big business, launched out on a campaign of systematic mass violence against the working-class movement, confident that they had at length begun to get the hated Socialists and Communists on the run. Two years were still to pass before the Fascist March on Rome, which brought Mussolini to office as head of the Government. But in September 1920 the Socialists failed to take their one real chance of making a bid for revolution ; and thereafter their strength and their hopes alike steadily and rapidly faded away.

At the very moment when the Socialists and the Trade Unions were shrinking back from actual Revolution, the Comintern delivered to the Socialist Party the bombshell of the 'Twenty-one Points' agreed to at its Second Congress. The Moscow ultimatum, already described,[1] was published in *Avanti* on September 21st, 1920, accompanied by an editorial strongly criticising its terms and saying that whoever had drafted them could have known singularly little about Italy or its Socialists. The issue that counted for most in the reception of the 'Twenty-one Points' arose, not out of the policy the Socialist Party was required to follow, but out of the explicit demand that it should expel the leaders of its right wing, including the deeply respected Turati, its outstanding international figure. Turati, despite his complete disagreement with the revolutionary policy to which the Party stood officially committed, had remained attached to it as a firm believer in the need for working-class unity — a belief which he shared with most of the leaders of the Centre and of the less extreme left. To expel him and his fellow-reformists would mean a split that would by no means stop short at the eviction of the reformist wing. It would involve at the least a considerable proportion of the Socialist deputies and a large part of the Trade Union following of the Party, and would divide the whole working-class movement at a moment when, in face of the developing aggression of the Fascists, it seemed more necessary than ever to close the ranks. Accordingly, many of those who had been enthusiastic advocates of the Third International and its policy found the 'Twenty-one Points' too much to swallow. They were not, indeed, prepared to renounce their support of Communism or to give up their wish to become part of the

[1] See p. 334.

Comintern ; but they felt that that body was behaving un-reasonably towards them and that a determined attempt must be made to induce Moscow to alter its policy, at least to the extent of leaving it to the Italian Socialists themselves to decide whom to expel and when. G. M. Serrati (1872–1926), the editor of *Avanti*, who had played the leading part in the earlier negotiations with the Comintern and had been the most prominent advocate of affiliation to it, was of this opinion ; and his view carried great weight with the main body of the left and centre.

The Socialist Party did not meet in full Congress to settle the terms of its answer to the Comintern until January 1921. But immediately after the receipt of the Twenty-one Points the Party Directing Committee met and voted by 7 votes against 5 in favour of acceptance. Thereafter the debate within the Party took place to the accompaniment of a series of violent clashes with the Fascist blackshirts, who in one town after another set to work to raid and destroy Socialist, Trade Union, and Co-operative buildings and equipment, to beat up working-class militants or dose them with castor-oil, and to commit all these outrages practically without interference from the police, and often with their connivance. The most spectacular of these affairs was the Bologna raid of November 19th, 1920. On that day the Blackshirts, after posting notices ordering all persons except Fascists and Communists to remain indoors, occupied the city and engaged in an orgy of breaking-up and administrations of castor-oil which the organised workers were too ill-prepared to resist. Similar events followed in other places : the workers resisted when they could, but Mussolini's hired thugs had all the advantage of discipline and ample resources on their side, and the extreme brutality in which they gloried paid rich dividends in disintegrating the solidarity of the resistance.

Meanwhile, the wave of romantic nationalism which had carried d' Annunzio to Fiume in 1919 had ebbed, and many of d' Annunzio's followers had transferred their allegiance to the Fascists, who had taken to speaking more and more as the defenders of the nation against the threat of Bolshevik inter-national Revolution. In social matters, d' Annunzio had never been a man of the right : his ideas were in many respects closely akin to Syndicalism, with a dash of radicalism, more than a flavour of personal autocracy, and even some admixture of Soviet influence. Left in possession of Fiume by Giolitti, he had been at work devising a constitution for the quasi-independent State he was attempting to set up ; and by a coincidence this Constitution for the Italian 'Regency' of the Quarnero, with himself as Regent, was published on the same day as the occupation of the factories in Northern Italy began. It included the often-quoted Article 9, which ran as follows :

> The State does not recognise property as an absolute domination of the individual over matter, but looks on it as the most useful of social functions. No property can be reserved by any person as if it were part of him : it is in-admissible for a lazy proprietor to have his property unused or badly used, to the exclusion of others. Labour is the only title to power over any means of production or exchange. Labour alone is master of the goods it has rendered fruitful in their highest degree and most profitable to the general economy.

D' Annunzio, in effect, was seeking to make himself the apostle of a kind of nationalist Syndicalism appealing in foreign affairs to the more intransigent warriors of the mainly right-wing nationalist movement and in home affairs to the mainly left-wing sentiment of Syndicalists and opponents of the politicians and of the bourgeois State. In 1919 there had been great scope for such an appeal to the militant elements of the disbanded army and to the young ; and d' Annunzio had seemed too formidable for the Government to dare take strong action against him. But as the Fascist movement grew and provided an alternative and more spectacular outlet for lovers of violence, d' Annunzio's following fell away, and many of his admirers, such as Count Dino Grandi, went over to the Fascist movement, in which their advent soon led to a serious idternal crisis. For, paradoxically, at this point Mussolini was playing with the notion of calling off his campaign of violence and of coming to terms with the Popular Party and the right wing of the Trade Unions and even of the Socialist Party, in order to form a Government in which he himself hoped to play the leading part. The Grandi section, on the other hand, while proclaiming its adherence to the national Syndicalism of the d' Annunzian Constitution of Quarnero, was determined to carry on with the campaign of violence until both the Socialist Party and the Socialist Trade Unions had been entirely destroyed ; and in the end this faction prevailed, drawing Mussolini after it into more and more aggressive nationalism combined with warfare to the bitter end against the organised working-class movement in all its forms.

Despite this development of aggressive nationalism, d' Annunzio's own position was steadily weakened as the main centre of activity was diverted from Fiume and the Italian 'Irredenta' across the Adriatic to the internal struggle between the Fascists and the Italian working-class movement. Within a month of the Fascist raid on Bologna, Giolitti felt strong enough to bring the Regency of Quarnero to an end by dispatching armed forces to dislodge d' Annunzio from Fiume ; and, when it came to the point, a very few shots proved enough to induce d' Annunzio's legionaries to surrender. Their leader abandoned Fiume and ceased to count as a major figure in Italian affairs ; most of his supporters went over to Fascism and swelled its more extremist wing.

This was the situation when the Socialist Congress met at Leghorn in January 1921 to decide on its answer to the Comintern in respect of the disputed 'Twenty-one Points'. There were again three factions — the 'Pure' Communists, who were for complete acceptance, involving the exclusion of the right wing ; the 'Unitarian' Communists, who were for adhesion to the Comintern and accepted its general policy, but refused to be dictated to in deciding whom to expel, or when any expulsions should be made ; and the 'Concentrationists', who were against any expulsions and made the continued unity of the Party their primary objective, and were therefore thoroughly against the 'Twenty-one Points'. This last group included, besides the reformist Socialists headed by Turati, a considerable part of the leadership of the C.G.L., led by Ludovico d' Aragona. Serrati, Lazzari, and most of the older leaders of the Socialist left wing were in the middle group. The 'Pure' Communists were headed by the young Turin leaders, Antonio Gramsci (1891–1937) and Palmiro Togliatti (b. 1893), both intellectuals who had built up a big following among the Metal Workers and in the Turin Chamber of Labour.

At Leghorn the victory went to the middle group, largely under Serrati's influence. It got 92,028 votes, against 54,783 for the 'Pure' Communists and 14,695 for the Concentrationist right wing. The vote was followed immediately by the secession of the 'Pures', who met separately and set up the Italian Communist Party as a section of the Moscow International. The split spread to the Trade Unions. At the ensuing C.G.L. Congress delegates representing 433,000 workers seceded to Communism, whereas the majority, representing 1,436,000, remained in the C.G.L. Such splits as this were the easier because Italian Trade Unionism rested in the main on a local basis, so that each local unit could decide its own allegiance.

The victorious group in the Socialist Party, though it rejected Moscow's ultimatum, was by no means prepared to give up its desire to join the Third International. It sent the veteran Lazzari to Moscow to negotiate with the Comintern, in the hope of persuading it to modify its conditions; but Lazzari came back empty-handed, as Serrati had done before him. The Comintern did not want the adhesion of a Socialist Party containing even a powerless minority of outspoken reformists : it wanted a split, and preferred a Communist Party with no more than minority support, but of unquestioning loyalty to Moscow, to a Party including a large majority but insistent on maintaining its right to take its own line. Accordingly, from the beginning of 1921 the Italian working-class movement was not only seriously weakened by Fascist attack, but also split much more seriously than it had been by the earlier secession of the relatively small anti-parliamentarian Bordiga group. In this plight it fought the General Election of May 1921 with surprisingly little loss. In 1919 it had won 156 seats as a united Party : it now won 128, and the new Communist Party a mere 13. The Popular Party rose from 100 to 106 : the Fascists numbered only 33, while the National Bloc, a coalition of the right-wing and bourgeois Parties, plus a few Independents, together numbered 220. Giolitti, thus placed in a minority, tried to carry on the Government ; but when both the Popolari and the Fascists withdrew their support, he fell, and the former Socialist, Ivanoe Bonomi, became Prime Minister with the backing of the Popular Party. It was at this time, just after the election, that the big quarrel between Mussolini and Grandi developed inside the Fascist movement. Mussolini actually signed a pact with the Socialists promising to bring his campaign of violence to an end ; but he was repudiated by his own followers and thereupon resigned all his offices. But this curious state of affairs did not last for long. Mussolini speedily renounced the pact which most of his followers had refused to observe, accepted the Grandi policy of a war of extermination against the Socialists, and resumed his leadership of the Fascist movement.

The Socialist Party met again in Congress, in October 1921, to receive Lazzari's report on his unsuccessful journey to Russia. It was still not prepared to accept the Twenty-one Points, but it reaffirmed its desire to join the Comintern and passed a fresh intransigent resolution rejecting all parliamentary compromise and collaboration. The struggle inside the Party continued : the right wing, which was strong in Parliament but had very little popular support, wanted to work for a relatively liberal Government that would be prepared to take action against the lawless violence of the Fascists, but was prevented from doing anything effective by the attitude of the Party as a whole. The weak Bonomi Government remained in office until February 1922, when it was brought down by a complicated series of intrigues. Giolitti, who had hoped to return to power, was prevented by the refusal of the Popular Party to support him ; and a sheer nonentity, Luigi Facta, a Giolittian whom Don Sturzo was prepared to tolerate, took office at the head of a Cabinet of definitely more right-wing tendency than the last. With Facta's advent the Italian Government almost ceased to govern at all, and the Fascists had matters more than ever their own way. The Trade Unions, on the proposal of the Railway Workers' Federation, which was outside the C.G.L., formed a Labour Alliance including the C.G.L. and most of the independent Unions for the purpose of organising resistance to Fascist violence. The workers also began for the first time, but only here and there, to organise a force of their own — the Arditi del Popolo — to meet the Fascist gangs with disciplined resistance ; but, unlike the Fascists, the Socialist Arditi were dealt with severely by the police and were never able to become effective in more than a few areas — notably Parma. They were the less able to meet the Fascists on equal terms because the Communists refused to co-operate and even the Socialist Party failed to give whole-hearted support. Nevertheless, the Labour Alliance and the establishment of the Arditi del Popolo did something to help the workers' movement to hold out during the ensuing months. In August 1922 the Alliance made a desperate attempt to defeat the Fascists by calling a national strike; but the Fascists met the strike with an intensified campaign of organised violence, and the strikers were driven back to work in defeat and almost in rout, though in Parma and one or two other places where the Arditi del Popolo were well organised on quasi-military lines they succeeded in beating back the Fascist attacks. After August 1922 it was clear that the strength of Trade Unionism and Socialism had been thoroughly broken.

On the morrow of this defeat the Socialist Party, yielding to Moscow, at length expelled Turati and his reformist followers. Turati's final offence had been that in June, when the Facta Government had resigned, he had accepted an invitation from the King to go to the Quirinal for consultation about the formation of a new Government. The consultation had no effect, and Facta resumed office; but it brought on Turati a furious attack from the Socialist Party Direction, which accused him of 'collaboration with the monarchy and the bourgeoisie' and announced that his action had brought his connection with the Party to an end. This verdict was endorsed, in October, by the Rome Party Conference, though only by the very narrow majority of 32,000 to 29,000; and Turati and his followers reluctantly formed a new Party — the Socialist Party of the Italian Workers — which had some strength among the Socialist deputies, but not much outside Parliament. Indeed, the entire Socialist movement had by this time been reduced to a pale shadow of what it had been only a year or two before.

By this time the decisive victory of Fascism was very near. On October 28th, 1922, the Fascists organised their unresisted March on Rome, followed immediately by the summons to Mussolini to form a Government. The four years of confused struggle were over; the policy of violence which the Socialist Party had preached but not practised, whereas the Fascists had practised it as well as preached, had paid rich dividends to its practical exponents. For the first time since 1918 Italy had a Government which could at any rate make some attempt to govern, instead of being merely pushed about by extra-legal forces. The Fascists, however, were not yet in a position to rule alone, or even with support only from the industrialists and the Parties of the right. They depended on the parliamentary backing of the still unbroken Popular Party of Don Sturzo, which was impelled by the Papacy to support them against the still considerable parliamentary contingent of the Socialist Party. The Popular Party still professed to be an upholder of liberal and democratic principles, but had moved a long way rightwards under pressure from the Vatican and the Catholic hierarchy ; and the advent of a reactionary new Pope, Pius XI, drove it still further rightwards in 1922. It accepted representation in Mussolini's Cabinet and, while exerting some moderating influence, helped the Fascists to consolidate their power after the March on Rome.

The March on Rome was not, of course, the end of the story. More than two years had still to pass before the liquidation of the opposition was completed and the Fascist régime possessed of unchallenged power. Through 1923 the Socialist Party, greatly reduced in strength, continued its attempts to secure acceptance by the Comintern, now that Turati and the rest of the right wing had been definitely excluded. Serrati again visited Moscow, and came back to propose fusion between the Communist and Socialist Parties, but was defeated, largely because of the opposition offered by the rising young Socialist leader, Pietro Nenni (b. 1891). Late in the same year the Popular Party at length withdrew from the Government and passed into opposition. Their last act in support of the Government was to help Mussolini to pass a new election law, under which the Party or *bloc* securing the largest number of the votes was to get two-thirds of the total number of seats, even if it was in a minority — a system which enabled the Fascists, with right-wing nationalist support, to win a secure parliamentary majority at the General Election of 1924. This electoral change, together with the defection of the Popular Party, gave the signal for an intensified Fascist attack on the relics of Italian democracy. The election was fought under conditions of mass intimidation by the Fascists. The total opposition vote was about 2,500,000, of which about 1,000,000 went to the Communists and the two Socialist Parties combined. When the new Chamber met, Giacomo Matteotti (1855–1924), the secretary of the reformist Socialist Party, attempted to indict Mussolini for his conduct of the election; but he was howled down, and a few days later was murdered by five men in a car who caught him on his way from his home to the Chamber. His body was left in a ditch outside the city, and was not found for two months; but there were eye-witnesses who could bear testimony to the murder.

The murder of Matteotti gave rise to the last serious crisis the Fascists had to face on their way towards absolute power. It was impossible for them to prevent the arrest of the murderers or the holding of a criminal investigation which barely stopped short of legal proof of Mussolini's personal complicity. During the following months there was intense political excitement. A hundred and fifty opposition deputies attended a meeting at which Turati delivered a funeral oration in memory of the murdered Socialist; and by way of protest the whole parliamentary opposition seceded from the Chamber in what came to be known, from a passage in Turati's oration, as the 'Aventine Secession', under the leadership of the southern liberal, Giovanni Amendola. But the opposition deputies, having thus expressed their revulsion, did not know what to do next, beyond continuing to meet and record their belief in democracy. It was legally possible under the Constitution for the Chamber of Deputies to indict Mussolini; but there was, of course, no possibility of a Fascist-controlled Chamber acting in this way, and Mussolini could safely challenge it to do so. At the beginning of 1925 he issued this challenge, denying that he had been personally responsible for Matteotti's murder, but accepting full 'political, moral and historical responsibility' for the whole violent course of Fascist policy and action. Mussolini went on to propose and carry the exclusion from the Chamber of the entire Aventine opposition, on the ground that they had forfeited their seats by absenting themselves for six months from its proceedings. He then procured an amnesty for all those who had been sentenced or charged in connection with the murder, and followed this up with a spate of repressive legislation. The opposition Parties were suppressed, the press was made subject to severe censor-ship, special tribunals were set up to try political offenders, and the free Trade Unions were practically destroyed by the grant to the newly established Fascist Labour Unions of exclusive rights of negotiation with the employers. From this time on, active resistance to Fascism became nearly impossible ; and the remaining leaders of the Communist and Socialist Parties either escaped abroad or found themselves in prison or in concentration camps. Gramsci, the outstanding leader of the Communists, went for a time to Moscow in 1924, but returned to Italy and attempted to carry on underground propaganda. In 1928 he was caught and sentenced to twenty years' imprisonment, from which he never emerged. He died in prison in 1937, leaving behind him a number of writings, smuggled out of prison, and published only after the liberation, which have given him the repute of the principal Italian con-tributor to modern Marxist theory. The best known of his writings is his *Il materialismo storico e la filosofia di Benedetto Croce* (1948), in which he attempted to integrate Croce's philosophy into a new interpretation of Marxism. Much earlier, in 1919, he had founded in Turin his own journal, *Ordine Nuovo*, in which he attempted a fundamental restatement of Socialist doctrine in relation to current problems from the standpoint of Leninist Communism. With him on this journal was another highly original thinker, Piero Gobetti (1901–26), who became dramatic critic on *Ordine Nuovo* at the age of 20 and, when its premises were destroyed by the Fascists the following year, founded his own paper, *Rivoluzione Liberale*, which lasted till its suppression in 1925. The following year he was beaten up on Mussolini's orders, but was allowed to escape to Paris, where he died of his injuries only a few weeks later, at the age of 24. Gobetti had thrown himself passionately into the Turin revolutionary movement. He laid the blame for the Fascist victory on the errors of the old Socialist Party, with its incoherent and planless insurrectionism and its con-sequent futility in action. As against this, he idealised the new Communist Party, but preached a gospel of 'liberal Com-munism' which had little in common with its practice, based as it was on a repudiation of dogma and a strong insistence on the creative common sense of the ordinary worker, when he did not allow himself to be misled by planners. Gobetti's plea was for a Communism that should be ever open to receive new impressions and to try out new ways of action. Like Gramsci and Togliatti, Gobetti was an 'intellectual' and not a workman. He wrote very well, and apart from his journalism was a notable pamphleteer. His death was a serious loss to the none too plenteous stream of post-war Socialist and Communist thought.

Of other outstanding personalities of the left wing, Togliatti found refuge in Moscow after the collapse. Serrati and his left-wing followers of the Socialist Party at length came to terms with the Comintern, into which they were admitted in face of fierce opposition from Bordiga and his extreme left-wing group. Serrati died in 1926 ; and Lazzari the following year.

Of the right-wing Socialists, Giuseppe Emanuele Modigliani (1872–1947), who had been among the Italian delegates at Zimmerwald in 1915, and his wife Vera made their way to Paris, where they were joined first by Claudio Treves, then in 1927 by Turati, and in 1929 by Carlo Rosselli (1899–1937). In 1927 the exiles in the West founded a common organisation of Socialists and Republicans, the Concentrazione Antifascista, which published in Paris its journal *Liberta*, edited by Claudio Treves. The Concentrazione was an attempt to sink differences for the time being both between the rival Socialist Parties and between Socialists and other progressives who were prepared to carry on the struggle against Fascism from abroad. This collaboration helped on the reunion of the two Socialist Parties — the Unitarian Socialist Party headed by Turati and the Maximalist Socialist Party, in which, after its reconstitution in exile, Pietro Nenni was the leading figure. Nenni, like Treves, had escaped from Italy by walking over the Alps, and had refused to accompany Serrati and his group into the Communist Party. In 1930 the two Socialist Parties, both reformed and re-named in exile, amalgamated ; and the combined Party became a member of the Labour and Socialist International, to which the Unitarians had attached themselves from the beginning.

Meanwhile Carlo Rosselli, discontented with both the exiled Parties, had taken the lead in forming, not a third Party, but a group, Giustizia e Liberta, which issued both a journal of the same name and a number of pamphlets for smuggling into Italy. Its programme, devised mainly by Carlo Rosselli, was a 'liberal' Socialism in which the ethical rather than the economic aspect was particularly emphasised ; and it had much closer relations than the Concentrazione with the resistance inside Italy and particularly with Ferruccio Parri (b. 1890), who, after helping, together with Rosselli, in Turati's escape, decided to stay on in Italy and became a most important figure in the 'underground', and subsequently leader of the Action Party which took over and developed Rosselli's ideas. He was for a short time Prime Minister after the liberation, in 1946. In 1931 Giustizia e Liberta joined the Anti-fascist Concentration, which then became predominantly Socialist, so that the Republicans withdrew the following year. Later in the 'thirties the Giustizia e Liberta group was among those which rallied to the anti-Fascist cause in the Spanish Civil War : Carlo Rosselli was on his way back from Spain when, with his brother Nello (b. 1900), he was murdered by Fascist agents in Normandy in 1937. Nenni, too, was among the Italian Socialists who took part in the Spanish War, in which he was accused of acting as an extreme partisan of the Communists in their campaign against the P.O.U.M. Turati died in exile in 1932, and Treves the following year. Bruno Buozzi (1881–1944), who had been the secretary of the Metal Workers and thereafter the last secretary of the C.G.L., got to Paris in 1926 and there contrived, with the help of the French C.G.T., to carry on a skeleton organisation which catered chiefly for Italians working in France. It continued until, in 1943, Buozzi returned to Italy and set to work secretly to reorganise the C.G.L. He was caught and shot by the Germans the following year.

As one looks back over the story of the Italian working-class movement from the end of the first world war in 1918 to the complete eclipse of 1926, the first temptation is to say that almost everybody who held any position of influence or authority in relation to it behaved very foolishly indeed. Surely, one is tempted to say, there were two courses open to the Italian Socialists in 1919 ; and they followed neither. One course was to attempt by violent Revolution to destroy the existing State and to establish a proletarian State on its ruins — that is, to follow the 'Moscow road', while adapting both the methods used and the character of the new society to Italian conditions and Italian temperaments. The other was, rejecting this course, to collaborate with the more radical bourgeois groups, including the socially radical wing of the Popolari, in establishing a Government under Socialist leadership, and to attempt in this way to tackle the fundamental problems of land reform and economic development, and to adopt a 'good neighbour' policy in external affairs in the hope of overcoming Italy's problem of shortages of food and materials, and of rendering possible the gradual development of a Welfare State. But as soon as these alternatives are plainly stated, it becomes evident that neither of them was in effect any more practicable than what the Socialists, or a majority of them, actually tried to do. It is easy enough to show that the occupation of the factories could not have been successful unless it had been followed up by real revolutionary action ; for it was impossible to keep the factories going without the means both of paying wages and of assuring supplies of materials and sales, and these assurances were unattainable without control of the Government. But had the Socialists the strength needed to turn the occupation into a Revolution ? Many of those who were revolutionaries by belief and profession thought not ; and those who took this view included the majority of the Trade Union leaders. The main difficulty was not that the Government was too strong to be overthrown. It was in fact exceedingly weak, and might very likely have succumbed. But what would have happened then ? The Socialist Party and the Trade Unions had almost no strength in southern Italy or in Sicily. Even if they had been able to seize power in the industrial towns of the north, and to hold it, the south would have remained as a base for the gathering of the anti-Socialist forces, and there would have been a civil war in which the weight of the Allied Governments, including the United States, would have been thrown into the scale against the Italian 'Bolsheviks', and the north would have had nowhere to look for help and would have been speedily starved out. Moreover, even in the north the Revolution would have had to reckon, not merely with the weak Government, but also with the rising forces of both Fascism and intransigent nationalism, and even immediate success would have been by no means a foregone conclusion.

The other policy, that of abandoning revolutionism and setting to work to promote gradualist Socialism and social reform with non-Socialist help, presented no less formidable difficulties. It involved coming to terms with the Popolari, whose support was indispensable for establishing a parliamentary majority ; but this would have meant a break with the deeply rooted anti-clerical tradition of Italian Socialism, and would never have been accepted by more than a minority of the Socialist Party, even if the Popolari had been prepared to play ball. The Popolari, for their part, could hardly have entered as junior partners into such a league with the Socialists without being disowned by the Pope and the clerical hierarchy — which would have meant a split in their ranks, even had the majority been ready to follow such a lead. It would, however, have been quite impracticable for the Socialists to have formed or joined a Government of the left without the Popolari. Even if Turati had been prepared to attempt this — and he was not — a Government under his leadership would have been turned out of office if it had attempted to follow even a mildly socialistic policy ; and a Government headed by Giolitti or Nitti with Socialist support would not even have tried to solve any of the major problems. It would merely have continued the traditional do-nothing policies that had brought Italian parliamentarism into discredit before the war. Turati, moderate though he was, always took the line that the Socialists could afford to co-operate with the bourgeois Parties only if, in doing so, they could speak in the name of a really united working-class movement ; and this was, of course, entirely out of the question. Even if the out-and-out Communists are left out of account, Serrati and Lazzari, and not Turati, had the support of the majority in the Socialist Party and of a very large part of the Trade Union movement. If Turati had entered or formed a Government committed to co-operation with either the Popolari or the other parties of the parliamentary left, he would merely have precipitated his own expulsion from the Socialist Party. Knowing this and believing that a break-up of the working-class movement into a number of contending factions would make its defeat certain, Turati clung to the Party, though doing so involved him in accepting again and again policies which he utterly disliked and disapproved.

The two main alternatives — outright revolution and reformist collaborationism — being alike impracticable, what remained? In effect only one course — the rapid building up of a working-class force capable of meeting the Fascists on equal terms. As soon as the Fascists began to establish a disciplined force of blackshirt thugs and to use them for organised raids on working-class premises and systematic beating up of working-class leaders, and were allowed to do this without hindrance from the regular police — and sometimes with their positive connivance — while successive Governments stood by and allowed the reality of power to slip out of their hands, the Socialists and the Trade Unions were bound to be defeated unless they could organise and bring into action a force of their own capable not merely of defending their property and the persons of their leaders but also of overmastering and destroying the Fascist storm troops. This was, no doubt, a very difficult task ; for the Fascists were not only before long supplied amply with money by the industrialists but were also able to draw upon large numbers of angry demobilised soldiers and thwarted nationalists who could be brought into the struggle against 'international Communism' and positively enjoyed the violence to which they were encouraged to resort. The working-class movement could not afford to keep large forces of full-time para-military fighters in its pay : nor could it in any event have made the same uninhibited appeal to sadism and violent action as the Fascists were fully prepared to make. If it had fought back in an organised way, it would have done so under severe handicaps and would very likely have got the worst of the struggle. It might, however, at least have compelled the Government to take some action against the Fascists as well as against itself, and to make some attempt to restore order ; and this would have greatly benefited the Socialists against their opponents.

Unhappily, nothing of this sort was attempted until too late, when the Fascists had been allowed to grow much too strong to be beaten back, and when the working-class movement itself had already been divided by the Communist split. By the time the left wing set about organising the Arditi del Popolo, the battle of the streets had been already lost ; and even then the organisation was much too localised and based on too narrow a support to be able to meet Mussolini's nationally organised thugs on equal terms. The C.G.L. and, later, the Labour Alliance were too divided in counsel and too localised to be capable of building up an effective national resistance movement. Their localisation allowed the Fascists, by mobilising their forces over wide areas and then concentrating them on a single centre at a time, to defeat the workers city by city, moving on from Bologna to Genoa, from Genoa to Milan, and from Milan to Turin with their weapons of incendiarism, rubber truncheons, and castor-oil, and leaving each devastated centre of working-class power irretrievably weakened and depressed.

This localism was very deeply rooted in the Italian working-class movement, in which the local Chambers of Labour, and not the national Trade Unions or Federations, were the main points of focus for working-class loyalty. Naples could never concert measures with the cities of the industrial North ; and even within the famed 'triangle' based on Turin, Milan, and Genoa there were constantly recurring differences and disputes. The South, where the Popolari were strong, participated hardly at all in the great Fascist-Socialist conflict, except in a few isolated centres : the Socialists and the Trade Unions were alike too isolated from the peasants to know how to set about appealing to them across the barrier of religion ; whereas the Fascists, who had begun as anti-clericals and denounced the Catholic Church as roundly as the Socialists, found no difficulty in changing their tune and invoking the name of God when it became important to them to win the support, or at least the friendly neutrality, of the right wing.

There is indeed, as one looks back on the events in Italy after 1918, a certain impression of the near inevitability of the working-class defeat. From the very beginnings the Italian Socialist and Trade Union movement had been chaotic in organisation and, though rich in intellectual supporters, deficient in more than local working-class leadership. In a country which had remained mainly agricultural, it had been an essentially urban movement, resting mainly on the support of the industrial workers of the North, who were only a minority of the exploited classes. Anarchists, rather than Socialists, had attempted to break down the barriers between town and country and to stir up peasant revolt : the Socialists had done little except among the *braccianti* — the day labourers — on the large estates close to the industrial areas. Left-wing Catholics, among whom Romolo Murri [1] was the great pioneer in the early years of the twentieth century, had made greater and more successful efforts to enlist a peasant following, but had been bitterly opposed by the Papacy and the Catholic hierarchy until, in 1919, Don Sturzo was given his head to form a mass Catholic Party — only to find its relatively progressive and democratic majority more and more repressed by the reactionary influences of the Vatican and the more conservative Catholic groups.

Moreover, even in the industrial areas, there had been constant internecine struggles inside the working-class movement. In the days of the First International, the Marxists had been outdistanced by the followers of Bakunin ; and even after Andrea Costa had changed sides there had been considerable working-class groups which continued to be very suspicious of 'intellectuals' and to insist on keeping the mass movement under strictly working-class leadership. In the Socialist Party this antagonism had been quickly thrown into the background, and the intellectuals had dominated the Socialist Party in the Chamber of Deputies. This, however, had contributed to widening the gap between the Party and the Chambers of Labour, which formed the main basis of Trade Union organisation ; and as the Anarchist influence waned its place was increasingly taken by Syndicalism, which developed as a gospel of 'direct action' largely affected by French ideas. The Italian Syndicalists never became powerful enough to detach the main body of Trade Unionists from the Socialist Party ; but they became involved, during the years before 1914, under the leadership of Arturo Labriola (1859–1904) and Enrico Leone (1875–1940), in a growingly acute conflict with the C.G.L., which led to the breakaway of the Italian Syndical Union in 1912. The U.S.I. was never very large, and the Railway Workers' Union, though under Syndicalist leadership, remained aloof both from it and from the C.G.L. But it was influential enough to play a big part in the strike movement of 1913–14, which led to fierce conflicts with the police and was disavowed by the C.G.L. When the European War came and

[1] See Vol. III, Part II, pp. 725 and 731.

Mussolini was expelled from the Socialist Party, a section of the Syndicalists, headed by Alceste De Ambris (1874–1934) supported his interventionist policy and broke away from the U.S.I. to form a new body as the forerunner of the Union movement built up later under Fascist auspices. After the war this group and some other former Syndicalists gave their support to d' Annunzio in his Fiume adventure ; and the Constitution of Quarnero embodied a considerable admixture of Syndicalist ideas as well as of intransigent nationalism. After the retirement of d' Annunzio from Fiume a large part of his following transferred its allegiance to Fascism and, as we saw, provided some of its most uncompromising elements in the campaign of violence against the Socialist Party and the more orthodox Trade Unions.[1] But these elements, while nationalist *à outrance* and furiously hostile to international Communism, kept a good deal of their social leftism and played a considerable part in developing the theory of a corporative society on which Mussolini said the Fascist structure was to be based. The corporative element was never, in practice, more than a façade ; but there was always an element in Fascism that took it seriously and this element came largely from the former Syndicalists who had gone over to the Fascist side. After their defection, outright Syndicalism lost most of its hold on the Trade Union movement ; but the demand for workers' control of industry, which had extended far beyond the Syndicalist organisations, remained strong and found renewed expression in the demands put forward at the time of the occupation of the factories in 1920. The Trade Union movement continued to include, besides groups mainly interested in ordinary collective bargaining and industrial reform within the capitalist order, large elements which disbelieved in parliamentary action as a means to Socialist advance and saw in Trade Unionism a potential instrument for the overthrow of capitalism, or at least for the winning of a real share in the control of industry. These latter groups maintained within the C.G.L. and the Chambers of Labour an uneasy partnership with the Trade Union right wing which, under the leadership of Ludovico d' Aragona (1876– ?), was in close sympathy with the parliamentary, reformist wing of the Socialist Party. In the Trade Unions as

[1] See p. 382.

well as in the Party there was a continual struggle between reformists and left wingers, the latter being further divided into revolutionary Communists, or near-Communists, and advocates of democratic industrial control.

In some respects Italy must have appeared in 1919 and 1920 to be one of the most hopeful areas in Europe for the success of the Communist Revolution, both because of the evident weakness and tendency to disintegration of the existing State and of capitalist industry, and because its working-class movement stood, in the main, a long way to the left of those of other Western countries. But whereas in Russia it was possible for the industrial proletariat to seize and hold power with the support of a large part of the army and by taking advantage of the general condition of mass unrest and revolutionary feeling among the peasants, in Italy neither of these elements could be brought to the rescue of the Revolution from its enemies. The returning soldiers were much more susceptible to nationalist than to Socialist appeals ; and the peasants were for the most part kept away from the Revolution by the success of Don Sturzo in building up the Popular Party. Had the industrial areas risen in open revolution, the South would have provided a basis for rallying the counter-revolutionary forces ; and even in the North the workers would have needed to settle accounts not only with Mussolini's Fascists but also with a large body of intransigent nationalist feeling which before long rallied to the Fascist movement. In Russia, as Lenin fully realised, the Bolsheviks could not have won without giving the soldiers and the peasants what they wanted — peace and land. In Italy, too, the soldiers and the peasants wanted these things, but peace came, except on the frontiers, before the revolutionary wave had gathered force ; and there was no equivalent to the left wing of the Social Revolutionary Party to urge the peasants on to seize the land for themselves. Land seizures did occur ; but they were sporadic and lacked the backing of an organised movement of revolt, so that they were suppressed without great difficulty and prevented from spreading far or fast. Italy, though it possessed, like Russia, a small but highly organised sector of advanced industrialism, lacked a State of the utterly repressive and detested type of Czarism ; and no really nation-wide revolt against the Italian State at all resembling the revolt against Czarism was able to develop. Moreover, the Allies, in their hour of victory, were able to exert much more pressure on Italy than they had been able to use against the Russians in 1917 and 1918, both because Italy was much more dependent on imported supplies and because the Italian middle classes and intellectuals were much more integrated in spirit with the Western world.

In the sphere of Socialist thought, too, Italy was on the whole uncreative and imitative, not for want of a large body of thinkers, but because its leading theorists were for the most part imitators rather than originators of new ideas. Antonio Labriola had been a considerable Marxist thinker, but had had no successor of comparable ability. Croce, after a brief association with the French Syndicalists, had turned his back on Socialism and become in effect a liberal conservative. Turati was a notable intellectual influence, but wholly within the orbit of a Western Social Democracy which failed to fit Italian conditions or to appeal to the main body of Italian workers. Errico Malatesta (1853–1932), a great name in the international Anarchist movement, never succeeded in building up a mass following.[1] The Syndicalist leaders, such as Arturo Labriola and Leone, were only second-rate. The Italians translated and published a great many of the classical European Socialist writings ; but their own contribution was limited and not seldom confused. The years after 1918 found them in an ideological muddle, as well as in one of organisation. They were conscious of their weakness in both fields ; and no personality capable of driving them forward towards Socialism in face of doubts and difficulties appeared. Therefore, during the critical period immediately after the war, they showed themselves irresolute and divided when their only chance lay in forthright united action. The Comintern, for its part, contributed greatly, during these years of crisis, to making certain their defeat because its leaders, set on forcing the pace of revolution throughout Europe, repelled the Socialist Party when it was eager to throw in its lot with the Revolution and thus forced a series of splits which fatally weakened the movement just when it needed most to exert its united strength. The story of Italian Socialism after 1918 has its comic elements ;

[1] For Malatesta, see Vol. II, p. 356 and Vol. III, Part II, p. 727.

but it is essentially a tragedy of frustration and rudderless navigation of terribly stormy seas.

Nor must it be left out of account that Italian Fascism, which destroyed the Socialist movement in Italy, had at its head and as its leading theorist a former left-wing Socialist, who was able to carry with him a substantial body of working-class support and continued in certain respects to carry on a sort of perverted Socialist, or at all events Syndicalist, tradition. Mussolini's version of the 'Corporative State' was no doubt in the main only a façade behind which capitalism could maintain its authority and ride roughshod over the workers. The essence of Fascism lay, not in the corporative structure which purported to bind employers and workers together in the common service of the nation, but in the strident assertion of militant and militarist nationalism and its embodiment in an authoritarian structure presided over and dominated by the figure of 'Il Duce' as the embodiment of the spirit of the nation. In its assertion of the supreme rôle of the Fascist Party and its General Council which executed the inspired orders of the leader, it bore certain resemblances to the attitude of that very Communism of which it proclaimed itself the foremost enemy. True, Communism had in theory no 'Duce' — no 'cult of personality' such as Fascism ostentatiously professed ; yet Lenin, and much more Stalin after him, became in practice hardly less charismatic 'leaders' than Mussolini. Fascism, for its part, had no theory of party democracy, such as Communism at any rate at the outset professed ; but Italian did differ from German Fascism in assigning a considerable degree of autonomous responsibility to the Fascist collective leadership and to the corporative structure, and was much less a purely personal autocracy of a single man. The root difference between Italian Fascism and Communism was that where Communism stressed, at any rate in theory, the absolute predominance of class, Fascism put in the place of the class-struggle the 'national idea', involving the 'sacred egoism' of the nation in the struggle for power. Communism was aggressively international, with World Revolution under Russian leadership as its objective : Fascism was aggressively nationalist, seeking to create a nation united in aggressive hostility to the world outside its frontiers.

Internally, as well as externally, this militant nationalism required that the people, regardless of class, should act unitedly as the champions of the national cause. The entire resources of the nation had to be mobilised so as to make the nation formidable to others ; and this meant that its internal structure had to be based on a sharp subordination of all sectional interests to the national will embodied in the Fascist Party. This, however, could be achieved only by enlisting the sectional interests as far as possible on the side of Fascism, while repressing ruthlessly such groups and interests as could not be brought to act in conformity with the Fascists' will. Unable to secure the compliance of the Socialists or the Trade Unions associated with them, Mussolini stopped short of nothing that could be done to destroy these anti-nationalist agencies root and branch. In doing this, however, he did not forget his own Socialist and proletarian past, and did attempt to create a Fascist Party and a range of new Fascist Trade Unions capable of exercising an attraction for former supporters of militant Socialism and Syndicalist, or semi-Syndicalist, Trade Unionism. The Fascist Trade Unions, even though they exercised no real power over working conditions, did bear a good deal more resemblance to real Trade Unions than Hitler's Arbeiter-Front, which was much more directly and completely subordinated to the rôle of the Party. There was in Italian Fascism, at any rate in its earlier phases, a real element of semi-Syndicalist self-regulation that was wholly missing from its German counterpart. Mussolini's attacks on parliamentary pluto-democracy and his affirmations of corporative doctrine were largely reminiscent of Sorel and of the more extreme forms of Syndicalism, and did in fact attract an appreciable number of former Syndicalists to his support. Such men as Giuseppe Bottai, his Minister of Corporations, did combine with their intransigent nationalism a real hostility to the old forms of capitalism, and did attempt to invest the corporative structure with some degree of real authority and control, within the limits imposed by the overriding requirements of Fascist nationalism. The corporative system never really worked, because it proved impossible to induce the capitalists, when their old antagonists, the Trade Unions, had been destroyed, to share authority with the new Fascist Unions, or the workers to place any real trust in these new Unions in face of their evident subordination to the Fascist Party. Nevertheless, there was a real difference between Italian Fascism and German Nazism in their attitudes towards the forms of labour organisation they found it necessary to create as *gleichgeschaltet* auxiliaries of their respective Parties. True, there appeared among the Nazis exceptional figures, such as the Strassers, who had something in common with the more Syndicalist elements of Italian Fascism ; but Hitler, unlike Mussolini, had no sort of sympathy with them, and they were speedily liquidated or driven out.

I am not suggesting that Mussolini remained in any sense any sort of a Socialist after he had assumed the leadership of the Fascist movement. I am saying only that his long and close association with Socialism influenced the shape of his anti-Socialist ideas, and helped to mould his conception — never realised in practice — of the corporative State, in which Hegelian State Nationalism jostled with notions of corporate organisation on the Hegelian plane of 'Civil Society'. There was, in one of these respects, more in common between Mussolini and the Syndicalists than between Mussolini and Hitler, just as in the other there was more in common between both Mussolini and Hitler and the Communists than between either and the exponents of parliamentary democratic Socialism. Mussolini's Socialist past helped him to success in liquidating the Italian working-class movement because it enabled him to win over a section of the old Italian left to belief in the reality of his corporativist intentions. Hitler, too, fought the German Socialists by demagogic appeals that won over many workers to his side. But Hitler's demagogy was of a different order, at once more charismatically pursued and much more totalitarian in its aggressive nationalist and racialist appeal. Incidentally, there were far too few Jews in Italy for anti-Semitism to become a major issue.

CHAPTER XII

GREAT BRITAIN FROM 1914 TO THE GENERAL STRIKE

IN the affairs of the Second International up to 1914 the part played by the British was in no respect comparable with that of the Germans or the French, or even with that of the Belgians or the German Austrians. The great battles of the International were fought mainly between a united German delegation and a part of a sharply divided French delegation ; and on no really significant occasion did the British section exert a decisive influence. Only one British delegate effectively impressed himself on the Congresses of the International as a figure comparable in stature with Bebel or Jaurès, or with Vandervelde or Victor Adler. That one was Keir Hardie (1856–1915), who made his position by the intensity of his anti-militarist convictions, by his determination to rouse the International to action against the threat of war, and by his advocacy of the use of the strike weapon for this purpose. But Hardie, unlike these others, could not speak in the name of a mass Socialist Party or even, like Jaurès, of a preponderant section of such a Party. The only body in Great Britain that was even the beginning of a mass Socialist Party was the Labour Party ; and the British Labour Party of the years before 1914 neither possessed a nation-wide organisation of its own nor was committed to Socialism as an objective. It was mainly the Party of the Trade Unions in partnership with certain quite small Socialist bodies, of which the I.L.P. was the most important and the Fabian Society the outstanding contributor in the realm of Socialist theory. Neither of these Socialist bodies was by profession Marxist, whereas Marxism was the basic creed, at any rate by profession, of all the leading Parties of the other countries connected with the International. Great Britain, too, had its Marxists, represented in the Second International by the Social Democratic Federation and, after

1911, by its successor, the British Socialist Party. But the S.D.F. had left the Labour Representation Committee almost immediately after its formation in 1900 ; and the B.S.P. remained outside the Labour Party until 1916, when it was at length admitted to affiliation despite its opposition to the war. This exclusion from the Labour Party did not prevent the S.D.F., or later the B.S.P., from forming part of the International's British Section ; but these bodies, despite their Marxism, were prevented from having any influence in the International by the strong anti-German attitude of their best-known leader, H. M. Hyndman (1842–1921), who in 1916 seceded from his own Party because of its anti-war attitude and formed a rival, strongly pro-war National Socialist Party, but enlisted only an insignificant group of supporters. In any case, the S.D.F. and the B.S.P. were alike too weak to have any considerable influence on the British Section as a whole. The Section was indeed quite incapable of following a common policy. Keir Hardie's advocacy of an international strike against war did not even command the assent of the whole of his own I.L.P. — MacDonald and Snowden were both against him on this issue. Even less could he speak in the name of the Fabian Society or of the Labour Party as a whole, or in that of the Trades Union Congress Parliamentary Committee, which also sent its delegates to the Socialist International Congresses. Apart from Keir Hardie, the British delegates played only a minor part in the really critical debates of the International before the first world war ; and in the pre-war Trade Union International the British participation was even less, for the Trades Union Congress did not belong to it, and the British representation was in the hands of the much smaller and less important General Federation of Trade Unions, which had no mandate at all to speak for the British Trade Union movement as a whole. Great Britain was in fact regarded, in respect of Socialism, as a backward area, which had so far failed to establish a Socialist Party comparable with those of the leading continental countries. The Labour Party and the T.U.C. had been admitted to the International on the ground that, though they were not formally Socialist and would not even declare their support of the class-struggle, they were nevertheless engaging in that struggle on the basis of a Trade Union-Socialist alliance and did represent a mass working-class movement which the Socialist Parties of other countries could not afford to ignore. They were admitted, but hardly more than on sufferance ; and their ambiguous status practically ruled them out from playing a significant rôle. Moreover, at the Congresses of the International up to 1914, the great majority of the British delegates came from either the S.D.F. or the I.L.P. The Labour Party and the Trades Union Congress sent only quite small delegations and played, as a rule, only a minor part in the proceedings.

When war came, the Labour Party and the Trade Unions, in face of only small minority opposition, rallied to the national cause, as did the majorities in the Socialist Parties of Germany and Austria and of France and Belgium — but not, as we have seen, of Italy or of Russia. As against this, both the I.L.P. and the B.S.P. took up an anti-war attitude, though not without internal dissent. But whereas in Germany, by 1917, the anti-war Socialists had been expelled from the Social Democratic Party and had been forced to form an Independent Party (the U.S.P.D.), in Great Britain no such expulsions occurred, despite the strong feeling against the dissentients in many of the Trade Unions and among the pro-war Labour M.P.s. Indeed, the anti-war B.S.P., as we saw, was actually admitted to affiliation to the Labour Party in 1916, well before feeling in favour of a negotiated peace had gained any considerable body of fresh support. The maintenance of this attitude of tolerance was, I think, largely due, at first, to the deep respect in which Keir Hardie was held by almost the entire movement, except the most rabid jingoes, among whom were some members of the *Clarion* and S.D.F. groups, and later to the personal influence of Arthur Henderson (1863–1935), who toiled unremittingly to hold the Party together with a view to the need for united action after the war. Henderson had succeeded James Ramsay MacDonald (1866–1937) as leader of the Labour Party on the outbreak of war ; and, though from 1915 to 1917 he held a succession of offices, first under Asquith and then as a member of the War Cabinet under Lloyd George, he never relaxed his hold on the party machine, which, after his removal from the Government as a result of his activities in Russia and his support of the Stockholm Conference project of 1917, he played the main part in building up into an instrument capable of making a real bid for political power. A further factor making against a split was the position of MacDonald, who, after Hardie's death in 1915, held the leading place in the I.L.P. as well as the important office of Labour Party Treasurer. For MacDonald, though widely denounced as a 'pro-German' and a 'traitor' to the national cause, in fact took up, at least at the outset, a somewhat equivocal attitude, highly critical of the diplomacy which had led Great Britain into the war, but at the same time saying that the war, having come, must be won, and holding himself apart from the more intransigent anti-war partisans both in the I.L.P. and outside it.

The war-time I.L.P., indeed, represented a number of widely divergent points of view. Of the minority who refused to accept its anti-war line, quite a number, such as J. R. Clynes (1869–1949), remained members, though they ceased for the time being to play any active part in it and transferred their activities to the Labour Party instead. Of the outstanding leaders, Philip Snowden (1864–1937), F. W. Jowett (1864–1944), J. Bruce Glasier (1859–1920), and a number of others stood together, well to the left of MacDonald on the war issue, but remained, even after the Bolshevik Revolution, primarily parliamentarians and certainly not advocates of Revolution at all on the Russian model. Another significant group — headed by Clifford Allen (1889–1939), later Lord Allen of Hurtwood, as a reward for his support of MacDonald in 1931, but in 1914 a young intellectual from Cambridge who had become manager of the ill-fated *Daily Citizen* — proclaimed themselves absolute pacifists opposed on conscientious grounds to all forms of war and violence ; and it was this group that attracted a considerable fraction of the new recruits, especially from the middle classes, who joined the I.L.P. during the war years. The I.L.P., as a body, never became fully pacifist in this absolute sense ; but pacifism became very strong in it and powerfully influenced its reaction to the Bolshevik Revolution and, after the war, to the demands for universal civil war that went out from the Comintern.[1] There were other recruits to the I.L.P. who took a more revolutionary line and demanded after 1917 that it should throw in its lot with the Soviets and the Comintern ;

[1] See p. 307.

but they were always in a minority, and after 1920 most of them went over to the newly founded Communist Party, though a good many soon saw cause to leave it. The predominant tone of the I.L.P., despite the efforts of this left-wing group, never became Marxist. The I.L.P. had been from the outset primarily a grouping of ethical Socialists who denounced capitalism as a moral enormity and preached a gospel of Socialist fellowship rather than of economic determinism, though they did not scorn to make use of materialist arguments as well. The war, by shocking the consciences of many of these ethical Socialists, impelled them strongly towards making peace, rather than Socialism, their primary immediate objective ; and such Socialists were only repelled by Lenin's insistence that the way to peace must lie through world insurrection and universal civil war. Having suffered no oppression at all comparable with that of Czarism or even of imperial Germany, they had not been forced to see in violent Revolution the only hope of an advance towards Socialism. They wanted to end the war and to bring the world's workers together again in a peaceful crusade for the conquest of political power. Some of them had imagination enough to see that no such choice had been open to the Russian Socialists, or even in reality to those of Germany or Austria-Hungary ; but that did not make them ready to accept the Russian gospel as applicable to countries in which democratic institutions, however defective, did appear to leave the road open for peaceful change. At the same time they felt themselves sharply divided from those Socialists who, in the hour of trial, had forgotten their internationalism and cried out for war to the bitter end against their national 'enemies'. In this spirit the I.L.P., shedding its extreme left wing to the Communists and at the same time losing a part of its right wing to the reorganised Labour Party, rallied in 1921 to the Vienna Union, but felt the need to dissociate itself from those parts of the Vienna 'Statement' [1] which contemplated the use of force as a means of achieving Socialism.

In these matters the British Socialist Party, shorn of its Hyndmanite wing, stood a long way to the left of the main body of the I.L.P. and found no difficulty in swallowing the Communist doctrine entire. The B.S.P., such as it was, formed the

[1] See p. 339.

largest single element in the Communist Party of Great Britain set up, after several false starts, in 1921. The other elements were the main body of the Socialist Labour Party, which had almost its whole strength in the industrial belt of Scotland — mainly on Clydeside — Sylvia Pankhurst's (1882–1958) Workers' Socialist Federation, which had grown out of the London East End Federation of Suffragettes — a militant working-class secession from the Women's Social and Political Union of Emmeline and Christabel Pankhurst, Sylvia's mother and sister —the small but active South Wales Socialist Society, and the more extreme elements of the war-time Shop Stewards' movement. These groups were joined by seceders from the I.L.P., by a section of the Guild Socialists, and by a number of scattered individuals ; but in view of the rapid disintegration of the Shop Stewards' movement after 1918 they had no mass following.

As we saw, there was no split in the Labour Party during the war ; and the I.L.P. remained formally affiliated to the Labour Party and its M.P.s members of the Labour Party in the House of Commons. In practice, however, both in and outside Parliament, the I.L.P. during the war acted virtually as an independent Party, and the small group of M.P.s who sat under its auspices took their own line, though this was not followed by a number of its members who sat in Parliament under the auspices of their Trade Unions. The handful of I.L.P. Members — MacDonald, Snowden, F. W. Jowett, W. C. Anderson (1878–1919), Tom Richardson (1868–1925), and, up to his death, Keir Hardie — both pressed continually the cause of peace by negotiation and took a stand against many of the Government's wartime measures that endangered working-class liberties or economic conditions. They continued, however, to work with their Labour Party colleagues in many matters which did not raise such issues of Socialist principle ; and MacDonald in particular took an active part in the reconstruction of the Labour Party that was engineered mainly by Henderson and Sidney Webb. The I.L.P., however, was not able to maintain under war conditions its pre-war position as an active independent member of the British Section of the Socialist International, not only because the International itself was virtually out of action but also because, when the question of participation in the Stockholm Conference arose, the Miners'

Federation successfully made it a condition of the Labour Party's acceptance of the invitation that the British delegation should represent only the Labour Party and the Trades Union Congress, to the exclusion of the Socialist bodies which had belonged to the British Section of the Second International on equal terms. Henderson vainly sought to oppose this exclusion, which was contrary to the terms of the Stockholm invitation : the Trade Unions outvoted him. The exclusion, however, did not prevent the Labour Party from choosing MacDonald as one of its own representatives ; and MacDonald actually took part both in the Inter-Allied Socialist Conferences held during the war and in the Berne Conference at which the initial attempt was made to re-establish the International after 1918.[1] This was one of the factors which caused MacDonald, after the war, to identify himself less with the I.L.P. and more with the reconstituted Labour Party, of which he was within a few years to become again the leader.

To the British Labour movement, especially on the Trade Union side, the war brought a great accession of strength and influence. In the absence of military conscription in 1914, there was much less disruption of either the Socialist or the Trade Union movement than occurred in other belligerent countries — though there was, of course, a very large voluntary enlistment, including not a few skilled workers who could have been better employed at home. In 1914 there was an almost entire failure to anticipate the economic consequences of warfare or the shortage of man-power to which it would give rise. Indeed, at the outset there was substantial unemployment, and a continuance of this was widely feared. The notion was widespread that the fighting would not last long, and that the German offensive in the West would be speedily beaten back. Within a few months, however, the situation had greatly changed : the shortage of munitions at the front made it imperative to mobilise all the available resources for war work, to introduce large numbers of women into the war factories, and to come to terms with the Trade Unions concerning the relaxation or suspension of working rules and practices that stood in the way of mass production of weapons and other necessary supplies. At the same time rising prices made it

[1] See p. 290.

necessary to agree to wage advances, which were for the most part given as temporary 'war bonuses', on the mistaken assumption that prices would return to the pre-war level after the war. There were strikes on wage-issues, and also disputes arising out of the 'dilution' of labour by promotion of less skilled workers to jobs ordinarily done by skilled men. In March 1915 the Government negotiated a 'Treasury Agreement' with the Trade Unions, which agreed to accept relaxation of Trade Union practices for the period of the war, on condition that they should be restored when it was over, and also endorsed the temporary suspension of the right to strike in the war industries. A little later, on July 2nd, 1915, these provisions were given the force of law by the Munitions of War Act, which was promptly defied by the South Wales Miners' strike later in the month. This was a wage-dispute with the colliery owners : despite the Act, it was decided in the miners' favour, because the Government could not face the consequences of a prolonged stoppage in the coalfield which was the main source of supply for naval fuel.

It is astonishing in retrospect to see to what an extent, for more than two years, the Asquith Government attempted to carry on the war with a minimum of interference with the working of industry. The railways, indeed, were taken over at once and put under the management of a Railway Executive Committee which consisted of the general managers of the principal railway companies ; and under the Munitions of War Act the factories making war munitions were subjected to state control from the middle of 1915. But the rest of industry, including the coal-mines, was left in private hands until Lloyd George ousted Asquith from the Government at the end of 1916. Thereafter, as the problems of man-power and supplies became more and more acute — especially as the Germans resorted to unrestricted submarine warfare — state control was rapidly extended ; and military conscription, which had been introduced for single men only in March 1916, was applied generally and much more stringently enforced by 'combing out' increasing numbers of workers from the factories, and replacing them by women or disabled or elderly men. The Labour Party, from June 1915, had a small representation, headed by Arthur Henderson, in the Asquith Government. In

December 1916, in return for concessions which included the establishment of a Ministry of Labour, it agreed to support Lloyd George in ousting Asquith, and was given a considerably increased representation, including a seat for Arthur Henderson in the small War Cabinet that assumed responsibility for organising the war effort. Henderson, however, did not long retain his position. As we saw,[1] he was forced to resign when, after visiting Russia as the emissary of the Government in the spring of 1917, he returned to advocate British support for the projected Stockholm Socialist Conference. The Labour Party, however, did not leave the Lloyd George Government : the engineer, G. N. Barnes (1859–1942) — who had been active in the I.L.P. in earlier days — replaced Henderson in the War Cabinet, and the Party withdrew from the Government only after the armistice had been signed in November 1918. It then left the Government in order to fight, as an independent Party, the General Election which Lloyd George, as the organiser of victory, had determined to hold at once. Barnes and some of his colleagues, refusing to accept this decision, thereupon left the Labour Party and formed a coalition National Democratic Party which continued to support Lloyd George and won a small number of seats at the Election, but thereafter speedily melted away.

Although the Labour Party continued to participate in Lloyd George's Government, and the Trade Unions to co-operate with the Government in the war effort right to the end of the fighting, anti-war feeling grew rapidly during the latter stages of the struggle, especially after the Russian Revolution of early 1917. This was partly because, by the end of 1916, the vast majority of those who felt any will to serve in the armed forces had already been called up, so that the successive 'comb-outs' of those who were left in civil employment had to be applied to more and more reluctant recruits. It was also because, as the war of attrition dragged on to an unexpected length, more and more people came round to the view that a negotiated peace, without either defeat or victory, was to be preferred to a seemingly endless struggle involving so many deaths and mutilations, as well as an increasing pressure of shortages of foodstuffs and other supplies. Moreover, there

[1] See p. 49.

was a growing scepticism about the Allied war aims and, after the Revolution in Russia, a great deal of enthusiasm for the exhausted Russians' insistent cry for peace. Both the Independent Labour Party and the Union of Democratic Control, which was supported by a contingent of Radical intellectuals as well as by Socialists, gained strength rapidly, though without enlisting at any stage a mass following. George Lansbury's (1859–1940) weekly *Herald* — the left-wing *Daily Herald* had been forced for financial reasons to become a weekly after the outbreak of war — reached a large circulation and became a powerful organ of the anti-war movement. But more important than any of these as a mass influence was the rise of the unofficial Shop Stewards' movement, chiefly in the war factories.

This movement began on the Clyde, in connection with the unofficial strike of the Clyde munition workers in February 1915. For the conduct of this movement the Clyde workers' representatives from the leading establishments formed a Central Withdrawal of Labour Control Committee, out of which developed the more permanent body known as the Clyde Workers' Committee. Shop Stewards, appointed by local Trade Union organisations, had, of course, existed in many establishments well before 1915 as minor delegates with the task chiefly of seeing to the maintenance and extension of Trade Union membership in their particular workshops or departments, and had in a few cases undertaken minor functions of workshop negotiation on the Unions' behalf. What was new about the Clyde movement, and about the similar movements that soon developed in other areas, was the assumption by the shop stewards of independent functions and powers and also the appearance of unofficial stewards appointed not by the Trade Unions but by groups of workers in particular establishments, to represent these workers, in some cases without regard to the particular Union to which they belonged. Therewith went, in many cases, the setting up of Shop Stewards' Committees composed of representatives of all types and grades of workers in an establishment, and of local Workers' Committees made up of delegates from all or most of the establishments in a particular area — followed later by the federation of these local or area Workers' Committees into an unofficial nation-wide Workers' Committee Movement which challenged the official Trade Union leadership. The protagonists of this movement were left-wing Socialists who argued that the Trade Unions, by accepting an 'industrial truce' and allowing themselves to be bound by the Treasury Agreement and the Munitions of War Acts, had betrayed the workers' cause and abandoned the class-struggle. In the earlier stages the growth of this unofficial movement was fostered by the continual disputes arising over the 'dilution' of labour and the suspension of Trade Union practices ; but after conscription had been introduced it came to be more and more concerned with resistance to the increasing severity of the 'combing out' of the workers for military service and therewith took on a growingly political colour. After the Russian Revolution the Workers' Committees took up the cry for Soviets and played a large part in the Leeds Conference of June 1917, which issued a call for the formation of Workers' and Soldiers' Councils on the Russian model. This unofficial Conference, held some months before the Bolshevik Revolution, was participated in by many anti-war Socialists who were by no means really revolutionaries but only advocates of a negotiated peace ; but the prevailing temper at it was, at any rate on the surface, revolutionary and indicated the influence of the Russian Revolution in strengthening the British anti-war left wing. During the previous month there had been widespread 'May strikes' which had spread from one centre of war production to another and had seriously alarmed the Government. The unofficial movement never became strong enough to win control of the Trade Unions away from the official leaders or to gain a great deal of support in the Labour Party, which many of the unofficial leaders regarded as hopelessly reactionary. It did, however, become an increasingly powerful disturbing factor ; and control of it passed more and more into the hands of the extreme left. The termination of the fighting and the consequent cessation of mass production of war munitions struck at the roots of its power ; for in the post-war situation it became easy for employers who were cutting down their staffs to get rid of the principal 'agitators', and of those who escaped the sack, many, in fear of it, became much less active. The Shop Stewards' movement, after 1918, soon became a mere shadow of what it had been. The militant nucleus that was left, on the Clyde and elsewhere, furnished one of the significant groups that went to the making of the Communist Party of Great Britain. The revolutionary Shop Stewards — including, of course, those of Germany, France, and other countries as well as Great Britain — were specifically named in the call that went out in February 1919 [1] to the initial Congress of the Communist International.

Of course, by no means all the shop-steward leaders were, or became, Communists. The Shop Stewards' movement was composed throughout of mixed elements, some of which were opposed to the growing 'politicalisation' of it in 1917 and 1918, and were interested in it primarily as an instrument for the winning of 'workers' control' at the factory and workshop level. Many in these groups were supporters of Guild Socialism, or of some sort of Syndicalism, and not of Communism. A small fraction of the Guild Socialists did go over to Communism ; but the main body was strongly opposed to centralisation and to dictatorship and remained attached to the Labour Party or to one of its affiliates, such as the I.L.P. But this section, too, lost most of its industrial support with the general decline in shop-steward influence and activity. Guild Socialism found for a while a new centre of influence in the building industry, where it was able, with the aid of the builders' Trade Unions, to establish a widespread structure of Building Guilds in connection with the post-war housing scheme. But the Building Guilds were brought down in 1921 by the post-war slump, which led the Government to reverse its housing policy in such a way as to destroy their financial basis. Attempting to carry on without the aid of government capital, they soon became unable to meet their financial obligations ; and the whole movement faded away. The slump was also fatal to the smaller working Guilds which had been established in a number of other industries, such as engineering, clothing, and furniture-manufacture ; and these disasters were fatal to the entire Guild Socialist movement, which had gained for a time considerable Trade Union support and had exerted a large influence on Trade Union and Socialist ideas of socialisation, especially in the mining industry and in the railways.

An outstanding sign of this influence was the appearance in post-war socialisation plans, put forward by the Trade Unions,

[1] See p. 300.

of the demand for 'workers' control'. The main pressure for socialisation came at this time from two industries — coal-mining and railways — which had both come under unified state control during the war. The Miners' Federation of Great Britain had authorised in 1912 a draft Bill for the nationalisation of the industry, drawn up for it by H. H. Schloeser (b. 1883, later Lord Justice Slesser) and published by the Fabian Society, of which Slesser was an active member. This draft had provided for the taking over of the coal-mines by the Government and for their administration by a Minister, subject to parliamentary control. But at the end of the war the Federation came forward with a quite different plan, under which the administration was to be put in the hands of a National Mining Council to be appointed half by the workers in the industry and half by the Government. The National Union of Railwaymen similarly came forward with a demand for a nationalisation scheme under which the workers were to appoint half the members of the administration. These projects differed from those put forward simultaneously in France by the C.G.T., in that the latter asked for a tripartite form of administration by representatives of the producers, the consumers, and the Government, whereas the British projects treated the State as representing the consumer interest.

By February 1919 the Miners' Federation was threatening a national strike in support of its demands for higher wages, a six hours' working shift, and the nationalisation of the industry, with a large measure of workers' control, whereas the Government, though prepared to grant a small increase in wages, was offering only to refer the other demands to a committee of enquiry. After much hurried negotiation the miners were induced to postpone their strike notices and to take part in a Royal Commission of enquiry with wide terms of reference, on condition that the Miners' Federation should be allowed to appoint half the members, exclusive of the Chairman. It was finally agreed that half the members should be persons either appointed by the Federation or agreed upon between it and the Government, the other half to consist of three persons nominated by the colliery owners, and another three appointed by the Government to represent other employer interests, with a judge, Sir John Sankey (1866–1948) — subsequently, as Lord Sankey, Lord Chancellor in the Labour Government of 1929 — as independent Chairman. The Miners' Federation thus successfully insisted on the principle of parity of representation in the proposed enquiry ; and the Government, faced with the threat of strike action and with many troubles on its hands in other industries, as well as in connection with demobilisation of the armed forces, reluctantly gave way on this point.

During the next few months the Sankey Coal Commission was the centre of a great deal of public attention. The miners and their allies on the Commission — Sidney Webb, R. H. Tawney (b. 1880), and the former Liberal publicist, Sir Leo Chiozza Money (1870–1944), most effectively put the colliery owners in the dock for their mismanagement of the coal industry's affairs, and were able to convince not only Sir John Sankey but also the three other employer members that the pre-war control of the industry should not be restored. The Coal Commission did its work in two stages : its interim Reports, issued in March 1919, gave the miners a substantial wage advance and, more important still, reduced the working shift of underground workers from eight to seven hours, with a promise of a further reduction to six hours at the end of 1920 if the condition of the industry then allowed of this. Or rather, these proposals were contained in the Report of Sir John Sankey and the three non-colliery-owner, employer members, whereas the colliery owners offered only the seven hours and a smaller wage-advance, while the miners and their three allies stood out for the six hours' shift and for a bigger wage-increase, as well as for immediate nationalisation. Most significantly of all, the Report signed by the Chairman and his three colleagues declared for 'nationalisation or a measure of unification by national purchase and/or by joint control' and went on to say that 'it is in the interests of the country that the colliery worker shall in the future have an effective voice in the direction of the mine'.

After the Government, under strong pressure from the Miners' Federation, had declared itself prepared to carry Sir John Sankey's Report into effect 'in the spirit and in the letter', the miners withdrew their strike notices and the Commission took up the second stage of its work, in which it was chiefly concerned with formulating definite plans for the future conduct of the industry. It finally reported in June 1919 ; and on this occasion there were no fewer than four rival Reports, signed respectively by the six Labour members of the Commission, by the three colliery owners and two of the other three employer members, by the remaining employer member, Sir Arthur Duckham, and by the Chairman. Thus there was, strictly speaking, no majority Report ; but Sir John Sankey agreed with the six Labour representatives in proposing nationalisation of the industry, and all four Reports advocated public owner-ship of the coal itself — that is to say, nationalisation of coal royalties payable to the surface owners of the land. Sir John Sankey's Report also provided for workers' representation in the direction of the industry, both on Pit Councils and at higher levels, but so as to leave these representatives every-where in a minority. The Report of the six Labour members accepted most of the Chairman's recommendations, but re-quired a larger measure of workers' representation and control. The colliery owners and their two allies in effect rejected all major change in the control of the industry, and were not pre-pared to go beyond an advisory structure of joint committees. Finally, Sir Arthur Duckham proposed a scheme of regionally unified mining companies, on which workers' representatives were to sit in a minority, and provided for limitation of profits.

In view of the fact that a majority had declared for nationalisa-tion, the Miners' Federation at once demanded that the Govern-ment should carry out its promise by transferring the mines to public ownership. This, however, it soon appeared, the Government had no mind to do. Instead, Lloyd George came forward with a proposal, based on a watered-down version of Sir Arthur Duckham's Report and promptly nicknamed 'Duck-ham and Water'. When the miners rejected this, Lloyd George took his stand against doing anything at all to alter the structure of the industry, which still remained under temporary state control ; and the Miners' Federation thereupon appealed to the whole Trade Union movement to support it in measures designed to force the Government's hand. In the first instance, the Miners asked, not for strike action, but for the concentration of all the Labour movement's resources on an educational campaign to convert the public to the cause of nationalisation ;

and the Trades Union Congress of September 1919 pledged its support to the miners and arranged for a Special Congress to meet in December to settle what action should be taken. This Special Congress agreed to back the proposed campaign and to convene a further Special Congress to consider further action when the campaign had been held. Accordingly, with the support of the Labour Party and the Co-operative Union as well as of the T.U.C., the 'Mines for the Nation' campaign was carried through during the closing months of 1919 ; but in the midst of other causes of excitement it had very little impact on public opinion. When the second Special Congress met in March 1920, it was confronted with a demand from the Miners' Federation for general strike action to enforce nationalisation ; but the Congress, knowing the miners themselves to be divided, rejected this demand and decided, instead, in favour of 'political action', in the form of 'intensive political propaganda in preparation for a General Election'. In effect, that was the end of the matter ; for before the year ended the post-war boom had ended too, and a slump was well in sight. It would have been impossible, in any case, to concentrate political attention on the coal question so as to make it the central issue at a General Election ; but, apart from this, by the latter part of 1920 the great labour unrest of the previous year was ebbing fast. The Government had successfully surmounted the dangers of the period of demobilisation and post-war readjustment, and were no longer in a mood to make concessions to any claim that ran counter to capitalist interests ; and the Trade Unions were more concerned with looking to their own defences, industry by industry, in face of the threatened depression than with supporting the Miners or any other section in essentially socialistic demands. The big working-class offensive had been successfully stalled off ; and British capitalism, though threatened with economic adversity, felt itself once more safely in the saddle and well able to cope both industrially and politically with any attempt that might still be made from the Labour side to unseat it.

It has been necessary to carry the record of events in the coal-mining industry on into 1920 because all the events so far discussed arose directly out of the mining crisis which followed hard on the armistice of November 1918. The coal crisis, however, was at the beginning only one part of a general crisis confronting Great Britain as soon as the fighting ended. Long before this, all the big Trade Unions had been getting ready their programmes of post-war demands, and the left-wing groups had been formulating their own more ambitious projects. Lloyd George, foreseeing trouble, made up his mind to hold an immediate General Election, in which he would be able to appear as the saviour of the nation at the head of a coalition of all good 'patriots', to the confusion both of the Asquithite Liberals whom he had driven from office two years before and of the Labour Party, unless it were prepared to remain a subordinate partner in a capitalist Government of national 'reconstruction'. The Labour Party, as we saw, decided, by a big majority, to leave the Coalition and to put the new electoral machine which Arthur Henderson had been constructing for it to the test; and only a tiny minority of Labourites broke away and appeared as 'Coalition Labour' candidates. But at the General Election of December 1918 the Lloyd George Coalition, with its 'coupon' candidates — mostly Tories, but including Lloyd George's Liberal following — had matters all its own way. The cries of 'Hang the Kaiser' and 'Make Germany Pay' went down well with the electorate; and the Coalition emerged with 359 Tory, 127 Liberal, and 15 'Labour' supporters, as against an opposition made up of only 51 official and unofficial Labour members, 34 Asquithite Liberals, 7 Irish Nationalists, and a few Independents — not counting 73 Irish Sinn Feiners, who refused to take their seats. Even this small band of Labourites was an advance on the pre-war position of the Labour Party, which had secured only 42 seats at the last pre-war Election. It was, however, a most disappointing outcome of the work that had been put into the building-up of the Labour Party on a new basis, with its new Socialist programme, *Labour and the New Social Order*, and of its changed status in Parliament in view of the dissolution of the great Liberal Party of pre-war days. For, with the Liberal Party in ruins and rent by deep internal divisions, the Labour Party, almost negligible up to 1914 as a political force, had become by 1918 the only possible challenger to the Tory-dominated Coalition as a candidate for governmental power — at any rate unless the Coalition were to break down and the

Liberals to succeed in re-establishing their unity, of which there was little sign. At no Election before that of 1918 had the Labour Party even fought more than a small minority of the contested seats ; whereas in 1918 it had 368 endorsed candidates, not counting another 30 or so who stood under unofficial Labour or Socialist auspices.

The new Labour Party of the 'workers by hand and brain' had indeed staked out its claim to be the official Opposition in Parliament, with the hope of becoming in course of time the Government ; and it had done this by drastic changes in both its organisation and its programme. Up to 1918 the Labour Party had been essentially the Party of the Trade Unions and of the I.L.P., which had served as a sort of individual members' section of it, at the same time as, aided by the Fabian Society, it had acted as a Socialist leaven within it. The Labour Party itself, save in one or two very special constituencies, had possessed practically no local organisation of its own : it had relied for its electoral work mainly on the local Trades and Labour Councils and on the branches of the I.L.P., and most of its M.P.s had been returned primarily as Trade Union nominees. In theory, it had insisted on its independence of all other Parties ; but in practice it had owed nearly all its seats to Liberal support and had been, up to 1914, in most matters an obedient satellite of the Liberal Government. By 1918 it had created at any rate the nucleus of an organisation of its own in the great majority of constituencies, and had begun on the task of building up an individual membership in competition with the Socialist societies, which thus found their status in the Party profoundly altered. The I.L.P., in particular, having acted virtually as a separate Party during the war — though it had maintained its affiliation to the Labour Party throughout — did not at all like the change in its position involved in the appearance of the latter as a Socialist Party claiming the work and loyalty of all democratic Socialists and thus threatening to push the relatively tiny I.L.P. into the background. The I.L.P. leaders, however, could by no means afford to break away from the Labour Party, with which they agreed on most questions now that the war was over. They were themselves too deeply involved in the Labour Party's fortunes, and indeed regarded it as their child. Ramsay MacDonald, though he had been driven from his leadership of the Labour Party on the war issue, was still its Treasurer, had represented it at Allied Socialist Conferences during the war, and had played his part, with Webb and Henderson, in drawing up its new Constitution and Programme. He at any rate was much more closely in sympathy with the new Labour Party than with the left, or even the centre, of his own I.L.P. ; and though Philip Snowden was still less a Labour Party and more an I.L.P. man, he too was utterly out of sympathy with the I.L.P. left wing, which was coquetting with Sovietism and loud in its hostility to the thorough-going parliamentarism in which he most devoutly believed. The I.L.P. was half-hearted in its support of Henderson's effort to build up the Labour Party organisation in the constituencies on a basis of individual membership ; but outside Scotland it did not positively oppose this, but sought rather to strengthen its own hold on the new Local Labour Parties that Henderson was busily setting up.

As for programme, the adoption of *Labour and the New Social Order* as the master statement of Labour Party principles involved a radical break with the Labour Party's past ; for it committed the Party to a definitely Socialist objective and thus converted it from a loose federation of Socialists and Trade Unionists into a Socialist Party with Trade Union support. The Socialism of *Labour and the New Social Order* was, of course, thoroughly gradualist and unrevolutionary : it was the Fabianism of Sidney Webb with concessions here and there to the new spirit of the times — for example, in its references to democratic control of industry and workers' participation. These concessions, as was presently to appear, did not mean much in practice : in essentials what happened was that the Labour Party committed itself to the objectives of Fabian Socialism and to working for them by parliamentary democratic means, as the inheritor and fulfiller of the progressive Liberal tradition rather than as the initiator of any new revolutionary doctrine. Moreover, *Labour and the New Social Order* was not an election programme but a statement of principles and long-term objectives : so that it did not bind the Labour Party to any particular immediate measures, but only to a general attitude. It was adopted with very little opposition, partly for this reason, but also because during the war years Trade

Union opinion had moved on a long way and the break-up of the Liberal Party had destroyed the very foundations of the old allegiance to the mainly nonconformist Liberal-Labour alliance.

The Labour Party, then, came forward in 1918 as a claimant for political power, still a very long way off success, but with immensely widened ambitions and with greatly increased prospects of popular support. Before 1914 its candidates had never mustered more than about half a million votes; in 1918, with an electorate two and a half times the pre-war size and for the first time including women, it mustered nearly $2\frac{1}{4}$ million as against $5\frac{1}{2}$ for the Coalition Parties and less than $1\frac{1}{2}$ for the Independent Liberals. With many voters away from home and many soldiers unable to vote, the entire poll in 1918 was very low; but, heavily though most of the Labour candidates were defeated in view of Lloyd George's prestige, it was clear that for the future the Labour Party would need to be taken seriously as a political force. It could, however, be reckoned on to play the parliamentary game strictly in accordance with the established rules. In no country in all Europe was there so little sign as in Great Britain that the shape of politics had been altered by the Russian Revolution or by the holocaust of dynasties and empires in Central and Eastern Europe.

The British General Election of 1918 came so hot on the heels of the armistice that it was all over before there had been a chance for the workers to assert themselves in the industrial field, or for troubles to develop over the demobilisation of the armed forces or the munition workers. Accordingly these troubles, when they did develop, appeared in the environment of a political régime already decided on and of an anti-Socialist Government seated firmly in power. This Government, conscious of difficulties to come, was set above all on gaining time and on preventing too many problems from coming to a head at once. It therefore made haste to stabilise wage-rates for the time being and to provide emergency 'donation' benefits not only for demobilised warriors but also for discharged munition workers till they could be absorbed into peace-time jobs; and it also tried to strike a balance between the clamour of the soldiers for speedy demobilisation and the ability of industry to re-employ them — on the whole, with considerable success. Its next most urgent task at home was to stave off the insistent claims of the Trade Unions for improved conditions and, in some cases, for nationalisation and some sort of 'workers' control' as well, and to make a beginning with the provision of new houses in view of the acute shortage and of the great numbers wishing to set up new homes. We have seen already how a threatened national miners' strike was averted by the appointment of the Sankey Commission and by the concessions made after its interim Reports ; and we have now to study what took place in other leading industries.

The first open signs of mounting industrial unrest were the unofficial strikes on the Clyde and at Belfast for shorter working hours — on the Clyde for the 40, and at Belfast for the 44 hours' week, as against a pre-war standard varying in most places from 50 to 54 hours. The railwaymen had already been promised a week of 48 hours ; and negotiations for 47 or 48 hours were already proceeding in a number of industries when the Clyde and Belfast workers, chiefly in enterprises affected by the cessation of war demand, threw over their national leaders and, in January 1919, called local general strikes on their own. These movements were defeated — on the Clyde after some scenes of violence — and the engineering and shipbuilding Trade Unions thereafter negotiated a national agreement for a standard week of 47 hours. But in January 1919 it looked likely that the strike movement would gain momentum unless prompt action were taken to check it ; and the Government, in February, called together a National Industrial Conference of representatives from all Trade Unions, employers' associations, and joint bodies such as the recently established Whitley Councils, to consider the means of improving industrial relations and procuring industrial peace. A number of the most important Trade Unions — the Miners, Railwaymen, and Transport Workers, who had banded together in a Triple Industrial Alliance, and also the Engineers — refused to attend this gathering, on the ground that they were already engaged in negotiations of their own. But the majority of Trade Unions and employers' bodies did attend ; and the Conference set up a Joint Committee to produce a report on the questions remitted to it, including those of working hours, minimum wages,

and joint machinery to represent 'industry' in its dealings with
government departments and with the Government itself. This
Joint Committee sat for many months — it did not finally disperse until July 1921 — first preparing its Reports and then
arguing endlessly with the Government about their adoption.
Its real function, when it was set up, was to keep the Trade
Union leaders arguing and negotiating until the immediate
post-war ferment had died down and the danger of serious
industrial disturbances had gone by. In order to achieve this,
the employers' representatives were prepared to be accom-
modating during the earlier stages and to concede in principle
what later many of them were to oppose in application ; but
as the tension in the country lessened, they grew less and less
co-operative, and, long before the Trade Union side decided
to bring the farce to an end, they had in effect joined hands
with the Government in refusing to act on the recommendations
which they had appeared earlier on to accept.

After the immediate threat of a national miners' strike had
been removed, the principal remaining danger-point in industry
was on the railways. The railway Trade Unions were demanding both full recognition of their bargaining rights and considerable wage-improvements, and also the nationalisation of
the railways under a system that would give the Trade Unions
half the representation on the new management. The railways,
as we saw, had been put under state control during the war
and had undergone a considerable amount of co-ordination : so
that it was barely possible for them to be handed back to the
numerous separate companies. It was generally agreed that
there would have to be, at the least, consolidation into a small
number of big concerns, if not complete unification ; but there
was strong opposition to nationalisation, and the railway
workers were pressing more urgently for immediate wage-
concessions, including a national re-grading of labour, than for
public ownership. Thus the wages issue came to a head first,
in the summer of 1919, when negotiations with the Government broke down and, on September 26th, 1919, the railway
Unions declared a national strike. As the National Union of
Railwaymen was at this time associated with the Miners'
Federation and the Transport Workers' Federation in a Triple
Industrial Alliance designed to bring about united action by the

three groups, the railway strike threatened to bring the other two bodies into the field. The N.U.R., however, made no appeal to them to join the strike ; and what actually happened was that a special conference of Trade Unions, summoned by the Transport Workers' Federation, set up a Mediation Committee to help in reopening negotiations between the railwaymen and the Government. With the help of this Committee, a basis for a settlement, favourable on the whole to the railwaymen, was reached on October 5th, 1919 ; and the strike ended, though the subsequent detailed negotiations took several months to complete. The question of railway nationalisation did not enter directly into these negotiations, but was present throughout in the background, as the Government was considering ways and means of bringing the war-time state control to an end and of reorganising the railway system by some measure of unification.

At length, in 1920, Sir Eric Geddes, as Minister of Transport, propounded a plan, not unlike the Duckham plan for coal, under which the railway companies were to be amalgamated into a small number of big concerns and the workers were to be allowed a small representation on the governing bodies of these concerns. This project, shorn of its provisions for workers' representation, later took shape in the Railways Act of 1921, which set up four big grouped companies under private ownership and brought state control to an end. The railway Trade Unions, unwilling to accept the small share in 'control' offered to the workers under the Geddes scheme, accepted in lieu of it a system of consultative Councils and statutory negotiating machinery, which at any rate conceded the full Trade Union recognition the companies had hitherto refused to grant. The railwaymen did not give up their demand for nationalisation ; but they did, under the right-wing leadership of J. H. Thomas (1874–1949,) allow it to be pushed aside when their other claims, for improved wages and conditions, had been partly met.

Thus, the nationalisation issue was pushed into the background both on the railways and in the coal industry ; and the Government was allowed to return both industries to capitalist ownership and control. There was still much industrial unrest ; and there were big strikes and lock-outs still to come after the railway strike of 1919. But in none of these was nationalisation a direct issue : they arose out of disputes about wages and conditions and involved no challenge to the re-established capitalist system.

The first big dispute of 1920 arose at the docks and had to do with wages and conditions of employment and with nothing else. It was settled in the workers' favour without a stoppage of work after Ernest Bevin (1881-1951), the rising leader of the Transport Workers, had persuaded their Federation, instead of declaring an immediate strike, to ask for their claim to be referred to a Court of Inquiry under the recently enacted Industrial Courts Act — the first such Court to be set up. Before this Court, over which a high-court judge presided, Bevin argued the dockers' case with remarkable skill and flair. They got the 44 hours' week and the 16s. a day minimum they had demanded — indeed, everything except the scheme of de-casualisation for which they had to wait another twenty years ; and Bevin, previously no more than a minor Trade Union figure, leapt suddenly to the very front of the Trade Union movement at the head of what became before long the biggest Trade Union in the world — the Transport and General Workers' Union, based on an amalgamation of many of the Unions which had formed the Transport Workers' Federation. Bevin was fortunate in that his case was argued and won while prices were still rising and before the breaking of the post-war boom. But he deserved his success, and well earned his nickname of the 'Dockers' K.C.'

Then came, in the summer of 1920, the great excitement arising out of the threat of British intervention in the Russo-Polish War. The Poles had launched an offensive against the Russians in April and had captured Kiev early in May. Then the tide had turned. Kiev had been retaken in June, and the following month the Russian armies were nearing Warsaw and appealing, vainly, to the Polish workers to rise against their Government and so extend the Russian Revolution to the frontiers of Germany. The French sent General Weygand to help the Poles ; Great Britain sent only munitions, but a series of troubles arose when Trade Unionists objected to handling such supplies. In particular, the episode of the *Jolly George*, a vessel under charter to carry arms to Poland from Harwich, acquired world-wide celebrity when the dockers successfully refused to load its cargo, and it became clear that any attempt to defeat the boycott by the use of blackleg labour would result in a widespread sympathetic strike. The wildest rumours spread abroad. In Russia it was even reported, and for a time believed, that the Revolution had broken out in Great Britain. There was indeed a sudden wave of feeling among the British workers, for whom the affair of the *Jolly George*, small though it was in itself, had a symbolic significance as standing for international solidarity in support of the Russian Revolution against its capitalist-imperialist enemies. There were, moreover, widespread fears that the Government, in conjunction with the French, was contemplating armed intervention on the Polish side. So acute did these fears become that early in August a special Conference representing the entire Labour movement met and set up a Council of Action, at the same time telling the Government plainly that any attempt to make war on Russia would be met by the united resistance of the movement, up to and including a general strike. On this issue the movement felt well able to act strongly, being aware that it had the overwhelming support both of the working class and of many sections of non-Labour opinion. This determined attitude caused Lloyd George to have second thoughts and to declare that he had never entertained the idea of making war on Russia. Consequently the Council of Action and the local Councils, which had been set up in connection with it throughout the country, were not called upon to carry out the threat to strike, though they remained in being until a Peace Treaty between Russia and Poland had been drawn up and accepted in October 1920. What would have occurred had not General Weygand helped the Poles to save Warsaw and to drive the Russians back, and if, in face of the threatened Polish defeat, Great Britain had attempted to send armed forces to fight on the Polish side, it is not easy to know. The men who endorsed and helped to form the Council of Action included the leaders of the British Labour right wing, who would assuredly have approved of using the strike weapon only in the very last resort.

The Polish crisis was barely over, and the Irish crisis which had accompanied it was still unresolved, when, in the autumn of 1920, trouble came to a head again in the mining industry, in connection with a renewed wage-demand put forward by the Miners' Federation. After complex negotiations, in which the Government offered only wage increases conditional on increased production, the miners in October 1920 declared a national strike and called on their partners in the Triple Industrial Alliance to give them full support. The Railway and Transport Workers' leaders, however, were most unwilling to become involved in a national strike on the miners' behalf ; and they set to work to mediate between the Miners' Federation and the Government. The outcome was a temporary settlement, under which the miners got certain concessions ; but the industry's fundamental problems were left unresolved, and it became clear, when the Government announced its intention of ending the war control and handing the collieries back to their private owners on April 1, 1921, that a much more serious crisis than that of 1920 was brewing. The colliery owners announced that it would become necessary both to reduce wages drastically and to increase working hours as soon as government control ceased to operate ; for it would no longer be possible to subsidise the weaker pits at the cost of the more profitable. The owners insisted that, for the future, wages would have to be settled separately in each coalfield, in accordance with local ability to pay ; whereas the Miners' Federation argued that, if the Government refused to nationalise the mines, there would have to be a 'national pool' out of which living wages could be paid to the workers in the pits and areas that could not afford to meet them out of their own resources.

On April 1st, 1921, a national coal strike, or rather lock-out, began, when the miners refused to go to work on the terms offered by the colliery owners. Once more the Miners' Federation appealed to its partners in the Triple Industrial Alliance ; and again the Railway and Transport Unions' leaders were not at all eager to call a strike in the miners' support. Nevertheless both groups did declare their readiness to act in support of the miners unless negotiations were re-opened on a basis satisfactory to the Miners' Federation; and when that body refused to accept a proposal by the Government that wholly failed to meet its claims, the N.U.R. and T.W.F., reinforced by several other Unions, reaffirmed their intention to strike. At this point, however, a number of attempts were made to bring the parties together again, and it was suggested that there might be a temporary settlement of the wages issue, leaving the questions of the proposed National Pool and National Wages Board to be dealt with by subsequent negotiations. Frank Hodges (1887–1947), the Miners' Secretary, was interpreted as giving some support to this suggestion in answer to a question put to him at a meeting of M.P.s which he addressed ; but when Lloyd George wrote to the Federation asking whether it was prepared to negotiate for a temporary settlement on this basis, the Miners' Executive definitely refused, reiterating its demand for the establishment of a National Pool and a National Wages Board. On the excuse of this refusal, the Triple Alliance Unions and those which joined them, meeting on April 15th, 1920, cancelled their strike instructions and left the miners to continue the fight alone. This day, April 15th, was thereafter known in Labour circles as 'Black Friday', because it was regarded as the day on which the great Triple Alliance had ignominiously collapsed and as bringing the period of post-war industrial militancy to a decisive end. Certainly, these were the immediate effects : after Black Friday the whole Labour movement was forced back on the defensive. The Miners' Federation, left to itself, continued its hopeless struggle right on into July, when it had at length to admit defeat. By that time, industrial recession had set in everywhere ; and one Trade Union after another was being forced to accept severe wage-reductions. Unemployment, which had averaged only 5 per cent among insured workers in 1920, averaged 17 per cent in 1921 and 14 per cent in 1922, rising to well over two millions during the coal stoppage of 1921. Wage-rates, which at the end of 1920 had been from 170 to 180 per cent above the level of July 1914, fell by stages to but 65 to 70 per cent above that level in 1923. Total Trade Union membership dropped from 8,334,000 in 1920 to 4,328,000 in 1923. The struggle was to be resumed and was to reach a new culmination in the General Strike of 1926 ; but for the time being the slump and the miners' defeat between them had brought the period of positive struggle to a definite end.

Nor was the defeat confined to the industrial field. In the political field the depression ushered in a great campaign for 'national economy', which found its main expression in the 'Geddes Axe' proposals of February 1922, put forward by a Committee which had been appointed to recommend cuts in public expenditure. The 'Geddes Axe' was used to slash not only unemployment benefits, but also education and other social services, and to cut down spending on public works just when it was most urgently needed. In an endeavour to obtain redress, the unemployed workers began to organise on a considerable scale in the industrial areas ; and the Trade Unions, by their failure to take effective measures, allowed unofficial leaders, many of whom were Communists, to take command of the movement. The Communist Party, definitely constituted only in 1920, went through a drastic reorganisation in 1922, when it accepted the Comintern's instructions to reorganise itself as a disciplined, centralised Party. The National Unemployed Workers' Movement began to organise 'hunger marches' on London from the industrial areas, holding demonstrations as they marched and converging on London in an endeavour to bring more pressure to bear both on the Government and on the Labour Party, which they accused of lukewarmness in supporting their claims. By December 1922 there were also extensive rent strikes of tenants on Clydeside and in other areas. Meanwhile, in October, the Conservatives had ousted Lloyd George from his position as Prime Minister and had put their own leader, Bonar Law, in his place at the head of a purely Conservative Government. A General Election followed immediately ; and the Labour Party increased its poll from 2·2 to 4·2 millions and its seats from the 57 won at the 1918 Election to 142. The Conservatives were still a long way ahead, with 5·4 million votes and 347 seats : the Independent Liberals polled 2·5 millions and the National Liberals, who supported the Conservatives in most matters, 1·7 millions ; and each Liberal group had 59 seats. The Communists fought only 5 seats, of which they won one. In the new House of Commons the Clydeside M.P.s, badly mistaking their man, succeeded in bringing Ramsay MacDonald back to the Labour Party leadership, with J. R. Clynes, whom he defeated, as his deputy.

The new Parliament lasted only a year. Stanley Baldwin succeeded Bonar Law as Prime Minister in May 1923 and decided to appeal to the electorate for a mandate to introduce a general system of tariff protection. With employment still bad and working-class discontent rising, this decision favoured the Labour Party ; and at the General Election of December 1923, though it polled a vote only slightly above that of the previous year, it raised the number of its M.P.s to 191, as against 258 Conservatives and 158 Liberals, the two Liberal groups on this occasion joining forces as a single Party. The Communists lost their one and only seat. Thus, Labour was not even the largest Party ; but the Conservatives lost their clear majority and the Liberals decided to put the Labour Party into office. Ramsay MacDonald formed his first minority Government, in the knowledge that the Liberals could turn him out whenever they pleased.

There was much debate within the Labour movement on the question whether the Labour Party should agree to accept office on these terms, and also about the policy it should follow if it did accept. Most of the Labour politicians favoured acceptance ; but some of them wanted the Party, when it had accepted, to proceed at once to introduce a drastic Socialist programme that would involve certain defeat in the House of Commons, and then to appeal to the electorate on the basis of this programme and to put the blame for turning the Government out on the Liberals, in the hope of winning over an appreciable part of the Liberal left. MacDonald, however, was not at all minded to act in this way. He favoured taking office and going forward with a moderate reformist programme in which the Liberals would find it difficult to discover a good pretext for turning him out. Even though this was the spirit in which the Labour Government of 1924 took office, its advent made a deep impression on the minds of a great number of persons, including many of its supporters. So little time had passed since the Labour Party had been regarded as hardly more than a subordinate appendage of the Liberal Party, depending on Liberal voters for nearly all its seats despite its professed independence, that its accession to office served as a clear sign of the changed status of the working class in political and social affairs, and of the passing of an order in which political office had been regarded as a prerogative of the upper and middle classes. That the illegitimate child of a domestic servant, brought up in poverty, should have risen to the position of Prime Minister, and should so thoroughly look the part, seemed to many the portent of a new era, even if, for the time being, nothing very far-reaching of a practical sort was likely to result from it in view of the Labour Party's position as a minority in the House of Commons, and as not even the largest Party. It was not expected that the Labour Government would take up any revolutionary attitude ; but there was none the less an excited waiting to see what would in fact happen in this entirely novel political situation.

Ramsay MacDonald, in forming the first Labour Government, included in it most of the Labour Party's leading personalities, except George Lansbury, who was offered only a post not carrying cabinet rank, which he rejected. The principal representative of the left wing was John Wheatley (1869–1930), who became Minister of Health, and was thus put in charge of the urgent and difficult housing problem. For a few offices MacDonald went outside the ranks of his party, appointing Lord Chelmsford as First Lord of the Admiralty, the former Liberal Minister, Lord Haldane, as Lord Chancellor, and Lord Parmoor as Lord President of the Council, and also filling the Scottish Law Offices with non-Labour nominees. The Cabinet was weighted on the side of the right wing ; and MacDonald kept Arthur Henderson out of the Foreign Office by taking the Foreign Secretaryship as well as the office of Prime Minister into his own hands. Philip Snowden went to the Exchequer, Sidney Webb to the Board of Trade, and Henderson to the Home Office. On the whole, the Ministry looked competent as well as moderate, but unlikely to attempt any adventurous courses, except in the field of housing. The Labour Government of 1924 was to some extent fortunate in that its advent coincided both with some improvement in economic conditions and with a swing to the left in France, in revulsion against Poincaré's action in occupying the Ruhr the previous year. Aided by these developments, the Labour Government was able to carry through some useful social legislation, especially John Wheatley's Housing Act, which made the first serious attempt to enable the local authorities to provide new houses for letting at rents that ordinary workers could afford to pay. Wheatley also successfully negotiated with the building Trade Unions an agreement under which they accepted effective arrangements for increasing the supply of skilled workers through upgrading of less skilled employees to skilled positions, and special measures for the training of additional workers. This was the most ambitious and successful of the Government's domestic measures, its effects persisting for some years after its fall from office. Other important measures improved the conditions for the receipt of unemployment benefit, and restored the system of agricultural wage-regulation which, instituted during the war, had been swept away during the post-war slump. The Government was also able to help in bringing into force a new wage-agreement which did a little to improve conditions in the coal-mines — which had profited from the shutting down of the German mines during the occupation of the Ruhr. In addition, after considerable pressure had been put on MacDonald by the left wing, it recognised the Soviet Union, sent an ambassador to Moscow, and proceeded to negotiate an Anglo-Soviet Treaty and to enter into discussion about a projected loan to the Soviet Union. It helped to secure the adoption of the Dawes Plan for dealing with reparations from Germany and thus at any rate to initiate a less unrealistic German policy ; and at the League of Nations it did its best to strengthen the League Covenant and to further the causes of disarmament and general arbitration. As we saw, from June 1924 it was aided by the presence in France of the left-wing Radical Government led by Édouard Herriot.

These were sound steps as far as they went. But in August the Government landed itself in an awkward predicament by arresting and charging with sedition the editor of the Communist *Workers' Weekly*, J. R. Campbell (b. 1894), and then dropping the charge in face of the protests that the action had aroused. This incident led to an inquiry, on the report of which the Government was defeated at the end of the month, under heavy attack over both the dropping of the Campbell prosecution and the proposed loan to the Soviet Union. MacDonald resigned office, and a new General Election was held only a year after the last. It is impossible to say how the General Election would have gone but for an incident which, immediately before the poll, put the Labour Party in an almost hopeless position. This was the affair of the 'Zinoviev' or 'Red Letter', an alleged communication from the Comintern to the British Communist Party in which, amid the normal precepts of the Comintern to its affiliates, there appeared passages definitely inciting the British Communists to conspiratorial action for stirring up disaffection in the armed forces and inciting revolt. Whether this 'Letter' was genuine or a forgery has never been clearly established. No original was ever produced : only an alleged copy which had got into the hands of the *Daily Mail*. The Foreign Office got to know that the *Mail* meant to publish the 'Letter' on the eve of the Election and called on MacDonald, who was Foreign Secretary as well as Prime Minister, to provide it with an answer requiring the Soviet Government to discipline the Comintern. MacDonald, who was on an election tour, received the Foreign Office communication only after some delay, and then himself delayed before taking any action. Meanwhile, the Foreign Office published the draft reply it had sent to MacDonald for approval, subsequently explaining that it had felt it to be impossible to allow the *Daily Mail* to publish the 'Letter' without any official answer. Naturally, when the reply was officially issued, everyone supposed that MacDonald had authorised its publication, including the threat to withhold ratification of the Anglo-Soviet Treaty unless the Comintern were disowned and brought to book. But when MacDonald himself at length offered what purported to be an explanation, the obscurity about what had occurred became deeper than ever ; for he left it uncertain both whether he regarded the 'Letter' as genuine and whether or not he had actually approved or authorised the Foreign Office's reply, which seems, in fact, to have included both of two drafts intended to be alternatives, so that it appeared almost to contradict itself by its mixture of mildness and severity.

The effect of this extraordinary and discreditable affair was to put the Labour candidates, in the election campaign, in an impossible position. My own view, for what it is worth, is that the 'Red Letter' was most likely a touched-up version of a much less damaging original which did not contain the definite incitements to revolt ; but anyone's guess is as good as mine. Some say that there never was an original, and that the alleged letter was concocted from reports of what had been said at a meeting of the Comintern. At all events, the 'Red Letter' and MacDonald's imbecile handling of the affair finished all chance the Labour Party had of even holding its electoral gains of the previous year. The Party emerged with 151 seats instead of 191, though, on a much higher total poll, its actual vote rose by over a million. The Conservatives gained two million votes and won 415 seats, regaining a large clear majority. The Liberals lost a million votes, and tumbled from 158 seats to a mere 42. Baldwin came back as Prime Minister and proceeded, with Winston Churchill at the Exchequer, to take Great Britain back to the gold standard on terms of parity which severely damaged British overseas trade and brought on the crisis of 1925–6.

The first Labour Government of Great Britain thus ended in inglorious fiasco, despite the relatively favourable conditions under which it had taken office and the positive merits of some of the measures it had enacted ; and the blame for this fiasco rested squarely on MacDonald, who had played straight into its opponents' hands. It is a moot point whether the Party was wise or unwise in taking office under conditions which made it the prisoner of the Liberals ; but it must not be left out of account that a situation which rendered it impracticable to attempt any really socialistic legislation was by no means unwelcome to MacDonald and to many of his colleagues, who wished to proceed with the utmost caution and were provided with a strong argument with which to meet those who demanded a more forthright Socialist policy. To MacDonald and to many others it probably seemed all to the good that the first Labour Government should set out to win the confidence of the 'moderates' by following an essentially reformist policy that involved no challenge to the basic institutions of capitalism. They hoped, no doubt, to be able at a later stage to advance towards more socialistic measures, of a gradualist kind, but only when they had won over a much larger part of the electorate and reduced the Liberals to a negligible rump. After all, they were complete parliamentarians, and thought of Socialism as something to be contended for only by strictly parliamentary means — that is, by winning a majority of the electors over to the Socialist side. Though, under pressure of opinion in the Labour movement, they recognised the Soviet Union and were prepared to make a treaty with it, they deeply detested Communism (and were deeply detested by the British Communists in return). Quite apart from any 'Red Letter', MacDonald and many others probably had qualms about entering into friendly relations with the Soviet Union, and such Labour men were proportionately disturbed when they found themselves charged with making friends with a country which, through the Comintern, appeared to be only too ready to stab Great Britain and its Labour Government in the back.

Lenin died in Russia the day before the first Labour Government took office ; and while it held office the struggle inside the Soviet Union among Lenin's successors was running on to the climax of Trotsky's resignation of all his offices in January 1925. In Great Britain, the Communist Party was loudly denouncing the Labour Government, while persisting in its attempts to be allowed to affiliate to the Labour Party — attempts which were rebutted by enormous majorities at successive Labour Party Conferences. At the General Election of 1922 the Communists had put up 6 candidates, only one of whom stood in opposition to a Labour candidate ; and 2 of them — J. T. Walton Newbold (1888–1943) and the Indian Shapurji Saklatvala (1874–1936) — had been elected — the latter as a Labour M.P. In 1923 they had lost both these seats ; and in 1924 they had only a single electoral success. On the Trade Union side, the Communists did rather better. In 1923 the Trades Union Congress General Council was persuaded to set up a Joint Committee with the National Unemployed Workers' Movement, which lasted until 1926. In 1924 Arthur Cook (1884–1931), their leading Trade Union figure, was elected secretary of the Miners' Federation ; and during the same year they launched, with the veteran Socialist Tom Mann (1856–1941) as leader, the Minority Movement, whose function was to act as the British supporter of the Red International of Labour Unions, in opposition to the Amsterdam I.F.T.U. Moreover, in November 1924, the British and Russian Trade Unions agreed to establish an Anglo-Russian Trade Union Committee to work for friendly relations between the two movements ; and this decision was ratified in April 1925 at a joint meeting of delegates in London well after the Labour

Government's fall. In the matter of relations with the Soviet Union, Trade Union, if not political Labour, opinion was moving definitely towards the left ; and in home affairs also there were signs of increasing militancy on the industrial front. All this was far from meaning that the workers of Great Britain were going Communist ; but it did mean that there was a trend to the left away from the extremely right-wing policy of the Labour Government and towards a more challenging attitude to capitalism. In January 1925 George Lansbury (1859–1940) resigned his position as manager of the *Daily Herald*, which the Labour movement had taken over officially in 1922, and proceeded to start his own journal, *Lansbury's Labour Weekly*, as the advocate of a left-wing Socialist and industrial policy. The forces of the left were moving into position for a renewed struggle. The Independent Labour Party, breaking away from MacDonald's influence, set to work, under the leadership of H. N. Brailsford (b. 1873) and Clifford Allen, to formulate its new policy of 'Socialism in Our Time' ; and the Trade Unions which had allowed the Triple Alliance to break down in 1921 began to draw up plans for a new Industrial Alliance.

A fresh mining crisis developed during the summer of 1925. With the reopening of the German coal-mines after the Ruhr crisis, the temporary prosperity of the British mining industry had come to an end, and the colliery owners put forward demands both for large cuts in wages and for the substitution of local for national agreements, and also for an extension of the working day. British costs, they said, were much too high, and export trade was seriously threatened, especially after the restoration of the gold standard at the pre-war sterling-dollar parity. The Miners' Federation, smarting from the effects of its defeat in 1921, had succeeded by 1925 in rebuilding its organisation in most of the coalfields, though there were still weak spots, especially in the Midland fields. The Federation rejected the owners' demands and appealed to the whole Trade Union movement for support. On July 10th, 1925, its leaders met the Trades Union Congress General Council, and the two bodies issued a joint appeal to all Trade Unions to rally to the miners' aid. On July 14th the Government set up a Court of Inquiry into the dispute ; but this was abortive and, with the lock-out notices due to expire at the end of July, the Special Committee set up by the General Council met the railway and transport Unions and agreed with them to impose a general embargo on the movement of coal, both on the railways and at the ports. On July 30th, at a meeting with the miners' representatives, the Prime Minister, Stanley Baldwin, told them that 'all the workers of this country have got to take reductions in wages to help put industry on its feet'. His argument was that such reductions were indispensable for the maintenance of exports and of the newly restored gold standard ; but naturally his words produced a strong reaction throughout the Trade Union movement.

Up to this point the Government had taken the line that wages and hours were matters to be settled between the miners and the owners and that no responsibility rested on it to intervene. Baldwin had declared it impossible for the Government to grant any sort of subsidy to ease the situation ; but at the last moment, in face of the imminent lock-out and of the embargo decided upon by the transport workers, he suddenly changed his mind and declared the Government's readiness to grant a temporary subsidy to ease the transition to the greatly worsened conditions which the owners stated to be unavoidable. The subsidy was to last for only nine months, and in the meantime a Royal Commission was to report on the whole mining problem. On this announcement the colliery owners withdrew the lock-out notices, and further action was postponed until after the Royal Commission had made its Report.

The reasons for the Government's sudden change of front are clear enough. They had been taken by surprise by the evident will of the Trade Union movement to support the miners ; and they were not ready to deal with the crisis that would follow a general mining stoppage accompanied by an embargo that might easily lead to a general transport stoppage as well. Fully determined though they were to support the colliery owners and to bring about a general reduction in wages, they needed time to organise resistance, so as to be able to maintain essential supplies even in face of a widespread cessation of work ; and the temporary subsidy was given for the sole purpose of gaining time to organise the requisite measures for defeating the Trade Unions. The Royal Commission, under the chairmanship of Sir Herbert Samuel (later Lord Samuel), began its work in September, and reported on March 10th, 1926. Meanwhile, using powers conferred by the Emergency Powers Act of 1920, the Government arranged for the establishment of a voluntary agency — the Organisation for the Maintenance of Supplies — which set out to enrol large numbers of recruits, chiefly from the middle classes, who would be prepared to serve as blacklegs in the event of an extensive stoppage of work. The Government also set to work to mobilise a fleet of lorries and to train emergency drivers for railway engines and lorries and emergency telegraph and telephone operators to meet a possible postal stoppage.

On the Trade Union side no corresponding preparations were made for the coming struggle, though it was evident that the crisis was bound to recur when the subsidy came to an end. The Royal Commission could hardly be expected to arrive at a solution that either the colliery owners and the miners or the Government and the miners would accept. The miners were set against either wage-reductions or an increase in working hours and were determined to maintain the principle of national bargaining. The owners insisted on local bargaining and on their inability to carry on without lower wages and increased hours of work. The Government was against both nationalisation and any renewal of the subsidy beyond the nine months, and had committed itself to a general reduction of wages as a necessity. This meant that the Government and the owners were ranged solidly against the miners, who had the support of the rest of the working class because it was felt that their defeat would usher in a general attack on the Trade Unions. The Royal Commission had therefore an unenviable task ; for nothing it was in a position to propose could remove the deadlock — unless indeed it could persuade either the miners to give in or the Government, with or without nationalisation, to assume responsibility for running the industry at a loss ; and neither of these solutions was at all likely to be accepted.

By November 1925 the Government had made its main arrangements for the contest. The country had been divided into ten regions, each under a Minister or Civil Commissioner with wide powers. The Trades Union Congress, on the other hand, though militant speeches dominated the proceedings at its annual meeting in September, did next to nothing by way of preparation, presumably because it did not know what it could do without being accused of organising for open rebellion against the Government's authority. Its leaders, while insisting on their right to support the miners by strike action, were determined to do nothing that might even seem to give their resistance any appearance of assuming a revolutionary character. Either they supposed that, when the time came, the Government, despite all its preparations, would yield to the threat of general working-class action without an actual strike being declared, or they believed that a general strike could succeed against the Government without passing outside the bounds of strict legality. Or, perhaps, they were simply bewildered and paralysed by the course of events, and did nothing because they could not make up their minds what to do.

Lansbury's Labour Weekly, as well as the Communists, upbraided the T.U.C. for its inaction, and demanded that the whole Labour movement should be mobilised so as to be prepared itself to take over the running of essential services when the moment came. In October the Government raided the Communist Party's offices and arrested a number of the Communist leaders for incitement to unlawful acts ; and the following month it published and communicated to all public authorities its plans for dealing with the threatened emergency.

In March 1926 the Royal Commission published its recommendations. On the immediate issue of wages and hours, it saw no alternative to large concessions by the miners, but argued that was for the miners themselves to choose between maintaining the seven hours' day and accepting heavy wage-cuts and agreeing to increased hours so as to make the wage-cuts less severe. On the larger issue it reiterated the view of the earlier Sankey Commission in favour of nationalising coal royalties, but rejected colliery nationalisation and recommended only that the colliery owners should be encouraged to amalgamate into larger units, with a vague suggestion that some sort of compulsion to do this might need to be invoked later if the owners failed to take voluntary action. It also proposed steps to develop research in order to raise productivity, but came down definitely against any prolongation of the subsidy. The

Miners' Federation at once declared its inability to accept the Report, reiterating its slogan, 'Not a penny off the pay; not a second on the day', and appealing to the other Trade Unions to carry out their pledges of aid. The T.U.C. General Council was more hesitant and, while reiterating its declaration of 'support for the various efforts to obtain an equitable settlement', added that 'matters have not yet reached the stage at which any final declaration of the General Council's policy can be made'. What this meant was that the General Council was still hoping that reopened negotiations would lead to a settlement which the Miners' Federation could be induced to accept. Undoubtedly, some of them had reached the conclusion that there was no practicable alternative to wage-reductions and that the best hope lay in negotiating for a compromise. They could not say this openly, in face of the miners' attitude ; but it was what they meant.

The miners, however, led by their President, Herbert Smith (1863–1938), a remarkably stiff-minded Yorkshireman, though by no means a left-winger in his general attitude, and by their fiery secretary, Arthur Cook, were determined not to yield an inch ; and in this the main body of Trade Union opinion was definitely behind them. The colliery owners too were in an intransigent mood : in face of the Miners' Federation's insistence on a national settlement, they attempted to open district negotiations with the separate local Miners' Associations. This helped to harden Trade Union feeling ; and in face of the deadlock the T.U.C. General Council summoned, for April 29th, 1926, a special Conference of Trade Union Executives to decide what should be done. It also set up, with Ernest Bevin as chairman, a special Committee to draft plans for the emergency that was now imminent. When the Conference met, it adopted a resolution urging that the lock-out notices issued to the miners should be suspended while negotiations were renewed with the General Council's as well as the Miners' Federation's participation. Hurried negotiations followed between the miners, the General Council, and the Government ; but the lock-out notices were not withdrawn, and on May 1st the negotiators reported to the Conference of Executives that a complete deadlock had been reached. In these circumstances the Conference decided to call a 'general' strike in support of the miners, who had already been locked out from that morning.

The 'general strike', which began on May 3rd after the Government had broken off further negotiations, was not in fact general. In the first instance it was limited to transport workers, the printing and newspaper trades, the iron and steel and other metal-manufacturing and chemical industries, and the building industry with the exception of work on housing and hospitals. The electricity and gas services were called upon to co-operate by refusing to supply power to the stopped undertakings. A second line was held in reserve, to be called out later if the conditions seemed to require its aid. The Trade Unions were directed to assume responsibility for the continued operation of public health and food services; and the local Trades Councils were instructed to take action locally in support of the strike. But, though the great strike was called, there was a condition attached to it — that the Miners' Federation should hand over its conduct to the T.U.C. General Council. To this the Federation was said to have agreed; but there was evidently a misunderstanding, which has never been thoroughly cleared up. The General Council interpreted the condition as meaning that it was authorised to arrive at a settlement even without the miners' consent: the miners, on the other hand, insisted that the Trade Unions had called the strike in support of their claims and that these could not be altered without their agreement. For the moment, in face of the Government's refusal to negotiate, the issue did not practically arise; but it was to do so within a few days.

The excuse used by the Government for finally breaking off negotiations with the General Council was almost ludicrously trivial, and showed plainly that the Government had made up its mind to a fight. The excuse was that the compositors of the *Daily Mail* had refused to set up a leading article vehemently attacking the proposed general strike as a 'revolutionary movement intended to inflict suffering upon the great mass of innocent persons in the community', and stating that it must be combated by every resource at the community's disposal. On receiving news of this refusal, the Cabinet negotiators presented an ultimatum to the General Council rejecting any further discussions unless the strike were unconditionally called off. The General Council was prepared to disavow the compositors' action ; but the Government refused to meet them again. The strike was therefore called on May 3rd, 1926, and lasted for nine days.

The response to the strike call was remarkable : almost all those who had been called upon came out and remained out to the end. Even more remarkable was the absence of violence, despite the numerous arrests made by the police during the early days — until the gaols were over-full — and also despite the large-scale organisation of blacklegs on the government side. Though the strikers were clearly challenging the Government, nobody made any attempt to turn the movement into a revolution, even of a peaceful kind. The General Council insisted throughout that it was engaged in a 'purely industrial struggle', with no political implications ; and the strikers followed its lead. Strikers and police arranged football matches ; and there was no organised interference with the emergency services organised by the Government. The Trades Councils readily issued permits for necessary transport services, and carried on some services of their own ; and the whole affair was conducted for the most part in an atmosphere of astonishing good-humour. This good-humour did not extend to the emergency newspaper, *The British Gazette*, which the Government issued under Winston Churchill's control ; but it did in the main to Labour's rival news-sheet, *The British Worker*. The B.B.C., brought under government control during the strike, was used exclusively on the official side : the strikers made do with improvised local stencilled newspapers, devoted almost entirely to strike news.

Meanwhile, though no negotiations were supposed to be in progress, the Government brought in Sir Herbert Samuel, the Chairman of the recent Commission, and allowed him to play the part of an unofficial go-between. After consulting Baldwin and other Ministers, Sir Herbert drew up a Memorandum, based on the Commission's proposals, and laid it before the T.U.C. General Council as the outline of a settlement, saying that he had no authority to commit the Government, but hinting strongly that the Government would be prepared to accept a settlement on the suggested lines. This Memorandum brought the latent misunderstanding between the Miners'

Federation and the General Council to a head. The miners rejected it out of hand, whereas the General Council was prepared to advise its acceptance as a basis for resumed negotiations. When the miners had made their refusal clear, the General Council, which had just previously decided to call out the 'second line' — mainly the engineering and shipbuilding workers — not only cancelled this call but waited on the Prime Minister and announced to him their decision to bring the general strike to an immediate end. They then arranged with the Trade Unions concerned to issue orders for an immediate resumption of work, though it had been made plain to them that the Samuel Memorandum did not bind the Government and that they were in fact making an unequivocal surrender.

Thus, on May 12th, the great strike ended, except for the miners, who fought on right into November, though no hope was left to them after the collapse of their allies. It had been plainly demonstrated, on the one hand, that a general strike, necessarily directed against the Government, could not succeed unless the Government panicked and gave way, or unless it turned into a revolutionary movement in which the strikers were prepared to take power into their own hands. On the other hand, the strike had shown no less clearly the strong sentiment of solidarity that united the workers, but at the same time the wholly unrevolutionary character, not only of their leaders, but also of the main body of those who felt this solidarity and were prepared to act upon it when the call came. This did not mean that the rank-and-file activists were all out-and-out parliamentarians, such as Ramsay MacDonald, who scarcely concealed his intense dislike of the general strike, even while it was in progress. There were no few left-wingers who believed ardently in 'direct action' and welcomed the strike as a proletarian challenge to the Government and the capitalist system. But very few, even of these, even considered the possibility of making the strike the opening gambit of a social revolution, or hoped for more than the success of the miners in resisting a further deterioration in their lot. There were many who hoped, even to the end, that the Government would take fright and give way in face of the display of working-class solidarity ; but few of them expected that the Government would be forced to resign or considered what would happen if it did. The workers rallied instinctively to the miners' side, fighting the Government because they felt they had to, rather than because they had any intention of overthrowing it.

The general strike of 1926 could not have succeeded unless the Government had panicked; and this it was never likely to do. Ever since the previous summer it had been preparing for a decisive struggle; and it could not easily have drawn back when the crisis came. No doubt, some of its members hoped that the General Council and the rest of the Trade Union leaders would take fright and call the strike off without ever declaring it; and there were, no doubt, Trade Union leaders who would have liked to do this. But they, too, were carried along by a current they were not strong enough to resist, and found themselves forced into the strike against their will by the temper displayed at the decisive Conference of Trade Union Executives. All they could do was to watch out for the first opportunity of asserting their right, now that they had come to the aid of the miners, to have the decisive voice in determining the terms of settlement; and the refusal of the Miners' Federation to concede this claim gave them their chance to bring the movement to an end. Such leaders had been afraid throughout that the control of the strike, once it had been declared, would slip out of their hands into those of unofficial left-wing leaders: indeed, a number of them advanced this danger as a justification for their action in calling the strike off, though there was no indication either of an impending breakdown or of the strikers getting out of hand.

With the collapse of the general strike, received at first almost with incredulity by many of the strikers, the post-war movement of industrial militancy came to a final end. It had almost come to an end before, after the defeat of 1921: the events of 1925 and 1926 were only a final flare-up, brought on by the deliberate attack on wage-standards that accompanied the restoration of the gold standard. The excitements of 1925–6 did indeed enable the Communist Party temporarily to double its membership; but the increase, which was speedily lost again, was only from a handful of 5000 to 10,000 members. The unofficial Minority Movement in the Trade Unions made greater headway and, under Tom Mann's leadership, was able to get together an unofficial Conference representing about a million organised workers to call for action on the miners' side. But this following ebbed rapidly away after the defeat. In effect, the Communists, though very active as individuals, simply did not count : they had no influence even over the main body of the Trade Union left wing.

This left wing had indeed been enthusiastically behind the joint Anglo-Russian Trade Union Committee set up in April 1925 and behind the attempt of the British Unions to persuade the Amsterdam I.F.T.U. to agree to a 'Unity' Conference from which it was hoped that a United Trade Union International might emerge. But in December 1925 the I.F.T.U. rejected the British proposals ; and though the Soviet Trade Unions gave the British miners financial help the following year, the movement for unity lost ground rapidly after the collapse of the general strike had thrown the British Unions back upon a policy of discomfited defence. From 1926 onwards, though the T.U.C. of that year voted — without practical effect — in favour of a reform of Trade Unionism on Industrial Unionist lines, the British Trade Union movement passed over definitely to a policy of industrial peace.

This was partly because the British employers, instead of launching an all-out offensive against the Trade Unions in the moment of their defeat, for the most part refrained from pushing their advantage to the limit and preferred taming Trade Unionism to attempting to overthrow it. The protagonist in urging this conduct on the employers was Sir Alfred Mond (later Lord Melchett), the head of Imperial Chemical Industries, who in 1927 invited the Trades Union Congress General Council to confer with an influential employers' group with a view to the improvement of industrial relations. The account of these developments belongs, however, to a later section of this narrative.[1]

Though the employers refrained from launching a general offensive, wages were reduced in many industries, and the Trade Unions, which had suffered heavily in membership, accepted moderate reductions rather than resort to strike action. Meanwhile, in the political field, the Government

[1] See p. 667.

447

showed no similar forbearance, but did its best to undermine the Labour Party as well as to curb Trade Union power by the Trade Unions and Trade Disputes Act of 1927. This Act declared general strikes to be contrary to law, hedged round the right to take sympathetic strike action with disabling restrictions, severely limited the right of picketing, and forbade Unions organising mainly workers in the public services to belong to either the Trades Union Congress or the Labour Party. Over and above this, it struck a direct blow at the Labour Party by altering the law relating to Trade Union contributions to political funds. Under the Act of 1913, Trade Unions had been authorised to raise levies for political purposes provided they allowed those who objected to such payments to sign forms 'contracting-out'. The Act of 1927 altered the system to one of 'contracting-in', so that political contributions could be levied only on those who actually signed forms agreeing to pay them. These changes reduced the Labour Party's affiliated Trade Union membership from 3,388,000 in 1926 to 2,077,000 in 1928 — though some of this fall was due to the general decline in Trade Union membership from $5\frac{1}{2}$ million in 1925 to 4,804,000 three years later.

The Independent Labour Party, as we saw, had launched, after the fall of the Labour Government in 1924, an active campaign in favour of a more determined Socialist policy under the slogan, 'Socialism in our Time'. The main points of this policy were the demands for a 'living wage' and for far-reaching measures of industrial socialisation. It was expounded in a number of pamphlets and in a book, *Socialism for To-day* (1925), written by H. N. Brailsford, the editor of the I.L.P.'s journal, *The New Leader*. This campaign brought the I.L.P., for the time being, a substantial acquisition of strength, and made it the chief spokesman of the political left wing inside the Labour Party. But the defeat of 1926 reacted adversely on the I.L.P. as well as on the Trade Unions ; and the impetus behind the movement died down with nothing achieved. The main immediate point in the I.L.P.'s programme had been that a living wage for all should be made a first charge on the national income and that the Labour Party should make this its first, overriding objective. MacDonald and other former I.L.P. leaders had attacked the entire 'Socialism in our Time' programme as 'flashy futilities'; but when the 'Living Wage' resolution was brought before the Labour Party Conference in October 1926, the Party Executive, instead of attempting to defeat it directly, secured its remission to a joint Labour Party-Trades Union Congress Committee, in whose unending proceedings it was quietly buried. Thereafter, the I.L.P. continued on its left-wing but unrevolutionary way, still within the Labour Party but less and less of it, up to the final break which severed it from the Party in 1932.

It seemed necessary to carry on the record of British Socialism in a continuous narrative right up to 1926 because the general strike of that year was a decisive turning-point and there was no earlier stopping-place that seemed convenient. I have tried to make plain that there was no point at all at which there was any possibility of a British Revolution. Great Britain emerged from the first world war with its social structure essentially unchanged and the power of its governing classes intact. Labour, indeed, was in process by 1918 of becoming a considerable political force, and the power of the Trade Unions had increased a great deal; but the Labour Party had still to get used to being a really nation-wide Party and a claimant to political power, after serving up to 1914 as little more than an auxiliary of the then united Liberals, and it was much too intent on replacing the Liberals as the second major parliamentary Party to feel critical of the parliamentary system. Moreover, some of its outstanding leaders — notably Arthur Henderson — were former Liberals who had by no means shed their liberalism with their party allegiance; and others, such as MacDonald and Sidney Webb, were convinced gradualists who held that Socialism would have to be built on the basis of the Liberal progressive tradition, and not by revolt against it. Even Philip Snowden, who sometimes appeared more extreme, was a thorough parliamentarian, and most of all out of sympathy with every form of industrial leftism. Only George Lansbury among the leading figures and F. W. Jowett and John Wheatley among those of the second stature were consistently on the left; and of these Lansbury combined his leftism with Christian pacifism, and Jowett and Wheatley both found their main interests in local government and social legislation rather than in industrial militancy or international affairs.

John Wheatley, whose death in 1930 after a prolonged illness was a very serious loss to the British movement, was the outstanding success of the Labour Government of 1924, his Housing Act being the most constructively successful of its measures. Wheatley was a Clydeside Roman Catholic, the most intelligent of the group of Clydeside M.P.s associated with the I.L.P. and, while he lived, the chief inspirer of James Maxton (1885–1946), the exceedingly popular orator who became the leader of the I.L.P. in its crusade for 'Socialism in Our Time'. Wheatley, by profession a publisher, was no great orator : he preferred to act in committee, or behind the scenes. Housing reform was his passion, as it well might be in view of the appalling housing conditions on the Clyde ; and he showed great skill in negotiating with the building Trade Unions a treaty under which they were prepared to co-operate actively in his housing drive. The Wheatley Housing Act, of which the effects were seen only after the fall of the Labour Government, was highly successful in stimulating the provision of local authority-owned houses that were to be let and not sold outright. He did not get on with Ramsay MacDonald, who disliked his leftism and was glad to be able to leave him out of the Labour Government of 1929.

Other prominent figures in the I.L.P. of these years were E. F. Wise (1885–1933), Clifford Allen, and H. N. Brailsford. Brailsford, who very ably edited the *New Leader* — successor to Keir Hardie's *Labour Leader* — from 1922 to 1926, was a Radical veteran who had made his name as a writer on foreign affairs and a strong opponent of imperialism, had taken an active part in the campaign for women's suffrage, and had been a Socialist from his schooldays. Originally a Fabian, he had left the Fabian Society because of its attitude to the Boer War and had joined the I.L.P. in 1906. He had travelled widely in Europe, including Eastern Europe during the troubled years before 1914, and had written extensively upon international affairs as a fierce opponent of militarism and imperialism in all their forms. His book, *The War of Steel and Gold* (1914) had given the best account of the forces making for war and of the Second International's endeavours to preserve the peace. He had been to Russia, since the Revolution, and had written about it with real sympathy ; and he was a man who could be relied upon to rally on the highest principles to every good, humanist cause. Wise, who had held high Civil Service posts during the war in connection with the state control of wool and then of food, was an intellectual who had given strong support to the movement for Anglo-Russian trade and had made himself the leading advocate of state trading in time of peace. By instinct he belonged more to the centre than to the left ; but circumstances and his friendship for the Russians had impelled him leftwards and given him a leading place as the I.L.P.'s specialist in economic planning. Finally, Clifford Allen was a young Cambridge graduate who, as a conscientious objector, had led the 'No Conscription Fellowship' during the war. He, too, was by instinct a Centrist ; but his war attitude had ranged him with the I.L.P., and his great organising initiative led him to attempt to reassert its claims to provide the driving force for the Labour Party. Always in poor health, he had nevertheless great energy ; but after a few years of left-wing activity he moved rightwards and finally followed MacDonald in the crisis of 1931, becoming as a reward Lord Allen of Hurtwood and passing out of the Labour movement into the well-merited obscurity of his later years.

The Labour Party itself, after issuing *Labour and the New Social Order* in 1918, produced no further general statement of aims and principles until *Labour and the Nation* appeared in 1927. In the interval, however, it issued a long series of pamphlets, either expounding particular aspects of its policy or dealing with immediate matters, such as unemployment. In all these it appeared as an essentially reformist Party, seeking piecemeal ameliorations rather than any catastrophic social and economic change. Internationally, it took part in the Berne Conference of February 1919 and played a leading part in the reconstruction of the revived Second International, with the German Majority Socialists as its most active colleagues. In view of the strong anti-German feeling that had existed during the war — above all, after the resort to unrestricted submarine warfare — it is remarkable how easily the British Labour Party settled down to this post-war collaboration, which rested largely on a common belief in the superior virtue of parliamentary democracy and a violent hostility to every form of proletarian or party dictatorship. The I.L.P., on the other hand, threw itself into the 'Two-and-a-Half' Vienna International, till that body agreed to merge itself in the Labour and Socialist International established at Hamburg in 1923. Thereafter, as a part of the British contingent in the L.S.I., the I.L.P. ceased to play an independent rôle until it seceded from the Labour Party in 1932 and was left poised in a vacuum between the L.S.I. and the Comintern.

Guild Socialism, which had for a time seemed capable of emerging as a major economic force and of exerting a wide influence on Trade Union policy, had practically vanished as an organised movement well before the first Labour Government took office. Beginning as a social doctrine in the columns of A. R. Orage's *New Age* and receiving its first full exposition in the book *National Guilds* (1914) by S. G. Hobson (1864–1940) and A. R. Orage (1873–1934), it had developed during the war under the auspices of the National Guilds League, in which William Mellor (1888–1942) and the present writer (b. 1889) were outstanding figures. It had won substantial support both in the Shop Stewards' Movement and among the miners, railwaymen, and postal workers, and had largely influenced the policies put forward by the Trade Unions in these industries after the war. From 1917 onwards, the Bolshevik Revolution had caused considerable dissensions in its ranks, though not to the extent of a split, which came only with the foundation of the Communist Party and the secession of a minority of its adherents to that body. Further dissensions arose when Major C. H. Douglas (1879–1952) came forward with his projects of credit reform as a panacea, and won Orage's support. The end of the fighting and the disbandment of the munition workers weakened its hold among the engineering workers ; but when S. G. Hobson, with the support of the building Trade Unions, launched a National Building Guild in 1920, the Guild movement suddenly emerged as the sponsor, not only of a theory of social reorganisation, but also of a practical attempt to put workers' control of industry into operation within the framework of the capitalist system. The Building Guilds, set up and controlled by the Trade Unions, offered to help to meet the acute housing shortage by erecting houses on a non-profit basis under the government housing scheme, offering guaranteed employment at Trade Union wages. At that time, the finance of public housing was mainly a government responsibility, and it was possible for building firms to receive payment as the work proceeded, though always in arrears of work done. This made it practicable for them to operate with relatively little capital ; and for a time the Building Guilds were able to borrow such capital as they needed from the Co-operative Wholesale Society's Bank, with Trade Union backing. All went well as long as these conditions lasted, and excellent house-building work was done by the Guilds at relatively low cost to the public. But then came the post-war slump : and in the middle of 1921 the Government suddenly altered its housing policy, shutting down on all new housing contracts and, when it reopened the door, changing over from the system under which it met the residual costs after a fixed contribution from the local authority concerned, to one under which it paid the local authorities a fixed subsidy and left them to meet the balance. Under the new arrangement it was no longer possible for the Guilds to get the greater part of their working capital from the Government ; and they found themselves faced with the need to raise large sums which they could not persuade the Co-operative Bank or the Trade Unions to supply. Attempting to carry on under the changed conditions, they were soon faced with insolvency, and the entire movement collapsed, dealing a mortal blow to the Guild Socialists whose leaders, except S. G. Hobson, had had no share in the management of the Building Guilds, but were none the less discredited by the collapse. Most of the relatively small working Guilds which had been set up in other industries, such as engineering, clothing, and furniture-making, also came to shipwreck as a consequence of the slump ; and the remaining Guild Socialists decided to wind up the movement rather than await its gradual dissolution. Many of them, including the present writer, kept their Guild Socialist convictions ; but after 1923 there was no longer an organised Guild movement, though something of its influence remained in the continuing Trade Union claims for workers' participation in control.

Guild Socialism, though predominantly a left-wing movement, was never revolutionary in the sense of seeking the violent overthrow of the existing social order. It had its revolutionary wing, which passed over to Communism and included such notable Communist figures as Rajani Palme Dutt (b. 1896) and Robert Page Arnot (b. 1890), and, for a time, William Mellor. But it had also a right wing, most of whom became converts to the Major Douglas plan of credit reform. Its largest group, however, consisted of left-wing, non-Communist Socialists who were strongly critical of reformist parliamentarism and put their main hopes on Trade Union industrial action as a means of building up organisations of the workers 'by hand and brain' capable of taking over the management of industry under nationalised ownership. The Guild Socialists were not Syndicalists : they recognised the need for public ownership and for control of high economic policy on behalf of the whole community and not merely of the workers in each particular industry or service. But they held that the community should entrust the actual management to the workers by hand and brain engaged in each type of undertaking, and that social democracy would be a sham unless the workers became self-governing in their daily work as well as through the possession of political rights. They differed among themselves in their attitude to the political State. Orage and Hobson wanted the Guilds to be 'chartered' corporations, acting under licence from the State ; whereas others, of whom I was one, were Social Pluralists, and believed that the Sovereign State should in due course be replaced by some form of federal authority, resting on a partnership between producers' and consumers' and other 'functional' representatives. It was a favourite slogan of the Guild Socialists that 'economic power precedes political power' — by which was meant that the workers could achieve real freedom and democracy only by getting economic self-government.

Like other Centrists in many countries, the Guild Socialists found themselves after 1918 squeezed out between the contending factions of Communism and parliamentary social democracy ; and their influence was also eroded by the post-war slump, which rendered impracticable advances towards 'workshop control' as a first step towards the realisation of their larger objectives. The same fate overtook the movement of the French C.G.T. for *la nationalisation industrialisée* [1] and the Building Guilds which developed in Germany after 1918.

[1] See p. 470.

Only in Palestine did an analogous movement, led by the Histadruth, the Jewish Trade Union organisation, strike firm roots which have continued to grow up to the present time.[1]

[1] For a fuller account of the earlier stages of the Guild Socialist movement, see Vol. III, Part I, p. 242.

END OF PART I

PRINTED BY R. & R. CLARK, LTD., EDINBURGH